ADVANCES IN
LIBRARY ADMINISTRATION
AND ORGANIZATION

Volume 2 • *1983*

ADVANCES IN LIBRARY ADMINISTRATION AND ORGANIZATION

A Research Annual

Editors: GERARD B. McCABE
Director of Libraries
Clarion State College

BERNARD KREISSMAN
University Librarian
University of California, Davis

VOLUME 2 ● 1983

 JAI PRESS INC.

Greenwich, Connecticut   *London, England*

CONTENTS

INTRODUCTION

One year ago Carl Jackson wrote the introduction to the initial volume of *Advances in Library Administration and Organization*. Almost immediately thereafter Carl was reported as missing at sea and the profession had lost one of its most adventuresome and respected colleagues. In that initial essay Carl listed a number of issues confronting individual librarians such as economic welfare, status and the work environment which, at first blush, may not appear to be the appropriate territory for exploration by a professional publication concerned with administration and organization. However, it does not take protracted deliberation to realize that such individual concerns, translated to institutional and professional levels, are distinctly elements of administrative and organizational interest.

In the very first formative days of *A.L.A.O.*, the editors were engaged in a definition of the purposes of our forthcoming publication. Those purposes were eloquently summarized by Jackson as recognition of and responses to "challenges to the effective operation of our libraries." Indeed, that effort at definition began with the title, the initial descriptive word of our work, namely "Advances," which we recognized would betoken research exclusively for some of our readers. The editors, early on, rejected the concept of "research exclusively" as far too narrow for our objectives. As Volume 1 has demonstrated and as this volume shows, *A.L.A.O.* is to be a medium for the publication of meritorious essays of description, history, philosophy, observation, bibliography and research; concerned with or applicable to the effective operation of our libraries. We decided, nonetheless, that "Advances" in the title was quite appropriate for our ends and we denied the current sense of confining the term to its single pigeonhole of research. We have the highest authority for our usage: *Webster's Third* provides a definition for the verb "Advance"— "to bring forward for notice, consideration or acceptance: bring to view." We took the liberty of utilizing that verb in a nominative sense.

A.L.A.O.'s eclectic approach obviously transcends the subject matter of our standard courses in administration, but for that circumstance we make no apology—we simply apply Carl's yardstick. As you will discover in this volume, *A.L.A.O.* differes from other serials in the profession in its conscientious but congenial consideration of articles and research papers which either by their length or their nature would find other publication sources unreceptive.

The editors of *A.L.A.O.* intend, as Carl Jackson wrote, to have our publication serve "to the ultimate benefit of librarians, as well as the libraries and the publics they serve."

Bernard Kreissman
University of California at Davis

MANAGEMENT TRAINING FOR RESEARCH LIBRARIANSHIP

Deanna B. Marcum

I. RESEARCH LIBRARIES: BACKGROUND

If we accept the assertion that, when compared to the present, research libraries will be fundamentally different organizations in both form and function in the year 2000, it follows that those individuals responsible for management and operations of those libraries will need additional skills and capabilities as well. Further, librarians will bear much of the responsibility for forming the library of the future, so those who are presently at work will have the difficult task of maintaining the present services and resources, while simultaneously shaping what is to come.

Because the mix of forces now at work affecting the future of libraries is complex (there are pricing and funding issues, a set of technologies that is rapidly changing, shifting relationships within the scholarly communications system, unresolved legal and policy issues, and even inadequate

Advances in Library Administration and Organization, volume 2, pages 1–19.
Copyright © 1983 by JAI Press Inc.
All rights of reproduction in any form reserved.
ISBN: 0-89232-214-4

definitions of organizational objectives), it seems almost useless to attempt a detailed description of the research library of the future.

Rather, it seems more useful to look at those forces most likely to influence the direction and nature of research libraries: changes in higher education, changes in economics, and changes in technology.

A. Changes in Higher Education

The *Chronicle of Higher Education* contains almost weekly predictions of the future of higher learning. Most forecasting experts agree that enrollments in colleges and universities will peak by 1982–83 and then decline before rising again late in the century. There will be a significant increase in the number of older students, part-time students, and students enrolled in skills-based or vocational programs.

A principal factor will be the increased longevity of adults, which will have enormous implications for educational policy and planning. The demand for adult education programs is expected to grow, while the proportion of young people in the total population will decrease markedly. Recruiting efforts, of necessity, will be aimed at an older audience. Within research libraries the resulting changes in curricular options will cause significant shifts in both scope of collections and demands for services.

B. Changes in Economics

Costs of running research libraries are increasing at a faster rate than university budgets can accommodate. Recent Association of Research Libraries statistics indicate the magnitude of the cost increases for both library materials and personnel—the two major costs in research libraries. From 1968/69 to 1978/79, ARL member libraries spent 91% more for library materials, yet added 22.5% fewer books to their collections. Personnel costs have increased 106% in the same period, yet essentially no new positions have been added. When such data are corrected for inflation, the magnitude of the problem doubles.

Other factors exacerbate the financial crisis. The amount of material being published is increasing at about 2.5% each year; hence, libraries are losing ground in the proportion of new information they are able to purchase. Expectations and demands of faculty and students for library materials are constantly increasing without regard to the economic constraints.

The economic difficulties are not expected to ease in the near future. Instead, research libraries will, of necessity, attempt to "do more with less." Alternatives for providing immediate access to materials will be explored by many libraries.

C. Changes in Technology

Virtually every research library is undergoing a transformation because of computer and telecommunications technology. Information is now disseminated in a variety of formats, including machine-readable formats, and research libraries can no longer concern themselves with only printed materials. Data bases that were once available in print are now available only in machine-readable form, making it necessary for the library to purchase equipment in order to make the information available. Pricing structures have consequently changed. No longer is there a one-time cost for such a publication. Machine-readable data bases are accessible on a per use cost. Each time information is sought, a charge is levied. Budget implications for the library are very difficult to anticipate.

In a more general sense, the creation of bibliographic records in machine-readable form has the greatest impact on research libraries. Individual records once kept in each department of the library are now often combined in a single source, the computer. Standards for creating records and protocols for gaining access to those records become library-wide matters when access is through a centralized source.

In addition, these machine-readable records make such innovations as automated circulation systems, on-line catalogs, and automated acquisitions systems possible. The resulting changes in procedures, consolidation of activities, and organizational structure create enormous staff training needs.

II. STATE OF MANAGEMENT IN RESEARCH LIBRARIES

Charles McClure in "Library Managers: Can They Manage? Will They Lead?" indicates that the most important aspects of academic libraries are the organizing and managing of the physical resources to meet the changing information needs of society. He predicts that the central most important concept for library and information professionals in the next century will be management.[1] He goes on to offer this analysis:

> Academic library managers have not provided leadership in the solution of societal information problems, nor have they effectively utilized innovative managerial techniques to administer the library. Instead, a hybrid between "concerned paternalism" and "crisis management" impedes the library from serving as a problem solver and limits the librarian from utilizing his/her full potential to improve the performance of the library.[2]

In "Requirements for Middle Managerial Positions," Martha Bailey notes that current library managers responding to a survey found little or no value in the library administration courses offered in their library schools.[3] Other writers have reached similar conclusions: most managers in research libraries do not possess, at the time of appointment, the necessary skills and training for peak managerial effectiveness. Most of the "management training" comes from doing the job.

A. On-the-Job Training

A number of writers have pointed to the "crisis of management" within research libraries. The reasons are varied, but one of the most often cited inadequacies is the failure of the library manager to view him/herself as a manager. Too often it is assumed that the quality librarian can become a quality manager simply because a new title is bestowed.

Many librarians have observed that one of the greatest deficiencies is managerial training for middle management staff in the research library. Most reluctantly agree that the manager in a library is almost always trained on the job.

Faced with this reality, many research libraries have attempted to provide better managerial skills to their new supervisors by seeing to it that they receive instruction in basic management practices. Over and over again, it is noted that librarians feel relatively comfortable in their technical roles, but quite uncomfortable as managers of people. More and more librarians are making the transition from a subject or technical specialist to that of manager. What looked so easy and obvious from the operational librarian's position becomes very difficult when that librarian is promoted to a managerial position and peers become subordinates in the process.

The very nature of managerial positions in libraries contributes to this difficulty. In the vast majority of promotions into library supervision, the primary consideration is technical or subject competence and expertise. The candidate's ability to perform most or all departmental jobs is often paramount in the hiring decision. This is natural and understandable. The supervisor must be able to train others, assign responsibilities, and monitor job progress. So, job knowledge is clearly important to supervisory success.

Closely allied to job knowledge is departmental experience. In reviewing the candidates for a position, library administrators and search committees within a research library are strongly inclined to consider the degree to which the person has experienced that particular situation or similar situations.

The candidate's interpersonal skills usually rank third in consideration. Ability to communicate, to get along well with others, and establish an informal leadership style are evaluated. Top management usually considers the personalities of other departmental employees and makes a judgement as to how well the candidate will be likely to gain their confidence and respect.

A lesser factor in promotional decisions is the knowledge the candidate has of other departments as well as broader organizational goals. These are typically perceived as learnings which the supervisor can help develop on the job.

The factor probably least considered is knowledge of and ability to use management skills. The previous nonmanagement position usually does not require demonstration of these skills, so the candidate's likely abilities are unknown and untested. Top management makes an educated guess and hopes these skills will be acquired in time.

Since few supervisors have had any formal exposure to management principles at the time of promotion, their new role is usually unclear. It is not surprising that most new library supervisors feel awkward or uncomfortable.

It is a common practice to fill a first line supervisory position with a person who is already an employee in the department. The advantage from the library's point of view is that the new supervisor knows most, if not all, departmental tasks. Little technical training is required.

The new supervisor is likely to concentrate his/her effort on what he/she already knows how to do well, namely departmental tasks. The typical problem is establishing a leadership position among former peers while also attempting to do too much operational work.

In those cases where a supervisory appointment is made from another department or from the outside, the major problem will be the technical orientation period—or how-it's-done-here training. An advantage of the "newcomer" is that he/she is an unknown quantity and as such is usually granted a honeymoon period in which to establish a leadership style.

Planning, organizing, and control activities cause difficulties for most new supervisors. The paperwork procedures that link the department to all others and to the library administration must be mastered. Priorities have to be established and job sequence determined. Tasks must be assigned according to staff abilities and new priorities and demands. It is likely then, that the new supervisor will feel overwhelmed by the many requirements and apparent conflicts that develop.

Another major problem is in the supervisors' overall dealings with people. It is very difficult to know how firm or how casual to be with people. If the supervisor stresses authority excessively, both morale and productivity may drop. If the supervisor is too relaxed, the department may quickly develop a casual attitude toward productivity. In a short period of time, the new supervisor must assess the situation, his or her own capabilities, and the capabilities of the staff, and based on the combination of people and circumstances, begin to establish a leadership style.

Typically, the new supervisor will tend to withdraw from staff contact whenever possible because he/she really does not know what behaviors are appropriate. Any comfort this provides will be short-lived as the staff soon begins to complain that the new supervisor is aloof and uninterested in their problems or concerns.

Staff perception is not the only concern of the new supervisor. The new supervisor is being monitored and evaluated by his/her superior, as well. At the first counseling or performance appraisal session the new supervisor is usually faulted for:

- poor delegation
- poor time management
- confused priorities
- lack of planning and organization
- insufficient time spent dealing with personnel
- bias or favoritism

Fortunately, most new supervisors will develop both the skills and confidence needed for good management. The length of time this takes will be partially dependent upon their unique differences and upon the help or assistance they are given in personalized or group supervisory training.

Training needs are not limited, though, to managerial skills. An increasing number of libraries are faced with massive staff training and retraining efforts because of technology. Virtually all areas of the research library are affected by computer technology. university libraries are involved with bibliographic utilities and other automated efforts that require learning new procedures and new ways of operating. If librarians are to contribute to the development of these systems, in addition to benefiting from their use, they must learn the basics of how such systems operate and how they might be used. Many librarians have attended workshops and conferences devoted exclusively to the understanding and use of computer technology. The library schools and the information industry sector have been equally active in providing opportunities in these areas for practicing librarians who need additional skills in order to perform well in their jobs. Finally, many research libraries have initiated staff training programs to teach the use of automated systems on-site.

B. Workshops and Professional Meetings

The most active participant in the management training and organizational development arena continues to be the Office of Management Studies (OMS), an affiliate of the Association of Research Libraries. This organization provides services including institutes for individuals wishing to enhance their managerial skills; a film training program, which is offered to participants for use in their local staff development efforts;

publications designed as self-help techniques in such areas as planning, staff development, budgeting, and so on; and a topically focused self-study program that builds competencies of staff while simultaneously solving problems in a specific library. These services in combination result in a comprehensive approach to staff and organizational development. The OMS has been instrumental, too, in developing a training program for consultation skills, in which twenty talented librarians are recruited per year and trained to become library consultants of the type who work with staff in identifying alternatives rather than simply providing answers. In the process, these librarians greatly enhance their own skills as the work in their local situations.

Other organizations have realized the importance of providing staff development programs to enhance the managerial skills of their members. In nearly all surveys conducted concerning the greatest needs of the membership, management skills rank at or close to the top. In 1981, the Association of College and Research Libraries offered staff development programs to its members just prior to the annual ALA conference. The topics, though wide-ranging, had at least a component of managerial effectiveness. The Staff Development Discussion Group of ALA spends much of its meeting time sharing ideas for promoting effective supervision within the research library. Techniques are analyzed and program plans are critiqued.

C. Academic Programs

While it is true that each research library carries the major responsibility for training its managers, many have voiced concern abut the lack of academic preparation of library school graduates. It is clear that the library schools, in general, do not prepare librarians to assume managerial positions. In fact, it seems quite unreasonable to expect library schools to turn out graduates who are fully effective the first month after commencement. This has never been, nor will it be, the case. Today, even the best-trained library school graduate will require six to twelve months of on-the-job experience with careful supervision before becoming a reasonably effective cataloger or reference librarian in a research library. And no matter how much theory he/she absorbs in a library school (or even in a graduate school of business), one is not going to fill a responsible administrative position successfully without some seasoning.

III. THE RESEARCH LIBRARY IN THE NEXT DECADE

While the nature of the times is a valid explanation for present difficulties, it is incomplete. From the viewpoint of research librarianship, the profession itself seems ambiguously defined, a fact that possibly constrains both educational innovation and effective recruiting and that also accounts, at least in part, for traditionally low salary levels that are, in themselves, a key source of a self-fulfilling prophecy. Further, the professional school structure is not without problems. It has been greatly expanded in the last twenty-five years and is, primarily for this reason, uneven in quality and presently hard-pressed to maintain high enrollment levels in a time of shrinking demand. Finally, while there is no shortage of librarians per se, there is a severe shortage of individuals with certain needed skills and of exceptional, experienced individuals for major management posts.

With these perceived difficulties in mind, the Council on Library Resources established in 1980 a program called Professional Education and Training for Research Librarianship (PETREL). Following discussions with practicing librarians, library educators, and others, several possible steps were proposed to build professional strength. Although the items listed below vary widely in purpose and means, they are complementary. Together, they are intended to improve the performance of research libraries by raising the overall quality of professional skills.

- Recruit to academic and research librarianship an appropriate share of the best and brightest college graduates and provide them with a rigorous and stimulating basic professional education.
- Identify in the present ranks of librarians those who, through their skills and other qualities, show clear promise for professional leadership and then provide them with exceptional opportunities for additional training.
- Focus attention by librarians and others who should be concerned on the fundamental issues now facing research libraries.
- Raise the quality of and make more pertinent the research related to library matters and increase the involvement of librarians and others outside the profession in the research process.
- Promote more effective communication between practitioners and professional school educators.
- Influence the content and structure of professional education for research librarianship to enhance its pertinence to present and projected concerns of academic and research librarianship.
- Continue to press for improvement in library management, with special attention to capitalizing fully on professional staff skills.

If these goals are to be achieved, actions of several kinds over an extended period of time seem essential. In no other way will short-term manpower problems be addressed and more fundamental matters be attended to in durable and intellectually acceptable ways. A substantial but not unreasonable commitment of funds over a period of years will be necessary and, equally important, research libraries, library schools, and the profession's leadership will have to assume responsibility and demonstrate their willingness to be held accountable for results.

Several projects funded by CLR and other institutions and professional organizations are now under way, including work related to professional education, continuing education and training, and research.

A. Basic Professional Education

Many librarians and at least some library school administrators support the idea of establishing a rigorous professional education program geared specifically to research librarianship in two ways: course content and an integrated internship in a research library setting. If it can be demonstrated that research libraries have fundamental distinguishing characteristics, it is important to include an understanding of them in the curriculum. To create a responsible base for developing and implementing this kind of program, it may be necessary for research libraries to join forces with library schools to build the concept and substance of research library specialization into the more general structure of professional education.

As a start, the Council on Library Resources has awarded a grant to the University of Michigan's School of Library Science for a program designed to attract a small number of highly qualified students to research librarianship. An extended academic program, additional course work in related disciplines, research library internships, and placement assistance will be included in this new basic professional education program.

On their own, a few library schools have extended the length of the master's degree program, prompted by the expanded basic knowledge now required for librarianship, and the increasing pressure on students to achieve some competence in a specialized area while in library school. UCLA, North Carolina, Washington, Chicago, and the Canadian library schools have extended their programs for these reasons. Columbia University convened a conference in 1980 to discuss the results of its study of the issue. Other library schools are investigating the possibility of extending their programs, but they remain concerned about the additional cost to students in an economically depressed profession.

One change in nearly every library school has been a renewed emphasis on internships or field study. Research libraries, recognizing the value of practical experience, have sought ways to cooperate with library schools to offer practical work opportunities.

B. Continuing Education and Training

Most major administrative appointments in research libraries during the next two decades will be made from the ranks of those now at work. It is essential that the best talent in this group be identified early and provided with exceptional opportunities to build skills, particularly in management, and gain experience.

The CLR Management Intern Program, now in its eighth year, has identified thirty-five promising professionals, typically with five or more years of experience, and has supported them during a year away from their own institutions while they work as management interns under the direct tutelage of distinguished library directors. The program is expensive, in large part because it covers the salaries of interns as well as direct costs, but it continues to receive high marks from both interns and directors as an effective way to produce "total immersion" in the management process for at least some of the best young professionals in the country. The need to be away from "home base" for an extended period is disruptive, personally and professionally, and as a result, constrains participation by some. Currently, a study is being conducted to determine the most beneficial aspects of the Management Intern Program and to evaluate its benefits as well as costs.

Within a specialized area, the Council has administered a Health Sciences Library Management Intern Program under contract with the National Library of Medicine. This program follows the same pattern as the Management Intern Program, although it lasts for one year instead of ten months, and it includes two weeks of orientation at the National Library of Medicine.

Two recent CLR grants have been made to support the continuing education and training for outstanding librarians.

At the University of Chicago, the Graduate Library School, in cooperation with the Graduate School of Business, has established a special postgraduate program leading to a certificate of advanced study in library management. The course work includes interdisciplinary study in library science and management, a focused seminar to continue throughout the period of study, and investigative internships at several participating research libraries. The first students will be enrolled in June, 1982.

Another program, designed by UCLA, will provide an opportunity for specialized training for individuals who have recently assumed senior management posts in research libraries. A six-week course emphasizing managerial skills with periodic follow-up sessions during the year of the fellowship will be developed as a prototype for a continuing training program. The first session is scheduled for August/September, 1982.

C. Research

The quality of library research has been widely criticized. Most librarians agree that research is an area that needs substantial improvement. Library managers often comment that the research should be more directly applicable to the problems they face in day-to-day activities.

A recent study of libraries as organizations indicated that the research literature supporting the profession is generally inadequate. Although there are a number of notable exceptions, the research methods employed, the methods of data analysis, and the extraction of policy implications reveal an unfortunate lack of experience and expertise in the methods of research and policy analysis.

In another related study, the impact of an increased number of doctorates awarded in library science or research related to the profession is explored. Among the findings are excessive compartmentalization (little mobility between operations and education), a low level of experimental or innovative research, and inactivity in research by a significant portion of those who hold the doctorate.

One promising approach to improve research is reflected in a PETREL grant to UCLA for support of a conference (December 1981) designed to explore and describe the frontiers of research librarianship. Commissioned papers explored characteristics of research universities in the 1980s and subsequent discussions served to relate research library development and operations to the economic, technological, political, and intellectual factors that promise to dominate policy-making for the next decade, at least.

CLR has also funded a host of individual research topics over the years. The Council has been a primary source of funding for the librarian needing supplemental funds to carry out research projects aimed at addressing the fundamental problems of research librarianship, including management.

Another agency concerned about the quality and amount of library research is the U.S. Department of Education. The Office of Library and Learning Technologies commissioned a project to develop a "Library and Information Science Research Agenda for the 1980's." Although the agenda does not focus on research libraries exclusively, the results will be of interest.

All of these projects reflect common themes—to provide distinctive opportunities for exceptional research librarians, both present and prospective, to develop improved capacities for professional education, and to establish and help carry out a research agenda pertinent to the functions and future of research libraries.

IV. MANAGEMENT TRAINING METHODS

Various traditional methods have been tried to convince middle and senior management of the importance of managing human resources efficiently, such as in-department courses, courses run in conjunction with other parts of the university, sending staff to workshops and courses arranged by some section of ALA, and a considerable amount of coaching by top management on a one-to-one basis. Training methods used have included lectures, seminars, working groups, case studies, and audiovisual presentations. While all of these have contributed in some way toward improving the situation, many feel a totally new approach will be required.

Experiential Learning Theory

The philosophy behind experiential learning is that the most effective way of learning is to place the learner in an environment where he/she can assimilate information from being personally involved. Not only does this assist in the retention of information, but it is also an effective motivator.

Features of experientially based training include:

1. an attempt to simulate working conditions
2. a trainee-centered environment
3. group discussions and interactions
4. short theoretical lectures (maximum, 30 minutes)
5. intensive periods of interaction in a relatively risk-free but not anxiety-free environment
6. lengthy self-directed participation to achieve

   - greater motivation
   - increased self-awareness
   - increased empathy
   - improved critical faculties
   - increased involvement in the working situation.

Experiential learning, as the name implies, is learning through experience, or rather by experiencing various situations individually and in groups and in testing other people's reactions to them. In this way, the individual learns a lot about him/herself and about other people in the group. It is not group therapy or a vehicle for massive catharsis, but it does use the process of group dynamics to teach managers the issues in management, as it highlights the problems of working with people and how to get the best from them. The effectiveness of group exercises depends upon the participants being honest and candid about themselves, and this tends to trigger a defensive mechanism in most people. But if this honesty and openness can be achieved in the work situation, the quality of relationships improves, and consequently the quality of work also improves.

Management is working with and through people in an effort to achieve organizational goals. To achieve these goals, a manager must first be able to diagnose his/her own leadership behavior or style, and also appreciate that the type of leader behavior may vary with differing situations. Each manager will, through experience, develop his/her own style, and this is not necessarily the style he/she perceives it to be, but rather how the staff see it. They will react and behave according to their perceptions of the manager's behavior.

An important element of management training, then, is the opportunity to test perceptions of others in various managerial situations. A variety of workshops and conferences are designed in one way or another to assist the librarian in discovering those perceptions.

Resources for Improving Managerial Skills

The rapidly occurring changes in research libraries dictate that those responsible for managing them be informed of opportunities for managerial and supervisory training for new persons assuming those positions. The responsibility for managment skills is shared by the library schools producing new librarians, the research libraries, and the individual librarians seeking and assuming management positions. The following sources of training are listed as examples of supplementary training beyond the academic preparation.

A. Management training for librarians

Several library schools and professional library groups offer continuing education and staff development opportunities designed specifically for librarians. Nearly all of the library schools have as one of their purposes providing continuing education opportunities for practicing librarians and, quite often, they offer management-oriented workshops. Some of these organizations have offered management training on a continuing basis. Among the better known programs are:

1. Maryland Library Administrators' Development Program. Offered annually, this two-week program provides management training in the areas of decision-making, motivation, formulating objectives, political processes, marketing information services, and other related issues.

2. Executive Development Program for Library Administrators and the Advanced Executive Development Seminar. These programs, spon-

sored by the School of Business Administration of Miami University in Oxford, Ohio, are week-long sessions designed to improve managerial effectiveness. The advanced program is for the benefit of experienced managers in libraries.

3. Office of Management Studies, The Association of Research Libraries. The Office of Management Studies offers a number of training opportunities for librarians: Management Skills Institutes, Advanced Management Skills Institutes, topically based supervisory skills workshops, organizational development programs in the form of self-studies for libraries, and a Consultant Training Program.

4. Academic Library Management Intern Program. Each year, until now, the Council on Library Resources has sponsored a competitive program of internships for up to five librarians who wish to be administrators. A ten-month internship is provided in a major research library for the successful candidates.

B. General Management Training Programs

Within the public and private sectors, a broad range of management training opportunities are available. While the programs are not designed exclusively for librarians, the management principles addressed are easily transferred to a library setting. Among the more popular programs are:

1. American Management Association. Each year the AMA produces a complete catalog of course offerings. Many of the management courses and workshops are designed for managers within nonprofit organizations, and many librarians have found them to be worthwhile. The programs are offered in a number of locations each year.

2. University Associates. University Associates offers management training and personal development programs for all types of organizations, but many of the participants work in nonprofit organizations. The training is highly experiential. Internship programs are also offered.

3. National Training Laboratories (NTL). NTL is the oldest, most firmly established training organization to develop personal growth and highly interactive skills-based programs. It, too, offers workshops in a variety of locations each year, provides internship opportunities, and offers consultant training programs.

C. Contractual Programs

Many business and management schools of universities, educational associations, and consulting groups offer training programs for a library staff or a library group. Training offices attached to personnel departments within the university may be a source for contractual training programs for the library, as well.

D. Professional Meetings and Publications

At every professional meeting, a variety of continuing education and training programs are offered. In general, these are excellent "refresher courses" or introductions to a topic. Few are long enough or detailed enough to do much more than point out a need for the individual librarian. But the importance of them as introductions to topics cannot be over-emphasized.

Similarly, professional publications play an important role in alerting librarians to the management training programs and workshops that are of potential interest. CLENE's *Communicator* is a publication devoted exclusively to this purpose. Regular columns in *Library Journal, American Libraries*, and others also provide excellent sources of information about such opportunities.

V. FUTURE DIRECTIONS

Management Skills

The library manager responsible for certain aspects of the library's performance must analyze, appraise, and interpret the performance of others, relating that performance to the unit's effectiveness and the library's goals. Essential components of the manager's job are planning, organizing, directing, staffing, and controlling, and these are just as important in a library as in any other organization. The techniques used by an individual library manager to perform these functions will vary, depending upon the particular library environment, the department and the nature of its work, and the abilities and personal skills of the manager.

In order for the library to accomplish its mission, library managers must be able to reduce the conflicting goals and forces that exist in the library. To ensure that conflict is reduced so that organizational goals can be attained, control mechanisms are employed, centered on the process of authority, power, and leadership.

Bureaucratic authority, which assumes that the subordinate has little interest or expertise in the activities for successful performance of the unit, may not be the most suitable model for research libraries, although it has been used and eventually accepted in some. But this model of the autonomous professional also assumes that the librarian has little interest in the overall effectiveness of the unit or the library; the work of the individual librarian is the most important function. Yet, the effectiveness of the unit and of all other units is essential to the library's success. Considering all factors, the library will employ the management model that will best ensure organizational effectiveness.

What are the implications, then, for management training? Certainly, it is important that librarians learn to make collective decisions that are in the best interest of the library. Several libraries have emphasized consensus decision making, in the belief that questions needing answers in research libraries today are of such importance that all concerned must be involved. Unfortunately, lack of skill in group decision making and lack of preparation for participatory management have led to some poor decisions and a diminution of confidence in group decision making as a technique. If librarians are going to be able to function as effective team members, they must have adequate training for that role.

Before training in group decision making will have a lasting impact, the individual manager must become aware of personal strengths and weaknesses, tendencies, and preferred management style. Management or supervisory skills workshops and institutes can be enormously helpful in identifying these traits and for taking preliminary steps in making modifications or acquiring new skills. But if these new skills are not reinforced on the job, even the enthusiastic new manager will have difficulty developing and refining effective management practices.

Technical Competence

In view of the rapid changes occurring in research libraries, new skills and competencies must be acquired by their leaders. Computer technology alone will have a marked influence on the organization of research libraries over the next decade. Just as library schools have not prepared their graduates to assume major management posts, neither have they prepared them for fundamental changes in technology.

Librarians who plan to play leadership roles in the future must arm themselves with technical knowledge. While it is not necessary for every librarian to learn computer programming, it is essential that the librarian/manager has enough understanding of technology to make the best possible decisions for the library's directions. Otherwise, the future of the library will be determined by technicians who do not have the full range of understanding.

It is equally important that the managers of research libraries have an understanding of accounting techniques and financial planning principles. Accountability for decisions often resides in the budget arena, and if librarians are unable to participate fully in financial decisions, the library's effectiveness is eroded. In almost all instances, training in accounting and finance must be provided for the new library manager.

Organizational Knowledge

It is not enough that research library managers know the basic techniques of management and supervision. They must also understand how the library operates, both internally and externally. It is essential that the library manager understand the nature of the work being done in his/her department. Equally important is understanding how that work relates to the work of other departments, and to the library as a whole. An increasingly important element is understanding how the library operates in the university environment. The circumstances of the university will, in large measure, dictate the changes necessary in the library. It is the forward looking manager who anticipates and even influences these decisions who will be most effective.

Training for organizational understanding cannot be conducted in a classroom. It is more likely that the new manager will be most helped by working with an experienced top-level administrator within the library. Internships can serve a useful purpose of guiding prospective managers in this area. Once a manager has assumed a new post, it is probably most helpful if the head librarian engages in frequent discussion about the internal and external environment in which the library operates.

VI. SUMMARY

Research libraries are facing a complex and probably difficult future. The requirements of their users, the scope of collections, and wide-ranging activities breed both a unique dynamism and operational complexity. Their sheer size, driven by a growing world-wide production of information, is awesome. The independence of research libraries, which stems in large part from the character of their parent institutions, fosters distinction on as many fronts as it threatens fiscal disaster. New formats for storing and distributing information, born of computer and communications technology, are a demanding and exciting overlay on traditional forms, and new endeavors by book and journal publishers and a host of entrepreneurs in the self-styled information "industry" complicate library operating and economic environments.

But despite the backdrop of current turmoil, general research libraries are still solid contributors to important social objectives. At their core, they are collections of books, journals, manuscripts, maps, archives, photographs, pamphlets, and other such materials essential to scholarship, all assembled with intent, organized with care, responsibly preserved, and made accessible for use. They are also buildings suited to storage and supportive of use. They are organizations that reflect a unique heritage; yet, they are capable of responding to change, making full use of always inadequate financial resources, and depending upon, at least in part, the understanding and support of their constituents. Most of all, they are the people who, over time and in many ways, help carry the past towards the present, often with no sense of motive other than knowing it is the thing to do.

What is required of the profession to meet the challenges of the future is to provide the best possible training and education for its leaders. Research libraries have unique requirements and they must be part of any planning that is done to upgrade professional education or to design continuing professional education or training programs.

It seems unlikely that workshops and conferences will be enough. New understanding of the complex environment in which libraries now operate is a prerequisite for any type of skills training. The legal implications of new methods of dissemination of information must be understood. Adapting the organization structure to meet different service demands cannot be accomplished without substantial knowledge of the effects—and requirements—of certain patterns of organization.

In effect, recasting the profession is what is called for. The brief, however intense, training programs offered currently are extremely valuable for imparting skills to those librarians facing immediate problems. But over the longer term, research libraries will be significantly different organizations from what they are today.

Assistance in the transformation process will be required from many other professions if the library profession continues to provide a valuable service. Research librarians of the future must be trained to perform all of the new roles, without losing sight of the very nature of a research library.

Research libraries as a group are a costly enterprise and the quality of their performance is of great importance to intellectual work of many kinds. Both costs and performance are now matters of concern. Libraries, by their skill, energy, and imagination, must take the lead in responding to these concerns and forming their own future, and their numbers must be augmented by individuals working in related fields and by scholars who are dependent on research libraries in their own work.

NOTES

1. McClure, Charles R. "Library Managers: Can They Manage? Will They Lead?" *Library Journal* 105 (Nov. 15, 1980):2388.
2. Ibid.
3. Bailey, Martha J. "Requirements for Middle Managerial Positions." *Special Libraries* 69 (September, 1978):324.

REFERENCES

Bailey, Martha J., "Requirements for Middle Managerial Positions." *Special Libraries* 69 (September):323–31, 1978.
DeGennaro, Richard. "Library Administration and New Management Systems." *Library Journal* 103 (December 15):2477–82, 1978.

Galvin, Thomas J. "The Crisis in Management." *Idaho Librarian* 27 (October):121–25, 1975.

Heibing, Dorthea, "Sharpening Management Skills—A Resource List for Continuing Education." *Wisconsin Library Bulletin* 75 (November):300–303, 1979.

Holbrook, Anthony. "Librarian as Manager." *New Library World* 77 (May, 1976):95–97.

Lynch, Beverly P. "Libraries as Bureaucracies." *Library Trends* 27 (Winter):259–67, 1979.

McClure, Charles R. "Library Managers: Can They Manage? Will They Lead?" *Library Journal* 105 (November 15):2388–91, 1980.

White, Herbert S. "Management: A Strategy for Change." *Canadian Library Journal* 35 (October):329–39, 1978.

SUBJECT DIVISIONALISM:
A DIAGNOSTIC ANALYSIS

J. P. Wilkinson

THE " SICKNESS"

Apparently subject-divisionalism is currently out of favour in North American libraries, not only in practice but also even as a topic for theoretical discussion. If so, then perhaps the profession (or discipline, if you prefer) of librarianship is in more serious trouble than our most pessimistic critics have supposed. Subject-divisionalism undoubtedly presents difficult, some would say insurmountable, challenges to its proponents; but to dismiss it out of hand may be to surrender our last chance to become an independent intellectual discipline capable of existing concurrently with the newer, more rigorous, and certainly burgeoning discipline of "information science."

Indeed, one is tempted to see in our abandonment of precepts and justifications of subject divisional theory a manifestation of what may be

Advances in Library Administration and Organization, volume 2, pages 21–38.
Copyright © 1983 by JAI Press Inc.
All rights of reproduction in any form reserved.
ISBN: 0-89232-214-4

described as a malaise in librarianship in the second half of the twentieth century. If one takes such a view, it could be predicated upon the assumption that our field in its modern form began healthily enough as a legitimate response to nineteenth-century social needs, with sufficient impetus to carry it thus far into the twentieth century; but that such an impetus, lacking the vital regenerative force of a definable intellectual focus and a widely utilized research base, is now running down. We are becoming the sick discipline of North America, and our malaise is evidenced by our lack of professional curiosity, aggressiveness, and flexibility. The symptoms are as serious as the lack of basic research, which hobbles our attempts to develop a unique theoretical framework, and as trivial as the absence of frequent scholarly discussion in the meetings of too many of our library associations.

The malaise itself is remarkably pervasive. It reaches into our library schools, whose academic relevance and research impact are not seen by many universities as comparable to those in most other disciplines.[1] It reaches into our libraries, where specific subject competencies are so lightly regarded that many employees care little what subjects an applicant has mastered as long as he or she possesses the requisite degrees.[2] It infects the status accorded by society to librarianship and the regard librarians have for the social value of their services;[3] and it militates against the effectiveness of those services.[4] It is an insidious and contagious malaise, and it may indeed eventually kill librarianship as an intellectual discipline.

The sickness does not by any means affect all, or even most library school faculty, students, or librarians; but it is present in every one of these populations. It manifests itself in the routine pragmatism of many technical courses; in the lack of a theoretical base in our discipline;[5] in the sparcity of scholarly publication in our schools;[6] in the predominantly vocational outlook of most students;[7] in the failure of too many libraries to develop explicit goals, let alone operationalized objectives; in the lack of intellectual stimulation at a discouraging number of our library conferences; in the prevalence of limited, "conservative" service in the field;[8] and in the relative lack of in-depth client relationships in most of our libraries.

The causes of the sickness are much harder to describe than its symptoms. There is undoubtedly a "vicious circle" operating, in that the traditional reputation of librarianship itself causes difficulties in attracting highly motivated self-starters to the discipline. There is probably still an historical cause in that librarianship was for so long an opportunity for "gentlewomen" to earn a respectable living, and a legitimate refuge for less aggressive men (who nevertheless became administrators). There is a societal cause in that recreation rather than information has too frequently been seen as the determinant for the social recognition and support of public libraries, and recreation (while desirable) is comparably less measurably valuable than information.[9] There is an intellectual cause in that the relationship between vital social needs and the potential of information studies to meet those needs has eluded, indeed has only relatively infrequently concerned, librarians.[10] These causes, however, are themselves generally unresearched, little understood, and quite possibly not exhaustive. They are rarely if ever, for example, seen in the context of the basic organizational requisites of libraries themselves; and herein, finally, lies the ultimate significance of (the failure of) subject-divisionalism in North American libraries.

THE "CURE"

It is not the purpose of this paper to trace the history of subject-divisionalism in North America. The topic has been well treated by such writers as E.R. Johnson and Margaret Hocker;[11] but a definition of "subject-divisionalism" is needed here, and the one by Johnson is probably as good as any.

> In its most common form the subject-divisional plan is based on subject matter rather than on function or form. A precise definition of the subject-divisional plan covering all instances is [however] difficult. In order to obtain a homogeneous group of libraries for a study of libraries organized by the subject-divisional plan, a somewhat arbitrary set of criteria was established: (1) the service functions of the library are arranged by broader-than-single-subject areas (usually two or more related subject departments are grouped under one librarian responsible to the chief librarian or his deputy; for example, humanities, social sciences, and sciences); (2) the library has made a commitment to open access to most library materials for all levels of students and other patrons; (3) the library employs specialized book selection personnel and provides specialized, as contrasted with general, subject assistance to readers.[12]

The third of the above criteria is particularly important in the context of this paper. The use of specialized personnel and the provision of specialized subject asistance for readers moves subject-divisionalism out of organizational theory as such and into the realm of psycho-organizational dynamics; and here again a definition is needed. "Psycho-organizational dynamics" is a term developed by the present writer to describe a blending of basic psychological concepts and current organizational theory into a "new" and dynamic approach to (library) management.[13] Applied to libraries, the approach provides a perhaps novel rationale for the utilization of professional personnel.

> The modern library is clearly not a homogeneous organization, either in terms of its objectives, the demands it makes upon its personnel, or the mental sets its requires to achieve its goals. Why, therefore, attempt to impose a single authority structure, a

single communication pattern, or a single personnel policy throughout a library? Why not instead let those parts of the library that develop complex objectives be organized along highly participative (if not collegial) lines involving an all-points communication pattern and striving towards adult/adult transactions based upon conceptions of individual "professional" conscience derived from logical comprehensiveness and universality? On the other hand, let those parts of the library that develop routine, task-oriented objectives requiring adherence to regulations and subordination to administrative authority be more structured, with chain communication regarded as acceptable, with Kohlberg's conventional stages regarded as entirely acceptable, and with conventional parent/child transactions not regarded as dysfunctional.[14]

Librarians, by which we mean "professional librarians" in a North American context, are thus to be involved very largely in a complex, participative, externally oriented, judgement-making and decision-taking occupation. The value to society of such an occupation rests upon the depth and perceived importance of the client relationships involved, and here we turn to the contrast between the "forms-and-process" library organization and subject-divisionalism. "Forms-and-process" divides the library by the form material takes and the processes to which that material is subjected. Thus we have a microform division, a periodical division, a newspaper division, a catalogue division, a reference division, and so on. Such divisions may be easier to administer, but, it may be argued, they tend to look inwards to the library's convenience rather than outward to the needs of the user. The user, after all, is normally not primarily interested in format but in the information itself; and, unless his search is to e exhaustive, he or she wants the quest to be as simple as possible, ɔncomitant with results. Moreover, in the quest for information the role of the information expert should be of continual importance. The relationship between a complex information taxonomy (as distinct from a directional or one-source informative item) and the needs of a client is rarely self-evident, and to optimize the required interface should surely require an intermediary capable of appreciating the full potential of any interaction between a subject-user and the subject: that is, should require a subject specialist librarian.

The role of the subject specialist in libraries has, however, been very often misunderstood (outside of some "special" libraries) because that role has been subjected to the overriding acceptance of the "forms-and-process" structure. Thus libraries may utilize subject-specialization in book selection, or cataloguing, or reference; but they fail to integrate such specialization into a concept of overall responsibility for, and authority over a total functional stream based upon subject coverage. Worse, they fail to distinguish between the building plan of a library and its intellectual contribution and they confuse the "division" of responsibility with the purely physical "divisions" of the building.

Frank A. Lundy of the University of Nebraska Libraries, though he was by no means the first exponent of subject-divisionalism,[16] became the outstanding spokesman for the concept and fully understood most of its implications.

> He and his staff were convinced that they had a superior concept of library organiza-
> tion and service and they began explaining and publicizing the plan with a missionary-
> like zeal over the next twenty-five years. So successful were these efforts that to
> many librarians today the phrase "subject-divisional plan" is still synonymous with
> the University of Nebraska. . . . [To the end, Lundy] continued to maintain that a
> number of the ideas which had been modified or dropped were still good in theory,
> even though the library could no longer afford to continue them in practice. He had
> also come to believe that the subject-divisional plan had been misunderstood in
> academic library circles because, in his view, it was not merely a building plan. He
> held that it could be applied virtually anywhere, more or less regardless of the
> physical facilities available. For him, it was essentially a philosophy of librarianship
> and of library administration and it was, therefore, capable of nearly universal appli-
> cation.[17]

Lundy, indeed, went far towards recognizing the psycho-organizational importance of subject-divisionalism (although the term itself postdates him, Lundy would almost certainly have appreciated the value of psy-chological research in organizational development).

> The librarians at Nebraska would not be merely "custodians" in the "warehouse" of
> knowledge but real educators, competent in their own right, and active members in
> the academic community. Because of the subject-divisional plan "reference li-
> brarians" were to become "humanities librarians" or "social science librarians."
> . . . [Secondly] The divisional plan was the foundation for extending some of the
> traditional ideas and philosophies of librarianship. One way of doing this was to
> combine reference, book selection, and cataloging functions in the duties of each of
> the subject-divisional librarians. This is what Lundy called "the practice of librarian-
> ship clear across the board." The idea came to be known at Nebraska as the "dual
> assignment," attracting a great deal of attention in the library world.[18]

Here, then, is the all-important connection between subject-divisionalism and the malaise in librarianship referred to at the start of this paper. The subject-divisional plan, at least as it developed at Nebraska and later at the Dalhousie University Library in Nova Scotia, Canada,[19] represented a challenge to the whole image and psychology of librarianship in North America and, this chapter suggests, the decline of subject-divisionalism provides a sharp delineation of the very malaise with which we are concerned.[20]

First let us examine in greater detail the challenge of subject-divisionalism as it affected the librarians working with and within it at, for example, Nebraska and Dalhousie. Both libraries attempted to provide an all-points communication environment. In both, the operation of the library was entrusted to a library council which included all subject-division heads. In both, the members of council were communicative equals, and the library director chaired the meeting as the supportive "linking-pin" with higher administrative echelons, rather than as an authoritarian director.[21] At Dalhousie, in particular, the role of the director changed over a period of five years from that of director-*and*-council to director-*in*-council, so that eventually no major administrative decision was implemented without majority agreement, and the director became largely a peer member of the group with particular responsiblity for obtaining support for library policy outside the library.

Such communicative equality did not stem from mere idealism. Each professional member in a subject-divisional organization is a specialist with a unique contribution to make to the effectiveness of the group. The "foreman" concept borrowed from the industrial model, in which the higher levels of management are assumed to possess much of the knowledge and experience of the workers they supervise, simply cannot hold in the atmosphere of specialization inherent in a truly professional organization (if indeed it retains validity in any complex organization).[22] Subject-divisionalism not only requires a unique contribution from each professional member, but also tends to provide each member with the self-esteem and adult-adult transactional plane suitable to his or her level of psycho-intellectual development.[23] In return, the subject-divisional plan also expects that its members will relate to the objectives of the group at a higher level than merely that of an orientation to power or authority as such (an orientation typified by Kohlberg's lower levels of moral development).[24]

Subject-divisionalism, then, at least as conceived of by Frank Lundy and the present author, may justifiably be described as "a new philosophy of librarianship."[25] Certainly, as Lundy repeatedly emphasized, the subject-division is *not* merely a building concept. It is a model for professional development, and the "dual assignment," as a part of this development, ensures that every librarian simultaneously practices several library functions and is therefore better able to understand (and eventually presumably to supervise) most of those functions. The crucial developmental role of subject-divisionalism lies, however, in the demands it makes upon the total motivational and psychological strengths of its adherents, for the specialist in a peer-communication environment has literally no place to hide. He or she must stand or fall on the contribution made to and recognized by the group; and such contributions must be based upon a solid foundation of constantly up-dated knowledge. Participative management, which is what subject-divisionalism requires and what it received at Nebraska and Dalhousie, is therefore a most demanding concept for every member of the group, not least for the leader who must coordinate, adjudicate, and convince. To a great extent, therefore, subject-divisionalism requires of librarians the same teaching, research, and expressive attributes that the academic ethos requires of the university professor. For this reason, it tends to resolve the dichotomy between the academic librarian and the professor—what Daniel Bergen once referred to as the "bipolarization of the academic enterprise"[26]— and is particularly suited to the needs of the academic library (although its value to the larger public library is almost as great). By the same token, however, the ambitious expectations of the plan place a premium upon the most effective use of the professional's time. Moreover, the objectives of subject-divisionalism put heavy emphasis upon constant initiative and judgement and call for such psychological strengths as that level of morality which emphasizes equality and mutual obligation within the relevant group (Kohlberg); highly fulfilled needs for belonging and esteem (Maslow); and a well-developed "adult" state (Harris). These strengths must be fostered, moreover, within a compatible "all-points" communicative environment, as described by Alex Bavelas[27] and referred to in my own "Psycho-Organizational Approach."[28]

Yet subject-divisionalism in North America is in decline and, where it does still exist, it tends to be in a diluted form, which sharply reduces the overall responsibility of the subject specialist. Why, then, did "the Lundy dream" fade, even at Nebraska before his retirement?

REJECTION OF THE "CURE"

Johnson attributes the decline of subject-divisionalism to several factors. Many librarians never were convinced of its universal applicability. There was, for example, a great deal of skepticism concerning the assumption that subject specialists could offer really significant advice to users in their division outside their own specific discipline. As A.L. McNeal stated:

> In theory the subject specialist provides means of giving better service to a particular clientele. The fact that a Science Librarian has a degree in Chemistry may support the theory so long as his services are sought in that field. If the questions come from the area of Physics, Zoology, or Botany, he may have little more background than the average reference librarian. It can be claimed that he will have training in the scientific method, and that he will understand the needs of the scientist. This can also be true of the good general reference librarian.[29]

Again, as Johnson points out, "the subject-divisional plan represented a compromise in the eternal battle between teaching departments and librarians over the question of centralized or decentralized library facilities. Like all compromises, it did not satisfy everyone."[30] The continuing growth of interdisciplinary fields, particularly in the sciences, was seen as placing an unmanagable strain on *any* centralizing concept and to argue for departmental collections.

Moreover, the claim of subject-divisionalism to help unsophisticated undergraduates through reading room collections and service, while at the same time assisting advanced scholars through subject specialist library personnel, was challenged both because it might "spoon-feed" the undergraduate and also because it did not recognize, as did the undergraduate library concept, the unique nature of undergraduate needs.

[Finally,] several other factors contributed to the decline of the subject-divisional movement. Some argued that it was too expensive or too difficult to administer because of its requirement for well-trained subject librarians, the duplication of certain library materials it involved, and its demands on space properly to house collections and reading rooms for the subject divisions. Of all the factors contributing to the decline of the subject-divisional movement, the problem of space was the most important.[31]

Categorizing the above factors as either physical or intellectual, the present writer is tempted to minimize the physical factors, although Lundy himself placed them high on his own list.[32] The subject-divisional concept was never, at least at Nebraska or Dalhousie, primarily a building plan. Of course, a growth in student enrollment and in collections will place stress on subject-divisional libraries; but so will it also, as McAnally and Downs clearly point out,[33] on *any* type of academic library organization. As far as the physical structure of the library is concerned, maximum flexibility is just about all a university can provide, as Lundy himself believed;[34] and this regardless of the type of service approach involved.

It is, therefore, the psychological factors in the demise of subject-divisionalism which are of critical importance, and these can be divided into three groups highly relevant to our present thesis. First, there are the attitudes of library management. The basic conservatism which has typified many of our approaches to the library organization and management appear to apply also with respect to the present issue and perhaps with good reason, for the psycho-organizational adjustment to subject-divisionalism may in fact be, as we shall see, greater than our present capability for change.

Secondly, there are those psychological factors pertaining to the role of the subject specialist in the library. These factors would seem to concern the role-set of the specialist, his or her relationship with undergraduates, and the degree of perceived compatability between library subject specialists and teaching faculty (and postgraduate researchers).

Thirdly, there are the professional perceptions and psychological characteristics of the subject specialist librarians themselves. Subject-divisionalism, in its fullest sense, requires a personal as well as a managerial adjustment which may be the most difficult of all for librarians to achieve.

POST-MORTEM ANALYSIS: MANAGEMENT ATTITUDES.

To refer to the traditional conservatism of library management is admittedly to treat this important area in much too sweeping and simplistic a fashion. If many senior librarians have questioned the management implications of subject-divisionalism, their suspicions deserve deeper analysis. The effective diffusion of "expertise" throughout an organization inevitably requires a redistribution of the elements of authority since each subject specialist will expect, and in cost-effectiveness terms warrant, a greater degree of individual responsibility and authority. Subject-divisionalism embodies, in other words, an explicit recognition of that professional competence and self-awareness which the late Arthur McAnally described in his 1973 discussion of the pressures currently exerted upon academic library directors:

> Nowadays the library staff, both the academic or professional and the non-professional, are far better educated than in the past. Most librarians hold at least a master's degree, and many higher degrees. They also are more socially conscious, action-oriented, and impatient—in common with the rest of our society. They want and expect a share in policy decisions affecting themselves and the library. The rise of library specialists in university libraries also is producing severe strains on the library's administrative structure, and represents a force for change in administrative practices.[35]

McAnally was writing of those pressures which increasingly affect every academic library, regardless of its organizational library structure. How much more forceful will they be in an organization which places high priorities on discrete, individual subject expertise. Indeed, chief librarians, and by extension the more senior levels of library management, are apparently becoming more authoritarian rather than less in the face of the increasing pressures and complexities of modern library administration. On this point it is worth quoting McAnally further and at some length.

> Writers on management agree that to a certain degree stress stimulates executives to better peformance. But they also agree that excessive stress is harmful. As the pressures on the director increase, he has a tendency to become more and more decisive in attempting to cope with the growing multitude of problems alone, until he ultimately offends too many people or else concludes that the rewards are no longer worth the cost. The growing pressures on the director are exerted by five different groups. They are, in probable order of magnitude, the president's office, the library

staff, the faculty, students and, in publicly supported universities, state boards of control. It may seem odd to list the library faculty as high as second, but in those cases in which the principal cause for the director quitting his position can be identified, the library staff ranks second. . . . A particular problem that has not yet surfaced fully is that the director has two staffs, one academic or professional and one clerical or nonacademic. The latter is the larger of the two. Different administrative styles are neded for each.[36]

The point is, of course, that management suspicions derived from subject-divisionalism's encouragement of shared decision making and implemented expertise are misdirected. The professional librarian's growing awareness of his or her new potential is the result of many factors not connected with the subject-divisional approach; and such an awareness can be channelled through, but does not result from subject-divisional planning.[37]

Subject-divisionalism, far from threatening library administrators, offers, therefore, a means of ending the administrator's isolation from the grass roots of the library—from the users and the library staff who directly meet user needs. The chief librarian, thus seen as the link between his peers in the library council and the senior levels of the parent community, is in an extremely strong integrative position. He or she speaks for and truly represents the library; is but the apex of a subject-oriented organization which closely approximates the taxonomy of user informational needs; and is an expert among experts rather than an individual possibly holding on to an illegitimized (because no longer recognized for itself alone) authority.

POST-MORTEM: THE SUBJECT SPECIALIST

The concern as to whether or not the subject specialist can "offer really significant advice to users . . . outside their own specific discipline" involves two related concerns. First, we must ask whether alternatives to subject-divisionalism have led to an awareness among librarians that the services they offer are socially significant; and secondly we must ask how the services of subject specialists increase or decrease this awareness.

The dismaying evidence appears to be that public librarians at least do not presently regard their services as socially important. Mary Howrey, in her 1978 study of Illinois public librarians, found that their

belief in public service is low in relation to the other . . . professional dimensions, indicating that in general public librarians do not feel their profession is an indispensible service to society . . . [but] librarianship will never be an important occupation or profession unless the practitioners *themselves* believe it to be important. Librarians must first convince themselves of their professional status if they are to convince others.[38]

Certainly one may wonder if such lack of self-recognition does not contribute to the lack of reliability in library service found by such researchers as Bunge, Crowthers, and Childers. Moreover, poor information service is a self-fulfilling death wish, for unreliable products are clearly *not* socially important or in demand. It is at least arguable, therefore, that, even if the subject specialist can offer reliable service only in his or her own discipline, such limited service is better than inaccurate service which presumably leads to a decreased level of expectation on the part of the recipient, and which may result in a preponderance of relatively undemanding (and unimportant?) "one and two step questions" put by clients to their libraries.[39]

Moreover, there is a basic fallacy in the argument that subject-divisionalism can serve only a narrow range of clients. Because, as Samuel Rothstein has intimated,[40] successful responses to multistep research-type questions can lead to dramatic increases in the proportion of such questions, and because the subject specialist can thus serve an ever broadening client base, the (subject-divisional) library can constantly increase the justified expectations of its clients and thus increase the level of support it can legitimately ask for in meeting those expectations. If ten subject specialists can develop a satisfied clientele of societal leaders and opinion-makers, then that clientele will support (and encourage others to support) the addition of ten more subject specialists; but if the opinion-makers have low expectations of library service they will question (and lead others to question) the need for even the initial ten professional librarians. The psychology of service found among practicing librarians probably has much to do with the demand for numbers of librarians and for the services they provide.

If the above is true, it follows that well-qualified, well-paid, self-confident and willingly accountable subject specialists will increase the self- and socially perceived significance of the services they offer. They will then more than justify the initially higher costs of their service to the community and will enable the library to afford and attract more such truly professional personnel. Such an approach to personnel development is intended to be extremely practical; but also, and equally importantly, it provides a major premise in one future theoretical justification of librarianship in a post-industrial society.[41]

This theoretical framework clearly provides for compatibility between subject specialists and researchers (be they in special, university, or public libraries). It also, however, accommodates a higher-level relationship between the supposedly less demanding requirements of undergraduates, casual clients, and other nonresearch-oriented library users. In so far as such users do not need the services of subject specialists, they should interrogate library technicians (or on-line services). At the point where their needs are perceived as complex and judgement-taking, they should be referred to professional subject specialists. The latter does indeed have a legitimate role with respect to the nonresearcher; but that role is more limited and should be subject to preliminary screening. To argue otherwise is to negate the value of trained support staff in the public services, misuse (in cost-effectiveness terms) the highy paid, highly qualified specialist, and denigrate the social importance of professional information services in libraries.

POST-MORTEM: PROFESSIONAL PERCEPTIONS

We should not, and do not intend to, here become involved in the often fruitless and emotion-charged question of whether librarianship is a true profession. Some, such as John North, have argued that it is not,[42] but such arguments are probably peripheral to the concerns of the present paper. Whatever we call ourselves, we must choose between either offering services based upon independent, accountable judgements that arise from individual expertise and a body of specialized, expanding knowledge, or offering ingress to institutionally generated and controlled collections. The first choice corresponds to, for example, Amitai Etzioni's understanding of a true profession, while the second more closely approximates his criteria for a "para-professional" role.[43] What matters more than terminology, however, is that the self-perceptions of the librarian in the first instance will probably be more estimable, demanding, and involved than in the second instance.

Moreover, in that situation in which information services are based upon individual subject-specialization and a freedom to make judgements based upon that specialization, society's clear perception of the individual as an individual becomes paramount only if the "professionals are provided with the instruments, facilities, and auxiliary staff required for their work."[44] Relevant work, in this instance, involves the creation, application, and communication of knowledge. To the extent, therefore, that a library fails to provide its professionals with the necessary facilities and support staff, it becomes "nonprofessional"; and, to the extent that the library rejects the use of subject specialists (for who else can specialize in the creation, application, and communication of subject knowledge?), that library rejects not only subject-divisionalism but also professionalism.

The reader may tend to react instinctively against the above sequencing of generalized arguments. Let us, therefore, emphasize once again the logical sequence of our case. Librarianship may or may not be a profession; but it does involve the communication of information. In so far as such information is selected, interpreted, and prepared for dissemination, it may be regarded as knowledge. To adequately communicate knowledge, an organization needs to provide an environment of individual intellectual freedom, responsibility, and accountability for its employees. The employees in their turn must feel a commitment to subject knowledge and judgement-taking; but a non-subject-divisional plan cannot, we are arguing, provide such an environment or expect of its employees such a commitment. Indeed, the history of the hierarchical forms and process library would seem in retrospect to typify the failure of librarians to acquire subject specializations and to accept responsibility for the production, application, and communication of knowledge.[45]

Librarians have thus traditionally failed to bring to their "discipline" the professional perceptions and psychological requirements for subject-divisionalism; and libraries have consequently typically failed to develop organizational environments conducive to the fostering and utilization of subject specialization. Both the personal and managerial adjustments necessary to the successful growth of the subject-divisional plan have been absent; and it is for this reason, as much as for the reasons suggested by Johnson, that subject-divisionalism has failed to dominate library thinking and development.

CONCLUSIONS

There is, then, a "cure" for the malaise which afflicts librarianship, and that cure is subject-divisionalism; but we have rejected the cure and our reasons for doing so are revealed in post-mortem analysis to be deep-rooted and pervasive. Yet, though we are as a group conservative and insecure, we are presumably open to argument and the foregoing diagnosis has attempted to make several, we hope, persuasive points.

First, the library user, insofar as he seeks information, is less concerned with format than with data. Second, the dissemination of such data normally involves selection, interpretation (active or passive), and communication. Third, the importance *to the user* of the selection, interpretation, and communication processes will depend to a very considerable extent upon his or her perception of the communicative librarian's credibility and responsibility. Fourth, the credibility granted to the "mentor" function[46] of the librarian results in large part from that librarian's organizational environment and self-image. The self-image of the librarian with respect to the social importance of services provided rests upon the perceived complexity and/or importance of the enquiry, upon the depth of knowledge (expertise) required to respond effectively and upon the independence of judgement and decision-taking (span of discretion) provided by the library organization. Fifth, the degree of *subject* expertise, responsibility, and accountability necessary to an increasing societal recognition of the importance of the library's information services can only exist where the subject specialization of librarians, rather than their knowledge of format *per se* or their line function, is reflected in the basic administrative structure of the library. Finally, the common theme linking the above five points is drawn essentially from psycho-organizational theory and not from traditional structural concepts as such. The *psychological* environment of the subject specialist is as important as his postgraduate training or his hygienic security, and only a subject-divisional approach to library organization can optimize such an environment.

Thus, only when the effectiveness of (subject-divisional) library service is socially perceived to warrant major public expenditures can the costs for such service be justified and forthcoming. Public service in libraries can rarely be analyzed in cost-benefit terms, but it can be justified in terms of cost-effectiveness, and the effectiveness of such service will increasingly be measured in terms of the subject information supplied. Only the subject-divisional approach can provide the necessary framework and stimuli for such effectiveness.

Subject-divisional planning has failed in libraries because the necessary psychological conditioning and environment have been lacking at the organizational level, the management level, the service level, and the user level. The obstacles to remedying these lacks are far greater than would be presented by physical or fiscal barriers alone. The individual commitment and self-improvement which will be needed if librarians are to reverse their tradition of benevolent authoritarianism may seem too great in the short run. The heritage of Van Hoesen and Ellsworth and Lundy is, however, of greater depth and dimension than many of their successors may realize. It will overshadow librarianship in all aspects and through all its future. It cannot be ignored.

NOTES AND REFERENCES

1. The present writer is more familiar with the Canadian library scene than with those of other countries. It is his impression that much of what he describes and prescribes is applicable outside Canada, but if he inadvertently generalizes inappropriately from his own limited observations, he hopes readers will be quick to so advise.

2. At least one chief librarian, for example, has stated publicly to incoming Canadian library school students that today's library employers are interested in the personality and overall grades of applicants rather than in their specific course or subject background, and this statement is in line with a recent finding by academic librarians attending a regional conference of the Canadian Association of University Teachers that "willingness to enter the administrative structure of the library when positions are open is rewarded, while increasing specialization in one area is not." (*Feliciter*, 26, 2 (February 1980):4.)

3. Note, for example, the recent findings of Mary M. Howrey, referred to later in this paper.

4. It is at least arguable, for example, that the high rate of reference "misses" reported by researchers such as Bunge, Crowthers, and Childers results in part from the belief of many librarians that the responses they give are "not all that important"; and one of the more revealing symptoms of the malaise referred to here was the alarm expressed by many of us over the possiblity, raised by Allan Angoff's apocryphal "Library Malpractice Suit: Could It Happen To You?" *American Libraries*, 7, 8 (September 1976):489, that librarians might actually be sued if they disseminated dangerously inaccurate information.

5. Fifteen years ago Neal Harlow, addressing a meeting of the Canadian Library Association, spoke of our lack of such a base. "Problem one in the education of librarians is that no general theory of professional behaviour has been widely accepted . . . no theoretical base, no prototype upon which to pattern education and practice. We have been content to do what comes naturally." ("The Educational Problem," *Canadian Library* 22 (September 1965:87.) Sadly, this statement is probably as applicable today as it was a decade and a half ago.

6. Thus, the present author found that, from 1970 to 1975, the median number of publications for Canadian library educators indexed in *Library Literature* was, for assistant professors, 0; for associate professors, 2; and, for full professors, 4. (J.P. Wilkinson, "Trends in Library Education—Canada," *Advances in Librarianship*, Vol. 8 [New York: Academic Press, 1978], p. 221.)

7. At the University of Toronto's Faculty of Library Science, for example, elective courses such as those dealing with the library in politics, and communication and documentation theory rarely attract half as many students as do the more specifically "vocational" electives covering such areas as advanced cataloguing, reference, and government publications. The same appears to be generally true of continuing education workshops.

8. See Samuel Rothstein, *The Development of Reference Services Through Academic Traditions, Public Library Practice, and Special Librarianship* (Chicago: Association of College and Reference Libraries, 1955, ACRL Monograph, 14), pp. 94–95.

9. Clearly the controversial issue of recreational versus informational justifications for public libraries is too complex and, in context, too peripheral to warrant fuller discussion in this paper. Interested readers are referred, for starters, to H.C. Goddard's unpublished Ph.D. thesis, "A Study in the Theory and Measurement of Benefits and Costs in the Public Library" (Indiana University, Department of Economics, 1970); and, in particular to Goddard's argument "that recreation is not a service with which there are attached public or collective benefits of such magnitude to merit public support" (p. 177).

10. The relationship between developing information needs in post-industrial societies and the role of librarianship has indeed so eluded librarians for so long that William Knox was moved fifteen years ago to observe

[A] large number of professionally trained people entered the information services business [after the second world war] but not as librarians. And a number of competent entrepreneurs more sensitive to the changing market found a real opportunity to provide information services and with profit to themselves. This turn of events was not preordained. It took a positive turning away from the problem by the general library community to bring about this situation. ("The Changing Role of Libraries," *American Library Association Bulletin* 59 [8 September 1965]:720–25.):723.

11. E.R. Johnson, "Subject-Divisional Organization in American University Libraries, 1939–74," *Library Quarterly* 47 (January 1977):23–42. Margaret Hocker, "A Study of Library Organization with Special Emphasis on the Subject-Divisional Type" (Unpublished A.M.L.S. Thesis, University of Michigan, 1950).

12. Johnson, p. 24.

13. J.P. Wilkinson, "The Psycho-organizational Approach to Staff Communication in Libraries," *Journal of Academic Librarianship* 4, 1 (March 1978):21–26.

14. Wilkinson, p. 26.

15. For a fuller discussion of one-step, two-step and multistep measurements of reference questions see J.P. Wilkinson and William Miller, "The 'Step' Approach to Reference Service," *R.Q.* 17, 4 (Summer 1978):293–300.

16. The concept of subject-divisionalism has, indeed, a long and honourable history. William F. Poole, the "father of subject departmentation," proposed as early as 1881, "a classification of books into four grand divisions or departments of knowledge, each one of which would have a floor and reading room to itself." ("The Construction of Library Buildings," *Circulars of Information of the Bureau of Education*, no. 1. [Washington: U.S. Bureau of Education, 1881], p. 12). The Boston, Cleveland, Los Angeles, Baltimore, Rochester, and Toledo public libraries had all experimented with subject-divisional departments before 1940.

17. Johnson, pp. 33, 34.

18. Johnson, p. 33.

19. The present writer learned subject-divisional theory and practice as assistant director (Social Sciences) at the University of Nebraska Library under Frank Lundy from 1957 to 1960; and, as the Director of Libraries at Dalhousie University, Halifax, Nova Scotia, initiated an expanded version of the Lundy concept at Dalhousie between 1960 and 1965.

20. To thus equate the decline of one organizational concept with the decline of an entire profession may strike some readers as an overreaction. However, current management theory does indeed stress the integral relationship between organizational structure and professional effectiveness. Jane G. Flener, for example, concluded her article on "Staff Participation in Management in Large University Libraries" by noting that, "Ahead lies the challenge of how best to establish the climate and communications necessary to use most effectively the talents within the staff to meet the changes ahead for libraries and their patrons." (*College and Research Libraries* 34, 4 [July 1973]:279.); and M.M. Howrey stresses that, "Professionalization, in essence, means that *all* librarians assume responsibility for the quality of service to patrons, . . . such responsibility cannot be limited to decision-making within one's immediate work situation." ("Professionalism of Librarians: an Exploratory Study," *Illinois Libraries* 60, 5 [May 1978]:465).

21. The term "linking pin" is drawn from the work of Rensis Likert. See especially his *New Patterns of Management* (New York: McGraw-Hill, 1961), p. 113.

22. As Keith Davis has pointed out in *Human Relations at Work*, 3d ed. (New York: McGraw-Hill, 1967), pp. 101–102, "Technical skill . . . is the distinguishing feature of job performance at the operating level; but as employees are promoted to leadership responsibilities, their technical skills become proportionately less important. . . . They increasingly depend on the technical skills of their subordinates and in many cases have not practiced the technical skill which they supervise."

23. For primary readings on the concepts of "level of self-esteem" and "adult-adult transactions" see respectively A.H. Maslow, *Motivation and Personality* (New York: Harper, 1970) especially Chapter 4, "A Theory of Human Motivation"; and T.A. Harris, *I'm O.K.—You're O.K.* (New York: Avon, 1973).

24. For primary reading on this concept of moral development see Lawrence Kohlberg, "A Cognitive–Developmental Approach to Moral Education," *Humanist* 32, 6 (November–December 1972):13–16.

25. F.A. Lundy, "The Divisional Plan Library," *College and Research Libraries* 17, 2 (March 1956):148.

26. Daniel Bergen, 'Librarians and the Bipolarization of the Academic Enterprise,'' *College and Research Libraries* 24, 6 (November 1963):467–480.

27. Alex Bavelas, "An Experimental Approach to Organizational Communication," *Personnel* 27, 5 (March 1951):366–371.

28. Wilkinson, "The Psycho-organizational Approach to Staff Communication in Libraries," p. 26.

29. A.L. McNeal, "Divisional Organization in the University Library." *University of Tennessee Library Lectures*, no. 12 (1960):45–46.

30. Johnson, p. 38.

31. Johnson, p. 39.

32. F.A. Lundy, *The Divisional Plan Library*. (Kent, Ohio: Kent State University, Department of Library Science, 1959), p. 5. (Aspects of Librarianship, 18)

33. A.M. McAnally and R.B. Downs, "The Changing Role of Directors of University Libraries," *College and Research Libraries*, 34, 2 (March 1973).

34. Frank Lundy himself was a strong exponent of modular planning, believing that a library should resemble an "airplane hangar" with only the exterior walls fixed and weight-bearing.

35. McAnally, p. 111.

36. McAnally, p. 110.

37. Indeed, the directors' tendency to become authoritarian under pressure runs counter to the very professionalism which creates such pressure. As Jerald Hage and Michael Aiken, for example, have noted ("Relationship of Centralization to Other Structural Properties," *Administrative Science Quarterly* 12, 1 [June 1967]:72–92) "Presumably the greater the professional activity, the greater the demands for participation in organizational decision making. A number of case studies have suggested that professionals demand not only more job autonomy, but more power in general. Conversely, as the job occupants in an organization demonstrate more competence and expertise, men with power are more likely to consult with them, thus sharing decision making to a greater degree" (p. 84).

38. M.M. Howrey, pp. 463, 465.

39. Wilkinson and Miller, "The 'Step' Approach to Reference Service," p. 298.

40. Samuel Rothstein, pp. 95, 96, cites two indicative cases in this connection. *Ad hoc* Carnegie Corporation grants to the Pennsylvania and Cornell University Libraries enabled those libraries to offer specific in-depth services to faculty members engaged in research. The two "research librarians" involved had no connection with the regular reference staff and limited themselves to bibliographic and critical analysis research of considerable magnitude. Their efforts, regarded at first with skepticism by the faculty, led to widespread approval of their contribution because their specialized knowledge *as librarians* enabled them to find information which the faculty "could not have found for themselves at all." Despite such success, however, the Carnegie experiment had little impact upon library thinking. At Pennsylvania the position was discontinued upon termination of the grant; at Cornell it was not developed and apparently languished to its demise. "Most disheartening of all was the fact that the whole venture attracted surprisingly little emulation from other university libraries. . . . [Possibly] most librarians and university administrators . . . simply felt that they could not attract the personnel competent to offer such service."

41. The implications of a "diagnostic" approach to subject-divisionalism are apparently as numerous as they are controversial. The theoretical framework referred to here, though it clearly cannot be developed in the space of this paper, would involve the type of unique user-information relationships implicit in Edward Howard's rationalization of the social role of the public library: "In any given community the viable role of the public library is defined for it by the information resources already existing in other institutions, organizations, and agencies. The public library legitimately can do no more than occupy that part of the local

information network which is not already occupied." ("Toward PPBS in the Public Library," *American Libraries* 2, 4 [April 1971]:386–387)

42. John North, "Librarianship: a Profession?" *Canadian Library Journal* 34, 4 (August 1977):253–257.

43. Amitai Etzioni, *Modern Organizations* (Englewood Cliffs, N.J.: Prentice Hall, 1964), p. 78.

44. Etzioni, p. 78.

45. See, for example, the recent attack by Lloyd Houser and Alvin Schrader on the propensity of library educators and librarians to continue on without any theoretical framework: a course of action which can sustain the profession "only as long as society is willing to continue to tolerate their confused enterprise." (*The Search for a Scientific Profession: Library Science Education in the U.S. and Canada.* [Metuchen, N.J. Scarecrow Press, 1978]. p. 158.)

46. For a provocative discussion of the contrasting views of the librarian's "mentor" function in America and in the U.S.S.R., see W.M. Peters's "The Mentor Librarian," *IPLO Quarterly* 12, 4 (April 1971):173–184.

VIDEOTEXT DEVELOPMENT IN THE UNITED STATES

Michael B. Binder

Britain, France, Canada, and Japan were the first countries to recognize the potential of videotext; in the 1970s, each mounted sophisticated government-sponsored tests to develop and promote this new technology. The United States, although a late starter, has been quickly catching up in videotext development by expanding networks that already exist in computing and communications while utilizing the British, French, and Canadian technologies in its own development activities.

In comparison to the beginning of 1980, when it could be said of the United States that no cable television company had a cabletext channel operating, no full-channel teletext had been tested, no full-scale research efforts had explored the social implications of videotext, no serious explorations of the public service potential of teletext or viewdata had begun, no formal government proceeding had been convened to consider the knotty regulatory and policy issues, and no systematic evaluation of

Advances in Library Administration and Organization, volume 2, pages 39–68.
Copyright © 1983 by JAI Press Inc.
All rights of reproduction in any form reserved.
ISBN: 0-89232-214-4

current tests had taken place,[1] by the beginning of 1982, frenzied activity was occurring in all of these areas.

To help librarians gain a firm grasp of videotext development in the United States, following a review of system basics, this chapter focuses in detail on the areas where major development is transpiring—the newspaper and telephone companies, commercial and public broadcasting, cable television and OCLC.

SYSTEM BASICS

The reader should be aware that much confusion and disagreement over terminology exists in this field, as might indeed be expected of such a potentially significant, newly emerging technology-based service. There appears, however, to be a consensus that the field generically refers to a class of computerized information systems which, from a user's perception, are low cost, simple and easy to use. The use of color, graphics, and a television set or video terminal as the display device are additional salient features.

Early development of videotext was directed along the lines of systems using either telephone or broadcast transmission. The British, who pioneered in this area, used "viewdata" to describe its telephone-based system and "teletext" for its broadcast system. To give some idea of the inconsistencies now found in the jargon, the terms videotext, videotex, teletext, and teletex are often used by different authors to mean the same thing. Which term is used appears to be a result of either the author's personal preference or that of his or her publisher. The country where the development is taking place is also a determining factor. Britain and the United States, for example, still prefer to use viewdata to describe telephone-based systems despite the adoption by the CCITT (the International Telephone and Telegraph Consultative Committee of the International Telecommunication Union) of "videotex" to describe such systems.

Videotext (the generic choice for this essay) is increasingly being used, at least in the United States, as a generic term for viewdata, teletext, and hybrid systems. As Sigel observes in *Videotext: The Coming Revolution in Home/Office Information Retrieval*, "It combines two simple English words known to all and accurately describes the essence of the new service—the display of textual information, both words and numbers, on a video display screen."[2]

Compounding the lexicographical problem is the fact that individual systems have their own names (often trademarked). Among the commercial videotext services operating outside the United States are Prestel (Britain), Telidon (Canada), Antiope (France), and Captains (Japan), as well as Bildschirmtext (West Germany), Telset (Finland), Datavision (Sweden), and Viditel (Netherlands). In the United States, systems being developed carry such names as Viewtron (Knight-Ridder), Video-Text (Oak), Extravision (CBS), and Viewtel (OCLC).

A description of the general characteristics and operating procedures associated with the two principal forms of videotext—viewdata and tele-text—follows.

Viewdata

Viewdata basically refers to electronic information systems using tele-phone lines to tie television sets to mainframe computers. The TV sets however must be equipped with a microprocessor unit called a "de-coder." The decoder unit, which is separate from or integral with the TV set, incorporates several key functions including: isolation circuits to prevent the television interfering with the telephone system; a modem which converts the digital signals in the decoder to analog signals for transmission on telephone lines and vice versa; input and memory control to accept and store the signals from the modem; memory to store the transmitted information; a character generator to transform the data in memory into the patterns required by the television display; and syn-chronization controls necessary for the display. Thus, the decoder con-nects the TV to the telephone line, provides memory for storing the transmitted information and displays that information on the television screen.

A keypad, which has a set of buttons similar to a pocket calculator in addition to the program controls (channel selection, brightness, volume, etc.), is used to select information located in the viewdata mainframe computer and can work by remote control or can be connected directly to the TV set. The information in the computer is formatted as discrete numbered pages. A "page" denotes a screenful or frame of information, the amount displayed on the screen at one time. Organizations providing information to the system (called "information providers") are connected to the viewdata computer and input data directly from their own offices using special editing terminals, or by a direct line from the source of the information, for example, computers at the stock exchange, airlines, or news services.

To access a viewdata system, using Prestel as an example, the user first presses a special viewdata button on the keypad which activates an auto-dialler inside the TV set that dials the telephone number of the Prestel computer and identifies the TV set and user's pass number to the com-puter (for billing purposes). The computer then displays a "welcome" on the screen and asks the user what is wanted. The user has two ways to obtain information. One is through an index or "menu" with numbers beside the index entries, the use of which will usually result in a second, more refined index that asks the user to make a second choice. This process will continue until the user reaches the page providing the information sought. The other access method takes advantage of the system's numbering of pages. If the user knows the page number for a specific item, the page number can be keyed on the keypad along with two special control keys, thereby avoiding consultation of the indexes.

Within the viewdata data base, the pages are arranged in a hierarchical manner. The basic structure is a tree but the addition of cross-references results in a multiple connected graph. Viewdata as an information retrieval system is relatively unsophisticated due to its lack of inverted files and Boolean operators, two elements credited with giving online information systems a retrieval capability unmatched by print products. Viewdata is intended for the masses to use to meet their straightforward information retrieval requirements. Viewdata development, however, should be perceived as still in its infant stages; should the cost-benefit perception of the system designers regarding more complex information retrieval systems ever change, we can anticipate that they will add keyword and even Boolean search capabilities to their systems.

A typical page in Prestel contains 24 lines, each with 40 characters, producing a total of 960 characters, of which only 858 are in practice actually used in page creation (character space is also taken up by system use at the top and bottom lines and by color coding at the beginning of each line). With a maximum of about 130 words, it is a very small page compared to the printed page. The maximum page content consists of two short paragraphs or a few columns of figures. In addition, attempts are made to ensure that each page is self-contained and well organized, as well as having short sentences, a clear single message, and visual continuity with similar pages. The use of up to seven colors adds to the potential of the medium; pages are made easier and more attractive to look at and their information content clearer. By differentiating columns and categories of information, color can also tighten and improve the presentation and, in effect, make up for some of the inherent limitations of the viewdata page. It should be noted that it takes several seconds to build up a single page.

Because of these characteristics of viewdata, it has been used mainly for lists of various types. Examples on Prestel range from weather reports to real estate listings, to flight information, and to abstracts of newspaper business stories, with each type of page updated at different frequencies. Pure text, that is, filling up the screen with words from top left to bottom right, is not used often since it is considered hard on the eye. Even the Prestel system designers admit that viewdata is not a reading medium in the way that a newspaper, book, or magazine is.

Moreover, scanning is severely restricted to a maximum of about 10 pages of 10 items or 100 items per minute, which is one-tenth of the rate for the printed page. Designers have tried to circumvent this inherent shortcoming by applying a more sophisticated search process to a more carefully classified set of items. But this is a tough nut to crack and, in general, it should be recognized that viewdata is poorly suited to material which is normally scanned.

Because telephone transmission is used, the signals themselves are audio bandwidth signals, thereby enabling the user to have two-way or interactive communications with the viewdata computer. The volume of available information is limited only by the size of the data base or of the computer. The user can also make transactions with the data base such as placing orders, making reservations, paying bills, and so on.

Teletext

Teletext is both similar to and different from viewdata. Rather than the telephone, it uses a television signal for transmitting text and graphics. Information is also organized into pages which, in most systems, are formatted and displayed the same as viewdata. Access is through page numbers obtained from either a printed directory or a teletext directory (the menu) called up on the screen. Teletext systems are noninteractive, meaning that while users can "select" pages of information—the receiving equipment "grabs" the page keyed from the electronic flow of data and stores it in memory—they are unable to interact with the data base.

Teletext pages are sent cyclically at the rate of four pages a second from the originating center of the television station. Similar to the viewdata information provider terminals, editing terminals (comprising a keyboard and display monitor) are used to enter information into a computer. The pages are cyclically accessed by a computer and turned into teletext format signals by a data encoder. The final step in origination of teletext occurs when the pages are inserted into the vertical blanking interval (VBI) of a television signal by a data inserter. The VBI appears as the black band separating the top from the bottom of the picture when the TV receiver is not properly tuned; under normal conditions it is located at the top of the screen (the part of the picture tube hidden by the cabinet). Technically, the VBI is the time taken by the beam of electrons forming the picture to go from the bottom of the screen to the top. Most importantly, the VBI can carry digital information which can be decoded to the analog television signal and displayed on the screen by a teletext decoder.

Similar to viewdata, a user requires only a special decoder and a keypad to access the pages. The viewer's set must be equipped with the decoder to capture the digital signals and reconstruct them to appear as pages of information on the screen. Without the decoder, only the regular TV program would appear. By using a hand-held keypad or control unit, the viewer can shut off the regular TV program and consult instead pages of teletext information, which can be displayed either in place of or over the picture (the latter being especially applicable to captioning regular television programming).

Besides lacking interactive capability, teletext systems are also severely restricted in the amount of information transmitted due to the limit set by the sequential method of access. In contrast to viewdata, which theoretically can have an infinite data base, teletext, most experts concur, is limited to about 100 pages. Although more pages could be transmitted, the waiting time also would increase proportionately since pages are transmitted in a continuous cycle at the rate of four pages a second. A sequence of 500 pages, for example, may continuously be transmitted in a two-minute cycle, requiring the viewer to wait an average of one minute for the page selected. One hundred pages, which take only 25 seconds to transmit, require an average wait of 12.5 seconds, generally considered to be the limit for a viewer's patience.

Because of these additional constraints, teletext systems have been used for different purposes than viewdata. It is felt that the medium lends itself best to current news material; hence much of teletext information consists of the sports, weather, and stock exchange data in addition to other kinds of time-sensitive, regularly updated material.

Although broadcast teletext has used only a few lines of the VBI, it should be recognized that it is not limited to use of the VBI. Any number or even all the active television lines could be used, but because broadcast channels are filled with program material, this has not been done (with only a few exceptions). *Cabletext* (refers to teletext delivered over one- or two-way cable television systems), however, offers larger data bases at acceptable response rates due to the availability for information transmission of large numbers of unused channels. Employing a full-channel (either over-the-air or cable TV) for continuous transmission greatly increases the capabilities of teletext; as many as 20,000 pages can sensibly be made available at one time.

U.S. DEVELOPMENTS

What follows is a description and explanation of U.S. viewdata, teletext, and cabletext services since the late 1970s when U.S. interest in videotext first emerged. The section is organized according to developments in the telephone, newspaper, broadcasting, and cable television industries. An especial effort has been made to include information pertaining to the field trials, the data bases, and the potential of individual systems for further development and expansion.

Telephone Companies

The American Telephone and Telegraph Co. began in 1979 to experiment with its Electronic Information Service, which included an electronic Yellow Pages, in "concept trials" held in Albany, New York and Austin, Texas. Since directory data is now machine-readable and made available through special terminals to Bell System operators, AT&T wished to determine the reactions of its customers in having a similar service at their home or business. Accordingly, a randomly selected group of New York Telephone business and residential customers in the Albany area were given test use of a video terminal, which included a telephone set, visual display screen and a typewriter-like keyboard. In addition to the regular White and Yellow Pages listings, information on brand names and advertising, the weather, the time, and sports were all made available electronically. AT&T's test in Austin was on-again, off-again due to protracted opposition from Texas newspaper publishers before the state's public utilities commission. AT&T finally decided in July, 1981 to cancel its planned 14-month trial, which was to have included 700 Austin business and residential customers, and for which $6 million had already been spent.

The Albany and Austin field trials have been the only sites where AT&T was involved in all aspects of viewdata development, including information content. The fact that AT&T was getting involved in the provision of electronic information services alarmed the publishers. Despite the Texas experience, AT&T has continued to actively pursue its interest in viewdata by taking responsibility for telecommunications in jointly sponsored market tests with the videotext divisions of Knight-Ridder Newspapers and CBS Inc. in Coral Gables, Florida and Ridgewood, New Jersey, respectively.

General Telephone & Electronics (GTE), the second largest telephone company in the United States, in 1979 acquired Telenet, a major packet-switched network and also U.S. marketing rights for the British Prestel system's software. It appeared that GTE was preparing to become a major viewdata operator in the United States. However, the company has maintained a low profile with respect to its intentions and in fact never made real use of the British software. In August 1980, GTE made its agreement with Aregon Viewdata, Inc. (U.S. representative of the British Post Office) nonexclusive, thereby enabling Aregon to pursue U.S. home and business markets freely.

GTE has developed a concept for a viewdata service called "Infovision." If it ever gets off the ground, the Infovision service would utilize local newspapers as local viewdata operators in a national viewdata system linked by Telenet. The local viewdata centers would be responsible for tying together various local computers (banks, retailers, etc.) and establishing "gateways" to computers in other communities in addition to providing local news and classified ads from the newspaper data bases. A GTE-supplied electronic telephone directory service would comprise another part of this service.

Continental Telephone, based in Atlanta, which serves 2 million customers in 37 states, announced in 1981 its plan to test the home electronic information market in 1982 with its system, "ConTelVision." In a two-phase viewdata experiment, 50 Continental customers in Manassas, Virginia will receive a decoder for their home television set and an alphanumeric keypad, while another 50 will have a video display terminal and keyboard. The company hopes to determine which display device is the most appropriate information terminal and also if customer perceptions of the television as a source of entertainment detract from its use for information purposes. A variety of information and transactional services will be made available through the existing telephone network. In the second phase, a commercial service will be tested, with the number of customers increased, the amount of information in the data base expanded, and a charge made for use of the ConTelVision service.

Newspapers

As shown by the Texas battle with AT&T, newspaper companies have become actively interested in pursuing the opportunities offered by electronic information systems for their industry. In fact, four newspaper companies—Knight-Ridder, Times Mirror, Field, and Dow Jones—have formed subsidiaries to concentrate solely on the development of videotext and other forms of electronic publishing.

Videotext Subsidiaries

Knight-Ridder Newspapers, Inc. (publisher of the *Miami Herald*, the *Philadelphia Inquirer* and the *Detroit Free Press* and owner of four VHF television stations) established Viewdata Corp. of America in 1979 following the company's investigations of viewdata systems in Europe and Japan, which included experience as an information provider in the British Prestel service. The new company's first task was to implement in 1980 a test of an electronic home information system called "Viewtron." AT&T jointly sponsored the test, taking responsibility for the telecommunications aspects; Western Electric built the home terminals designed by Bell Labs; and Southern Bell Telephone provided the communications links between the homes. Viewdata Corp. of America provided the computer, wrote the computer programs for information storage and retrieval, and also selected the information providers and advertisers to be included in the Viewtron data base. The six-month test involved the rotation of 30 AT&T terminals among 175 homes in Coral Gables, Florida.

A 15,000-page data base was created for the test with 13 publishers and 16 advertisers inputing information for either the Home Information/ Management Services or Home Transactions portion of the data base. Information provided by the publishers included, for example, a baseball encyclopedia (MacMillan), a tourist guide to New York City (The New York Times), a cook book (HP Books), 500 selected stocks (Associated Press), daily report of the U.S. Congress (Congressional Quarterly), and a family medical guide (Addison-Wesley). Advertising information included such items as local real estate listings and Eastern Airlines flights to and from Miami. Family members were also able to use the system and their credit card to make purchases from J.C. Penney and Sears as well as from local merchants. Participants also received continually updated information on the news—information from the *Miami Herald, Wall Street Journal*, and Associated Press—the weather and the sports. In addition, they were able to use the interactive feature of the system to conduct banking transactions, place classified ads, play video games, and even communicate (through an electronic bulletin board) with other test participants.

Thus, a variety of transactional and information services, including library-type information, were encompassed by the system. Users called up screens of information by selecting topics from a self-instructive menu and choosing a numbered option. They were also able to retrieve pages by typing in one of 100 keywords such as "news," "sports," "travel," or "Sears."

While much of the research data from Knight-Ridder's viewdata experiment has not been made public because of its proprietary nature, the company's 1980 annual report contained the following statement from Viewdata Corp. of America's president: "We are encouraged by what we have seen so far. Users have quickly mastered the use of the keypads and keyboards. Their response to and use of the data base has provided invaluable insight and guidance for the further development of the service. The Viewtron team itself has gained unique experience in developing and managing a prototype service like Viewtron."[3]

Editor & Publisher reported the test results for the amount and types of news accessed by the Viewtron participants. They revealed that news accounted for 25% of all Viewtron use and that local news provided by the *Miami Herald* was a significant portion of this 25%. The data also showed that news provided by the Associated Press accounted for 50% of total news accessed, or one-half of the 25%. Of the Associated Press total, national news predominated (20%) followed by: stocks (10%), Mideast stories (10%), people stories (9%), weather (8%), sports scores (7%), world news (7%), market narratives (4%), business news (4%), science news (4%), sports stories (3%) and entertainment news (2%). From these results, the editor of Viewtron concluded that the home information system has the potential to become a viable news medium.[4]

The $2 million test, which originally was planned for six months (July to January), was extended to run an additional nine months (at an undisclosed sum). As an indication of further events to come, Knight-Ridder has disclosed plans to conduct another test of its Viewtron home information service, to 5,000 South Florida residents in mid-1983. Unlike the Coral Gables experiment, where participants received all information free, the company's second test will charge both customers and advertisers for the service to determine their willingness to pay. Other changes planned include more offerings in each category of information and service, a much larger data base (100,000 Viewtron screens versus the 10,000 created for the original test) and more sophisticated text and graphics.

Following completion of the 1980–81 Viewtron test, Knight-Ridder announced agreements to share the results from the Coral Gables test and the much larger market test scheduled for 1983 with two other newspaper companies, Affiliated Publications and Capital Cities Communications. Knight-Ridder also agreed to provide the companies with the computer software for permitting keyword searching and for banking, retailing, electronic mail, and other two-way transactional services in addition to training in viewdata marketing and data base creation. These agreements are significant; should the 1983 Viewtron test be positive, it appears certain that viewdata services will be offered in Kansas City, Fort Worth, and Boston (where Capital Cities and Affiliated publish newspapers) as well as in the 24 cities Knight-Ridder reaches with its 33 daily newspapers (with a circulation of almost 4 million, the country's largest newspaper company).

In February 1981, Telidon Videotex Systems, a company established by Toronto-based Infomart to sell Canadian-developed Telidon videotext systems to the U.S. market, sold a complete turnkey system to Times Mirror Co. for $1 million. Times Mirror, whose holdings include the *Denver Post*, *Newsday*, *Popular Science*, and *Sporting News* in addition to major broadcasting and cable operations, subsequently established a subsidiary, Times Mirror Videotex Services, and planned a major videotext field trial in the Los Angeles area. The trial, scheduled to begin in March 1982, will operate for 150 homes in Mission Viejo over two-way cable and for 200 homes in Palos Verdes by telephone. Rather than the simple demographics used in most videotext experiments, Times Mirror Videotex Services conducted in-depth interviews in the test locations to select participants based on attitudinal criteria.

Times Mirror does not believe that consumer revenues will provide sole support of its videotext service and that subsidization by banks or others will be necessary to recoup the significant costs of maintaining the computer hardware and software, according to a Western Cable Show panel discussion reported in *Broadcasting*. Times Mirror's videotext system, similar to Knight-Ridder's Viewtron, includes a wide range of information retrieval services as well as banking and shopping at home and electronic mail. As an alternative to using the menu, keyword access will also be provided to the 20,000-page data base. To help answer the questions concerning willingness to pay, participants will have free use of the service for 4 months, but after that the company has reserved the right to charge a maximum of $35 per month. It also plans to experiment with different ways of charging users, such as by the hour, the page, and the month to determine the effect of each on information use.

Dow Jones & Co. is another newpaper company that has entered the home information market. The company has been gradually changing its orientation from publisher to information provider and distributor, and has been heavily involved in the development of one- and two-way home information services for the cable television market.

Its one-way service, Dow Jones Cable News, provided 24 hours a day on one-way cable, is billed as a miniature electronic *Wall Street Journal* which deals with Americans and their pocketbooks. It has been projected to reach 250,000 people in 1982. Through its subsidiary, Ottaway Newspapers, the company has been involved in a one-way cabletext experiment using French technology with the *News-Times* (Danbury, Connecticut).

Dow Jones has established Dow Jones Cable Information Services to foster its development of two-way cabletext. In anticipation of offering its Dow Jones News/Retrieval data base to two-way cable systems, the company has been progressively adding to and enriching the content of the data base. A much wider range of information is already encompassed. The data base now contains the *Wall Street Journal Highlights Online*, which consists of summaries of key stories from the *Wall Street Journal*, various kinds of cultural material (including book, theater, and movie reviews), highlights from the *Asian Wall Street Journal*, and material from Dow Jones Books, in addition to information previously available on the system, that is, company profiles, 10K extracts, stock prices, Merrill Lynch reports, and *Barron's* articles.

Because coaxial cable is capable of delivering information less expensively than the telephone lines, Dow Jones anticipates that rapid spread of its service will accompany increased penetration of two-way cable television nationwide. In comparison to charges for the telephone-delivered personal computer service whose users currently pay $60 an hour, subscribers to the cable-delivered home service will pay only $12 per month ($40 per month for business hours use).

Dow Jones is proceeding with expansion of its two-way cable information service and has announced plans to offer transactional banking and shopping services and a wide range of information services, including information on entertainment, education, health care, sports, the weather, and the news in addition to the varied offerings of the News/ Retrieval data base. Originally started as an experiment in three Dallas suburbs, the Dow Jones two-way cable service is now being included in interactive cable systems in Fort Lee, New Jersey and Clearwater, Florida; scheduled for inclusion in new cable systems for St. Louis, Missouri and Pasadena, California; and being considered for inclusion by additional two-way cable operators. Dow Jones also has initiated contacts with local newspapers regarding offering local information and news through its data base in all areas with two-way capability.

Field Enterprises, publisher of the *Chicago Sun-Times*, is the fourth newspaper company to form a subsidiary to develop videotext publishing opportunities. Utilizing Field's commercial TV station in Chicago, WFLD, Field Electronic Publishing has been conducting with Zenith Radio Corp. an experimental teletext service called "Keyfax" over the vertical blanking interval of WFLD since April 1981. The service makes 100 screens of information available on demand to viewers who use a frame-grabbing device to obtain their information after consulting special indexes on the screen. Decoder-equipped television sets, using British technology, have been placed in Chicago private homes and in 110 "information kiosks" in high circulation public areas—libraries, colleges, transportation terminals, and shopping centers—and made accessible 24 hours a day. Field Electronic Publishing started a second experimental teletext service called "Nite-Owl" in September 1981, which requires no special equipment to receive information. Every 20 minutes from 12 A.M. to 6 A.M., viewers are fed constantly rolling pages of information from the same data base used for Keyfax. In both services, updated financial, news, weather, sports, and entertainment information are made available.

City and Town Dailies

In addition to the videotext services being pursued by large newspaper companies, options are becoming increasingly available to daily newspapers, both those with small and large circulation, for electronically delivering their news and advertisements to their customers and for providing additional information services.

Through an experimental project being conducted with Associated Press through the CompuServe Information Service, that began in 1980 with the *Columbus Dispatch*, eleven newspapers have been put online to home computer users. Newspapers whose electronic editions are currently on the CompuServe system include: the *New York Times*, the *Washington Post*, the *Los Angeles Times*, the *Columbus Dispatch*, the *San Francisco Chronicle*, the *Norfolk Virginian-Pilot and Ledger Star*, the *Minneapolis Star and Tribune*, the *St. Louis Post-Dispatch*, the *Atlanta Constitution & Journal*, and the *Middlesex News*. Typically offered in the electronic edition, using the *Atlanta Journal* as an example, are daily foreign exchange rates, airline flight schedules to over 30 cities, an Atlanta-area hotel guide with current room rates, late sports scores, closing prices on 20 selected stocks of interest to Atlantans and other market indicators, and news briefs that refer the reader to the *Atlanta Journal* for complete stories.

Yet another approach is being tried in Kentucky by the *Louisville Courier Journal* and the *Louisville Times* with Antiope Videotex Systems, Inc., which markets the teletext version of the French videotext system called "Antiope" in the United States. In this test of a teletext system for the Louisville papers, to be conducted in 1982, the French company is contributing one-half of the required $500,000. Several homes and public locations will receive decoder-equipped television sets to use to obtain information from the data base which will include news, sports and weather information and classified ads.

In Ohio, an experiment by the publisher of the Tiffin *Advertiser-Tribune* with an electronic edition of the newspaper holds possibilities for similar ventures across the country. Newspaper subscribers using their telephone and television set and a Radio Shack TRS-80 Videotex terminal (which sells for $399) will be able to retrieve the news electronically as a result of the publisher's $20,000 investment in appropriate Radio Shack equipment. Information that is more current or in more depth than it is possible to publish in the paper will be made available online, such as real estate listings that include floor plans and the complete stock tables on a daily basis. The publisher sees the electronic edition as complementing, not competing with his paper.

An option that has attracted the attention of about 30 newspapers concerns the leasing or owning of cable channels for news and advertising. The *Champaign News-Gazette*, Champaign, Illinois and the Yuma, Arizona *Daily Sun* exemplify this growing trend. The Champaign paper has leased two cable channels from the local cable operator; beginning in 1982, it offered classified advertising on one channel and news summaries, advertising graphics, the time, and the weather on the other. The one-way cable news is produced by interfacing the newspaper's computer with the character generator producing the textual format. Since the local cable system has two-way capability, the newspaper's future plans include interactive cabletext.

The Yuma paper leases four cable channels in order to provide on a 24-hour, 7-day-a-week basis: (1) a financial and sports update which utilizes the Reuters News-View Service, with information fed via phone line and attached directly to the newspaper's cable system equipment; (2) classified ads; (3) news from the Associated Press in 15-minute sweeps or rotations (thereby applying market research results which found maximum viewer interest to peak at 15 minutes); and (4) news briefs from its own paper, similarly utilizing the 60 pages, 15 minutes format. Interestingly, in the latter, although news is updated hourly, only basic facts of the story are provided to stimulate interest in the more complete story found in the *Daily Sun*; moreover, the electronic version will not "scoop" the paper in stories of major importance.

Commercial and Public Broadcasting

Beginning in the late 1970s with efforts by KSL-TV in Salt Lake City and by the CBS television network, the United States has been developing broadcast services for textual materials. Projects have been undertaken by both commercial and public television. The teletext systems being developed are based on British, French, and Canadian video technologies.

Commercial Television

Telext began in the United States with a 1978 test of the British Ceefax system at station KSL-TV in Salt Lake City following approval by the Federal Communications Commission. (FCC approval is required for all changes in television transmission including teletext, since it requires insertion of textual data in the vertical blanking interval of the television signal.) Seven decoders were placed in homes; through the system, news, weather, sports, stocks, and airline schedules were made available to the participants. While no decision has been reached to expand the experiment, station personnel have been able to determine that the number of pages (the teletext "magazine") should be limited to 100 to obtain a maximum response time of 15 seconds.

In March 1979, CBS received FCC permission to conduct its tests of teletext. The network began by comparing the French (Antiope) and British (Ceefax) systems using its KMOX-TV station in St. Louis. CBS eventually concluded that Antiope because of its variable format offers more flexibility than the fixed format of Ceefax and is more appropriate to U.S. needs, and later petitioned the FCC to accept a modified version of the Antiope system as the U.S. standard for teletext.

More recently, the Los angeles affiliates of CBS (KNXT-TV), NBC (KNBC-TV) and PBS (KCET-TV); and the West Coast office of the Caption Center of Boston's WGBH-TV have participated in a test of the

Antiope system with equipment supplied by Antiope Videotex Systems, Inc., the American subsidiary of the French firm that designed the teletext system. The test, which started in April 1981, was expected to last at least a year.

The CBS teletext magazine, called "Extravision," includes in its 80 pages such items as local and national news, sports, weather reports, stock market and financial information, consumer tips, airline flight information, entertainment lists, traffic conditions, captions, and various forms of advertising. In the initial phase of the test, decoders were placed in public locations with a second phase to involve private homes. Many of the teletext transmissions feature closed captioning for the hearing impaired. Early reports from the test site indicated that "perishable" information may be the type of teletext information most valued by viewers. A traffic trouble spot map, news headlines, and local information typify the kinds of up-to-the-second information that require frequent updating or local tie-ins and are also, coincidentally, well suited to teletext capabilities.

CBS has both teletext and videotex project directors, hence it is not surprising that the company is simultaneously developing both the Extravision teletext system and a viewdata system. CBS will test late in 1982, in cooperation with AT&T, which is handling both the telecommunications and computer aspects, a telephone-delivered home information system much like the one Knight-Ridder tested in Coral Gables. CBS, in addition to its television network, publishes 60 magazines (*Woman's Day*, *Mechanics Illustrated* and *Road & Track*, for example) and 6 book lines, all of which can be included in the data base, which CBS calls "Infovision." The test will involve 200 families in Ridgewood, New Jersey. Over a six-month test period, participants will have the ability to retrieve information as well as shop and bank at home, with no fees charged. Judging by the response of the media to the original announcement, the CBS-AT&T home information test will generate much attention, particularly since the many videotext analysts based in New York City are in close proximity to Ridgewood. Since many Ridgewood families subscribe to cable, and because the community is rated as "upscale," both in education and income, the test is expected to indicate to CBS and AT&T the potential market for their brand of videotext.

Taft Broadcasting Co. began a three-year teletext test, using British technology, in January 1982 over its WKRC-TV in Cincinnati. Teletext pages were initially imported from Field Enterprises, whose Chicago teletext test was described earlier. Similar to other teletext tests, television sets both in public areas and private homes will be equipped with teletext decoders. Local and national news, weather, sports, and advertising will be offered. Taft plans to feed its teletext service via satellite to its television stations in Birmingham, Buffalo, Columbus, Kansas City, Philadelphia, and Washington, D.C.

In addition to regular over-the-air, or free TV, such as employed by KSL, CBS, WFLD and WKRC in their teletext experiments, over-the-air subscription television (STV), multipoint distribution service (MDS), low power television (LPTV), and direct broadcast satellite (DBS) are also, or will become, available to the teletext broadcaster.

Public Television

Public television, similar to its commercial counterpart, has begun to regard teletext as a means of enhancing its regular programming service. Two Public Broadcasting Service affiliates, KCET-TV in Los Angeles and WETA-TV in Washington, D.C., and the Nebraska ETV Network are currently engaged in projects designed to demonstrate the potential benefits of teletext information services.

KCET is participating in the Los Angeles teletext project along with CBS and others. Taking a broad look at its public information role, KCET has developed a factual and educational type of teletext magazine called "Now!" Information included ranges from science to finance, from films to public affairs, and movies to medicine. In addition, the station is exploring linking teletext decoders and home computers.

WETA, in cooperation with the Alternate Media Center of New York University, has begun a $1 million teletext experiment in Washington, D.C. with funding received from the Corporation for Public Broadcasting, the National Science Foundation, the National Telecommunications and Information Administration, and the U.S. Department of Education. Using Canadian Telidon technology, the WETA/NYU project hopes to answer a variety of questions concerning public teletext information services and has both research and demonstration designs.

In the first phase of the experiment, which started in June 1981 and is scheduled to end July 1982, 50 decoders were placed in 10 public areas and 40 homes. A second phase, in which the number of decoders will be substantially increased, will begin in September 1982. The data base of 100 pages includes information provided by the Martin Luther King, Jr. Library, the *Washington Post*, the *Chicago Sun-Times*, the *New York Daily News*, and the National Weather Service. News, weather, sports, entertainment, horoscopes, a feature section (including information on books), and consumer information are all encompassed in the service. Of the total, 80 pages are changed daily and 30 pages weekly. The regular station programming is being coordinated with the teletext service; a NOVA program, for example, is being supplemented by a teletext-provided reading list.

Also in 1981, the Nebraska ETV Network began the demonstration phase of its Video Information Service (VIS) using line 21 of the television broadcast signal (used by the Public Broadcasting Service to provide close captioning for the hearing impaired). The Nebraska VIS is now available on all nine ETV channels in the state; the teletext service is accessible to any Nebraska viewer who purchases either a $269 Sears Telecaption decoder or a $500 television with built-in decoder. AGNET, the national interactive agricultural information service headquartered in Nebraska, which farmers have accessed by computer terminals, was the first information provider to participate in VIS.

Cable Television

Cable is hot and getting hotter. In comparison to 1968 when 5% of the nation's TV homes were connected to cable systems, by the beginning of 1982, it was estimated that 25 to 35% of cable television penetration had been achieved. Currently adding new subscribers at the rate of 250,000 a month, cable is expected to grow at a rapidly accelerating pace. Although invented in the late 1940s, until recently cable systems were primarily located in rural areas (such as mountain regions with poor reception) to improve the picture and bring in distant stations. In the mid-1970s, two key developments occurred which radically altered this situation. First, a variety of regulatory obstacles were lifted via FCC orders and court rulings. Secondly, with the launching in 1975 of the first domestic communications satellite, cable systems were able (by bouncing signals off the satellite to dish-shaped earth antennas) to deliver programs nationwide at a fraction of the cost of the broadcasting networks.

Of relevance to videotext has been the rapid growth of national pay-TV networks. More than 10 million subscribers in 1981 (triple the number three years before) were purchasing such extra "pay cable" packages, whose services are charged as additional fees to the regular monthly cable charge. These additional cable programming services, which so far have been limited mainly to entertainment, have the potential of being opened to a range of videotext services.

Cabletext can be provided in a variety of ways, including use of the vertical blanking interval of the cable channel, a full video channel, a two-way cable system or a hybrid system, such as a combination of telephone and cable. The inherent capabilities of cable systems enable a variety of teletext-type services. In comparison to telephone-delivered (narrowband) videotext, which operates at relatively slow data rates on a twisted pair of wires, the broadband/wideband feature of cable enables employment with large data bases at relatively high speeds and acceptable response rates. In comparison to broadcast-delivered (over-the-air) videotext, which utilizes only the VBI of the television signal, transmission via cable television permits a whole channel to be set aside for teletext.

The discussion that follows describes current efforts by the cable television industry to maximize the potential of their systems for the transmission, display, and retrieval of information.

One-Way Cable

In contrast to broadcast teletext, cable has few regulatory restrictions and is not subject to the same transmission standards as broadcasters, who currently must obtain FCC approval to conduct teletext experiments over the VBI. This means that cable operators can allocate full channels to nonprogramming services. Two practices are now well established for the transmission of the cabletext by U.S. cable operators.

One is the use of character generator channels wherein information suppliers (typically news agencies such as Reuters, UPI, AP, and Dow Jones) provide data signals over telephone lines to cable signal origination points. These signals are converted at the cable studio into synthetic video, using equipment called character generators, for modulation onto otherwise blank cable TV channels. The cable subscribing viewer, on tuning his receiver to one of these channels, sees pages of text roll or scroll by.

A second practice is the use of "super stations." The first super station, Turner Broadcasting System's WTBS-TV of Atlanta, is a formerly local TV station whose signal is now picked up and distributed by Southern Satellite Systems nationwide via satellite to 3,000 TVRO (television receive only) earth stations for use by cable systems. Data in the VBI is then decoded at the cable headend with Zenith-built decoders (trademarked VIRTEXT and VIRDATA) and placed on a normal cable channel. Because leased telephone line charges are avoided, this method facilitates the entry of smaller information providers. Since an adaptation of British teletext technology is used to insert the data into the VBI of the WTBS signal, the "CableText" system by Southern Satellite Systems is considered the first commercial, nonexperimental application of teletext in the United States. Another super station is WGN-TV of Chicago, which is distributed by United Video to 1,000 cable systems. In both of these types of cable transmission of teletext, true teletext control—such as the British Ceefax and Oracle systems provide, where the viewer can select pages on demand—is not possible.

Reuters was one of the first companies to develop videotext services on cable. Since 1979, its "News-Views" has been sent by telephone lines or satellite to subscribing cable systems. Both services are one-way noninteractive; the information consists of about 30 pages of general and financial news sent in rotation; the subscriber is unable to request or freeze any of the pages. Since 1978, Reuters has offered in the New York metropolitan area a one-way information retrieval service called "Reuter Monitor" over one of Manhattan Cable's channels. Similar to the British teletext systems, using decoders, viewers are able to retrieve information at high speeds. But unlike the British and other broadcast-delivered systems which insert data only in the VBI, making available data bases of only hundreds of pages, because an entire cable channel is dedicated to the Reuter Monitor service, data bases of up to 10,000 pages are available for transmission (in a round-robin manner for every few seconds). The data base is business-oriented and includes general market news, options, financial news, New York Stock Exchange and American Stock Exchange quotes, money markets, and commodities information. In 1979, Reuter Monitor became available on a nationwide basis when Reuters began to rent a transponder on the RCA domestic satellite.

Time Inc. is a major publishing and electronic communications company which has recently become heavily involved in testing cabletext for general in-home use. In addition to publishing seven major consumer magazines, Time owns Time-Life Books; Little, Brown; Home Box Office (HBO), a pay-TV service; and American Television and Communications (ATC), a basic-cable multiple system operator.

Early in 1982, at ATC's San Diego cable system, Time plans to market test a national teletext service that will deliver a wide range of textual and graphical information. Determining what people will want to read from their screen and also the advertising and subscription fees required to properly fund the service are among the company's objectives for the San Diego test. The service will make use of a full-text channel, that is, every line in the television signal will be used for teletext data. The 4,000-page data base ("Timetex") is being created by teletext service personnel with information derived primarily from Time Inc. magazines, which include *Time*, *Life*, *People*, *Sports Illustrated*, *Fortune*, *Money*, and *Discover*. The pages will be editorially grouped into a number of teletext magazines each with its own purpose and unique characteristics. Information in the data base ranges from current stock market prices and economic trends to encyclopedic information on U.S. companies and a series from Time-Life "how to" books.

In late 1981, Time's ATC and the *Orlando Sentinel Star* started a year-long test of a cable-delivered home information service in 200 Orlando homes. Although Time technical expertise and financial resources are being employed, the 6,000-page data base consists primarily of news and information from the *Sentinel Star*. Similar to Time's plans for the national teletext service, users will be able to select pages from the data base for display and also will pay for their information. In addition to advertising, several ways to fund the service are being explored, including monthly subscription fees, usage-based billing, equipment rentals, or a combination of these methods. ATC cable systems in Kentucky and Wisconsin are exploring with local newspapers the implementation of similar home information services.

Considering that Time-owned ATC and HBO are the nations' largest basic-cable and pay-TV systems, respectively, it is not unrealistic to expect cable-delivered home information services to become available throughout much of the country in the very near future. Of course this is predicated on the commercial success of the test services being adequately proven to Time.

Two-Way Cable

Promoters of two-way cable (denotes one line carrying signals from the cable headend to the subscriber, one line relaying the subscriber's responses back to the headend) describe their interactive systems as the key component in a computer-linked "home information center." Only recently described as innovative experiments, two-way cable today is the glamour child of the cable industry; two-way services have become a major factor behind the winning of big-city cable contracts by corporate bidders.

Although the design of the transmission system may differ, all two-way cable systems utilize a special terminal in the subscriber's home that sends signals over the return line to a central point. Terminal design ranges from the simple, such as sensors to detect changes in normal conditions (providing the capability to recognize a fire or burglary in process and send appropriate signals back to the central point), to the more complex, such as incorporation of a keypad to enable selection of one of various options. The latter type allows subscribers to conduct a variety of activities at home—for example, booking reservations for an airline flight, ordering tickets for the theater, placing off-track bets, playing video games, and sending electronic mail as well as retrieving information, banking, and shopping.

Two-way cable is beginning to be implemented in the United States. Warner Amex Cable first tested its service, "Qube," in 1977 in Columbus, Ohio. The company has spent $20 million on Qube and hopes to recoup its investment and begin to realize a profit on such operations. Thus, extensive efforts are being made to expand two-way cable to others of its 138 cable systems located throughout the country. In Cincinnati, in 1981, its second interactive cable system opened. Additionally, the company has been granted a two-way franchise in Houston, has applied for one in Pittsburgh, and has plans for another in Boston.

In the current Qube system, ten channels offer regular commercial TV; ten (at extra cost) offer first-run movies, live performances, sports, adult films, games, college courses, instruction in cooking, and so forth; and ten are reserved for community activities (local news and sports, consumer information, children's programming, coverage of town meetings and government hearings, etc.). The keypad used to access the service consists of three buttons from which to choose a main category and ten buttons for channel selection within each category. Qube's interactive services operate via five response buttons, which have been used mainly for polling, enabling subscribers to vote on community issues and play game shows or quizzes with the results announced in ten seconds. The system also has the facility to send a particular program to a specified list of subscribers.

Incorporated within the design, in the transition to Qube III, are a burglary and fire alarm system, an energy management service, home shopping and banking, and various computer processing services including simple information retrieval. Recently, as an indication of services to come, the company began field testing a consumer information service with Atari and CompuServe wherein selected Qube subscribers, using an Atari 800 personal computer, are able (during off-peak times for $5 an hour) to access pages from newspapers as well as recipes, financial information, computer games, and other items in the CompuServe data base.

Such futuristic two-way cable services have been incorporated by Cox Cable Communications in their system called "Index" (Interactive Data Exchange). Index is credited with Cox's winning of cable franchises in hotly contested battles in Omaha and New Orleans. It allows users to interact with a central computer by using a microprocessor-driven terminal (in place of the traditional cable television converter) and a keypad. Index services include provision for shopping and banking at home, interactive educational programs, home security, energy management and information retrieval (from The Source). In 1981, Index was offered to 300 Cox subscribers in San Diego, in a six-month pilot test, and was scheduled to be introduced in Omaha and New Orleans.

A different kind of interactive service has been developed by Rogers Cablesystems, Canada's largest cable system operator, for introduction into the United States through its U.S. subsidiaries. To surpass a major obstacle faced in videotext development, the cost of the decoder, Rogers designed a time-shared Telidon system wherein each display generator will be remotely located and shared by about 250 cable subscribers. As a result, the monthly fee to subscribers for interactive offerings will be reduced in half. However, a drawback of the system, as with any time-shared system, will be the tradeoff between the amount of information available to subscribers at one time and the length of access queues permitted. The time-shared service is being viewed by the company as a means for cable TV subscribers to gain familiarity with transactional and information retrieval services and also pave the way for eventual subscriber purchase of in-home decoders. Rogers two-way systems are currently under construction in Portland, Oregon and five suburbs of Minneapolis, Minnesota; the security portion of the Home Monitoring System is currently operating on the Syracuse, New York cable system.

Looking to the future, The Source and CompuServe, both of which provide a variety of consumer data bases, have established cable versions of their online information services called "CableSource" and "Info-Channel," respectively. CompuServe will initially be available only to cable subscribers with home computers and only as a two-way service; a field test to develop InfoChannel, in association with Atari and Warner Amex Cable, was described earlier. The development of CableSource, on the other hand, comprises both one- and two-way technologies. Source Telecomputing Corp. has arranged for The Source to be included in Cox Cable's San Diego system and has also reached an agreement with Viacom Cable to work together to deliver The Source to Viacom subscribers. The Source was included in Viacom's cable franchise proposals for Prince George's County, Maryland and Sheboygan, Wisconsin.

Both CompuServe and The Source have cooperative marketing arrangements with home computer retail outlets; the primary users of their services have been home computer enthusiasts. That picture may change dramatically as their cable versions become available to two-way cable multiple systems operators.

Two Notable Viewdata Experiments

Lest one think that except for the public TV stations, only private enterprise has been active in developing and finding applications for videotext systems, the roles of the U.S. government and the Online Computer Library Center, Inc. (OCLC) in videotext development through, respectively, "Project Green Thumb" and "Channel 2000" should be fully recognized. Project Green Thumb is notable since it represents the earliest videotext experiment funded by the federal government. Channel 2000 constitutes the first effort by a library-oriented organization to examine videotext and its potential for library services.

Project Green Thumb

In March 1980, the University of Kentucky began a two-year, $360,000 pilot test of the Green Thumb Dissemination System jointly sponsored by the Department of Commerce's National Weather Service, the Department of Agriculture's Extension Service and the Kentucky Extension Service. The project is testing viewdata delivery of weather, crop, market, and other kinds of information to 200 farmers in two Kentucky counties. A decoder (the "Green Thumb box") is the key to this dissemination system, in effect turning the farmer's television set into a computer terminal. (One set of wires of the Green Thumb box connects to the TV set and the other plugs into the telephone line.) The 1,000-page data base loaded on the county computer consists of a wide range of time-sensitive, highly perishable weather and weather-related information useful to the farmers in their day-to-day decision making. Vital updating of data in the county computer is accomplished both by the county extension staff with local information and on a dial-up basis by the state computer at the University of Kentucky, which itself is updated hourly by the computer at the National Meteorological Center in Washington, D.C.

The farmer, having attached his Green Thumb box to his TV set, next consults a menu of the data base offerings (available in print form or on the screen) and then accesses the system by keying in the desired screens and calling a special telephone number at the local extension agent's office to be connected to the computer. The information is sent in a burst over the telephone line and loaded into the memory of the farmer's Green Thumb box. The system allows for a maximum of eight screenfuls of information per telephone call. The farmer can display the information at his leisure; however, should more information be desired, the county computer again has to be called.

While some feel that the government should not be involved in supporting experimental videotext projects like Green Thumb because they may lead to the development of services duplicative of or competitive with those of private enterprise, the commercial sector has benefited already from this federally supported test. Besides providing both government and agribusiness with important data on the information needs of farmers, the project's Green Thumb box, which was manufactured by Motorola in conjunction with Radio Shack, is credited with spawning Tandy's now widely available TRS-80 Videotex terminal.

Channel 2000

Since its founding in 1967, "delivery of information to users when and where they want it" has been one of the tenets of OCLC. Until viewdata, however, it remained an idealistic goal of the future. Only a year after the establishment of OCLC's Research Department in 1977, a research program was initiated to bring this objective closer to realization, namely, the Home Delivery of Library Services Program. Under the rubrics of technology evaluation, service identification, and market analysis, OCLC has pursued varied research in remote or home delivery.

The first major research and development activity of the program, in cooperation with Warner Amex Cable, was to use the interactive capability of the Qube system in a "home book club" sponsored by the Public Library of Columbus and Franklin County. In 1979, Qube broadcast an hour-long show each month called "Home Book Club," which incorporated discussion of current novels by citizen panels. Through the interactive response buttons of the Qube two-way cable system, home viewers were able to voice both their opinions about the books and also vote on the novel to be discussed the following week.

Simultaneous with the Home Book Club project, OCLC researchers were busily engaged in initial investigations concerning the viewdata concept. As the story goes, the founder and then president, Frederick C. Kilgour, had returned from a business trip to London in 1978 carrying a *Times* article describing Prestel, the British viewdata system. Kilgour subsequently initiated a series of investigations to determine the promise of the technology for the delivery of library and information services. After OCLC staff had built a prototype viewdata system and determined that true operational feasibility would require a large-scale project, Channel 2000 was born.

The Channel 2000 final report[5] is itself significant since it provides the first publicly available information on the results of a U.S. videotext test. (Results, i.e., hard research data, from the numerous field trials and market tests conducted by private companies have remained confidential for proprietary reasons, except for occasional releases to the press.) While the test unfortunately was marred by technical problems, OCLC still considered participants' evaluation of the Channel 2000 service to be valid.

The test was conducted in Columbus, Ohio from October through December 1980. It accomplished its objective to design, develop, and evaluate an experimental home information service providing online access to a variety of data bases, including a library catalog. Participating in the test were 100 families randomly selected by OCLC and an additional 100 nonrandomly chosen by Bank One, OCLC's cosponsor, from its customers. Each family received free, a viewdata decoder with a keypad and also free use of the system. They were offered a variety of information services and educational programs from a data base of almost 2 million index and information screens.

The development of the Channel 2000 data base benefited from the automatic creation, using special OCLC software, from machine-readable records of the two largest portions, the catalog of the complete holdings of the Public Library of Columbus and Franklin County and the full text of the *Academic American Encyclopedia*, a 21-volume work published by Arete. Regarding the library catalog, users were able to search by author, title, or subject and select books to be mailed directly to their homes (with a postage-paid return envelope enclosed). If a book was not available, the library would leave a message for the user in the electronic mailbox, an additional feature of the system that allowed the library and OCLC to communicate with participants but did not also enable user-to-user communications (as in true electronic mail).

Also at the fingertips of the 200-household sample were home banking services from Bank One which also permitted payment of bills; a public information service from Com-tility (a local volunteer group), which provided information from city, state, and private sources about employment, environment, human services, and so on in the Columbus/Franklin County area; a community calendar from the Columbus Chamber of Commerce; and two educational programs developed by Ohio State University's College of Education, which were designed to help parents teach their children basic mathematics and reading skills.

The research design for the test included the administration of questionnaires before, during and after the test. Six focus-group interview sessions were also held in mid-January 1981. The results obtained included rankings according to "usefulness" (the library catalog and the public information service were the most useful Channel 2000 services, followed by banking services and the encyclopedia) and "purchase interest" (the encyclopedia and the library catalog were first, followed by home banking, public information, the calendar and the two educational programs).

Not surprisingly, since the classical viewdata method of indexing was used, 34% of the participants agreed that it took too much time to find a book or locate an encyclopedia article. OCLC chose this method of information retrieval and its accompanying standard 16-keypad to avoid a system having a more complex user language and more sophisticated, costly software to support it. Nevertheless, OCLC recognized that a full alphanumeric keyboard and its concomitant requirements would have allowed for keyword or direct access to information and also flexible phrasing of requests.

Significantly, for libraries, 41% of the respondents said their knowledge of library services increased as a result of their use of the viewdata system. In addition, 16% stated that they spent more time reading books than before the test.

OCLC hoped the results of its viewdata test would encourage similar efforts by libraries and, presumably, other library networks. To date, as the OCLC report on Channel 2000 recognizes, libraries have taken advantage of new technology to improve existing services rather than to provide new or enhanced services directly to patrons. The OCLC viewdata experimental project shows clearly that libraries have a new tool which can substantially raise their priority in the public eye and improve public awareness and knowledge of library services, as well as increase the reading of books.

As for OCLC, in the words of Tom Harnish, who directed the Channel 2000 project, "The findings are encouraging enough for us to continue to explore this new medium through Viewtel, a new in-home and in-office information project under way at OCLC. Channel 2000 has shown us that we're on the right track. There's an in-home information service in the future for libraries."[6]

CLOSING COMMENTS

It is apparent that in the United States, viewdata and teletext services are currently being market tested and readied for imminent introduction to the American public. Cabletext, both one-and two-way, has reached full service level, with some systems still undergoing improvement. A multi-billion dollar market is projected in numerous market research studies, although there are many who doubt that a significant market will ever develop. Numerous questions and unresolved issues remain, such as the need for system standards to enable mass market production of low-cost videotext receivers; the ultimate role of AT&T in electronic information services (a subject receiving intense debate and study in the courts, the FCC, and Congress); and policies concerning ownership of the VBI, copyright, privacy, and security.

It is also evident that, except for OCLC, these are systems being developed outside the library and information science community. In contrast to librarians' concern to develop information services to meet citizens' needs, videotext is technology-driven; the kinds of questions studied are market-oriented and concern what information consumers are willing to pay for, and how much.

The development of videotext presents both challenges and opportunities for libraries. Prior to the onset of videotext, libraries had only to contend with a "for-profit information business" composed of primarily information and computing companies. The surge of videotext development has already brought an increasing number of companies—from the newspaper, telephone, cable television, and broadcasting industries—whose primary interest in information is to develop new, profitable commercial services to market. In addition, public television stations have seen videotext as a way to expand their public information role. It is inescapable that to the extent information transmitted in videotext formats overlaps or duplicates information supplied by libraries, the potential for competition with libraries for information consumers exists.

However, the development of videotext should not be perceived only in a competitory light. As the Channel 2000 viewdata experiment of OCLC clearly illustrates, videotext also presents new opportunities for libraries and the potential for enhancing library services.

Kathleen Criner, director of telecommunications affairs of the American Newspaper Publishers Association, is one of the few who has expressed views on the implications of videotext for libraries. She sees various ways in which libraries can benefit from videotext development. According to Criner,[7] libraries can act in videotext capacities either as information providers, information brokers, or system providers.

In videotext, libraries have at their disposal a tool to use to directly deliver information services to the public. Similar to the role played by the Public Library of Columbus and Franklin County in Channel 2000 and by the Martin Luther King, Jr. Library in the WETA/NYU teletext project, libraries can act as information providers to viewdata and teletext systems. The information transmitted could be wide-ranging, from library-produced specialized bibliographies or lists of new acquisitions to library catalogs (portions or the whole catalog), to community reference data and to publicity on hours, services, equipment, meeting rooms, and so on. The possibilities are endless.

Libraries could, by contracting with companies providing the videotext systems, expand their service role to include acting as videotext service brokers. The library's responsiblity might include such activities as determining, updating, and indexing the information provided by the system. The library might generate some of the information itself as well as contract with other organizations to supply information that the library would put in videotext format. Again the possiblities are limited only by the library's ingenuity and initiative.

Library cooperatives could act as system providers for videotext-based library services. Following the example set by OCLC in its Channel 2000 experiment, they would handle all aspects of data base creation and design as well as system communications, management, marketing, and billing. The "library" would be extended well beyond its present physical boundaries directly into the homes and offices of its users.

The library profession must begin to focus clearly on what these developments mean not only for libraries, but also, and more importantly, what they mean for U.S. citizens and their information needs. At this point it appears that for the services to be profitable, the average and even the above average American income may find them difficult to afford. If videotext development is successful and becomes widespread, and the services are beyond the means of a large number of Americans, it will mean a greater gap between the information rich and the information poor. Greater governmental and institutional support for libraries will be required to enable them to provide videotext services for the public.

Videotext may prove to be only an evolutionary development. For the present, however, videotext is here, it appears to be growing in influence, and librarians should not only take it seriously but also devise means of exploiting it to their advantage.

NOTES

1. Michael J. Nyhan, Robert Johansen and Robert Plummer, "Videotex and Teletext in the U.S.: Prospects for the 1980s," *Telecommunication Journal* 47 (1980):398.

2. Efrem M. Sigel, ed. *Videotext: The Coming Revolution in Home/Office Information Retrieval* (White Plains, N.Y.: Knowledge Industry Publications, Inc., 1980), Preface.

3. Knight-Ridder Newspapers, Inc., *Annual Report*, (Miami, Fla.: 1980), p. 14.

4. "Viewtron Looks Good as a News Medium," *Editor & Publisher*, November 7, 1981, p. 11.

5. *Channel 2000: Description and Findings of a Viewdata Test Conducted by OCLC in Columbus Ohio, October–December 1980* (Columbus: OCLC Online Computer Library Center, Inc., April 1981).

6. OCLC Online Computer Library Center, Inc., News Release (June 9, 1981), p. 2.

7. Kathleen Criner, "Videotext: Implications and Applications for Libraries," in *Telecommunications and Libraries: A Primer for Librarians and Information Managers* (White Plains, N.Y.: Knowledge Industry Publications, Inc., 1981), pp. 87–89.

REFERENCES

Advanced Technology/Libraries, (March, May), 1981.

"ANPA Study Details Cable Lease Options." *Editor & Publisher*, (November 7):11, 1981.

"Atlanta Newspapers Start Year-Long Experiment of Electronic Edition." *Editor & Publisher*, (November 14):37, 1981.

Bolton, W. Theodore, "A Lesson in Interactive Television Programming: The Home Book Club on QUBE." *Journal of Library Automation* 14:103–08, 1981.

Boyd, Frederick W., "CBS, AT&T to Plug into Homeowner Data." *Newark Star Ledger.* (October 9):7, 1981.

British Videotex and Teletext, News Release. New York, (November 24), 1981.

"Cable TV: Coming of Age." *Newsweek*, (August 24):44–49, 1981.

CBS/Broadcast Group. News Release. Los Angeles, (April 8), 1981.

Cherry, Susan Spaeth, "The New TV Information Systems." In *Video Involvement for Libraries: A Current Awareness Package for Professionals*, edited by Susan Spaeth Cherry. Chicago: American Library Association:57–75, 1981.

Ciciora, Walter S., "Home Information Systems—Technically Speaking (An Overview)." Paper delivered at Electro '81. New York, April 7–9, 1981. Mimeographed.

———, "VIRTEXT & VIRDATA, A Present U.S. Teletext Application." In *Videotex '81: Proceedings*:77–84, Northwood Hills, England: Online Conferences Ltd., 1981.

Criner, Kathleen M., "Videotex: Implications for Cable TV." In *The Cable/Broadband Communications Book, Volume 2, 1980–81*, edited by Mary Louise Hollowell. White Plains, N.Y.: Knowledge Industry Publications, Inc.:208–21. 1980.

———, "Videotex: Threat or Opportunity." *Special Libraries*, (September):379–85, 1980.

————, "Videotext: Implications and Applications for Libraries." In *Telecommunications and Libraries: A Primer for Librarians and Information Managers*:69–89, White Plains, N.Y.: Knowledge Industry Publications, Inc., 1981.

Eissler, Charles O., "Market Testing Video-Text: Oak's Miami Teletext System." In *Videotex '81: Proceedings*:57–70, Northwood Hills, England: Online Conferences Ltd., 1981.

Ferrarini, Elizabeth A., "Videotex: The Race to Plug in." *Computerworld*. Supplement, (March 18):64–84, 1981.

Greenhouse, Lee R., "Marketing strategies for Viewdata/Videotex." Paper delivered at Electro '81, New York, April 7–9, 1981. Mimeographed.

"Green Thumb Ready for Harvest." *Viewdata/Videotex Report*:35–36, May 1981.

Gunn, Hartford, and Harper, Gregory W., "A Public Broadcaster's View of Teletext in the United States." In *Viewdata and Videotext, 1980–81: A Worldwide Report*:477–83, White Plains, N.Y.: Knowledge Industry Publications, Inc., 1980.

"Here and There in Anaheim." *Broadcasting*, (December 7):36, 1981.

Hirsch, Phil. "Videotex in the U.S.: The Portland Project." *Computerworld*. Supplement, (March 18):64–65, 1981.

"The Home Information Revolution." *Business Week*, (June 29):74–83, 1981.

IDP (International Data Base Publishing) Report, May 22, June 5, 19, July 3, 17, 31, September 11, 25, October 9, 23, November 20, 1981.

"Ill. Paper Leases Two Cable Channels." *Editor & Publisher*, (November 7):11, 1981.

Kleinfeld, W.R., "CBS and Bell Plan Video-Text Test." *New York Times*, (October 9):D1, 1981.

Lehnert, Howard F., and Scott, Harold A., "Agriculture Weather Program." *RQ* 20:63–65, 1980.

Lind, P.B., "Technical Basis for Inter-Active Service on Two-Way Cable Networks." In *Videotex '81: Proceedings*:277–286. Northwood Hills, England: Online Conferences Ltd., 1981.

"Lining up for Low Power." *Newsweek*:76, (December 21) 1981.

Lopinto, John., "Time Incorporated National Teletext Service." In *Videotex '81: Proceedings*:109–12. Northwood Hills, England: Online Conferences Ltd., 1981.

"LPTV Reality Seen as 18 Months Away." *Broadcasting*, November 16, 1981, p. 64.

"Ma Bell's Eye to the Future." *Newsweek*, October 19, 1981, p. 88.

New York University, Alternate Media Center. News Release. New York, February 18, 1981.

"Nielsen, Arbitron Cable Penetration Figures Vary." *Broadcasting*:82 (January 4), 1982.

Noll, A. Michael. "Teletext and Videotex in North America." *Telecommunications Policy* 2 (1980):17–24.

Norwood, Frank W., "The Emerging Telecommunications Environment." In *Networks for Networkers: Critical Issues in Cooperative Library Development*, edited by Barbara Evans Markuson and Blanche Wools:154–73. New York: Neal-Schuman Publishers, Inc., 1980.

Nyhan, Michael J., Johansen, Robert, and Plummer, Robert, "Videotex and Teletext in the U.S.: Prospects for the 1980's" *Telecommunication Journal* 46 (1980):396–400.

Plakias, Mark, "New Electronic Media: The Future and Cooperation." *RQ*, Fall, 1980, pp. 66–69.

Pollack, Andrew, "Dow Jones Expands Electronic Capability." *New York Times*, May 4, 1981, p. D4.

Robertson, Angus, "Teletext and Viewdata." In *From Television to Home Computer: The Future of Consumer Electronics*, edited by Angus Robertson:119–45. Poole, England: Blandford Press, 1979.

Roizen, Joseph., "The Technology of Teletext and Viewdata." In *Videotext: The Coming Revolution in Home/Office Information Retrieval*, edited by Efrem M. Sigel, 9–21. White Plains, N.Y.: Knowledge Industry Publications, Inc., 1980.

Sigel, Efrem M., "Videotext in the U.S." In *Vidotext: The Coming Revolution in Home/Office Information Retrieval*, edited by Efrem M. Sigel, White Plains, N.Y.: Knowledge Industry Publications, Inc., 1980, pp. 87–111.

Smith, Anthony. *Goodbye Gutenberg: The Newspaper Revolution of the 1980's*. New York: Oxford University Press, 1980.

Soldwedel, Donald N. "Opportunities for Small Newspapers." In *Videotex '81: Proceedings*:221–28, Northwood Hills, England: Online Conferences Lts., 1981.

Stokes, Adrian V. *Viewdata: A Public Information Utility*. 2d ed. London: Langton Information Systems Ltd., 1980.

Teletext and Viewdata in the U.S.: A Workshop on Emerging Issues. Background papers of the workshop, June 20–22, 1979, Pajaro Dunes, Calif. Menlo Park, Calif.: Institute for the Future, 1979.

Telidon Videotex Systems, Inc. News Release. Stamford, Ct., February 12, 17, 1981.

"Times Mirror to Start Videotext Trial in California." *Broadcasting*, (October 26):52, 1981.

Veith, Richard H. "Teletext (Broadcast Videotex) Begins in the United States." Paper delivered at Viewdata '81, London, October 6–8, 1981. Mimeographed.

———. "Videotex—The New Information Systems." Paper delivered at the Eighteenth Annual Clinic on Library Applications of Data Processing, University of Illinois, Urbana-Champaign, April 26–29, 1981. Mimeographed.

"Viewdata—A Review and Bibliography." *Online Review* 2:217–24, 1978.

Viewdata Corp. of America, Inc. News Release. Miami, Fla., July 16, 1980.

Waring, Paul C., "Cox's INDAX System—Delivering Future Two-Way Cable Services Today." *In Videotex '81: Proceedings*, pp. 287–94. Northwood Hills, England: Online Conferences Ltd., 1981.

Wicklein, John, "Two-Way Cable: Much Promise, Some Concern." In *The Cable/Broadband Communications Book, Volume 2, 1980–81*, edited by Mary Louise Hollowell, pp. 190–207. White Plains, N.Y.: Knowledge Industry Publications, Inc., 1980.

Williams, Ederyn, "Who's Who on the Prestel Data base." In *Viewdata in Action*, edited by Rex Winsbury:99–106. London: McGraw-Hill Book Company Limited, 1981.

Winsbury, Rex, "Editor's Introduction: Electronic Editing Database and Page Design." In *Viewdata in Action*, edited by Rex Winsbury:145–54. London: McGraw-Hill Book Company Limited, 1981.

———, "Editor's Introduction: A Lay Guide to How It Works." In *Viewdata in Action*, edited by Rex Winsbury:29–32. London: McGraw-Hill Book Company Limited, 1981.

THE ORGANIZATIONAL AND BUDGETARY EFFECTS OF AUTOMATION ON LIBRARIES

Murray S. Martin

When automation first became a realistic possiblity for business and industry in the late sixties a number of studies were carried out on its organizational effects. Nothing comparable has been undertaken for libraries, yet they face precisely the same kinds of problems and are in need of the same kinds of analyses. The salient points that emerged were: the need for involvement and understanding on the part of top management; the changes brought about in the decision making process, resulting from changes in the style as well as the quantity of new information now available; the shifts of various levels of authority and control; the difficulty in placing the computer people within the structure; and the renewed dangers of rigidity, this time of a different kind, resulting from the systemic requirements of computerization; but, above all, the in-

Advances in Library Administration and Organization, volume 2, pages 69–83.
Copyright © 1983 by JAI Press Inc.
All rights of reproduction in any form reserved.
ISBN: 0-89232-214-4

creased need for concerted planning at the top. None of these are new or startling conclusions, yet they indicate clearly that the computer was not the answer to management ills, only another tool that managers could use—if they took the trouble to understand it.

The primary characteristic of these early studies was their stress on the uncertainty of the future because of certain critical failures in top management. This judgment appears particularly relevant to libraries today, so it is perhaps advantageous to report these findings more fully.

The first and most important charge is the failure of top management to understand all the implications of a change to automation. The result in industry was that "many . . . top managers abdicated their responsibility by defaulting to their technically-oriented data processing managers in all matters relating to computers and computing systems."[1] In part this represents deferral to the expert, but it also shows a lack of understanding of the role of management in a computerized world. As Gilman says, "management can never be completely structured in a dynamic world. It cannot be replaced either by computers or by specialists in their use— though it must be increasingly supplemented by them."[2] This symbiosis is one of the central relationships of the future. How well it is handled may determine the health of the enterprise. By separating computer-related problems from other organizational needs, an unhealthy dichotomy can be created, leading to a split in goal setting. Gilman's words remain an ever-present reminder of this problem. "The real danger is not that top managers will *not* change their roles to fit the computer, but that they may."[3] The understanding of the role of management is a critical issue and on it may depend the success of any scheme of computerization.

Modern organizational studies assign a key role to decision making, and here the impact of the computer may be one of the most important determinants for the future. As Shaw describes it, "decisions are becoming increasingly complex because of the interdependency of relationships within the information system."[4] Computers can supply great amounts of information, can also to some degree manipulate it and derive some conclusions, but ultimately the most important decisions must still be made by management. It is necessary here to distinguish between programmable decisions and those which are of their nature political and not, therefore, freely subject to quantification. "While the computer is likely to absorb an increasing amount of the current decision making, managers will be motivated to seek new challenges in uncharted areas that, at least for some time, will not be susceptible to computerization."[5] Using Forrester's model, Tomeski and Lazarus project a future where creative management will be required always to explore new frontiers, a concept reinforced by Whisler's characterization of human, as against machine capacities as "the incomparable advantage of the human being at the boundary—at the interface of the organization with the physical and cultural world."[6] Decision making, then, is likely to become more, rather than less complex, particularly on the cutting-edge of any organization. Tomeski and Lazarus foresee the need for greater managerial involvement in setting up the rules for decision making and for asserting the notion of quality as against quantity.

Such changes clearly have an organizational impact and it appears most clearly in the isolation of different kinds of management. Top management must reassert its responsiblity for policy making and long-term planning. At'a middle management level the traditional role of vertical mediation within the command structure will be supplemented to a great extent by the need for lateral contacts, for guidance, and leadership. The computer will require middle managers "to be better managers. It will throw greater emphasis on innovation and leadership talent at middle and lower levels; and it will reduce the rampart of paper work behind which inadequate managers have always been able to hide."[7] The resulting fluidity will require changes in the information and communication network that sustains and guides any enterprise.

The ability to generate, retrieve, and interpret information is basic to the success of the organization. New ways of information gathering can be expected to have significant impact on older systems. "The characteristic pyramid structure, developed out of experience of centuries, has been determined by the requirements for executing decisions rather than for gathering information." Now, "the communications network of an organization is determined by who needs what kind of information and from whom, not by who tells whom what to do."[8] This kind of need parallels the older concept of the informal structure that lay behind the organization chart, only it now lays more emphasis on the former.

The questions of information and communication raise the issue of the relationship of computer and system personnel to the rest of the staff and here the consensus is that the "main-frame" movement has been deleterious because it separated responsibility and accountability and came to be an undesirable drag on momentum. "The effect on decision flexibility has been self-contradictory: Use of computers in decision-making stimulates ideas for change but greatly increases the costs of adopting these changes."[9] Whisler further warns that "continuing development of larger computer systems within companies will further exaggerate the problem of inflexibility and difficulty of change that already exists."[10] Eight years later Breslin and Taschenberg found the same problems in massive, centralized computer systems. "A centralized computer organization separates the systems executive from the systems user, confusing the responsibilities for timeliness and accuracy. . . . We must return systems responsibilities to the users, we must get the computer back in phase with the business at hand and we must cut escalating costs."[11] While this is in part a plea for recognition of the newer mini- and micro-computer technology, it is also a salutary reminder that in the past most managers have been content to be guided by self-interested computer professionals in their choice of computer systems and programs.

Diebold forthrightly lays the blame on a lack of sophistication, "the failure of top management to ask the right questions."[12] The real need is for greatly increased managerial knowledge about computers, not the assigning of responsibilities to computer specialists although the latter will be needed in increasing numbers. Decisions on the use of automation must however be dictated by the logic of the situation, to use Drucker's phrase. "The only real criterion for using data processing at all comes down to cost-effectiveness. If tasks can be performed manually in a quick, easy, and accurate manner, an expensive computer is not required."[13] In this context Diebold suggests that we may have been using quite the wrong criteria in deciding about automation. "The value of the information [derived from the computer] should be the determinant of system use. Yet, in lieu of adequate measures of the *value* of information, we continue to use cost displacement as the criterion."[14] What may have been appropriate for the simple transformation of book-keeping systems is inappropriate for far more complex information systems. In the de-veloping of such systems attention must be paid to the risks inherent in the computer's need for explicitness. What was implicit in the past must be made explicit now since the computer "not only permits us but requires us to carry the process of explication to the limit called for by the complexity of the organization, rather than to the one set by the manipu-lative ability of human thought."[15] It is at this point that the executive is in danger of resigning control to the expert, because he is the expert without recognizing that the responsibility of setting policy cannot be so abdicated.

If these are the kinds of problems still unresolved by industry in meet-ing the challenge of the computer, how well can libraries expect to fare? By now most readers should already be applying much of what they have read to library situations they are familiar with. There is, however, one characteristic of libraries that overrides all other considerations. The basic function of libraries is to organize and make accessible information of various kinds. In such circumstances automation is not simply an ex-terior tool to be used in promoting a business venture, it is a part of the business itself. Inasmuch as automation has irrevocably altered the whole nature of the information process, it has also altered the way in which libraries can and must work. This fact is the major, though not the only difference between libraries and other computer-using systems. Strangely enough, the librarians' response to this fact has been minimal and concentrated on marginal effects rather than on the central concern—how the change in the nature of information might change the nature of libraries. At the same time members of the information community have been only too vocal about the likely future of libraries,[16] perhaps another reason for librarians' silence, a well-publicized view of their imminent demise, along with their books and journals.

The future, however, is likely to prove by no means so simple. Walters, in a useful synopsis, provides sound reasons for expecting the book to survive and the library to absorb the new media. Examining the possibilities of the "electronic journal" he concludes that, if useful, it should be accepted into the canon of information carriers. "In so doing we should be mindful of the fact that no major communication format in the twentieth century has yet succeeded in displacing older forms that preceded it. They have merely moved alongside older forms as an alternative method of communicating."[17] That is to say, the new formats and their medium, the computer, challenge librarians to find ways of incorporating them into the existing communications complex of the library. There is no retreat, no way of reversing an already strong flow towards electronic information. It is, however, necessary not only to ride with the flow but to channel its course.

It is only to be expected that, faced with so basic a change in their stock in trade, libraries should be transformed by automation. These changes are widespread and affect virtually every part of a library's operation, even if librarians have not yet generally perceived this to be so. The introduction of automation requires new procedures, new staffing patterns, new budget and program priorities, shifts in certain kinds of authority and decision making, and extensive changes in a library's expenditure patterns. While each of these changes is important in itself, the most important change is their cumulative effect on the structure and organization of the whole library. Library management will do well to remember this in all planning for automation. In a recent statement on the quiet revolution in campus intellectual life, the Cohens placed the center of the revolution in the library because "of all campus institutions, libraries are the chief recipients of the benefits of technology. Computerization, miniaturization, telecommunication, and the audio-visuals are sweeping fresh air through musty halls."[18] Only too seldom has the library response to this wave of change been integrated or planned. The inbred pragmatism of the librarian has favored a piece-meal, step-by-step approach which has, in many cases, simply exacerbated the problems each step was meant to solve, as witness the many libraries which have come to recognize, belatedly, the inadequacy of the abbreviated records on which they based their circulation systems. To say this is not to lay blame on libraries and librarians, except insofar as they did not realize the meaning of the changes in their environment. The responsibility must be shared by the entrepreneurs and the utilities that sought to capitalize on the inchoate expectations of librarians.

The range of activities susceptible to automation is very wide. Immediately one thinks of cataloging and then the whole range of technical services. Circulation, too, is an obvious candidate with its large number of routine activities, but interlibrary loan and reference stand to benefit not only secondarily from improved bibliographic information, but primarily from vastly improved electronic communication. And behind all these is the possiblity of greatly increased managerial effectiveness deriving from access to a broader range of information. Although these are frequently thought of as independent activities—even listing them separately tends to perpetuate this idea—they are dependent on data generated and used in common. In the past this fact was not obvious, the computer has made it so and now reveals quite clearly the true interdependence of library activities. This fact alone would lead us to conclude that the need for top management to pay greater attention to policy making and planning is as urgent for libraries as for industry and business.

To date, however, libraries are still caught in the "cost displacement" mode of automation. Although it has long been realized that the true benefits of automation derive from its broad application to the entire spectrum of activity "most computers are used essentially for speeded-up routinized work previously done by manual or mechanical means."[19] Since libraries are not usually able to generate developmental capital it is not surprising that the first efforts are usually in the displacement mode. The commonest first step is to import a product—OCLC cataloging services being the most widespread example. The result can be changes as great or as small as the librarian wants. To many librarians OCLC (or any other utility) is still only a very expensive typewriter used to produce the traditional product—a card catalog. For such a situation the cataloger alone is not responsible, rather responsibility must be shared by library and institutional administrators who have failed to look beyond the immediate goal which was usually some mythical cost saving. Nevertheless the potential effects of automation elsewhere can be seen clearly enough in the catalog department:

1. a significant shift from people- to machine-generated data;
2. the need to reconsider entire procedures, including the rendering of previously implicit activities into explicit directions;
3. the creation of new classes of employees and new skills, (*e.g.* input operators), thus upgrading certain classes of employees, while reducing the professional cadre;

4. increased dependence on external sources (utilities; networks) for documentation, standards, advice, policies, and priorities, and the accompanying decrease in local autonomy;
5. a budgetary shift from personnel to equipment and contracted services.

The implications of these changes have not always been grasped. A very useful article by Holley[20] outlines the personal and institutional possibilities for cataloging, and sees a range of possible developments with profound implications for professional responsibilities. These range from development into a manager of the library's bibliographic control system to absorption into integrated subject units. The author elsewhere[21] has argued that the increasing complexity of bibliographic control and the need for continual updating makes the latter a remote possiblity for most libraries. Whatever the ultimate future may be, it is certain now that task differentiation will be forced on cataloging departments by economic necessity. Whether this will result in professional enhancement of the cataloger's role depends on the sophistication brought to the task of adaptation. The first generation of change has tended to be internal to technical processing, indeed almost exclusively internal to cataloging, which is odd since the catalog is only one end product of a flow of activity. To a large extent that decision was brought about by the utilities, which could rely on the standardization required by cataloging codes to generate large volumes of repetitive work. Finally, even they are beginning to work backwards into the acquisition process, but integrated technical systems are still few and far between because of the much greater differences between local business procedures. One external effect, however, has been noticeable: the division of budgetary support to provide necessary funds to purchase equipment and to continue payments for the ever-increasing costs of contracted services. Otherwise most parts of the library continued with business as usual.

What happens when any library, or any operation within a library becomes machine-dependent? The first result is a loss of flexibility in physical planning. Most libraries did not anticipate the electronic age and are not properly equipped electrically. Machines cannot be moved around as readily as people and the result is that people are moved to fit in with machine needs regardless of whether that encourages efficiency and effectiveness or not. The second result is more rigid timetabling to "maximize" the use of the machine. This restructuring of work times is usually the product of external forces, such as the availability patterns of the chosen utility. OCLC, for example, by manipulating its user fees, encourages libraries to undertake certain activities at off-peak hours, usually early morning or evening hours. While a change of this sort may not seem dramatic to industry, or even to the public service arm of the library, it represents a dramatic shift away from the customary office hours of the catalog department. Double shifts, or staggered working hours bring with them the need for changes in supervision and training. Other effects from participation in a "system" can also require considerable attention to staff needs, as outlined by Kallenbach and Jackson[22] in describing a switch from one utility to another. The pains of temporary disorganization, though frequently exaggerated, are real and compounded by the catalogers' anxiety that the change should not degrade the quality of their work or leave all kinds of loose ends.[23]

If the simple decision to contract out for cataloging can cause such profound shifts in a conservative department, how much greater are likely to be the changes as the library proceeds deeper into automation. The literature abounds with expressions of concern, but contains very little relating to the planning decisions that we require to implement any automated system. The chief new factors to be considered are external to the department: user needs and supplier capabilities. These require that close attention be given to the nature of the end-products desired and to the process that brings them into being. As suggested by Holley, these considerations call into question the whole basis of cataloging. Are catalog cards the most desirable product of automation, whether on cards or fiche, or even on the terminal screen? Is this the danger referred to by Tomeski and Lazarus when they claim "old manual and mechanical procedures are often duplicated in the new computerized systems?"[24] In part it is, but it is even more an example of system rigidity, because the end-product is defined for most libraries by what the utility is willing to provide. Further, it illustrates the rule-bound nature of librarianship, which tends to value adherence to codes and standards above user-service needs. One more instance of preferring means to goals.

On top of this the utilities and networks impose, currently at least, some very drastic constraints. Decisions by these outside forces, on which the individual library can have very little effect, may decide what kinds of bibliographic data will be available, what kinds of services will be provided, at what times, and at what cost. These problems frequently engender a feeling of helplessness and sometimes of rebellion, but they are merely symptoms of the fact that libraries no longer operate autonomously. There are no easy solutions, but finding any solutions requires much greater attention to the problems than library administrators have been wont to give in the past.

One very important fact must now be noted. The decision to automate tends to be irreversible. Once the process is begun, future alternatives relate only to choices between modes. Because libraries must, generally, dismantle their existing structures, procedures, and staffing patterns to pay for and accommodate to automated cataloging, they move into a dependent status. Henceforth they depend on a utility because there is no way of reestablishing autonomy except at prohibitive cost, both direct, say in terms of recreating vacated positions, and indirect, in terms of seceding from an increasingly cooperative bibliographic world. As a result, a sizeable element of the budget is now committed to a particular kind of program, *and* to any externally imposed changes and cost increases that may develop. The history of the relations between libraries, networks and utilities illustrates powerfully the problems that result from separating the decision making about automation from general decision making about library goals.

Until automated circulation systems became more reliable and their costs supportable, public contact with automation was very limited. Except for those few libraries which provided either public-access terminal[25] or on-line catalog access, the library appeared, to the user, not to have changed. The advent of the turnkey system changed all that. Borrowers are now much more likely to be aware that the library uses machines. They are also much more likely to know about the "rules"—and in academic circles much more likely to want to make and change them—and to find that they must follow them more precisely. Unfortunately many, if not most libraries, which installed circulation systems, until very recently ignored one of the basic rules in automation: to integrate activities as far as possible and particularly to create only one basic bank of information. True, alternatives were not readily available until recently, but one must have the strong suspicion that the salesperson rather than the librarian did the deciding. Now those libraries must pay for the reintegration and updating of records.

Insufficient attention has been paid to the important management information to be gained from automated circulation systems. Without them the investigations and proposals of McGrath, Kent, and others could not have been undertaken. While that may appear to be a mixed blessing, it is certainly true that never before (without unimaginable clerical labor) have libraries been in a position to know just what was being done with their collections. Interestingly, these systems have provoked much more thoughtful studies of a greatly neglected, yet basic aspect of library activity. One may cite, merely as examples, Mansfield on queuing[26] or Jestes on cost comparisons.[27] Such studies indicate a growing awareness of the need for research. So far we have not gone the next step to see what would-be borrowers did not find, to look at the problems in personal reserve queues, and, most important of all to reevaluate the connections between circulation, reference, and the catalog as suggested five years ago by Young[28] and Kazlauskas.[29] Internal access to materials has been improved but the price paid lies in more exacting and inflexible procedures, usually more restricted numbers of circulation points, increasing need for trouble-shooters (one of the predicted side-effects of automation on middle management), and the terrible conundrum of how to behave when the system is down.

Both cataloging and circulation tend to be internal systems. Except insofar as cataloging data is shared with other libraries, there are no external relations. Yet the very sharing of data has brought the pleasures and perils of automation into one of the most sophisticated but at the same time the least self-sustaining of activities—interlibrary loan. Here the effects of improved external and internal access to bibliographic data have first become visible. At a time when the costs and difficulties of handling an increasing interlibrary loan traffic were finally drawing managerial attention to this beleaguered department, the open screen increased the flood. Terminal access encouraged libraries to send requests anywhere. Regional agreements are breaking down, codes are disregarded and bibliographic centers are either going out of business or changing their goals to accommodate to change. In an attempt to cope, some libraries imposed heavy lending fees, others stopped lending at all or joined small preferential groups, while others simply got further behind in their work. The newest systems, OCLC and RLG, have begun to impose some order on this new chaos, but have in turn forced libraries to think much more carefully about what they could or would do for one another. It will be a long time yet before new patterns emerge, and those that do will have to be part of broader cooperative concerns. Interlibrary loan has been to date the victim of the directly contrary, simultaneous effects of automation, which made information about things much more widely accessible even while the things themselves becomes less accessible.

A similar quandary arises from the use of data base searching without concern for its side-effects. Access to unlimited numbers of citations, unaccompanied either by a sturdy acquisitions program or increased interlibrary loan, and without the necessary policy decisions, on what can or cannot be done to provide access to information that is not in conventional forms, can raise user expectations beyond the possible level of fulfillment. That of course increases user dissatisfaction and directly contradicts the on-line message. Part two of *The On-Line Revolution in Libraries* explores some of these implications,[30] but it does not cover adequately the vital issue of internal library planning, particularly the need for lateral integration. In his paper, De Gennaro[31] hints at the close relationship between economics and innovation by suggesting that many libraries may not continue to have the money to subsidize on-line access. This complex issue will require closer study, as library budgets decline, and directors will have to look carefully at the trade-offs between staff, materials, and on-line services.[32]

When all such changes and their accompanying problems are considered, it is clear that library managers face a whole new range of decision making. It is also clear that other parties—vendors, utilities, networks—are involved, even if silently. In a provocative article Moran[33] suggests that libraries must develop a structure that will respond to external as well as internal problems and lays the primary responsibility on top management. Little, if any, consideration has been given to the proper role of the systems staff in libraries, probably because very few libraries have any significant numbers of such people. Nevertheless, even if a library purchases all its computer services, or derives them from a separate service unit in the institution, the people who provide these services have become library decision makers. Where they fit into the hierarchy and how they participate in decision making become critical issues. This is particularly true when large mainframe computers, their costs, capabilities, and services are at the center of the relationship. Then, indeed, we have questions of mounting costs and increasing restrictions in choosing the future.

The focus of concentration tends to move from people to equipment, from process to product, from why to what. Because of this movement the decision-making power of systems or technical people tends to grow, while that of people-oriented librarians tends to weaken. To achieve the greatest benefits from automation, librarians should seek to reverse this trend, and learn from experience in industry. Fortunately the computer mainstay itself may have provided part of the answer, with new generations of mini-and microcomputers.[34] As Breslin and Taschenberg said, "we must return systems responsibility to the users, we must get the computer back in phase with the business at hand and we must cut escalating costs."[35] They saw in the new technology a way of overcoming domination by a central elite. The roles of the systems analyst and the systems manager need reassessment in order to increase responsiveness to user needs. They see decentralization as a major possibility. "The impact of distributed processing is to shift a significant amount of responsibility from one central organization to several user organizations."[36] A further gain is increased involvement by the participants. Admittedly, such changes are easier to implement in a business or industry that provides its own computing services, but the implication is clear: Systems that are developed as the result of joint effort are much more likely to be successful in a service organization than those imposed from the top. Utilities, service agencies, and networks are slowly learning this lesson, too. The first editorial in a new publication *Resource Sharing and Library Networks*, "Towards Broader Networks,"[37] summarizes the needs very well and stresses the need for cooperative solutions to problems which are now beyond the capacity of any individual library to solve.

The financial implication of automated access to computerized information provides the most pressing reason for reconsideration of the library's goals. Examination of ARL library budgets shows quite clearly a consistent and massive increase in expenditures for things. Some of this is caused by the incredible price increases in paper products, but much of it relates directly to automation. Even so simple a thing as an automated circulation system requires the provision of machine-readable labels and machine-readable borrower's cards. These are quite new expenditure items and, in large libraries, can be very significant. Similarly the detection strips to prevent theft simply add to operational costs. The costs of adopting OCLC (or similar services) are now well documented, but the rise in ongoing costs is not so well publicized. Counterbalancing decreases in people costs have not been as great as predicted, in part because libraries have never been generously staffed and the majority of library transactions remain individualized services. In some ways this parallels the history of miniaturization, where microforms were expected to decrease costs and provide relatively painless collection expansion for libraries. There the cost of equipment, the need for maintenance services, for proper user space and for librarians as intermediaries were grossly underestimated. Now libraries may be in danger of following the same path with public access terminals. The complexity of access to data bases, and so on, was underestimated and staff could not be reduced. Moreover if a library undertakes even a modest program of internal automation, the shifts in budgetary expenditures can be quite dramatic, particularly if new funding may not be available, even for the initial hardware investment, but also because the costs of systems staff, and for the maintenance of hardware and software are substantial.

The exhilaration expressed by the Cohens is very real, and libraries have no alternative but to embrace the new technology if they are to survive. As they suggest, the products sought in the new library will be qualitatively rather than quantitatively assessed by the user. To achieve such a turnaround will require money. They suggest that the money usually provided for expansion should now be invested on technology, but, as De Gennaro pointed out, such a switch is unlikely to take place at a time when most institutions are searching merely for enough money to survive.

Most of the changes noted in this article are associated with a transitional era. The true effects of automation still lie ahead in the period when on-line access becomes the standard. If libraries have coped only partially with today's changes, what can they expect of the future? The changes are likely be of such magnitude that ad hoc decision making will simply escalate the problems. Power will shift significantly towards those who are knowledgeable in automation.

The first need is to analyze the changes likely to take place and then to decide what library functions are likely to be affected and to what degree. This search should include looking for new linkages, whether via machine or not, to see what is the best way of providing any desired service in the most economical way. Obsolete functions should be examined for discontinuance, something like the old accessions book. Functions not presently being carried out should be evaluated for incorporation, according to the degree of appropriateness for the whole library. In a kind of zero budget process, the structure must then be put back together in a way that takes advantage of automation's good aspects and minimizes the effects of its imperfections, especially those unmeetable expectations so easily aroused.

The new structure must also recognize the new requirements of an automated library. Key questions of the past, such as the location, control, and use of the card catalog, are no longer critical when total information can be decentralized. The key questions now are how to staff and organize service points to take advantage of the new access. In the near future libraries will have to cope with the effects of the unfreezing of information. In its new, fluid state information can be redirected almost at will, can be reshaped, and, in effect, custom-tailored. The kinds of staff needed by this new age and the kinds of skills they will have to have are very different from those required now,[38] although paradoxically, they may reinforce the present trend towards greater subject knowledge and specialization. Independence will be the key-word for these new personnel and fitting them into the staffing patterns that must be maintained to meet the logistical needs of the library will be as great a challenge to library management as any heretofore experienced.

NOTES AND REFERENCES

1. Breslin, Judson and Taschenberg, C. Bradley, *Distributed Processing Systems: End of the Mainframe Era* (New York: AMACOM, 1978) p. 1.

2. Gilman, Glenn, "The Computer Revisited," in Boore, William F. and Murphy, Jerry R., *The Computer Sampler: Management Perspectives on the Computer* (New York: McGraw-Hill, 1968), p. 242.

3. Ibid., p. 294.

4. Shaw, Donald R., "What's Really Needed for Middle Management?" in Boore and Murphy, p. 207.

5. Tomeski, Edward A. and Lazarus, Harold, *People-Oriented Computer Systems: The Computer in Crisis* (New York: Van Nostand, 1977), p. 170.

6. Whisler, Thomas, *The Impact of Computers on Organizations* (New York: Praeger, 1970), p. 8.

7. Gilman, p. 301.

8. Ibid., p. 287.

9. Whisler, p. 93.

10. Ibid. p. 149.

11. Breslin and Taschenberg, pp. 10–11.

12. Diebold, John, *Business Decisions and Technological Change* (New York: Praeger. 1970), p. 51.

13. Breslin and Tomeski, p. 20.

14. Ibid., p. 49.

15. Gilman, p. 285.

16. Licklider, J.C.R., *Libraries of the Future*. (Cambridge: MIT Press, 1965); Lancaster, F. Wilfred, *Toward Paperless Information Systems*. (New York: Academic Press, 1978).

17. Walters, Edward M., "Electronic Journals and the Concept of a Paperless Library," *National Forum*, 60 (3): 135.

18. Cohen, Aaron and Cohen, Elaine, "The Quiet Revolution on Campus," *Chronicle of Higher Education*, Nov. 25, 1981, p. 56.

19. Tomeski and Lazarus, p. 165.

20. Holley, Robert P., "The Future of Catalogers and Cataloging," *Journal of Academic Librarianship*, 7 (2): 90–93.

21. Martin, Murray S., *Issues in Personnel Management in Academic Libraries*, (Greenwich: JAI Press, 1981), pp. 200, 214.

22. Kallenbach, Susan and Jackson, Susan, "Staff Response to Changing Systems: From Manual to OCLC to RLIN," *Journal of Academic Librarianship*, 6 (5): 264–267.

23. Martin, Susan K., "Upgrading Brief and Dirty Data," *American Libraries*, 10 (4): 213–214.

24. Tomeski and Lazarus, p. 165.

25. Friedman, Elaine S., "Patron Access to Online Cataloging Systems," *Journal of Academic Librarianship*, 6 (3): 132–139, provides an example of such a situation.

26. Mansfield, Jerry W., "Human Factors of Queueing: A Library Circulation Model," *Journal of Academic Librarianship*, 6 (6): 342–344. Although not directly concerned with automation, this article illustrates the kind of investigation that must precede the installation of any system, particularly since it is not possible to have spare terminals on hand sufficient to cope with peak periods, nor can computers handle partially complete tasks as effectively as people can.

27. Jestes, Edward C., "Manual versus Automated Circulation: A Comparison of Operating Costs in a University Library," *Journal of Academic Librarianship*, 2 (3): 130–134.

28. Young, Betty, "*Circulation Service—Is it Meeting the Users Needs?*" *Journal of Academic Librarianship*, 2 (3): 120–125.

29. Kazlauskas, Edward, "An Explanatory Study: A Kinesic Analysis of Academic Library Public Service Points," *Journal of Academic Librarianship*, 2 (3): 130–134.

30. Kent, Allen and Galvin, Thomas J. (eds.), *The On-line Revolution in Libraries*. (New York: Decker, 1978), Part two: "Impact of On-line Systems," pp. 75–204.

31. De Gennaro, Richard, "Impact of On-line Services on the Academic Library," in Kent and Galvin, pp. 177–181.

32. Smith, John Brewster and Knapp, Sara D., "Data Base Royalty Fees and the Growth of Online Search Services in Academic Libraries," *Journal of Academic Librarianship*, 7 (4): 206–212.

33. Moran, Robert F., Jr., "Improving the Organizational Design of Libraries," *Journal of Academic Librarianship*, 6 (3): 140–143.

34. Blair, John C., Jr., "Micros, Minis and Mainframes . . . A Newcomer's Guide to the World of Computers—Especially Micros," *Online*, 6 (1): 14–26.

35. Breslin and Taschenberg. p. 11.
36. Ibid., p. 139.
37. *Resource Sharing and Library Networks*, 1 (1): 1–9.
38. Das Gupta, K., "The Impact of Technology on the Role of the Technical Services Librarian of Academia in the U.S.A.," *International Library Review*, 13 (4): 397–408.

THE LIBRARIAN AS CHANGE AGENT

Tom G. Watson

"All things are in process and nothing stays still. . . . You could not step twice into the same river." Heraclitus, 217 A.D.

The rapid increase in the rate of change in our lives has been the most characteristic feature of our society in recent decades. No aspect of our experience and our world has escaped this phenomenon. In his book *Future Shock*, Alvin Toffler analyzed the impact of this intense rate of change on our technology, our physical environment, our social, political, and moral institutions, and the work place. Bombarded by mass media, by a wealth of available goods and ideas, and by the ever-changing scene to which our senses are exposed, each of us finishes every day having changed, even if the change has been ever so slight. A sociologist from the University of Wisconsin, Lawrence Suhm, observes, "We are going through a period as traumatic as the evolution of man's predecessors from

Advances in Library Administration and Organization, volume 2, pages 85–97.
ISBN: 0-89232-214-4

sea creatures to land creatures. . . . Those who can adapt will; those who can't will either go on surviving somehow at a lower level of development or will perish—washed up on the shores."[1]

Toffler further observes that people "attempt to withdraw from [change], to block it out as if it were possible to make it go away by ignoring it. They seek a 'separate peace,' a diplomatic immunity from change."[2] It is safe to assume that in any organization, no matter what size, there will be those whom the above description fits, people who cannot accept the fact of change. More importantly, in libraries, there will be persons who have not been able to grasp the notion that libraries, like all other social institutions, must adapt to the changes which society itself undergoes at an increasingly rapid rate. This means not only formulating new services to meet the new and different needs of ever-changing clientele, but it also refers to adapting to the needs of the ever-changing internal climate of organizations, which in many ways, are a microcosm of society as well as a macrocosm of the human organism.

Given the topic, "The Librarian as Change Agent," it would have been possible to have taken either of two distinctly different approaches in dealing with the subject. I could have dealt with the role of the librarian, working within the institution, the library, serving as an agent to change the segment or segments of society which the library serves and of which it is a part. Indeed much has been written in recent years about the so-called new librarians, particularly in the public libraries, who, not content to sit passively waiting to interpret and respond to the demands society makes on the library, view their roles to be the reshapers of society; they often see the library as an activist organization, using information service to point society in new and different directions. Much too, has been written about the librarians of the academy, who are not content passively to support the curriculum, but rather perceive their role as shapers and molders of the curriculum, who are not followers of the faculties, but leaders in their own right. The purpose of this paper is not to quarrel with this view of librarianship, because this approach has done much to improve library service. Rather I have chosen to address the other facet of the problem: How do librarians, specifically those in administrative roles, foster change *within* the library as a formal organization. For libraries as institutions are generally noted, among other characteristics, for their resistance to change, for their tendency to be comfortable with the tried and familiar. The problem of how effectively to bring about needed and meaningful change is a particularly pertinent one to the librarian who finds himself stepping into a new directorship, particularly if he is following a director who has been incumbent for a long time. And given the fact that until quite recently, library directors tended to remain in one library for years, any new director is likely to encounter this situation when assuming a new position.

It is likely that the previous administrator has realized that change is painful both to the initiator and to those who are being subjected to the change; consequently, he frequently has tended to put off for years the much needed changes within the library. The administrator who replaces him is immediately confronted with the situation in which changes are long overdue, and so urgently needed that the change process is likely to be even more painful than usual, because it will be perceived by others in the organization as radical surgery or revolution.

While this paper is clearly directed to administrators in middle and upper level management positions who are obviously in a position to initiate needed organizational change, it should be no less pertinent to librarians at any level who, if they are in a vital and dynamic library, effectively attempting to meet the information needs of the community they serve, find themselves confronted daily with the necessity of effecting change, both major and minor.

Before proceeding further, it is necessary to examine more carefully the term, change agent. A change agent, according to the common definition, is one who is brought by management into an organization from the outside to analyze various aspects of the present operations and organizational activities and to recommend changes that will improve organizational efficiency, operations, production, and effectiveness. Most of the social scientists who have written about the change agent-client relationship have assumed that it is best for the change agent to operate from outside the client institution. However, often the client institution has adequate human resources of its own, people who are capable of planning and fostering change. Or, as is more likely to be the case in the library world, funds are not available to secure the services of a change agent from outside, and hence, the library is forced to rely on its own resources, adequate or not. The premise of this paper is that it is possible, even desirable, for the agent to be someone who is already a part of the library organization.

In general, someone brought into an organization such as a library from outside, to analyze it and suggest needed changes, will bring with him an objectivity that it is difficult, if not impossible, for anyone associated with the library to maintain. However, that degree of objectivity is not necessary for effective analysis of organizations. Moreover, it can be argued that any disadvantages arising from lessened objectivity are more than compensated for by the familiarity that the internal change agent already has with his organization, not to mention the trust level which he probably has already been able to achieve with most other members of the staff.

A distinction probably needs to be made at this point between a consultant and a change agent. Usually, the consultant visits the organization for a short period of time, returns to his own base of operations, reflects on what he has observed and then writes and submits his analysis and recommendations for change to the organization which has contracted for his services. The change agent, on the other hand, becomes a part of the client organization, usually for an extended period of time, and interacts closely with everyone in the organization.

Looking now at the change process itself, there are seven distinct phases to the change process as it applies to organizations:

Phase 1:   The organization discovers the need for change, sometimes with the assistance of an outside change agent.

Phase 2:   The helping relationship is established and defined.

Phase 3:   The problem areas requiring change are identified and clarified.

Phase 4:   Alternative possibilities for change are examined and change goals or intentions are established.

Phase 5:   Change efforts are applied to the problem situation.

Phase 6:   Change is generalized and stabilized.

Phase 7:   The helping relationship ends or a different type of continuing relationship is defined.[3]

These seven phases obviously assume the intervention of an external change agent, but they are no less applicable when the change agent is someone who is already a part of the organization, although in the latter instance, some of the steps assume less importance or are easier to accomplish.

One word of caution is in order at this point. The librarian as a change agent, operating within his own library, should examine his own motives for attempting to bring about change very carefully. Many people consciously or unconsciously feel the need to gain power and control and will engage in bringing about change so that they have that sense of power. Such change is seldom in the best interest of the library. Even if other members of the staff do not perceive the underlying motivation, the change is unlikely to bring about any long-lasting positive effects in the organization.

Anyone who seeks to initiate change in a group or among individuals must realize that the word "change" is not a neutral word for most people. For many, it evokes images of revolution, disruption, and chaos. The change agent in that context may come to be viewed as a revolutionary idealist, malcontent, or trouble-maker. This fact has some important implications on the way we label what we are doing, as well as how we go about doing it. Most managers should already be aware that the labels we affix to things, situations, and people determine the way others react to those realities.

Recognizing the negative connotations a word like "change" may have, it would be wise to label the change efforts with terms that generally have more positive connotations to a larger number of people—words like educate, motivate, train, orient, and guide. It is difficult to understand why people react to particular words the way they do, why a word like "change" is threatening to many people, whereas a word like "motivate" or "educate" is less threatening. Perhaps the latter terms suggest to some people the implicit asurance that the end result of the process will be basically beneficial; they may suggest improvement, whereas the very process of change itself is uncertain; there is no guarantee that the result of the change process will be a better situation than the one which previously existed. The term "change" may even imply to some people that basic values will be assaulted, that no respect will be shown for traditions and well-established and cherished values. Such an assumption, of course, tends to upset people. However, the assumption is unfounded because the less threatening words like "educate" and "motivate" also involve changing values, in fact may involve a more radical modification of basic values than outright and overt change, because the process is often more subtle, and those people most likely to be affected are not aware of what is happening and hence cannot effectively resist.[4]

Experience, as well as various management studies, have all demonstrated conclusively that there are right ways and wrong ways to attempt to foster changes in organizations such as libraries. I want first to examine some of the basic reasons that people, both inside and outside organizations, resist change, before addressing some of the more effective ways of overcoming resistance to change.

Sometimes some of the factors which may, under normal circumstances, contribute most to the vitality and life of an organization become the most serious barriers to needed change. For example, in any healthy organization that has existed for any length of time, there should be among a sizeable segment of the employees a strong sense of pride in the traditions that have grown up within and around the institution. Change, of course, always threatens these traditions. Therefore, it is wise to attempt to relate the new programs to the older traditions in as forthright a manner as possible, helping the staff to perceive that in very significant ways, the innovations are in actuality a variation on what has come to be most respected and revered in the organization. In a library which has had a strong commitment to service along rather traditional lines, for example, attempts to develop an outreach program may be viewed as a radical departure by the staff unless they can be helped to perceive that the new program simply constitutes a new dimension of the services to which they have been committed. Every organization is unique, with its own past history that determines what its distinctive characteristics are or will become. The person who would be an effective change agent must first recognize these unique elements and capitalize on them.

Research has demonstrated that people tend to develop subjective hunches about whether change in the work place will be harmful or helpful to them in their own job situations and will thus formulate their attitude about and behavior toward the change accordingly. Of course, the development of these hunches is not an entirely rational process, making them particularly difficult to combat. The prospect of the change in an individual's situation typically brings about some speculation about the nature of the various possible outcomes to him, the probabilities of the various outcomes, and the benefits or liabilities of the various possible outcomes. If these suggest the likelihood of advantage to the individual, either professionally or personally, he will probably adopt a favorable attitude toward the change. If, on the other hand, they portend disadvantage or liability to the individual, he will probably resist the change. And most important of all, if he is in a state of considerable uncertainty about the possible outcomes, he will almost certainly strongly resist any change, because fear of the unknown is one of man's strongest fears.[5]

Timing is fundamentally important in bringing about change. Either a significant number of the staff must already be aware of the need for change or they must be helped by the change agent to perceive the necessity for the change before he actually attempts to implement the change. Because of their overview of all levels and phases of the organization, it is often easy for management or supervisors to assume that the staff understand that a change in organizational behavior, goals, or objectives is necessary, when in reality they may not perceive this need at all. Such a situation requires that supervisors initiate an educational program among the staff, helping them to understand more fully the nature of the organization of which they are a part. This is necessary because frequently changes in one part of an organization with which many staff members may be unfamiliar will require changes in that part of the organization with which they are most familiar.

Another factor which change agents in all types of organizations, including libraries, have failed fully to appreciate is that a person who has worked in one job in a particular organization for a long time quite likely has come to identify his job and his job performance with the kind of person he perceives himself to be. The tendency is just as great in our society for people to derive a sense of their own identity and worth from their jobs as it is for them to measure their own personal worth by the size of their compensation for the work performed. Thus, a major change in a person's job or in the way he is required to perform his job is likely to conflict with his own self-image and hence some modification of his concept of himself will have to occur before he will be both an effective and a satisfied staff member. It is also necessary to recognize that there is great variation in the degree to which individuals can modify their self-image. Even those who are capable of changing their self-image, often cannot do so quickly enough to meet organizational goals and should receive help in finding another role that more closely accommodates their self-image.[6]

One of the most difficult and most frequent staff reactions the change agent must deal with is subtle or passive resistance. In fact, in such instances, the staff members may give every appearance of complying with the wishes of the change agent with respect to desired changes, while in reality, they are waging guerrilla warfare. Such resistance may take the form of procrastination in which the staff members promise to get things done, while somehow never quite managing to do so, or, after the proposed changes have been effected, the staff who are resistant may consciously slow down their own work pace or create an atmosphere of cold indifference to the organizational needs. This latter stance almost always precedes a crisis or a blow-up.

Other factors that cause resistance to change are worth noting briefly. A bad previous experience with changes that have occurred in the past will make people wary of even the most auspicious change. Fear of having to give up prerogatives and power which may have been dearly won produce strong motivations for resisting change. This is just one of the reasons it is so vitally important that the would-be change agent fully understand how things have developed to their present state in the organization and why people are where they are in the organization. Often, something as simple as the fear of failure in attempts to accomplish the change will produce resistance to change.[7] Finally, people become confused and bitter when change is imposed that is not necessary, that does not appear to be necessary, or that has not been properly prepared.

It is essential that the change agent be aware of the obvious and not-so-obvious reasons people fear and resist change. Knowing what to expect, anticipating how people will react when we attempt to reshape and redirect human institutions, is to avoid many of the obstacles to effective change. But if the implementation of change is to be completely successful, we must also understand the positive steps that can be taken to facilitate the change process.

If the factors that contribute to people's resistance to change are reexamined, it will be noted that most, though not all, stem essentially from lack of adequate planning and communication failure. Marshall E. Dimock has observed that the persons who are going to be most affected by the change (and incidentally, on whose efforts the success of the change process most depends), namely the line staff, must be personally, intellectually, and emotionally prepared for the change. They must be helped to understand in a clear and forthright way what the change is going to mean to them in terms of their own jobs, salaries, personal satisfaction, status, and so on. Any problems that the change agent perceives should be brought into the open and discussed frankly even if it may have negative effects on the staff. It is far better that they understand what these negative possibilities may be prior to the change than that they come upon them unexpectedly, when they will inevitably provoke problems.[8]

It is all too easy for the change agent to forget that individuals in leadership positions within organizations tend to feel more tolerant of change and the stress which accompanies it than do those in follower positions. In addition to being generally more receptive, members in leadership positions usually have access to information, which enables them to predict some of the important consequences of change. The staff member in the subordinate or follower position seldom has access to such information unless it is provided by management. Rumor, imagination, and speculation often lead to grossly inaccurate evaluations of the potential effects of announced change. Participation in planning change, on the other hand, provides at least a minimum base of information in terms of which a staff member may evaluate some of the possible effects of a given change on his work situation, his status, and his relationship to the organization. Generally speaking, staff members will be more receptive to change if they are involved in planning it.[9] Hence, in the change process, the role of communication becomes paramount. People need to be told what is going to happen and how it may affect them. But as important as open communication is, and it is the foundation of effective change, there are other steps which the change agent may take to reduce resistance to change.

First, coercive tactics should be avoided. It is a fact that resistance to change is often lowered by the expedient of coercing the people involved into accepting the change. Threatening to suspend the circulation asistant until he conforms to the new dress code for public service staff, reducing the cataloger's salary until he accepts and uses cheerfully the new OCLC terminal, and other such coercive tactics may serve to force the staff into conformity with the changes. However, the primary effectiveness of such power tactics is inevitably short range. The staff will no doubt conform on the surface while seeking other jobs. More importantly, such an approach to fostering change is likely to result in a situation already described, guerrilla warfare, which will ultimately undermine the library's newly established goals.

Second, it is important to minimize social changes within the organization. Dorwin Cartwright has warned that although we tend, at least on the surface, to place a good deal of emphasis in our society on the individual, it is necessary to keep in mind that most individuals gain their identity from groups, such as those formed by individuals in a given department within a library. Many people tend to view themselves in relationship to the groups of which they are a part and tend to form their values in the same way. Resistance to change can usually be softened if these social relationships important to the individual are not disrupted by the change. It is also possible to use this power of group relationships within an organization effectively by remembering that the power of the group is often very strong in its influence over the individual group members. Any efforts to change single individuals in a group can be thwarted by group pressure, so the change agent would do well to remember that the group can be used as an effective medium of change.

Axiomatic to lowering resistance to change is to allow people to participate in the changes affecting them. The underlying dynamics of this situation are uncomplicated. When an individual or group of individuals contributes ideas to a proposed change, disapproving or resisting that change later is equivalent to disagreeing with oneself. Of course, proponents of participatory management have learned that involving an entire staff in the decision making within an organization, without first properly preparing those to whom participation in decision making is foreign, provides a sure blueprint for disaster. This is the classic situation in which a change of people's perceptions of their appropriate role in the organization must be achieved before they can be involved in any meaningful way in planning the more substantive changes that will affect their corporate life.

Obviously, money is still important to many, if not most people, in organizations, McGregor and Theory X-Theory Y notwithstanding. Many people's fears about change stem from a concern that the contemplated change will reduce their personal income. The degree to which the change agent can reassure the staff that their incomes will not be negatively affected is often the degree of enthusiasm with which the staff will support proposed changes.

Another factor the change agent will do well to keep in mind is that finality has a mild shock effect upon many people. Thus, reversible changes are more palatable to most people than irreversible changes. We can learn something from the effective salesman who knows that he has broken down much of a potential customer's sales resistance, if he can just get him to take his product on a trial basis with the understanding that he can return it within a specified time if he does not like it. The same principle can work effectively in promoting change in organizations. Of course, there may not be many situations in the typical library setting where we would be willing to make the changes tentative, and nothing could be much more demoralizing or do more to destroy the credibility of the change agent than for the staff to accept a change on a trial basis only to discover later that, whether or not they like it, they are locked into it.

All of the techniques enumerated and described are useful tools for effecting changes in the hands of a competent change agent. But they basically share one common denominator. Essentially when a change agent or administrator attempts to bring about changes in an organization, he is faced with changing the attitudes of the individuals who comprise that organization. Abraham K. Korman has defined an attitude as a type of affective reaction, either pleasant or unpleasant, which a person may have toward some object in his or her environment. It should be helpful at this point to examine attitudes more carefully as they relate to bringing about change.[10]

Attitudes have at least three essential components. First there is the cognitive component, the knowledge or intellectual beliefs that an individual might have toward an object. For example, in a library setting, a head of technical services may have accumulated considerable factual information about statistics as they apply to technical services in such areas as evaluating work flow, cost effectiveness of various processes, and so on. Second, there is the feeling or affective component which involves the emotions that are connected with an object. For example, the same head of technical services may basically dislike statistical analysis because of some unpleasant experience connected with statistics in college or library school. Third, there is the behavioral component, which refers to how a person acts. In the example of the technical services head, this person might make negative statements about statistical methods or even avoid their use in various reports and technical services procedures.[11]

How then does one go about changing attitudes effectively when attitudes may be basic to the success of other changes that one wishes to bring about? Researchers have isolated five different approaches to bringing about attitude change: communication of additional information, approval and disapproval, group influences, inducing individuals to engage in discrepant behavior, and adapting change methods to individual differences. These methods are usually used in combination.

Let us take a specific example to which we can refer in illustrating and discussing these five methods. Let us assume that a 29-year-old female head of cataloging is appointed in a larger library to replace a male head of cataloging who has just retired. Let us further assume that she has appropriate education and experience for the position. Reporting to her are five male catalogers, ages 44, 46, 47, 51 and 56. Let us also assume that these subordinates have negative attitudes toward being supervised by someone younger, and quite possibly, are apprehensive about a woman supervisor as well.

1. Communication of additional information. In such a situation, the change agent would find it necessary to add to the base intellectual knowledge that these men have about the capabilities of female managers. This might involve informing the five male staff members that the new female head of cataloging has appropriate credentials for the position, along with any other pertinent information that might be helpful.

2. Approval and disapproval. Rewards and incentives should be reasonably related to desired changes in attitudes. In the situation that we are using for an example, to the extent that the department members exhibit positive attitudes toward being managed by a woman, they should receive rewards. This could include positive comments about their cooperative attitude with the department head in the evaluations. It is possible for the reward to be such that its value is greater than maintaining the original attitude of resistance to being supervised by the woman, that is, significant salary increase. In similar fashion, displays of negative attitudes toward the new head of cataloging should be countered with disapproval, and this could take many tangible forms such as failure to receive salary increases, choice assignments, and so on.

3. Group influences. Interaction between those who have positive attitudes and those who have negative attitudes about female supervision sometimes is an effective method of attitude change. If there is one person out of the five who has more positive attitudes or who has "come around," he might be encouraged to enter into informal discussion about the topic with coworkers.

4. Inducing individuals to engage in discrepant behavior. In a laboratory situation, test subjects have often been asked to assume the attitudes held by persons whose views are opposite to their own. Sometimes engaging in such discrepant behavior does bring about changes in attitude. In the illustration that we have been dealing with, the staff members will of course find it necessary to at least approach the new department head with administrative problems, no matter how difficult and abhorrent this may be. If these problems are handled in a manner satisfactory to the male staff members, gradual shifts in attitude are likely to occur.

5. Adapting change methods to individual differences. Few groups such as the five staff members described are identical in their feelings and their reasons for their feelings about being supervised by a woman. Such individual differences should be taken into account,

so that if one of the five men is highly defensive, he should probably be approached gradually and cautiously whereas another person might be quite open himself to be confronted directly about his attitude.

A good summary of the foregoing is provided by some observations about change made by ten junior executives who were asked to discuss methods of adapting to change while maintaining organizational vitality. Although apparently none of these ten executives was a librarian or a library director, they were all talking about phenomena that occur in institutions with which libraries have much in common. These ten managers, or change agents, observed the following:

Change is more acceptable when it is understood than when it is not.

Change is more acceptable when it does not threaten security than when it does.

Change is more acceptable when those affected have helped create it than when it has been externally imposed.

Change is more acceptable when it results from an application of previously established impersonal principles than it is when it is dictated by personal order.

Change is more acceptable when it follows a series of successful changes than when it follows a series of failures.

Change is more acceptable when it is inaugurated after prior change has been assimilated than when it is inaugurated during the confusion of other major change.

Change is more acceptable if it has been planned than if it is experimental.

Change is more acceptable to people new on the job than to people old on the job.

Change is more acceptable to people who share in the benefits of change than to those who do not.

Change is more acceptable if the organization has been trained to accept the change. [12]

What must be realized is that change not only is inevitable in organizations, but that it is also absolutely necessary if organizations are to survive and be anything other than shadows of their former purpose and goals.

Having said all this, it is necessary to add a warning voiced by Toffler. He cautions that there are discoverable limits to the amount of change that the human organism can absorb; by endlessly accelerating change without first determining these limits, we may submit masses of people to demands they simply cannot tolerate. It is this state which Toffler terms "future shock." It is possible to create within an organization a state for some individuals that is comparable to the future shock Toffler has described.

NOTES AND REFERENCES

1. Alvin Toffler, *Future Shock* (New York: Random House, 1970), p. 289.

2. Ibid., p. 381.

3. Ronald Lippitt, Jeanne Watson, and Bruce Westerley, *The Dynamics of Planned Change; A Comprehensive Study of Principles and Techniques* (New York: Harcourt, Brace and World, 1958), p. 123.

4. Dorwin Cartwright, "Achieving Change in People: Some Applications of Group Dynamics Theory," *Human Relations*, 14 (1951):381–82.

5. Joseph Tiffin and Ernest James McCormick, *Industrial Psychology*, 6th. ed. (London: George Allen and Unwin, Ltd., 1976), p. 425.

6. Floyd C. Mann and Franklin Neff, *Managing Major Changes in Organizations: An Undeveloped Area of Administration and Social Research* (Ann Arbor, Michigan: The Foundation for Research on Human Behavior, 1961), p. 23.

7. Lippitt, Watson, and Westley, pp. 180–81.

8. Marshall E. Dimock, *Administrative Vitality* (New York: Harper and Brothers, 1959), p. 237.

9. Harold Koontz and Cyril O'Donnell, *Principles of Management*, 4th. ed. (New York: McGraw-Hill, 1968), p. 310.

10. Abraham K. Korman, *Industrial and Organizational Psychology* (Englewood Cliffs, New Jersey: Prentice-Hall, 1971), p. 258.

11. John B. Campbell et al., *Managerial Behavior, Performance and Effectiveness* (New York: McGraw-Hill, 1970), p. 263.

12. Ralph M. Beese, "Company Planning Must be Planned!" *Dun's Review and Modern Industry*, 74 (April, 1957):62–63.

SATELLITE CABLE LIBRARY SURVEY

Mary Diebler

CABLE LIBRARY SURVEY RESULTS

Background

The Public Service Satellite Consortium (PSSC) conducted a survey of academic libraries in July 1980 to study their data communications needs and services. Results of that study, coupled with library interest generated by that study, convinced PSSC that: (1) libraries have a wide variety of communications needs which could be addressed with appropriate uses of telecommunications; (2) all types of libraries are affected, not just academic libraries; and (3) data transfer was but one of many types of library services in need of better communications.

This information motivated PSSC to take a broader look at library communications. That second look resulted in the identification of the "cable library" (CATVLIB) phenomenon and video library services.

Advances in Library Administration and Organization, volume 2, pages 99–118.
Copyright © 1983 by JAI Press Inc.
All rights of reproduction in any form reserved.
ISBN: 0-89232-214-4

In December 1980, PSSC launched a second survey directed to cable libraries; that is, libraries of all types which are connected to local cable companies. This study was aimed at determining: To what extent, if any, might a national satellite cable library network be already in technical existence? How many libraries are presently connected to cooperative cable companies with satellite hardware and excess satellite receiver capacity? And, of that number, how many cable libraries would be interested in participating in satellite-assisted library services and video-teleconferences?

To answer these questions, PSSC mailed questionnaires to 101 libraries that had been identified as potential cable libraries. In order to allow the participation of unidentified cable libraries, PSSC also advertised the survey in various library periodicals, including *American Libraries*, Cable-Libraries, and *JOLA*. That ad resulted in an additional 97 cable libraries requesting to participate in the survey, raising the total number of libraries receiving the questionnaire to 198. As of April 1981, 86 libraries have responded, yielding a 43% return. Follow-up phone calls have indicated that more surveys are forthcoming, or that the questionnaire proved to be irrelevant to present library conditions. In some cases, copies of the survey were requested and distributed for informational purposes only.

The Survey Instrument

The questionnaire incorporated explanations of terminology and was eight pages long. Additional enclosures furnished more specific information about PSSC and video-teleconferencing. The respondent was not only questioned about his/her library facilities, but also was asked to interview the cable company for necessary technical information. Though contributing to slower returns, this two-tiered approach did succeed in establishing contact between the library and the cable company, as well as provide all the data required to profile each library as a potential network participant.

Survey Participants

Since a national network is being pursued, an attempt was made to reach as many of the states as possible. Thirty-seven states received copies of the survey, while 31 had at least one responding library. All types of libraries were surveyed. Those surveyed included elementary school libraries, high school libraries, vocational school libraries, academic libraries, public libraries, regional library networks, state libraries, library systems, special libraries, and libraries which also double as their local community access center for cable television. Of the 86 who responded, 63 were public, 18 were academic, 4 were school, and 1 was a special library.

Responding libraries have been categorized according to their ability to be an active member of the network:

UF Usable Facility—This applies to those libraries which have met all the technical requirements for network participation. The library must be currently connected to an operational cable system which has a satellite receiving station and excess receiver capacity. In addition, the cable system and the library must have indicated an interest in participating in and hosting occasional satellite-transmitted events.

NXC No Excess RO Capacity—Libraries which meet all technical cable connectivity requirements, but whose cable system cannot presently accommodate any more activity on its satellite receiver(s), are grouped here. Should time become available in the future, these libraries are then technically able to advance to the usable facility group.

NRO No CATV RO—Here are placed those libraries who are connected to an operational cable system. However, the cable system has no satellite receiving station and therefore, no satellite access. In order to become a usable facility, these cable systems must install a satellite receiving station and be able to offer excess receiver capacity.

NCC No CATV Connection—While a cable system with all the satellite hardware requirements may be operating in the library's area, these libraries are not connected to the cable system. Reasons given in the survey are varied including logistics, economics, and disinterest. Depending upon the technical status of the cable system, a simple link may be all that is needed for the library to become a usable facility.

NCA No CATV in Area—Libraries in this group are located in areas which presently have no operational cable system. Some areas are now in the franchising process, some have awarded franchises but are not operational, and others have no idea if and when cable service will come to their areas. Libraries here have the advantage of knowing what requirements are necessary for network participation and can use this information when franchising negotiations begin.

NI No Interest—Here are grouped those libraries which are at various stages of technical capability, but have no desire to participate in a national satellite cable library network.

The following chart illustrates responses according to geographical location. (Numbers refer to the quantity of libraries from each state which fit into the above defined categories.)

STATE	TOTAL STATE RESPONDENTS	UF	NXC	NRO	NCC	NCA	NI
Alabama	0-NO RESPONSE						
Alaska	3				1	2	
Arizona	1					1	
California	5		1	1	3		
Colorado	2	2					
Connecticut	4	1		1	1		1
Florida	1	1					
Georgia	1	1					
Hawaii	1				1		
Idaho	0-NO RESPONSE						
Illinois	2	2					
Indiana	1	1					
Iowa	2	2					
Kansas	2	1					1
Kentucky	3	3					
Maryland	1			1			
Massachusetts	2	1				1	
Michigan	2				1		1
Minnesota	11	7			2	2	
Missouri	1	1					
Nevada	1	1					
New Jersey	4	1		2		1	
New York	14	5	3	3	2		1
North Carolina	2	1	1				
North Dakota	0-NO RESPONSE						
Ohio	1	1					
Oklahoma	0-NO RESPONSE						
Oregon	2				2		

STATE	TOTAL STATE RESPONDENTS	UF	NXC	NRO	NCC	NCA	NI
Pennsylvania	2	2					
Tennessee	2	1			1		
Texas	2	1	1				
Utah	2	2					
Vermont	0-NO RESPONSE						
Virginia	4	2	1			1	
Washington	2	1					1
Wisconsin	3	3					
Wyoming	0-NO RESPONSE						
TOTAL	86	43	7	9	14	8	5

Exactly half of these respondents are usable facilities. The largest hindrance to network participation is lack of connectivity between the library and the cable system.

Library/Cable Connectivity

Part One of this survey established the degree of connectivity between libraries and their local cable companies. PSSC's major concern was to find libraries wired to at least *receive* cable programming. PSSC also discovered that the highest percentage of libraries had two-way connection, usually for the purpose of cablecasting. Connectivity among the 86 respondents was broken down as follows:

33 (39%)*—two-way interconnection (transmit and receive video)
29 (34%) —one-way CATV drop (receive only-regular subscriber)
14 (16%) —no CATV connection
9 (10%) —no CATV in my area or presently operational in my area
1 (1%) —no answer to question

*All percentages have been rounded off.

Other questions in this section profiled the technical capabilities of the cable system. Specific hours of each day of the week a satellite receiver was available for occasional use were charted. Weekday mornings proved to be the most available time block.

It is also imperative for PSSC to know which transponders (channels) of the satellite cable systems can access. There are 24 transponders on SATCOM I, the main satellite used by cable. When PSSC coordinates a satellite telecast, time on a satellite transponder must be secured. Each transponder is leased to someone, such as Home Box Office (HBO), Ted Turner's Cable News Network, or the Appalachian Community Service Network (ACSN), to name a few, for the carriage of their programming. Time needed by PSSC for a two-hour satellite event, for example, can be sublet from a transponder lessee, subject to availability. However, finding time slots on SATCOM I transponders is becoming increasingly difficult as many lessees are expanding the number of hours of their own programming. As a result, PSSC must know which transponders each cable system can receive so that an attempt can be made, where possible, to accommodate the majority of survey facilities.

The ideal situation is for CATVs to own "frequency agile" satellite receivers; that is, receivers which can access *any* of the transponders. Some receivers can get only even-numbered transponders or odd-numbered transponders; others can access only certain individual transponders. Transponder accessibility is usually related to the type of programming the cable operator offers or plans to offer to the local cable subscribers, or to the age of the system. (Older systems often use twelve channel receivers, tunable to only even or odd-numbered transponders on SATCOM I.) For example, if a cable operator does not anticipate offering anything besides HBO now or in the future from SATCOM I, often he/she cannot justify the need for a frequency agile receiver. The following table outlines transponder accessibility for usable facilities only:

Transponder Number	Number of Facilities Able to Access Transponder
1	2
2	2
3	1
4	1
5	1
6	4
7	3
8	3
9	6
10	3
11	0
12	2
13	1
14	3
15	0

Transponder Number	Number of Facilities Able to Access Transponder
16	3
17	1
18	1
19	0
20	2
21	3
22	4
23	0
24	5
Frequency Agile	30
Not Sure	4

Note: These figures are for transponder accessibility on SATCOM I. Numbers for the specific transponders were tabulated from those surveys which indicated their satellite receivers were *not* frequency agile, but rather could access only those transponders they had listed.

This abundance of frequency agile receivers will provide the connected libraries with a greater amount of flexibility in receiving programming since their participation will not be dependent upon a certain transponder.

Another question probed the availability of provisions for closed-circuit, discrete delivery of satellite transmissions from the cable system's receiver into the library. Being able to provide closed-circuit capabilities would ensure the privacy of a satellite telecast. Some PSSC clients insist that their transmissions be safe-guarded through closed-circuit delivery.

As expected, this closed-circuit arrangement does not exist between very many libraries and their CATVs. Unless part of an institutional cable loop, most libraries cannot presently be singled out for closed-circuit cable reception. Under normal conditions, what is transmitted from the headend of the cable system travels to everyone subscribing to the cable service. Eleven of the 43 usable facilities claimed closed-circuit capabilities are currently available. Those 32 without described what technical considerations must be present before such provisions could be offered. These technical requirements included scrambling devices, midband channel usage, modulators, and demodulators. Such upgrading of the cable company's hardware was quoted as costing from hundreds to several thousands of dollars. No CATV indicated willingness to assume the expenses for such special capabilities, but a few did offer to investigate the possibility of temporary special links on a per occasion basis.

Library Facilities

The survey also asked about the library's facilities. Questions in Part Two centered on library accommodations and equipment. Answers here provided a description of each library, which gave PSSC an idea of how adaptable to hosting satellite teleconferences each might be.

A basic satellite program viewing facility consists of the viewing area, equipped with chairs and tables, at least one television monitor (wired to receive the cable programming), and, for interactive programs, a telephone. Survey libraries reported they had conference rooms, auditoriums, and classrooms available for viewing satellite telecasts. The number of viewers able to be accommodated at one time ranged from 6 to 400 with the average facility holding 75 people. Some libraries could provide simultaneous viewing in more than one room, which increased the total number of people they could accommodate for a single event. A majority of the libraries had more than one monitor; some as many as fifteen monitors. Three libraries indicated they owned a large-screen television projector. Forty-four percent of the usable facilities have no phones in the viewing rooms, but many explained that phones were either nearby or could be temporarily installed for an interactive event. In response to a question about the location and accessibility of the library within its community, the general comments described the majority of the libraries as being in a convenient part of town, with ample parking and barrier-free design. When given enough advance notice, most libraries were willing to schedule an event at any time, even during hours and on days the library was normally closed to the public.

Traditionally, as a part of its standard networking service, PSSC *rents* viewing facilities for the client, whether they are public television stations, hotels, or other facilities. Libraries, as another type of viewing resource, would be entitled to receive payment for use of their facilities. Obviously, this fact treads on controversial "fee or free" waters. Being aware of this, PSSC asked the libraries whether they could accept money for these purposes; and, if not, whether they might have some other mechanism, such as a "Friends of the Library" group, to which the money could be given instead. Those libraries which said they could accept money directly for the use of their facilities numbered 34. Oddly enough, 34 libraries also said they could *not* accept money directly for the use of their facilities. Of that group, 31 indicated they did have a "Friends of the Library" or similar group to which money could be given for indirect channeling back into the library. Eighteen libraries did not answer this question (many due to libraries not completing the entire survey once they felt the cable information made them technically ineligible for participation). Only 3 libraries might have a problem with financial arrangements for an event.

Program Interests

The final section of the survey (Part Three) gave each respondent the opportunity to list topics of interest to the library and community that could be presented via a satellite video-teleconference. General comments identified continuing education, organizational conferences, training, seminars, workshops, media distribution and information dissemination as major activities suitable for satellite-assisted delivery and distribution. Special target audiences included the following:

1. senior citizens
2. handicapped
3. minorities
4. the disadvantaged (economically, educationally, socially)
5. the abused (drug addicts and alcoholics; abused children and spouses, teachers and students; victims of crime; and the sexually harrassed)
6. the institutionalized (in hospitals, prisons, nursing homes, mental health centers, hospices).

These special patrons are often served through outreach programs and were named here as potential beneficiaries of satellite programming. The most frequently named special population was the elderly, with suggestions for retirement, social services, nursing home care, insurance, and other senior-oriented programming.

Three major classes of other potential users of satellite video-teleconferencing in the library were identified:

1. Education-oriented: preschool and nursery students; elementary, middle, junior high, and high school students; postsecondary and graduate students; vocational, technical, extension and cooperative education students; special education students; adult and continuing education students; educational administrators, faculties, and staff

2. Government-oriented: federal, regional, state, county and local government officials and employees

3. Employment-oriented: professional/nonprofessional; salaried/hourly; union/nonunion; management/staff; public/private sectors; employed/unemployed; full/part-time; permanent/temporary; big/small business; human services/trade.

Particular topics of interest felt to be ideal satellite program areas within each library's community included the following: (appearing in no rank order)

energy (solar and natural resources)   conservation
consumerism   genealogy
community services   religion
environment   business and industry
historic preservation/oral history   civil defense
legal aid   agriculture and forestry
librarianship   health and medicine
computers, data processing   mental health
technology   arts and humanities
communications/telecommunications   curriculum sharing
fund raising   therapy and rehabilitation
safety   real estate
recreation, physical education, sports, parks
language (bilingual, sign, foreign, literacy)
economics and finance (investment, banking, inflation, budgeting)

Several local associations, which have affiliates or branches located nationally, were listed as potential users of satellite video-teleconferencing: (appear in order of popularity)

1. American Association of Retired Persons
2. League of Women Voters
3. Historical Societies
4. American Library Association
5. Chamber of Commerce
6. American Association of University Women
7. Parent/Teachers Associations
8. Councils of Government
9. Jaycees
10. Boy Scouts
11. Friends of the Library.

Three questions concerning interest and ability to participate in future satellite video-teleconferencing activities were asked. The questions, vital to the outcome of this survey, follow, with their respective answers:

1. Would you be interested in helping set up one or more of these specialized teleconferences?
   Yes   —63 (73%)
   No   —10 (12%)

Maybe   — 5 (6%)
No Answer— 8 (9%)

2. Would you be interested in doing a local follow-up program after a national teleconference that is of interest to your community?
Yes   —65 (76%)
No   — 6 (7%)
Maybe   — 8 (9%)
No Answer— 7 (8%)

3. Periodically, nationally based organizations sponsoring teleconferences or special programs enlist promotional and site arrangement support from local site facilitators. Would you like to be listed as available to provide this support?
Yes   —54 (63%)
No   —18 (21%)
Maybe   — 3 (3%)
No Answer—11 (13%)

The interest of the libraries surveyed is well documented in questions one and two. However, their ability to presently participate is limited to financial and personnel resources as demonstrated by responses to question three.

General Conclusions and Recommendations

The majority of surveyed libraries recognize the need for libraries to expand their community service roles through some use of telecommunications. Many of the 86 libraries indicated that the idea of libraries becoming satellite program viewing facilities through their cable connectivity was so new to them that they could not fully understand or visualize the library in this novel role. Yet, the general consensus was that if joining with their cable systems to provide satellite program receiving locations was a method of improving community library services, while not making demands on the library's budget, then the concept was worth exploring individually on an operational basis.

To illustrate this concept of the CATVLIB as a satellite program viewing facility, a typical scenario would find participating CATVLIBs contacted by an organization or networking agent who wishes to reach the general community or a special segment with its satellite-transmitted programming. The CATVLIB, as the community contact, would have the option to respond negatively or positively. If the CATVLIB is interested, it must begin performing local coordination duties, most important of which is garnering the agreement of its cable system. CATVLIB and cable system discussions will determine five things:

1. Can the cable system access the satellite transponder on which the programming will be carried?
2. Will the cable system have a satellite receiver available on the date and time of the program?
3. Will the CATVLIB have its viewing facility available on the date and time of the program?
4. If desired by the program's sponsor, will the CATVLIB contact the local group who is to participate in the program and work with them prior to the satellite telecast to the extent needed by the requesting organizations?
5. Can the cable system and/or the CATVLIB handle special program considerations, if any? For example,

   - provide close circuit capability in the CATVLIB?
   - tape the program?
   - provide telephone(s) for interactive programs?
   - provide local site facilitation?
   - coordinate local follow-up activities?
   - provide refreshments?
   - coordinate advance publicity within the community?

Once the CATVLIB has determined whether or not it is able and desires to offer their services, the CATVLIB would be recorded as a satellite program "receive site." The CATVLIB will then assume the degree of local responsibility requested and contracted by the requesting organization, including all negotiations necessary with the cable system.

While there were survey indications of general support for such a national satellite cable library network, what are the pros and cons of its operation?

PROS

CONS

Pre-existing conditions. CATVLIBs need no investment for hardware, but merely take advantage of pre-existing cable connectivity.

Community service. Such CATVLIB participation potentially offers service to every member of the community.

Lack of SATCOM I occasional time. It is becoming increasingly difficult to sublease transponder time on this satellite for occasional satellite programs.

Dependency. The CATVLIB must depend entirely on the cable system to be able to be a network participant and offer this service.

PROS

Outreach to new patrons. Those community residents not previously using the library may find this new service applicable to their needs.

Economics. CATVLIBs could recoup any charges incurred through this service, as well as expect payment as a rented receive site.

Program interaction. Live satellite programming has the advantage over taped programming of allowing the option of offering viewers the opportunity to interact with the program's presenter(s).

Resource-sharing potential. This service has the future potential of providing CATVLIBs with an alternative method of accessing new information resources and data bases. Human resources can be shared now through this service.

Potential CATV expansion. More CATVs are expanding and upgrading their satellite access capabilities as usage of satellites by cable programming vendors increases. Some CATVs have already purchased WESTAR III hardware in addition to their SATCOM I hardware.

Future implications. If satellite-related services become valued by the community, the residents might decide the CATVLIB should have its own satellite hardware so that the community could take advantage of more programming available directly from satellite.

CONS

CATVLIB participation is dependent upon the cable system's satellite access capabilities which generally means SATCOM I only.

Lack of CCTV. Generally, most CATVLIBs cannot offer closed-circuit capability, so absolute privacy cannot be guaranteed to the program's sponsor.

CATVLIB policies. Some CATVLIBs will have to make decisions about various controversial items, such as:
    accepting money for use of facilities
    allowing some clients the right to limit viewing to only registrants
    hosting controversial groups.

Range of CATVLIB capabilities. Survey demonstrated that CATVLIBs cannot all offer the same degree of service due to the wide range of technical capabilities. At present, each satellite event would have to be judged individually to determine which CATVLIBS were equipped to participate.

A glance at the pros and cons of marrying libraries and satellite communications through cable connectivity suggests a national satellite CATVLIB network is a presently available and usable resource with potential for future expanded capabilities and unlimited programming uses. The obstacles imposed by the cons, however, are cause for a serious and objective look at the present and future viability of such a network.

Popular present uses of satellite video-teleconferencing are for telecasting continuing education and organizational conference interactive programming to special audiences. Some PSSC clients will often request to:

- *charge* his/her *special audience* for participating (course or conference fees, for example)
- have the satellite-transmitted event *closed-circuit* telecasted to the receiving locations only
- reach *specific geographical locations* (often large urban areas, such as New York or Los Angeles)

Charging Special Audiences for Closed-Circuit Satellite Event

The first two client requests are often related. If the client intends to charge the registrant-viewer a fee, he/she often expects the program to be viewed only at designated receive sites which are hosting the paying participants. (Why should a viewer pay if he/she could watch the same program at home on a cable channel for free?) Obviously, those clients interested in a "box office" approach to their event; that is, to make a profit rather than offer a service, are not suited for CATVLIB network use. However, how can the CATVLIBs accommodate those public service groups which must recoup expenses in order to offer such satellite program services?

Client-designed incentives such as giving the phone number for viewer interaction in a program only to the CATVLIBs rather than displaying or announcing the number during the program, requiring participants to have special materials and/or integrating local pre- or postevent activities in the CATVLIBs with the program, even offering course credit to registrants only are manageable alternatives for those CATVLIBs which cannot terminate the program in their facilities. Some CATVLIBs may be able to negotiate with their CATV for the provision of the necessary equipment to provide closed-circuit capabilities. However, this survey did not identify many CATVs that were willing to cooperate with the libraries to that extent.

For those CATVLIBs whose policies restrict their involvement with financial transactions, particularly money exchange among library patrons, advance registration fees paid directly to the client could enable the libraries to avoid being required by the client to "collect at the door."

Most libraries, however, by their very nature, cannot prohibit anyone from viewing a program within their facilities, thereby making it generally impossible for them to guarantee the client their requested selective audience.

Size, Location and Distribution of Receive Sites

Video-teleconference users generally want to reach as many of their members or special populations as possible, yet they must pay to rent *each* receive site. Economics influence their attempt to reach more people at fewer locations, not necessarily those most in need of the program. Therefore, it is no surprise that popular receive sites are located in heavily populated cities.

While cable television is finally coming to urban areas, present conditions find a lack of operational CATVs available. The typical CATVLIB *now* is located in a smaller city or rural area. Large states, such as California and Texas, have little or no CATVLIB representation. Only 23 states currently have a usable CATVLIB facility, which makes the network descriptor "national" not quite accurate. Expanding the CATVLIB network to include more and larger cities and all states is a must to make it competitive with other satellite networks available to a client. But, even if the network is able to expand, the previously mentioned inability of CATVLIBs to provide closed-circuit capabilities will lessen its desirability as a resource when that capability is offered by another satellite ground facility in the same city.

One competitive alternative a CATVLIB can consider is rental cost. Clients expect to pay a reasonable rate for the use of each facility. This rate differs among different types of satellite networks, and even within the same network. For example, renting a public television station is generally less expensive than booking a hotel. Yet, the rate for two public television stations can vary in the hundreds of dollars. If a CATVLIB chooses to offer its facilities for free, asking only for compensation of any expenses it might incur because of the satellite event, or charges a minimal amount, their facility becomes economically attractive. One factor the CATVLIBs must not overlook when contemplating such a decision is the *cable system*. Will the cable system expect remuneration for its services, especially if the CATVLIB is receiving payment? Libraries must remember they have entered into a cooperative arrangement with their CATVs in order to become a satellite program viewing facility.

Toward Future Independence

While a skeletal cable library network does technically exist, it is *imperative* that libraries work toward their own future independence before they can truly establish themselves as a viable satellite network.

Evolution of a CATVLIB network to a satellite library network might include the following two steps:

1. *Expanded CATVLIB network.* The survey instrument should now evolve into an interview tool for profiling additional libraries to become part of this network. Efforts should be made to encourage libraries within poorly represented states to join the network if technically feasible. Expansion is urged for two main reasons:

   - To allow *libraries* the opportunity to *experience* being a satellite program viewing facility without financial obligations.
   - To allow *community residents* the opportunity to *experience* a library service with great potential for all local population segments.

Once the library is regarded as the logical place for community communications, it will be much easier to begin a community drive toward supporting the outfitting of the library with the proper hardware necessary to function in that capacity.

Requirements for becoming part of the expanded CATVLIB net-work include:

- At least one-way connectivity between the library and the CATV. (A typical subscription for basic service will suffice.)
- The CATV must have a satellite receiving station.
- The CATV must have excess capacity available on its satellite receiver.
- CATV must be willing to cooperate with the library in providing satellite reception of occasional satellite telecasts.
- Library must have at least one viewing room available to seat those viewing the satellite program.
- Library must have at least one television monitor, wired to receive cable programming, available in the viewing room.
- Library must be willing to assume role of community contact to extent requested by client. (Need is for library interest in participating in these occasional satellite telecasts; degree of local responsiblity can be negotiated.)

Even though this network is designed to be a temporary method of allowing library participation in satellite communications, future implications could find these libraries expanding, improving, or beginning cablecasting on a library-designated cable channel. Thus, libraries deciding whether they should become involved with a temporary network, might contemplate the related activities available from library/cable system cooperation.

2. *Satellite Library Network.* At some point in the not too distant future, libraries will be faced with the decision of becoming independent from their cable system, and obtaining their own satellite hardware. A library with its own satellite receiving station will become more desirable to more users as a receive site for a satellite video-teleconference, since it will be more flexible and autonomous. Besides satellite video-teleconferences, libraries could investigate other uses of their satellite hardware including:

- direct satellite access (with permission recommended) for cable television fare,
- reception of nationwide satellite distribution of taped video programming for library use.
- facilitation of various library data communications.

If the library is able to prove the value and practicality of having community satellite access capabilities located at its facilities to the residents through participation in the CATVLIB network, local funding of a satellite library project might be realistic. If corporations are made aware of how such a satellite library facility could benefit their own communications needs, a corporate grant could prove to be another funding route. Other sources of support must also be explored.

Final Word

As a result of this survey, PSSC has profiled cable libraries of all technical capabilities for input into a data base of network resources. However, the limitations of a CATVLIB network have been noted. Effort will be made by PSSC *where appropriate* to use this network for client satellite telecasts. PSSC will continue to profile interested cable libraries for addition to the network, *upon request of the library.*

ADDENDUM

First Use of CATVLIB Network: American Red Cross Satellite Telecast

On May 21, 1981, the American Red Cross celebrated its one hundredth birthday by ending the annual conference in Washington, D.C. with a special two-hour nationwide satellite telecast. The PSSC coordinated distribution of the telecast, which originated from Constitution Hall in Washington, D.C., from 10 A.M. to noon ET. The program was carried on SATCOM I, transponder 16 (Appalachian Community Service Network) and made available to all cable systems able to receive this transponder. Those areas not able to schedule the live program were offered a satellite-transmitted taped feed later in the day. The American Red Cross had encouraged all its local chapters to initiate program reception in their communities by approaching the local cable system about carrying the event.

Since the American Red Cross was offering a *free* program and trying to saturate as much of the United States as possible, use of the CATVLIB network in conjunction with this telecast was appropriate. PSSC contacted 53 libraries in 23 states who were interested in assuming local coordination for bringing this event to their communities. As the local coordinator, the CATVLIBs' minimum responsibilities included alerting the cable systems to schedule receiving this program (if the local Red Cross chapter had not already approached the CATV) and contacting the local Red chapter to offer the CATVLIBs' facilities for their group viewing and concomittant local celebration.

Of these 53 CATVLIBs, only seven could not participate because of *technical* problems. Schedule conflicts, lack of CATV, Red Cross, or community interest, and Red Cross alternative plans were the major factors in prohibiting twelve others from directly participating in hosting the satellite-transmitted program. The remaining 34 CATVLIBs did host community residents in their facilities.

Evaluation forms revealed a variety of degrees of CATVLIB participation in coordinating their first satellite event participation. Several CATVLIBs, though no one came to the library for viewing, were instrumental in getting the program into the community and available to all local cable subscribers. Advance publicity, birthday cakes and refreshments, singalongs, taping for multiple showing, and joint library/chapter pre-and postevent activities are but a few of the ways the individual CATVLIBs participated. All of the evaluation forms indicated that the CATVLIBs wanted to be contacted as a potential local site for future satellite events.

The following list names the 53 CATVLIBs who were initially contacted to be local coordinators for the Red Cross one hundredth birthday satellite telecast. Though not all were successful, CATVLIB made an effort to bring the program to its community.

Colorado
Boulder Public Library, Boulder

Connecticut
Thomaston Public Library, Thomaston

Florida
Tarpon Springs Public Library, Tarpon Springs

Georgia
Tri-County Regional Library, Rome

Idaho
Pocatello Public Library, Pocatello

Illinois
Pekin Public Library, Pekin
Rockford Public Library, Rockford

Indiana
Fort Wayne Public Library, Fort Wayne
Monroe County Public Library, Bloomington

Iowa
Kirkwood Community College Telecommunications Center, Cedar Rapids
Iowa City Public Library, Iowa City

Kansas
Abilene Public Library, Abilene
Newton Public Library, Newton

Kentucky
Lexington Public Library, Lexington
Louisville Public Library, Louisville
Camden-Carroll Library, Morehead State University, Morehead

Massachusetts
Greenfield Community College Library, Greenfield
South Hadley Library System, South Hadley

Minnesota
Anoka County Library, Fridley
Cloquet Public Library, Cloquet
Crow River Regional Library, Willmar
International Falls Public Library, International Falls
Minnesota Valley Regional Library, Mankato
Marshall-Lyon County Library System, Marshall
Western Plains Library System, Montevideo
Rochester Public Library, Rochester
St. Cloud Public Library, St. Cloud

Missouri
St. Charles City County Library, St. Peters
New Jersey
Burlington County College Library, Pemberton
New York
Albany Public Library, Albany
Amherst Public Library, Williamsville
Bethelem Public Library, Delmar
Chautauqua-Cattaraugus Library System, Jamestown
Gates Public Library, Rochester
Mid-York Library System, Utica
Ridge Road Elementary School Library, Horseheads
North Carolina
Davidson County Community College Library, Lexington
Ohio
Greene County District Library, Xenia
Public Library of Columbus and Franklin County, Columbus
University of Toledo Library, Toledo
Pennsylvania
Altoona Area Public Library, Altoona
Lancaster County Library, Lancaster
Monroeville Public Library, Monroeville
Tennessee
Memphis/Shelby County Public Library and Information Center, Memphis
Utah
Merrill Library and Learning Resources Program, Utah State University,
   Logan
Weber County Library, Ogden
Virginia
Arlington County Department of Libraries, Arlington
Washington
Edmonds Community College Library, Lynnwood
Lynnwood Public Library, Lynnwood
Mountlake Terrace Public Library, Mountlake Terrace
Seattle Public Library, Seattle
Wisconsin
Middleton Public Library, Middleton
Nicolet College Learning Resource Center, Rhinelander

DETERIORATION OF BOOK PAPER:
RESULTS OF PHYSICAL AND
CHEMICAL TESTING OF THE PAPER
IN 2280 MONOGRAPHS FROM THE
COLLECTIONS OF THE UNIVERSITY
OF CALIFORNIA LIBRARIES

Richard G. King, Jr.

I. SUMMARY

This chapter reports the results of a study of over 2,000 monographs in the collections of the University of California (UC) Libraries. The monographs were tested to determine the remaining strength in the book papers. Test scores were then related to the level of paper deterioration

Advances in Library Administration and Organization, volume 2, pages 119–149.
Copyright © 1983 by JAI Press Inc.
All rights of reproduction in any form reserved.
ISBN: 0-89232-214-4

using categories developed by W. J. Barrow and the W. J. Barrow Laboratory. The major findings are:

1. Eleven percent of the paper samples tested scored in the Barrow categories "unbindable" and "unusable" (0–3 folds) for folding endurance, a test of the physical strength of paper. It is estimated that about 868,000 volumes in the collections of the UC libraries may have been in this category of paper deterioration in 1974, the year the study sample was drawn.
2. Monographs produced between 1850 and 1947 (30 years prior to testing), as a group, have the poorest folding endurance scores.
3. Seven percent of the tested paper samples yielded scores in the "unusable" range (0–12 grams) for tear resistance, a second measure of paper strength. It is estimated that 544,000 volumes in the collections of the UC libraries may have been in this category of paper deterioration in 1974, the year the study sample was drawn.
4. Monographs produced between 1860 (after the introduction of alum-rosin sizing into American paper making) and 1919 (55 years prior to testing), as a group, have the poorest tearing resistance scores.
5. When samples that had scores for both folding endurance and tearing resistance were compared, one percent had scores on both tests in the "unusable" range.
6. When the samples were tested for acidity level (pH, or hydrogen ion concentration), 86 percent were found to be in the unacceptable range for archival quality paper, that is, in the acid range of pH 6.0 or below. The median pH for all samples was 4.42 on a logarithmic scale, where 14 is very alkaline, 7 is the neutral point, and 1 is extremely acid.
7. Eighty-one percent of the samples tested were free of groundwood content. Groundwood, because of its acid content and ability to catalyze oxidation reactions is often suggested as one cause of the deterioration of book papers.

The following conclusions are offered:

1. Twenty-eight percent of the paper samples tested scored in the Barrow strength categories of weak and unusable on the folding endurance test and the tearing resistance test. The monographs represented by these papers, according to Barrow, should only be used in "a rare book room where users are cautioned to handle [them] with care."

2. Monographs produced between 1850 and 1947 (30 years prior to testing) should be the target group for any preservation program for monograph collections.
3. Statistical analyses show that neither bibliographic information nor nondestructive test results (e.g., pH or groundwood concentration) are sufficient predictors of the physical strength of paper. Analytical studies cannot point to either specific subject areas of the collection, or individual items which may be the most in need of preservation treatment. Evaluation by trained library conservators remains the only proven method for identifying specific books for treatment.

II. BACKGROUND

The deterioration of paper is a well known and lamentable phenomenon. As long ago as 1231, Emperor Frederick II of the Two Sicilies required that public documents be prepared on parchment and not paper "so that they may bear testimony to future times and not risk destruction through age" (Clapp, 1972, p. 2). Since that time, thousands of monographs and periodical articles have been written that deal with the causes of degradation in paper. Cunha's *Conservation of Library Materials* (1971) contains a bibliography of some 4,000 entries, many of which deal with this problem. The causes of paper deterioration are numerous: inherent acidity, visible light, ultra-violet radiation, variations and extremes of temperature and humidity, microbiological agents, animals, fire, flood, and people. Of this multitude of enemies of books, the most insidious is the acidity of most book papers. Beginning around 1870, the demand for large amounts of printing paper led to the introduction of mechanical or ground wood pulp and certain chemical wood pulps. These manufacturing processes placed a devastating time bomb in almost every book published by introducing destructive materials in the form of lignin (a natural constituent of wood fibers), chemicals from the pulping process, and alum in the sizing or surface finish.

By the 1890s serious concern was being voiced about the deterioration of books and newspapers then being published in the United States. Newspapers were a particular problem in that they disintegrated quite rapidly, a problem no less extreme today. Beginning with these complaints in the late nineteenth century, individuals and professional committees have called for the use of permanent archival quality papers in publishing. Papers are usually considered archival or permanent if their estimated life span is several hundred years or longer. Some samples of Chinese paper still extant were produced in the eighth century; this is the epitome of permanence. Early in the twentieth century, Alexander

Graham Bell and others proposed printing archival material on gold, platinum, or silver sheets; others proposed the use of pottery. The University of California Press, at an early date, began printing depository copies of its publications on "permanent paper." This printing effort continued formally until 1944. Today the Press remains concerned with this problem and prints on acid-free paper when it is suitable and available. Many other university presses, such as the University of Oklahoma Press, also pride themselves on the acid-free quality of their printing paper.

Although there was great concern about paper deterioration on the part of some individuals and groups for over seventy years, the enormity of the problem was not really understood until the 1960s. In the mid-1960s the W. J. Barrow Research Laboratory, using grant funds from the Council on Library Resources, began publishing a series of studies designed to assess the deterioration of book papers and to find methods to reduce or reverse this process (see listing under Barrow, W. J. in the reference section). In general, Barrow's studies showed that, of books which were printed between 1800 and 1899, 31 percent had to be accounted unusable by 1964. Books with imprint dates between 1900 and 1939 gave slightly worse results; 39 percent of the papers tested fell into the unusable category. Tests of book papers from the 1940–1949 printing years which had aged only 7 to 17 years showed that 57 percent of the samples had deteriorated to the strength level of newsprint, usable but rapidly deteriorating.

By the 1970s, having been spurred to action by the disturbing reports from the Barrow Laboratory and by the evidence of their own experience, curators of several large research libraries in the United States had evaluated the scope of the problem of deteriorating books in their collections. The New York Public Library reported (Kingery, 1960) that approximately half of its research collection needed conservation attention; the cost of coping with the problem of deteriorating collections at the New York Public Library was estimated at $12 million (Cunha, 1975). Williams (1971) reported that 6 million bound volumes of the collections of the Library of Congress were too brittle to be handled by patrons. Although the Library of Congress does not release detailed budget information for its preservation effort, in 1977 about 43,000 "rare books and related materials [were] bound, rebound, restored, reconditioned, or otherwise treated." In addition, 27,000 maps, manuscripts, prints, and photographs were preserved, restored, or otherwise treated. This same year saw 5,343,000 microfilm exposures taken of brittle books and serials, at a cost of $535,000. The preservation and restoration staff, including personnel involved in research, restoration, binding, and microfilming, was about 130 persons (Library of Congress, 1978). Of these, about 37 positions were allocated to restoration of rare books. The Library of Congress also estimated that accomplishing the restoration task would require 11,500 years of work for each of the 37 positions on the staff (Waters, 1977).

In 1975 a survey of the British Museum Library revealed that 10 percent of the collection—about 1 million volumes—was in need of repair, even though the conservation/binding budget was at a level of $3 million. This finding was of such intense concern that, subsequent to the 1975 report, the British Museum Library increased its conservation and binding budget in fiscal year 1977–78 to $4 million. During that year the library was employing about 133 people in the conservation/binding department; although the number of staff dedicated exclusively to conservation is not known (Barker, 1977).

As noted above, beginning in 1963, the W. J. Barrow Research Laboratory commenced publication of a series of booklets on the deterioration of paper. W. J. Barrow and his staff had been aware of the problem of paper deterioration for some time (Barrow himself since the 1930s) and with funding from the Council on Library Resources began scientific research on the problem in the early 1960s. The work of the Barrow Laboratory continued for about ten years after the death of W. J. Barrow in August 1967. Although the major emphasis of the Barrow Laboratory's work was on devising specifications for permanent/durable printing paper, the landmark achievement of W. J. Barrow and the Barrow Laboratory was the application of scientific testing procedures to the problem of deteriorating paper in library materials.

Because the Barrow work is the only quantitative work that exists on the topic of deteriorating library books, the results of the following study will be compared and contrasted to the earlier findings of Barrow and the Barrow Laboratory.

In 1976, the Library Council of the University of California system formed a Task Group on the Preservation of Library Materials. One charge to that Task Group was to "determine the extent and rate of deterioration of library materials in the University's library collections. The Task Group decided that the best approach to satisfying this charge would be to use the Barrow Laboratory procedures to evaluate at least part of the University's library collections. This approach would allow comparison with the Barrow findings and would provide empirical data for planning by the university. Because the books to be tested were those in the working collections of the university libraries the number of samples available from each volume was necessarily limited. That is, the books could not be cut apart to get large numbers of samples nor could pages containing textual material be destroyed. This limitation was known to increase the variability of the results for the proposed folding endurance test of paper strength. Therefore, several mechanical and chemical tests were chosen to increase the validity of the results. Papers that failed more than one test could be more confidently described as unsuitable.

The principal objective of the study was to use this series of tests to arrive at an overall view of the condition of monographs currently in the circulating collections of the University of California libraries. A secondary objective was to examine the adequacy of nondestructive tests and bibliographic data as predictors of the state of deterioration of the paper, as measured by the destructive tests of paper strength. This report gives the results of the testing study and describes the attempts to predict the physical condition of individual books from the results of the chemical test and bibliographical data.

III. METHODOLOGY

A. Sample Selection

Bibliographic records for items to be sampled were drawn randomly in 1974 from the most complete card catalogs of each general library unit on every University of California campus. At least 1,000 monograph titles were selected from each campus collection. These records were incorporated into a computer file which served as the source of the titles selected for this study. In 1977, when this study began, the data base was relatively current and significant savings in time and resources were achieved by using that sample population rather than creating a new one. When the samples were initially drawn in 1974, catalog sampling was also performed to estimate the number of monograph titles held in each campus collection. These estimates were then used to calculate the system-wide aggregate 1974 monograph numbers (Thompson, 1981). At that time the total collection size for bound volumes was reported to be 13,434,334 bound volumes in the general libraries (University of California, 1975). We therefore estimated that 6,447,099 volumes systemwide were monographs. Projections to current collection size may not be valid as the distribution of ages and paper qualities of items in the collections has changed during the intervening years. Further, materials in the 1974 collection have now had more time to deteriorate to a greater degree than was found in this study.

Because the time required for sampling and physical testing of paper samples was considerable (about 15 minutes per sample for removal from the bound volume, plus about one hour for testing) it was decided that the study would be limited to monographs only and that 300 titles per campus would be selected. An additional 300 titles were selected from the holdings of the Intercampus Library Facility-North. This facility stores many older, low-use monographs from the UC Berkeley campus libraries. This sample size was selected after discussion with the testing consultants as pushing the limits of the time and resources available for the study. The initial sample size was reduced as rare or otherwise valuable monographs were removed from consideration. This process allowed the study to be concentrated on the general collections of the libraries, the collection of interest.

The final sample sizes for each campus, given in Table 1, allowed for an adequate representation of the UC library collections.

Each selected monograph was retrieved and bibliographic information was recorded: title, author, country of origin, date of publication, number of pages, and so forth. After the bibliographic data were recorded, physical samples were removed from each book. If possible a full blank flyleaf was taken. Only paper that was the same as that used in the text-block was removed; end papers were not sampled. If a full blank page was not available, a strip of blank paper was pared from the front edge of the last printed page of the book. These areas of the book were selected for testing because they should most closely represent the condition of the paper nearest the spine of the book. That is, both the outer pages of the text-block and the portion of each page nearest the spine are in closest contact with acid materials of the binding case. Since the condition of the paper nearest the spine dictates whether the book can be rebound, it was desirable to select test paper which had aged in a manner similar to the spine paper. Strips of 15mm width were removed in this manner for physical testing. If a blank 15mm strip was unavailable, a small strip of blank paper was pared from the last printed page for chemical testing. Each sample was numbered, using a very soft drafting

Table 1. Number of Paper Samples by Campus

Campus	Number	Percent
Berkeley	178	7.8
Davis	231	10.1
Irvine	275	12.1
Los Angeles	177	7.8
Riverside	259	11.4
San Diego	219	9.6
San Francisco	164	7.2
Santa Barbara	224	9.8
Santa Cruz	248	10.9
ICLF-N	305	13.4
TOTAL	2,280	100

pencil, and was packaged in a neutral pH envelope with the bibliographic information stapled to the outside of the envelope. The samples were stored in an environmentally controlled room (TAPPI, 1970) at the University of California Forest Products Laboratory in Richmond, California for acclimatization and testing.

B. Testing Methodology

1. Folding Endurance

Each sample of sufficient size to meet the standards of the Technical Association of the Pulp and Paper Industry (TAPPI, 1969) was tested in an MIT-type folding endurance testing machine (Testing Machines Incorporated Model TMI-33-2). Each standard-sized sample was clamped in the test machine at 0.5 kilograms tension and a cooling fan was closed over the head jaws. The machine, when started, bends the paper at the head jaws through 270 degrees of arc (135 degrees right and 135 degrees left) until the sample breaks. The machine shuts off automatically when the sample breaks, and the number of folds through 270 degrees is automatically recorded by a counter mounted on the test machine. Since the moving web of a paper-making machine causes the fibers in the pulp to lie parallel with one another in the direction of the web movement, the paper acquires a "grain" or "machine direction." Fold tests in both the "machine" and the "cross-machine" direction of the paper samples were made. The number of folds that a paper can resist is termed "folding endurance." Folding endurance may range from several thousand folds for a high quality cotton-fiber paper to less than fifty folds for newsprint. Since the folding action of the test machine most closely replicates the repeated bending of pages in a book, folding endurance was chosen as the primary test for residual strength in the paper samples.

Although the TAPPI specifications call for testing of 10 samples per data point, the UC study was limited to testing from 1–3 paper samples per bibliographic item. The reasons for this limitation were discussed in section III.A. After consultation with the testing staff at the Forest Products Laboratory it was concluded that while the reduced number of tests would increase the statistical test error for an individual book, the test data would suffice for the description of the sample papers in terms of the Barrow strength categories.

2. Tearing Resistance

A standard-sized sample was placed in an Elmendorf Tear Test Machine which tears the paper sample in half (TAPPI, 1965). The machine automatically tears the sample and records the internal tearing resistance of the paper in grams. Tear tests were made in both the cross and machine directions of the paper. This test was chosen as a second measure of paper strength as it best duplicates the type of pull that occurs when a book page is turned. As noted by Barrow (1964), "like the folding endurance test, the tear resistance test is of much importance and ranks second among the physical tests for books."

3. Hydrogen ion Concentration

Hydrogen ion concentration, or pH, was recorded for each paper sample from a Chemtrix Model 50 pH meter using a flat-bulb combination glass electrode (Beckman Instruments Model No. 39507). In this test a drop of de-ionized water is placed on the sample and the electrode is lowered onto the sample at this point. The pH value is read from the meter when the indicator stabilizes. Hydrogen ion concentration is a measure of the acidity-alkalinity of the paper. The pH scale runs from 1 to 14 with values of 1.0–6.9 indicating active acidity, pH 7.0 indicating neutrality, and pH 7.1–14.0 indicating alkalinity. This scale is logarithmic so that a pH of 6.0 is ten times more acid than a pH of 7.0; a pH of 4.0 is 1,000 times more acid than pH 7.0. As described by Clapp (1972), pH values in the acid range can be exemplified by: cow's milk, pH 6.5; spinach, pH 5.5; bananas, pH 4.5; sauerkraut, pH 3.5; and hydrochloric acid, pH 0.01. A reading of less than pH 7.0 indicates that the material is in the acid range and is undergoing acid hydrolysis or deterioration. That is, acid inherent to the papermaking process or acid picked up from the environment is active in the paper, breaking down the cellulose fibers. The lower the pH the higher the acidity and the more rapid the deterioration (see for instance Langwell, 1952; Langwell, 1957).

4. Groundwood Content

The presence of unbleached groundwood, which contains the deteriorative component lignin, was assayed using a spot-test reagent of phloroglucinol in methyl alcohol and hydrochloric acid. In this test a drop of reagent is placed on the paper sample and the resulting color change is matched to a standard color chart (Barrow, 1969). The test result is recorded as a percent groundwood content of 0, 25, 50, 75, or 100 percent.

C. Statistical Tests and Classification of Test Data

1. Statistical Tests

All statistical tests were performed by computer using the Statistical Package for the Social Sciences (Nie, 1975). A weighting factor was applied to the test data when the data were used to estimate the number of volumes in a particular deterioration category. This adjustment was made to account for the individual campus differences in the percentage of monograph collections included in the sample.

2. Standard Classifications for Paper Testing Data

The restoration categories developed by W. J. Barrow were used to classify the data of the present study (Barrow, 1964). The following categories were developed by Barrow for describing the results of folding endurance and tearing resistance tests:

a. High strength. 1000+ folds and 75+ grams of tear resistance. "Many bond and ledger papers composed of strong chemical wood or cotton fibers fall in this category and can be expected to withstand hard usage."

b. Moderate strength. 300–999 folds and 60–74 grams of tear resistance. "Book papers of this strength have good potential use in the average library."

c. Low strength. 51–299 folds and 31–59 grams of tear resistance. "Many scholarly publications occur in the range of 51–75 folds and will soon need restoration because of the fast rate of deterioration due to high acidity."

d. Newsprint strength. 11–50 folds and 25–30 grams of tear resistance. "These papers have limited potential use."

e. Weak strength. 4–10 folds and 13–24 grams of tear resistance. "It is suitable only for a rare book room where users are cautioned to handle it with care."

f. Unusable strength. 2–3 folds and 0–12 grams of tear resistance. "Such a sheet breaks when creased by the thumb and it is difficult to sew if rebound. A leaf in a book of this strength should be turned with much care and is unsuitable for use unless restored."

g. Unbindable strength. 0–1 folds and 0–12 grams of tear resistance. "Restoration category, often unbindable."

W. J. Barrow (1964) also proposed a partial classification or categorization scheme for differing levels of acidity in book papers. Barrow noted that at a pH lower than 6.2 paper shows "a progressively faster rate of deterioration." In his 1967 work, the importance of the acidity of paper was emphasized: "It is the papers below pH 6.0 for which concern must be felt and which must form the subject of a paper-preservation program if they are to survive to meet the needs of research. For these papers are unstable to greater or less degree and are deteriorating with greater or less rapidity." "The anticipated rates of deterioration based on the pH values, can be classified as (a) . . . medium (pH 5.2–5.9), (b) high (pH 4.6–5.1), and very high (pH 4.0–4.5)." One must conclude that a recorded pH of less than 4.0 indicates extreme degrees of acidity and a consequently extreme rate of deterioration. At the other end of the scale the Barrow Laboratory (1967) noted that paper with a pH of 6.5+ "possess[es] sufficient stability to qualify it for library/archival use."

IV. DESCRIPTIVE STATISTICS: RESULTS AND DISCUSSION

A. Folding Endurance

1. Results of Testing

Table 2 displays the aggregate results for the folding endurance tests. Because of the way paper is printed and books are bound, the printing is normally at right angles to the grain of the paper. That is, the paper grain runs parallel to the spine of the book. As the leaf of a book is turned, the tendency is to fold or turn the page from the upper right hand corner. This leads to the folding stress being applied across the grain of the paper. Because of this and because it is ultimately the strongest direction (the

Table 2. Distribution of Folding Endurance
Scores: UC Samples

Barrow Category	Number	Percent of Samples
High strength (1,000+ folds)	25	2
Moderate strength (300–999 folds)	169	12
Low strength (51–299 folds)	361	26
Newsprint strength (11–50 folds)	435	32
Weak strength (4–10 folds)	234	17
Unusable strength (2–3 folds)	98	7
Unbindable strength (0–1 folds)	55	4
TOTAL	1,377	100

fold is across the body of most of the cellulose fibers) the folding endurance scores will be reported for the cross-machine (cross-grain) direction only (Barrow, 1964, p. 33). This may bias the test results somewhat toward the "best case." Only 1,377 of the 2,280 paper samples were of a sufficient size to meet the requirements for the folding endurance test.

2. Discussion of Results

In examining Table 2 it is important to note that 28 percent of the UC samples tested scored in ranges corresponding to the Barrow categories of "weak strength," "unusable," or "unbindable." According to the definitions of these categories noted earlier, these books are below newsprint in strength and are only suitable for use in a rare book room. Fifty-five samples or 4 percent had scores in the poorest Barrow category of "unbindable strength." These results are characteristic of paper in Barrow's "restoration" or unbindable category (Barrow, 1964, p. 15). The test results become somewhat more discouraging when one adds in all samples which tested at newsprint strength. The total of samples scoring at newsprint strength or worse is about 60 percent or 822 items. Conversely, about 40 percent of the UC samples scored in ranges above that of newsprint. This dichotomy may be explained by the disparity in ages of the two groups. The average age of the samples with a strength rating greater than newsprint is 13 years; the mean age for the samples of newsprint strength or worse is 29 years.

It is instructive to look at the relationship of publication date (or age) of the samples to the folding endurance test results. The data in Figure 1, taken from the work of the Barrow Laboratory (1974), allow one to visualize the decline in the folding endurance of book papers produced over the past 440 years. Figure 1 graphs the decline in median folding endurance scores across decades of publication. Folding endurance is generally taken to be the primary test of the strength of book papers. A good quality book paper should have a score of several hundred folds on this test. According to the plotted data, papers manufactured after about 1855 had apparently dropped to the strength of newsprint (11 to 50 folds) by 1974, the date of the Barrow Laboratory tests. The papers manufactured between about 1855 and 1930 were in the weak strength category (4 to 10 folds) and are, according to Barrow, suitable "only for a rare book room." The decrease in strength of papers manufactured after 1855–1860 is probably due to the introduction of alum-rosin sizing at that time into the United States. This point is indicated on Figure 1 by a vertical arrow. Alum-rosin sizing is used to harden the paper to better accept the printing ink; it is chemically acidic and deteriorates the paper. Another factor might be the introduction of poor quality, short-fiber groundwood pulp which is also acidic and consequently has a short usable life span. This

Figure 1. Fold Endurance of Book Paper (1507–1949)

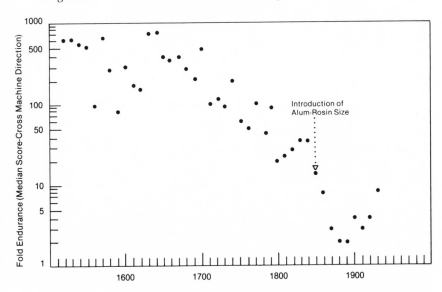

type of pulp is manufactured from mechanically shredded logs and retains many acidic noncellulose constituents such as lignin, an easily oxidized material that generates peroxides, leading to an easier breakdown of cellulose fibers (Williams, 1979). The increase in the levels of the scores for papers manufactured beginning about 1900 will be discussed later.

Figure 2 presents a similar pattern of declining folding endurance across time for UC monographs. It is also interesting to note that coincident with the introduction of alum-rosin sizing into the United States (1840–1860) the folding endurance test scores for the UC samples fall below the level of newspaper strength (i.e., median folding endurance scores fall below 10 folds). Testing for the presence of alum-rosin sizing was not undertaken in this study. The spot-tests are not easy to validate and are extremely time-consuming. However, later analyses using energy dispersive x-ray scans (EDXRA) indicated that high levels of aluminum existed in the acidic papers of low folding endurance. This finding presumably indicates the presence of alum-aluminum potassium sulfate.

Comparative examination of Figure 1 (Barrow data) and Figure 2 (UC data) suggests that books of adequate strength were published either before 1850 or in the thirty years prior to the testing date. Thus it appears that modern book papers decline to the weak strength level of ten folds in about thirty years, and that paper in books published after about 1850 and before thirty years ago should be the most badly deteriorated in any collection.

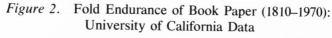

Figure 2.   Fold Endurance of Book Paper (1810–1970):
University of California Data

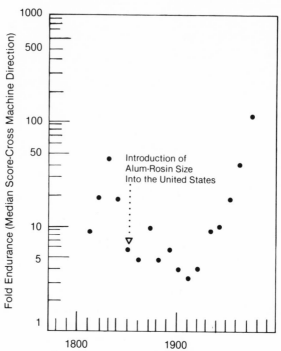

These findings from studies of paper samples in books that have been used in libraries can be compared to experimental data based on rapid heat aging of paper that was newly manufactured, unprinted, and unbound in 1963 (Barrow, 1963). Rapid heat aging duplicates the effects of long periods of storage at ambient temperatures by subjecting the paper to short periods of high temperature. The ratio is estimated to be 26 years of normal aging (at 20 degrees Centigrade) to 3 days of heat aging (at 100 degrees Centigrade). Figure 3, modified from the Barrow data (1963), indicates that the rate of deterioration of naturally aged book papers from the late nineteenth century and the first half of the twentieth century is similar to that found experimentally. Barrow (1963) also found that "typical modern book paper, with a pH of 4.8" reached a folding endurance score of about 10 folds in an estimated thirty-plus years.

The increase in median folding endurance scores which begins about thirty years prior to either the Barrow or UC test dates may arise from either of two factors. The papers that are less than thirty years old may not have had enough time to fall to the folding endurance level of the older papers. This notion is supported by the Barrow tests of heat aged paper

Figure 3. The Heat-Aged Folding Endurance Regression Lines of Two Typical Book Papers with Different Amounts of Acidity.

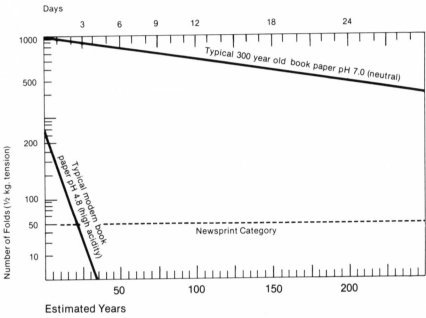

Note: Heat Aged @ 100°C.

described above. The second hypothesis regarding this recent increase in scores is that paper is, in general, getting better. If this is the case further testing later in this century should show little decline in the folding endurance test scores for the papers from these most recent three decades. Even if book papers are becoming "better" they are certainly not becoming much better. The test scores for the UC monographs with the most recent imprint dates do not reach much above those for the Barrow newsprint strength category.

Because the samples for the UC study were selected in a random manner, the data from the samples can be used to estimate some characteristics of the total collections from which the samples were drawn. The samples were initially drawn in 1974, at which time catalog sampling was performed to estimate the number of monograph titles held in each campus collection. These estimates were then used to calculate the systemwide aggregate 1974 monograph numbers (Thompson, 1981). At that time the collection size was reported to be 13,434,334 bound volumes in the general libraries (University of California, 1975). We therefore estimated that 6,447,099 volumes systemwide were monographs. By applying the data from Table 2 to this estimated collection size one can calculate

Table 3.   Estimated Folding Endurance of the Monograph
Holdings of UC Libraries in 1974

Barrow Category	Number of Volumes*	Estimated Proportion of Collection (%)*
High strength	90,679	1.4
Moderate strength	744,866	11.5
Low strength	1,541,550	23.8
Newsprint strength	2,014,378	31.1
Weak strength	1,217,695	18.8
Unusable strength	867,931	13.4

*Adjusted for campus differences in the proportion of monographs to total collection size. See subsection III.C.1.

the numbers of monograph volumes in each of the Barrow categories noted earlier. Table 3 gives the estimated numbers of volumes in each Barrow category for the 1974 monograph collection. Because some paper samples were too small to meet the requirements of the MIT Folding Endurance Test Machine the number of samples tested (1,377) fell below the number of samples taken (2,280).

We statistically examined the relationship between the samples tested and those which we were unable to test. That analysis reveals two pertinent facts:

a. There was no systematic bias by country of origin for those titles excluded from physical testing;

b. There was a statistically significant difference between the mean ages of the two groups.

If the difference in the mean ages of tested and untested samples causes a bias in the data, the bias is in the direction of greater deterioration. However, the mean ages for both groups fall within the period of maximum loss of folding endurance strength, that is, 1850–1924. From this we have concluded that even if the difference in mean ages results in a bias, the effect on our findings is negligible.

B.   Tearing Resistance

1.   *Results of Testing*

Table 4 presents the tear resistance test scores for the UC data by Barrow categories. Because of the way paper is made on paper-making machines it acquires a noticeable grain or machine direction. To enable the book to open properly, the page is usually printed so that this grain runs parallel to the spine of the book. When the page is turned it is folded across the grain as noted in the section above. At the same time force is being applied in the direction of the grain. As the tearing resistance of the paper deteriorates, this results in tears usually beginning at the top edge of the page and extending down. When the paper becomes extremely brittle the entire page will break off along the inner margin close to the spine of the book. Because of this factor the tearing resistance scores are reported for the machine direction only (tearing along the grain of the paper). There is some controversy about which grain direction exhibits the greatest tear resistance. If the machine direction tear test assays the weakest direction then we may be biasing the tear test scores to the low end. Because the Barrow tests were performed in the machine direction we have preferred to perform our tests in acordance with the precedent.

2. Discussion of Results

As Table 4 shows, 7 percent of the UC samples tested were in the Barrow category of unusable. An additional 21 percent were in the slightly better category of weak paper strength. According to Barrow, none of the books with papers in these two categories should be circulated to patrons. Therefore, according to the test results, 28 percent of the UC samples tested have so little resistance to tear that they should be restricted from circulation.

Table 4. Distribution of Tearing Resistance Scores:
UC Samples

Barrow Category	*Number*	*Percent of Samples*
High strength (75+ grams)	53	3
Moderate strength (60–74 grams)	165	8
Low strength (31–59 grams)	1,099	58
Newsprint strength (25–30 grams)	65	3
Weak strength (13–24 grams)	407	21
Unusable (0–12 grams)	130	7
TOTAL	1,919	100

In Figure 4 and Figure 5, the median tearing resistance scores by publication date are given for the Barrow and UC studies respectively. For the Barrow Laboratory data (1974) in Figure 4, one finds that the tearing resistance scores drop dramatically in the decades 1850–1870. This appears to coincide with the introduction of alum-rosin sizing in American paper-making (Clapp, 1972). The Barrow Laboratory (1974) found that, out of 100 books published in the United States between 1830–1849, 6 percent contained alum-rosin sizing. Of 100 books published between 1850 and 1869, fifty percent contained alum-rosin sizing. In Figure 5, which displays the UC data, one finds the median tearing resistance scores declining rapidly in the decade 1810–1819. This earlier decline in scores compared to the Barrow data is probably due to the fact that Barrow only tested American editions. The UC data includes volumes published in a number of countries where alum-rosin sizing was introduced much earlier. During the decade 1850–59, the UC data show a further decline in tear resistance scores. This appears to coincide with the time of the introduction of alum-rosin sizing to the American paper-making process.

When Barrow tested his samples (in the early 1960s), papers made during or after the decade 1900–09 continued to have a tearing resistance at least as good as newsprint. By the time the UC tests were conducted a little over 12 years later those papers produced during the decade 1900–09 had fallen in tearing resistance to the weak category. Papers from the two

Figure 4. Tear Resistance of Book Papers (1507–1949)

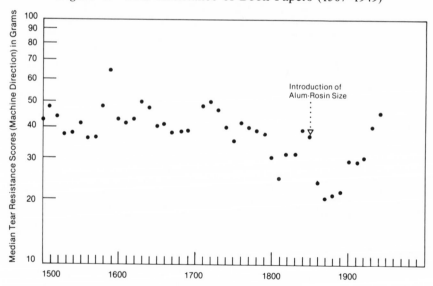

Figure 5. Tear Resistance of Book Papers (1810–1970):
University of California Data

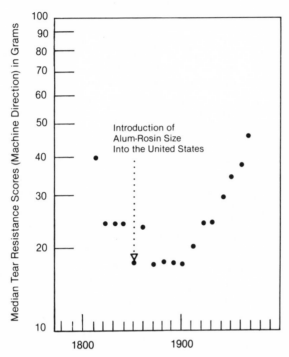

following decades tested slightly poorer in the UC study than papers from the same decades in the Barrow tests conducted 10 years earlier. Of course the same papers were not retested in the later UC study. However, if both the Barrow study and the UC study are assumed to be sampling the same population of book papers at different points in time, one can conclude that tearing resistance continues to decline as the paper ages.

In the Barrow data of Figure 4, the vertical arrow points to the decade which followed the introduction of alum-rosin sizing in American paper making (in that study Barrow only tested books of American manufacture). In Figure 5, the UC data, the situation is more complex. The test scores are for papers of both American and foreign manufacture. One could postulate that the decrease in tearing resistance scores seen between the decades 1800–1809 and 1810–1819 was because of the introduction of alum-rosin sizing into European paper-making after 1807. The further decrease in scores in the decades between 1860–1879 may reflect the effects of the subsequent use of alum-rosin sizing in papers of American origin. The increasing scores seen after 1920 in the UC data of Figure 5 are probably attributable to a slower deterioration time for tearing re-

Table 5.   Estimated Numbers of the 1974 UC Libraries
Monograph Holdings in the Barrow Categories for
Tearing Resistance

Barrow Category	Number of Volumes*	Estimated Proportion of Collection (%)*
High strength	161,928	2.5
Moderate strength	492,260	7.6
Low strength	3,601,267	55.6
Newsprint strength	220,221	3.4
Weak strength	1,457,347	22.5
Unusable strength	544,076	8.4

*Adjusted for campus differences in the proportion of monographs to total collection size. See subsection III.C.1.

sistance than for folding endurance. It takes about 30 years for folding endurance to reach weak strength, whereas it takes those same samples between 55 and 60 years to reach the same deterioration category for tearing resistance.

Using the data from Table 4 one can estimate the number of monographs in the 1974 UC collections that should fall into the Barrow categories of tearing resistance; Table 5 displays these estimated values. Once again we note that there is a disparity between the number of samples in this test and the number of samples originally taken. That is because there were a smaller number of samples meeting the size requirements for the Elmendorf Tear Tester than there were total samples taken. This was the case because many monographs of apparently cheap manufacture did not contain an unprinted paper sample of sufficient size to be used in the test apparatus. Thus, if this lack of paper was not random with regard to paper quality, there may be a bias in the test results which could lead to an underestimate of the numbers of deteriorated monographs.

C.   Folding and Tearing Resistance: Combined Results

In the two sections immediately above, results for the folding endurance tests and the tearing resistance tests are given independently. This is because of Barrow's (1964, p. 17) admonition that "failure in either folding endurance, through embrittlement, or tear resistance makes a sheet unusable." Although this may be true, the UC study found many papers that were quite good on one test but which tested poorly on the other. Because the current state of research in this area does not provide for inferences about the usability of those items that are strong on one

Table 6. Estimated Numbers of the 1974 UC Libraries Monograph Holdings in Two Barrow Categories of Folding Strength

	Estimated Number of Volumes*	
Test	Weak Category	Unusable Category
Folding endurance	1,217,695	867,931
Tearing resistance	1,457,347	544,076
Folding endurance and tearing resistance	414,534	97,156

*Adjusted for campus differences in the proportion of monographs to total collection size. See subsection III.C.1.

Table 7. Distribution of Hydrogen Ion Concentration Scores: UC Samples

pH Range	Number	Percent of Samples
9.01–10.00	2	0.09
8.01–9.00	24	1.10
7.01–8.00	110	4.80
6.01–7.00	192	8.40
5.01–6.00	196	8.60
4.01–5.00	1,387	61.00
3.01–4.00	353	15.50
2.01–3.00	10	0.40
1.00–2.00	1	0.04
TOTAL	2,275	100.00

physical test and weak on another, it is of interest to look at the numbers of items that perform poorly on more than one test. Table 6 displays the estimated number of volumes which should score in the same Barrow categories for both folding endurance and tearing resistance.

D.   Hydrogen ion Concentration (pH)

1.   Hydrogen ion Concentration Test Results

Hydrogen ion concentration or pH is, as noted earlier, a measure of the alkalinity/acidity of a substance. The higher the acidity, the lower the pH. The more acid the paper the shorter the usable life span. Table 7, below, presents the frequency with which the test scores of the UC samples occurred in each pH range.

2. *Discussion of Hydrogen ion Test Results*

As noted in the methodology section, Barrow found that papers that tested less than pH 6.0 are "the papers . . . for which concern must be felt and which must form the subject of a paper-preservation program if they are to survive to meet the needs of research." From Table 7, above, it appears that about 86 percent of the UC samples showed a pH less than 6.0. Table 8 places the UC samples in the Barrow categories of deterioration based on pH. The categories are not continuous in that there was no category proposed for the transitional range of 6.00 to 6.50. Samples with a pH less than Barrow's worst category must be interpreted as having a very high rate of deterioration.

As can be seen in the Barrow (1974) data of Figure 6, no paper sample published after 1610 met the criterion for archival paper (pH 6.5+). After 1650, only the samples from the decade 1830–1840 tested better than the moderate deterioration category. After 1740, only the samples from 1820–1860 tested better than the high deterioration category. The slightly higher scores for the data points 1820, 1830, 1840, 1850, and 1860 remain unexplained. Figure 7 plots the median pH scores for the UC samples. These results indicate that the UC samples were somewhat more acid than the ones tested by Barrow. Median scores for only two decades of UC data were better than those for the very high deterioration range.

When the UC results for pH are plotted using only data from United States imprints, they are much more comparable to the Barrow data. However, the number of data points available is not sufficient to allow statistical comparison.

Table 8. Projected Deterioration Rate of UC Samples Based on Hydrogen Ion Concentrations

pH Range	Barrow Categories	Number	Percent of Samples
6.51+	Stable/archival	250	11
6.00/6.50	(No category)	86	4
5.20/5.99	Medium deterioration rate	122	5
4.60/5.10	High deterioration rate	425	19
4.00/4.50	Very high deterioration rate	1,052	46
3.99–	(No category, extremely acid paper)	340	15
	TOTAL	2,275	100

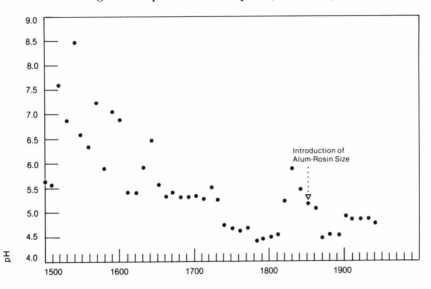

Figure 6. pH of Book Papers (1507–1949)

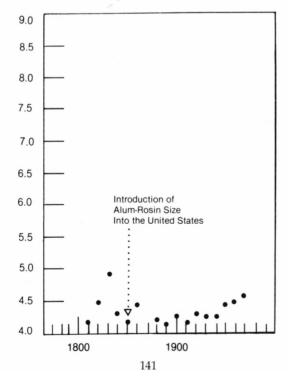

Figure 7. pH of Book Papers (1810–1970):
University of California Data

141

Table 9.   Estimated Numbers of the 1974 UC Libraries Monograph
Holdings in the Barrow Categories for Acid Deterioration

Barrow Category	Number of Volumes*	Estimated Proportion of Collection (%)*
Stable/archival	647,710	10.0
No category	207,267	3.2
Medium deterioration rate	317,378	4.9
High deterioration rate	1,055,767	16.3
Very high deterioration rate	3,031,282	46.8
No category, extreme acidity	1,224,172	18.9

*Adjusted for campus differences in the proportion of monographs to total collection size. See subsection III.C.1.

Table 9 indicates the estimated number of volumes from the 1974 UC monograph collections classified by the Barrow categories for acid deterioration rates.

E.   Folding, Tearing and pH: Combined Results

In the previous sections the poor performance of a paper sample on more than one physical test was proposed as validation that an individual item was indeed badly deteriorated. One can use the hydrogen ion content test scores as a further validity check on those items. To do this, the cases used to estimate the numbers of items in the same categories of both folding endurance and tearing resistance (i.e., Table 6) were cross-tabulated with the Barrow pH ranges of Table 8. Table 10 indicates the estimated numbers of monographs in the 1974 collections which would have been in the weak and unusable strength categories and in the "high deterioration rate" or "very high deterioration rate" categories according to their pH scores. Table 10 shows that over 92 percent of the samples in the weak category for both folding endurance and tearing resistance had high or very high acidity. For the samples in the unusable category on both strength tests 100 percent are in the high or very high acidity range. One cannot state that the levels of acidity are the cause of the weakened strength of the paper. However, one can say that high acid content will continue to degrade these papers, which are apparently already in a seriously deteriorated condition.

Table 10. Estimated Numbers of the 1974 UC Libraries Monograph Holdings in Two Barrow Categories of Tearing Strength

	*Estimated Number of Volumes**	
Test	Weak Category	Unusable Category
Folding endurance only	1,217,695	867,931
Tearing resistance only	1,457,347	544,076
Folding endurance and tearing resistance only	414,534	97,156
Folding endurance, tearing endurance and high or very high acidity	382,200	97,156

*Adjusted for campus differences in the proportion of monographs total collection size. See subsection III.C.1.

F. Groundwood Content

1. Groundwood Content Test Results

It was long thought that groundwood content was a major factor in the deterioration of paper. This notion was based on the inherent acidity of the lignin which was thought to lead to the rapid breakdown of the cellulose fibers. It is known that the presence of lignin does provide an enhanced substrate for direct oxidation of paper (Williams, 1979). Barrow (1967) reported that for books from the period 1850–1899 all-rag papers "suffered the same sharp loss in strength as did the part-rag." Groundwood content was assayed in the UC samples in order to confirm and extend this finding to papers from other years. The groundwood content, in percentage, was measured by the use of the reagent test described in the methodology section. Table 11 displays the measured groundwood content of the UC samples.

As can be seen from Table 11, 81 percent of the UC samples tested negative for groundwood content. If groundwood was the sole source of deterioration in the UC samples one would expect a better showing on the tests of paper strength than was found. Since this was not the case, one must assume as Barrow did that other sources of deterioration are at work in the paper.

Figure 8 graphs the percentage of UC samples containing groundwood for each decade of publishing. As can be seen from the graph, no samples tested positive for groundwood until the decade 1860–1869. The numbers of samples containing groundwood remained about the same until the

Table 11. Distribution of Groundwood Content Scores:
UC Samples

Groundwood Content (%)		Number	Percent of Samples
100		172	8
75		77	3
50		64	3
25		117	5
0		1,845	81
	TOTAL	2,275	100

Figure 8. Percentage of University of California Samples
Containing Groundwood

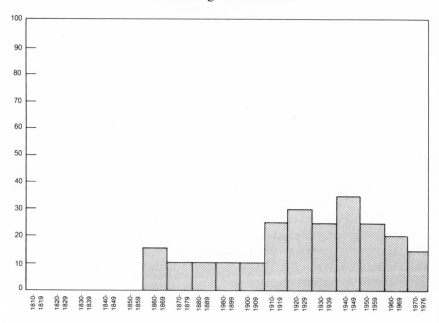

decade 1910–1919. From this time until slightly after World War II, the numbers of samples containing groundwood continue to rise. The largest number of samples testing positive for groundwood is found in the decade 1940–1949. After this period the percentages begin to decline to pre-1910 levels. Although this apparent decline in the percentage of samples containing groundwood seems good news, it is somewhat misleading. That is, even though there is a decline in the proportion of samples containing groundwood the numbers of books this represents in the collections is growing. In 1940–1949 the UC collections added about 1,000,000 bound volumes of which we can estimate 48 percent were monographs. Thus UC may have added 480,000 monographs of which, according to Figure 8, 32 percent or 154,000 volumes were printed on paper containing groundwood. During 1970–1976 UC added approximately 4 million bound volumes to its collections. If 48 percent of these were monographs then, according to Figure 6, 13 percent or about 250,000 monographs printed on paper containing groundwood were added to the collections.

2. Discussion of the Groundwood Test Results

The results of the groundwood testing lead to two interesting observations. First, the percentage of the samples containing groundwood is much lower than would be expected from the extant literature. The finding that only 19 percent of the samples contained any groundwood and that only 8 percent of the samples were from paper composed of 100 percent groundwood is better than expected. That these percentages are still important has been noted above. The second point of interest is the cross-tabulation of the groundwood scores with the Barrow strength categories. Table 12 shows the cross-tabulation of the groundwood test scores with the distribution of samples in the Barrow strength categories for folding endurance. One can see from the cross-tabulation in column one, row six, that the occurrence of groundwood in the paper sample is not necessarily associated with poor performance on the folding endurance test. Conversely, groundwood is found to occur in some samples that are not severely deteriorated, although none of the samples in the high strength category were found to contain groundwood. The first finding offers some support for the hypothesis that alum-rosin sizing is the more likely source of acidity in book papers.

Table 12.   Cross-tabulation of Barrow
Categories for Folding Endurance with
Groundwood Content

Folding Endurance Strength	*Groundwood in Percent*				
	0	*25*	*50*	*75*	*100*
High	25	0	0	0	0
Moderate	154	8	3	1	3
Low	306	14	10	15	16
Newsprint	345	31	10	9	39
Weak	172	22	8	6	26
Unusable	104	3	8	12	25

V. PREDICTIVE ANALYSIS: RESULTS AND DISCUSSION

While the data presented above can help establish the magnitude of the conservation/preservation problem the UC libraries may face, they do not enable one to select specific monographs for preservation treatment. This selection process usually occurs now in one of two ways: deteriorated books returning from circulation are sent to mending, or professional staff select items from the stacks for treatment. In the first instance only circulating items receive attention and then only after they have deteriorated to the point that they can no longer circulate. In the second instance materials can be sent for treatment before severe damage occurs but at high cost, in terms of professional staff time for selection. It would be of advantage if one could focus the selection process on likely candidates for treatment based on call number class or other bibliographic data such as imprint date or country of origin. Such a focus might be achieved if, using the data of this study, one could establish a definite relationship between one or more aspects of the bibliographic data about a book and the Barrow deterioration category based on folding endurance for a sample from that book. If such relationships could be established (e.g., monographs printed in Spain before 1940 are probably of unusable strength) then nondestructive tests might then be applied to these preselected items to determine the level of deterioration. A list of material needing preservation treatment could then be established and reviewed for priority of treatment.

A series of analyses of variance (ANOVAs) were performed to investigate the statistical relationship of the folding endurance scores to call number class, age of the paper, country of origin, and circulation history. The ANOVAs established that the bibliographical variables were statistically related to the folding endurance scores ($p > .01$) but that the relationship was extremely weak, with the R-squared equal to 0.10 or less. Thus the bibliographic factors were statistically related to the folding endurance scores but only explained abut 10 percent of the variance in those scores. Ninety percent of the variance in the folding endurance scores remained unexplained. A second series of analyses of variance was performed to assess the statistical relationship between the test scores for physical strength and those for hydrogen ion content, groundwood content, and paper thickness. The latter three scores are obtainable without removing paper from a book or causing significant damage to the book. Once again the ANOVAs indicated that there was a statistically reliable relationship between the folding endurance and the nondestructive tests ($p > .01$). However, the correlation between the nondestructive factors and the folding endurance scores was very weak with the R-squared equal to approximately 0.12, explaining only 12 percent of the variance in the folding scores.

These findings are discouraging. In the first place they indicate that there are unknown or untested factors at work in the deterioration of monograph papers that prevent one from using the data of this study to identify parts of the UC collections which may be the best candidates for preservation. The second conclusion is that even if one could focus on a selected portion of the collection the nondestructive tests and measurement could not be used to predict the deterioration level of the paper. Selection for preservation treatment will continue to be a matter of professional choice (for instance, see Magrill and Rinehart, 1979).

Given the amount of time necessary to complete the tests of physical strength used in this study, it appears probable that it would be extremely costly to extend this study to establish the correlations sought above in a statistically significant way. However, further studies are needed in this area to develop cheaper and more timely methods of selecting material for preservation treatment. Future studies should now concentrate on only the "brittle" books in the collection; these books may have bibliographic features in common that could enable one to select items for preservation by examination of the shelf list.

VI.   CONCLUSION

A.   Review of Findings

The test results show that 28 percent of the samples tested had scores in the Barrow categories of weak strength or unusable strength for folding endurance or tearing resistance. This represents 32.2 percent and 30.9 percent of the adjusted 1974 monograph collection sizes respectively. It was further found that 7 percent of the samples had test scores in these categories on both tests of paper strength. It was also found that 86 percent of the samples tested were in the acid range on pH. These papers will continue to lose strength as long as the acid condition persists. A reduction of acidity can only occur by the treatment of these materials with a deacidification process. It was estimated that as many as 479,000 volumes in the UC collections in 1974 were in the Barrow categories of weak or unusable strength and were of high or very high acidity. Groundwood was not found to be a significant factor in the low strength of the book paper samples. However, high strength papers did not contain groundwood.

B. Conclusions

The results of this study support the subjective reports of other investigators that about 30 percent of any large research library's book collection is in poor physical condition. Studies, including this one, that have tries to statistically examine the whole of a working collection have been unsuccessful in pinpointing classes or individual items in need of preservation treatment. Further studies are needed which examine closely the physical, chemical, and bibliographical aspects of "brittle" books.

REFERENCES

Barker, Nicolas, "Blight in Bloomsbury." *Times Literary Supplement* (November 18): 1359, 1977.

Barrow, W. J. *Permanence/Durability of the Book—I: A Two-Year Research Program.* Richmond, Virginia: The W. J. Barrow Research Laboratory, 1963.

Barrow, W. J., *Permanence/Durability of the Book—II: Test Data of Naturally Aged Papers.* Richmond, Virginia: W. J. Barrow Research Laboratory, 1964.

Barrow, W. J., *Permanence/Durability of the Book—V: Strength and Other Characteristics of Book Papers 1800–1899.* Richmond, Virginia: W. J. Barrow Research Laboratory 1967.

Barrow, W. J., *Permanence/Durability of the Book—VI: Spot Testing for Unstable Modern Book and Record Papers.* Richmond, Virginia: W. J. Barrow Research Laboratory, 1969.

Barrow, W. J., (Research Laboratory, Inc.). *Permanence/Durability of the Book—VII: Physical and Chemical Properties of Book Papers, 1507–1949.* Richmond, Virginia: W. J. Barrow Research Laboratory, 1974.

Clapp, Verner W., "The Story of Permanent/Durable Book-Paper, 1115–1970." *Restaurator,* No. 3: 1–51, 1972.

Cunha, George Martin, "Tripartite Concept of Conservation." In *Conservation Administration.* North Andover, Massachusetts: The New England Document Conservation Center, 1975. Pp. 19–48.

Cunha, George Martin, and Dorothy Grant Cunha, *Conservation of Library Materials.* 2nd ed. 2 vols. Metuchen, N.J.: The Scarecrow Press, Inc., 1971.

Kingery, Robert E., "The Extent of the Paper Problem in Large Research Collections and the Comparative Costs of Available Solutions," In *Permanent/Durable Book Paper.* Richmond, Virginia: The Virginia State Library, 1960. Pp. 36–41.

Langwell, W. H., *The Conservation of Books and Documents.* London: Sir Isaac Pitman & Sons, LTD., 1957.

Langwell, W. H., "The Permanence of Papers." *British Paper and Board Makers Association. Technical Section. Technical Bulletin* 29, No. 1 (February, 1952): 21–28.

Library of Congress. *Annual Report of the Librarian of Congress.* Washington, D.C.: Library of Congress, 1978.

Magrill, Rose Mary, and Constance Rinehart, "Selection for Preservation: A Service Study." *Library Resources & Technical Services* 24, No. 4 (Winter): 44–57, 1980.

Nie, Norman H. *Statistical Package for the Social Sciences.* New York: McGraw-Hill Book Company, 1975.

Technical Association of the Pulp and Paper Industry (TAPPI). *Folding Endurance of Paper (MIT Tester).* T 511 su-69, revised-1969.

Technical Association of the Pulp and Paper Industry (TAPPI). *Internal Tearing Resistance of Paper*. T 414 ts-65, corrected-1965.

Technical Association of the Pulp and Paper Industry (TAPPI). *Standard Conditioning and Testing Atmospheres for Paper, Board, Pulp Handsheets, and Related Products*. T 402 os-70, revised-1970.

Thompson, Donald D. Personal communication, 1981.

University of California. Systemwide Administration. *Size of the Libraries of the University of California on 30 June 1975*. Berkeley, California: University of California, 1975.

Waters, Peter. Personal communication, 1977.

Williams, John C., "Chemistry of the Deacidification of Paper." *International Institute for Conservation of Historic and Artistic Works* 12, No. 1 (October): 16–32, 1971.

Williams, John C., "Paper Permanence: A Step in the Addition to Alkalization." *Restaurator*, 3, No. 3(1979): 81–90.

EVALUATION AND THE PROCESS OF CHANGE IN ACADEMIC LIBRARIES

Delmus E. Williams

The economics of higher education are placing an increasing emphasis on the need for academic libraries and other components of colleges and universities to engage in serious planning efforts. But before efforts of this kind can begin, information must be accumulated on the current state of the organization, and consensus must be forged as to its strengths and weaknesses. For this reason, the academic library is being asked to integrate an ongoing process of program evaluation into a general planning process so that it might have the information at hand to meet the challenges of coming years.

The evaluation of library services is going on constantly in any academic library. Statistics are gathered in most areas of the library for one reason or another, user surveys are conducted on an occasional basis,

Advances in Library Administration and Organization, volume 2, pages 151–174.
Copyright © 1983 by JAI Press Inc.
All rights of reproduction in any form reserved.
ISBN: 0-89232-214-4

annual reports are prepared for submission to the general administration, and operational analyses are often required as the library justifies its budget requests. As fiscal restraint forces institutions to make increasingly difficult choices regarding their programs, efforts to coordinate all of these information-gathering devices are becoming increasingly important. To remain strong, academic libraries must develop within themselves the capacity to systematically get and control all of the information they need, to analyze that data, and to disseminate it in a way that will influence university policy. Program evaluation is designed to fulfill these requirements.

Evaluation is defined here as any process designed to delineate, obtain, and provide managers useful information for judging decision alternatives.[1] It is a pragmatic process that fits specific circumstances and that is tailored to meet specific information needs. On the one hand, an accreditation self-study mandated by a regional accrediting body may require an institution and its library to perform a thorough program evaluation. On the other, a consultant may be brought into an academic library to examine issues relating to automation or the implementation of a new cataloging code, and that person's report might provide insights into more general needs of the organization. In either case, the major impact of evaluation is to discover areas where change is needed and to help the organization develop alternatives to current operating procedures. In fact, this capacity of the evaluation process to act as a change agent is the central thread binding together the concept of program evaluation.

To understand how program evaluation works in an organization, one must first understand something about how organizations institute changes in their programs. It is not the purpose of this paper to advocate change nor is it the place of the evaluator necessarily to do so. Rather, both change and evaluation theory emphasize the need within healthy organizations to develop the capacity to adapt themselves to changing situations should the need arise. In this vein, a large body of research has begun to accumulate as people attempt to identify those factors that enhance or retard the capacity of the organization to change. Most of this literature relates to what J. Victor Baldridge calls the human relations school of management. This school believes that within an organization there are two separate structures. The first is based on the formal bureaucratic model and is designed by its managers to facilitate the use of their authority. The second is an informal one based on interpersonal relationships between members of the organization and designed to allow those individuals to exert their influence on its program. While advocates of this theory understand that some changes can and must be implemented through the use of power exerted by elements of the bureaucracy, they generally feel that change is most effective when it can be made acceptable to the components of the informal structure. As a result, change studies have attempted to analyze how innovation affects this structure and how adaptations can be made while placing the least possible stress on it.[2]

As a matter of convenience, David D. Dill and Charles P. Friedman have suggested four frameworks around which change literature can be organized. These are the complex organization model, the diffusion model, the conflict model, and the planned change model.[3] It is understood that the components of the change process do not necessarily break down neatly into discrete packages. All of the elements identified in any of these models are seen to impact on the process as a whole, and the division of them into schools of thought are more a matter of emphasis than an attempt to exclude the elements of the other models. Still, the use of these four paradigms does provide an orderly way to examine the literature that is available.

The first of these four is the complex organization model. The literature that falls within this paradigm relates the capacity of an organization to change to a variety of preexisting characteristics within that organization. The basic assumption is that certain variables, like the complexity of the organization, the degree to which its authority is centralized, its size, affluence, and stratification and its degree of formalization, all impact on its capacity to change. Therefore, advocates of this school suggest that any effort to change an organization should be preceded by an attempt to determine the extent to which these elements exist within that organization. Efforts then can be designed to lessen the effect of resistance that will be caused by them.[4]

The diffusion model also emphasizes that any change should be preceded by an analysis of existing situations in the organization, but it is less concerned with organizational characteristics than with the organization's communications network. Change agents who espouse this model focus on the identification of those people within the organization who are most likely to remain neutral through the process so that an active coalition can be formed to support it. These researchers have found that individual characteristics, like education and cosmopolitism, and characteristics of individual changes, like divisibility, can greatly influence the rate of acceptance. Proponents of this model feel that individual changes can be implemented with minimum stress by maintaining maximum contact with "gatekeepers" within the organization and by tailoring changes in such a way that they might be sold to less enthusiastic members of the organization.[5]

Both of these models speak directly to the need for an adequate evaluation process within a library. Both isolate factors that can be predetermined as the library begins to think about its future and plans to meet that future. The director must understand those features of a library that will enhance or inhibit the capacity to change if that person is to adequately plan for any innovation. The library director must also understand how best to sell the innovation to the staff and to other constituents of the library once it has been decided to proceed. However, neither of these models addresses local conditions and variations that can be expected within the context of individual organizations.

It is this limitation that is addressed by theorists whom Dill and Friedman place under their conflict or political model. This framework views the organization as a political unit whose decision making is based on temporary coalitions of interest groups within the organization. These interest groups, in turn, are based on specific issues. The idea is that, as issues change, membership in each group and the coalitions of groups within the organization will also change. Therefore, it is the obligation of the administrator to come to understand where support is available for proposed changes and to use that knowledge to build support for them. According to J. Victor Baldridge, this is best done by, first, evaluating the social factors contributing to the value structure of an organization's members; second, by determining how the interest groups bring their interests to bear on decision making; and, finally, by analyzing the process by which the organization implements decisions once they have been made.[6]

It is far more difficult to generalize the impact of the various elements of this paradigm, and Baldridge and others suggest that the best way to study it is on a case-by-case basis. In this way, a process can be developed to meet particular political situations within a specific organization and to conform to the circumstances that relate to a specific change. In this way, evaluative processes can be brought to bear in the development of an individual organization's capacity to adapt to changing situations.[7]

The last of Dill and Friedman's paradigms is the planned change model. This model focuses on the optimum procedure that can be used while intervening in an organization for the purpose of changing it. It is designed to isolate "process variables"—that is, those variables that relate to actions taken during the conduct of the evaluation that are likely to influence the acceptance of its results. The core of it is generally referred to as Organizational Development (OD), a process designed to assist the organization to work through its own change process with the assistance of a change agent. The change agent serves to encourage the organization to focus on the problems to be addressed and then assists members of that organization to work through the problems to solutions that are acceptable to the management of the organization and in keeping with the values of the informal organization. This process begins with the change agent working to develop a positive relationship with members of the organization and then helping them to identify the problems to be treated. Once this is accomplished, the organization is encouraged to develop a variety of solutions using a group-centered problem-solving process. After that, the group works to isolate those solutions that are most appropriate, to assist management with their implementation, and to evaluate their effectiveness. Finally, the change agent works with members of the organization to emplace within it a continuing process through which it can deal effectively with future problems of this sort without outside intervention. At the point that this is accomplished, the change agent's role is complete, and that person withdraws from the organization. Success is measured in relation to the degree to which basic problem solving in the organization evolves to the point that it can be left in the hands of a group consisting of management personnel and representatives from other areas of the organization.[8]

The planned change model is designed to take many of the elements of the other three models and to synthesize them into a single problem-solving process. This paradigm stresses both the need for better communications in an organization and the need for consensus building in the change process. Above all, it views evaluation efforts as processes that can be used to satisfy short-term objectives while developing the capacity to change within the organization. This emphasis on process is useful in building an understanding of the importance of open communications within an organization and of mutual trust between those who manage and those who are managed in the change process.[9]

Organizational Development as a process forms the basis for the kind of evaluation that is most likely to be required in an academic library. While one might argue that more "scientific" approaches like cost-benefit analysis or time-motion studies might be useful, the primary problems that face the librarian in an academic setting are people problems. They relate to the attitudes of library workers and of the clients those libraries serve. Statistical information is useful in determining, for instance, whether one can justify economically the installation of an automated library catalog. However, no aggregation of statistics is likely to satisfy the patron who maintains that the computer is likely to go down more often than the card catalog and that he does not have much use for any kind of machine anyway. Or, when the library is understaffed, it is easy enough to show that other libraries have more people. However, when the university that it is a part of is retrenching, rational arguments of this sort can be less useful than the capacity of the library director to phrase the request in terms that are acceptable to those who oversee the library and support the request with whatever kind of evidence enhances the library's capacity to compete in the political arena of the university for scarce resources. While more concrete information must be developed as input into the evaluation process, that process must be able to then digest that input, interpret it, and package its results if it is to have maximum effect. Even then, the published results of the study should only be viewed as a portion of the impact the evaluation process has had on the organization. By undertaking an evaluation, the manager shows a willingness to accept input into decision making from others in the organization, and, if the process is handled well, the fact that workers and managers have faced problems together may be as important to the health of the organization as the fact that some eventually were solved.

Much of the theoretical basis for program evaluation has been taken from the literature of organizational change, and much of the research relating to the evaluation process quite rightly parallels that literature. An evaluation, like a planned change intervention, is an attempt to open up the decision making process within the affected organization. However, the reasons for undertaking a program evaluation are somewhat more complicated. In a planned change intervention, the change agent is aiming specifically at making the organization more capable of accepting innovation. In a program evaluation, the evaluator has the dual responsibility of encouraging change while determining how effective operations actually are. This dual purpose of quality assurance and the enhancement of the capacity to change can cause serious problems. The first instinct of managers and others within an organization is to insure that the organization survives and that programs in which much has been invested will be maintained with minimal outside interference. While a library director might welcome someone into a library to help get more funding for reference service, that person might very well resist having an outsider determine where that money ought to be spent if it is provided. The old dictum that a good consultant is one who can tell the director what is already known and phrase it in a way that can be sold to the university administration is sometimes too close to the truth for comfort. For many managers in all kinds of organizations, the idea of a serious evaluation for the purpose of enhancing the capacity of their operations to change is about as pleasing as the prospect of an audit from those people at the Internal Revenue Service who are only there to help the taxpayer. An evaluation is after all a political instrument. Whether it is carried on from outside of the library or from within it, it must be done with an eye to the impact the final product is likely to have. Only in this way can one hope to get the cooperation necessary for success.[10]

In looking at the utility of evaluation, one must begin by looking at the evaluability of the library. The concept of evaluability grew out of concern expressed in the early 1970s that the results of program evaluations in the public sector were not being utilized to influence policy making. As a result, Howard Davis, Susan Salasin, Joseph Wholey and others came to the conclusion that not all organizations were equally in a position to benefit from evaluation. Wholey contended that the organization must be willing to accept the concept of evaluation and the idea that it might be helpful, if it hoped to use the process to full advantage. He suggested that an information-gathering process should precede the actual evaluation to insure that all that could have been done to prepare the organization for the evaluation had been done. During the preevaluation, it would be the responsibility of the evaluator to determine how amenable the organization was to the process, how well defined its goals and objectives were, how plausible the objectives were in relation to the program that was operating, and how well management had considered how it might use the results of the evaluation. To get this information, Wholey suggested the following steps:

(1) Define the program to be evaluated. In this stage, the evaluator works with management to decide precisely what is to be evaluated.

(2) Collect information on the intended project. At this stage, the evaluator documents the program objectives, how those objectives are to be achieved, and how the success of those methods are measured within the organization.

(3) Develop a concise description of the program. At this stage, it is necessary to synthesize all of the information previously collected about the library's objectives into a statement that reflects what various levels of the administration expect of it. If the views of the administration are in harmony, a single model might be constructed showing what the university is contributing to the library, what is being done with those resources, and what is expected from the library as a result. If the expectation of the various groups that contribute to library decision-making differ, several different models may be required to show these differences.

(4) Document the extent to which the library's program is documented in measurable terms. This will identify those areas where statistical data can show how well the library is performing its mission and will determine where information must be gathered as to its effectiveness.

(5) Collect information on program reality. At this point, the evaluator is tasked with determining precisely what is going on in the organization and how well this reality conforms to the model(s) constructed in (3) above. Also, at this point, the evaluator tries to determine the cost of obtaining the data required to perform a reasonable evaluation of the library's operations.

(6) Synthesize the information gained regarding the library's program into a more inclusive description of the library's operation. A new model is now constructed refining the earlier one to provide a better view of how the library actually operates, to clarify the kind of data that is available about those operations, and to comment on which of the stated objectives of the library can reasonably be met with its existing programs.

(7) Identify options for evaluation. At this point, the evaluator should determine the degree to which each element of the library is ready for evaluation and outline those steps that might be taken to increase the possibility of success for an evaluation effort. That person identifies those objectives that are not addressed by existing

programs and suggests others that are reasonable and feasible within the operations of the library. The evaluator may also recommend for consideration at this point appropriate measures that might be used in areas where inadequate measures are being used and ways in which data might be collected to test those measures.

(8)   The final step is to present the information gathered during the process to the library director or to the person outside the library who commissioned the study. This person will, in turn, verify the results and determine how to proceed. In addition to considering both the clarity of the organization's objectives and the capacity of its operations to meet those objectives, the evaluator should address the question of whether those who control the operation of the library have the motivation, ability and authority to use evaluation information.[11]

Wholey contends that no formal evaluation procedure should be undertaken without working through this process. There is, however, one major difficulty for librarians in applying his method. Wholey's model for preevaluation planning has a strong prejudice for the evaluation of programs in which there is a paper trail of evidence as to their results. Consequently, technical service operations that can be easily quantified will always have high evaluability ratings, while more abstract services like reference or special collections are never likely to rate as well. Even so, this process does provide the administrator who is considering an investment in evaluation an opportunity to determine the kind of program that has the best chance for success.[12]

Another approach to the idea of evaluability was developed by Howard Davis and Susan Salasin. They dubbed their technique A VICTORY using an acronym derived from the eight factors that they considered important in determining the evaluability of an organization. These are the Ability of the organization to carry out an evaluation well; the Values of the organization as they relate to change; the Information available to support an evaluation process; the Circumstances surrounding the organization that might relate to its capacity to accept criticism; the Timing of the proposed evaluation; the Obligation felt by member of the organization to find out how they are doing; the Resistance to evaluation in the organization; and the anticipated Yield that might be expected to come from a thorough review of the organization's programs. Davis and Salasin developed a questionnaire based on these factors to test the readiness of an organization for evaluation. This technique relies somewhat less than Wholey's on quantification of programs, emphasizes the need for good communications in an organization, and stresses the need for members of the organization to believe in the value of assessment for evaluation to succeed. While it is not perfect, the process it outlines provides an opportunity for a quick assessment of the current readiness of an organization for evaluation.[13]

Sharon Studer asks managers to consider several other factors before deciding whether an evaluation will be of use to a library. First, she stresses the personal factor in evaluation. Studer contends that evaluations are most successful when there is a commitment on the part of management to the process being used to make the assessment and agreement prior to its implementation as to how the results are to be reported. Second, Studer contends that there should be a clear understanding as to the kind of results that can be produced from the evaluation and how those results might potentially be used. Finally, this author argues that the organization must appreciate that the benefits to be gained from the evaluation will outweigh its anticipated cost prior to the start of the program if it is to enter into an evaluation wholeheartedly.[14] All of these considerations are critical to the potential success of an evaluation effort.

From the theories discussed above relating to change and evaluability, it can be seen that the success or failure of any evaluation must be judged in relation to the capacity of a library to absorb the results of that process. A number of factors have been isolated that relate to this capacity. For convenience, it is helpful to divide these factors into three groups—one relating to factors within the library at the time the evaluation takes place, a second relating to the way in which the process is carried out, and a third relating to the issues that are addressed during the course of the evaluation. First, consider those factors relating to the library that is being evaluated. As noted earlier, for an evaluation to have a reasonable chance for success, it must have the wholehearted support of the library director and, preferably, of the university administration as well. For this to happen, the director must be secure in the organization and must perceive that the library administration has the support of the university administration and the library staff. Additionally, that person must be comfortable with the idea that the library is changing. The organizational structure in which evaluation operates best is an open system where information is exchanged freely between managers and other staff members. People within the organization should be secure in the knowledge that their opinions are valued and that they have both the right and the obligation to express their views. It is best that the organization be one with a history of encouraging broad participation in decision making. It is also best if the management team does not have a great deal invested in existing programs of the library. For this reason, a major evaluation is most useful early in the tenure of a library director. Cooperation from other lower level administrators is also essential as is a willingness to participate at all levels of the library operation. Finally, it is absolutely essential that the library director have an understanding of the kinds of results that can be expected from the process and a commitment to implement those recommendations that can reasonably be applied to the library.[15]

An evaluation process must also have certain attributes if it is to produce useful results. Such a process must combine a system for gathering objective information in an orderly fashion with an appreciation of the political realities of the library. It must scrupulously protect those who give it information and insure that it maintains its fairness throughout. Information should be released systematically and predictably in accordance with agreements made at the beginning of the process. Progress reports as to where the process stands should be made available to managers in the system periodically, but the results of the study should not be made available until all of the evidence has been collected and analyzed. The data collection process should be as broadly based as possible. It should utilize all available sources for existing information and stress maximum participation on the part of the library staff in the search for new information. To be effective, evaluators must also have a good working relationship with library management. They must enjoy the confidence of the director and bring to the process an appreciation of the values of the library under examination. If the evaluation team comes from outside the library, it should be selected after careful consideration of the relative prestige of the individuals on it and the prestige of the institutions from which they come. If they are members of the library staff, care should be taken to insure that they are selected fairly and that they are compatible as a group with the library administration. Throughout the evaluation, emphasis should be placed on process and on potential uses of the results of the study. Throughout the assessment every effort should be made to hear all sides of the issues under study, and when the final report is filed care must be given to insure that it conforms to the values of the audience and speaks to the issues that concern those commissioning the study. Throughout an evaluation, efforts should be made to convince all participants that it is part of a long-term planning process designed to provide the kind of information that will contribute to the decision making process. Participants should also be made aware of the potential benefits that management expects to gain from the process, and it should be stressed throughout that those benefits will outweigh the cost of the study.[16]

The issues addressed within the context of an evaluation can also determine its potential utility. That is not to say that obvious problems should be glossed over in the final report of the evaluator. Rather, it stresses the importance of focusing the report on issues that are deemed important by the administration and behind which the support of the library staff and library users can be marshalled. Administrators will not address matters that do not concern them or that they consider trivial. Evaluation reports may convince them that a single issue that they have not previously considered or that they have chosen not to deal with is indeed important, but an overemphasis on matters that do not affect the overall capacity of the library to provide service or that are of minor importance in the context of the organization as a whole may weaken the impact of the study. The issues to address are those that can be expressed in terms that are understandable to the person commissioning the study and that affect that person directly. While a question concerning cataloging rules may be appropriate in a report to the library director, it is not necessarily going to impact on the opinions of an administrator outside the library who understands very little about a library beyond public services. Therefore, a report for an outsider might put more stress on collections and public services than one for in-house use. It is also helpful if the problems addressed can be stated in quantifiable terms. It is all right to say that a library has too few reference librarians or that it is woefully lacking in filmstrips, but it is far more effective if those shortages can be related either to standards of one sort or another or if norms can be established using like institutions against which the library can compare its statistics. It is also important that the library and university administration relate the changes that are recommended in the report to value structures with which they can reasonably expect to identify. Telling a regional university that it should do something because Harvard does it or because it is being done by a small liberal arts college is not likely to have the impact that can be expected by comparison with its primary rival. In short, the issues must be relevant, they must relate to the value structure of the university, and the solutions presented must be stated in terms that will be heard and understood by those who have the power to implement them.[17]

After the library has decided to undertake an evaluation, it is the responsibility of the administration to bring in the appropriate kind of evaluation team and to lay out a coordinated plan for the conduct of the program assessment. The choice of an evaluation process to be used should relate to factors identified in the evaluability assessment. It might include the importation of outside experts, the use of self-study teams from within the library or the university, or it might include some combination of the two. But whatever kind of team is used, ground rules should be established from the beginning outlining the process to be followed. It is critical that a contract in either written or oral form be negotiated before the evaluation begins laying out the parameters for the study. In this way, there can be mutual assurance between the administration and the evaluators as to what is expected of the process and how the assessment is to be done. This contract should include information about the time frame in which the survey is to be conducted and the limitations on data gathering that might be available to evaluators, and it should provide an outline of the reporting procedures to be followed during the study. On the one hand, this will serve to cement administrative confidence in the process, while, on the other, it will reinforce the commitment of the administration to allow the evaluator to work independently and objectively.[18]

As the evaluation begins, it is important to see the role that the evaluator plays in the process. A useful model for evaluator interaction is presented by Ronald Havelock as he posits the kind of roles that a change agent plays in an organization. These functions can be performed either by an outsider hired for the purpose or by someone working within the organization, and they are important for any evaluation. These roles, include a catalyst for change, a solution giver, a process helper and a resource linker. The role of the catalyst for change is one in which the evaluator serves to dislodge the *status quo ante* by asking questions that have not previously been asked or addressing issues that have been avoided. By opening new avenues for discussion and by broadening the decision making process, new questions can be addressed and nagging concerns can be brought into the open. In this way the real problems of the organization can be addressed.[19]

The role of the solution-giver is a bit more difficult. It is inevitable that people who chose to address problems are likely to bring to the discussion their own ideas as to how those problems might be solved. Since the evaluation process is designed to bring together all of the best opinions and information relating to an issue, this might be helpful. However, great care must be taken to insure that the pet theories of an outside evaluation are not applied arbitrarily to any problem found, or that the solution given by the loudest voice is not given precedence in discussions of the evaluation team. It is also important that alternative solutions should always be explored even if one is seen by the evaluators to be clearly superior to all others and that the final report of the committee should list those alternatives and the relative merits of each. Boxing in decision makers in the management structure of the university and the library can undermine the work of the committee, and providing options can add to the credibility of the report.[20]

Havelock viewed the role of process helper to be the most critical role to be played by the change agent, and this seems also to be the most important role for anyone heading an evaluation team. In this role, a person helps members of the organization to work through a process designed to identify needs, diagnose problems, set reasonable objectives, acquire data for decision making, develop options for meeting organizational needs, and selecting from among available options those that can most reasonably be implemented. The aim of this role is to assist the organization to develop through practice a problem-solving system and to integrate that system into the existing structure of the library.[21]

The final role envisioned by Havelock is that of the resource linker. Effective problem solving requires the bringing together of program needs and the resources that are required to meet those needs. The change agent in the person of the evaluator can use that position to convince the library administration and the general administration of the university of the validity of certain kinds of needs in the library. By developing the capacity of the organization to come together in its assessment of library problems and in support of reasonable solutions to those problems, political clout can be developed to bring in outside support in terms of funding. The evaluator can also serve to link the committee charged with the evaluation to expertise that is available elsewhere. In this way, the evaluator can insure that the evaluation program has the best possible chance of success.[22]

It should be understood that none of the roles Havelock envisioned for his change agent are exclusive. The evaluator is expected to serve each of the roles in the course of a study, and each role assists that person to succeed. Each is instrumental to the process, but the degree to which any or all of them are taken on depends on the particular circumstances in which the evaluation is performed.[23]

As noted above, the specific needs of the library and the circumstances in which it finds itself dictate the actual kind of evaluation that it needs to use at a given time. In some instances, it may be deemed appropriate to use an internal committee, while in others an outside evaluator may be more appropriate. Self-assessment is a useful technique in that it brings together people who are familiar with an organization to look at the organization. These people are likely to have a certain commitment to its success and certain insights into its operations. This process is also useful from a management standpoint, in that individuals can participate in the decision making of the library. This, in turn, can help build a consensus within the organization as to what its goals are and what its problems are. Self-study can also be used to orient new administrators and others in the organization, to open up the structure, and to nurture potential leaders within the organization. Above all, the use of internal staff and library users can communicate to the library's operation the concept of staff and user participation in decision making.[24]

There are drawbacks to this course of action, however. Individuals in an organization are generally viewed in a particular context within their environment, and it is often necessary for them to remove themselves from that context to function as good evaluators. Political pressures and peer perceptions often make this difficult, and this difficulty can damage the credibility of an evaluation. Library staffs may also not be able to bring to the process the kind of expertise that is required to properly evaluate more innovative programs. This is particularly true in those libraries in which the staff has not been active in the profession or on occasions when radical departures from standard operations are required. This lack of expertise can be transformed on occasion to a lack of imagination and limit the options that are placed before the final decision-maker.[25]

The use of an outside evaluator also has a place in the evaluation process. Professional evaluators bring to a situation an objectivity that is not likely to be found within the organization, and, since they are generally hired for specific skills, they can expand the vision of the organization considerably in their area of expertise. If the evaluator is hired for a capacity to develop the interpersonal skills within the library, that person can seek to build the kinds of process skills required for the evaluation. If the evaluator is hired for a knowledge of technical matters, that expertise can assist in developing within the library the capacity to assess reasonably potential changes that might be anticipated in that area of librarianship. External evaluation may also serve to link the library to others in the field who can assist it or serve as a model for it as the library looks to the future. A good consultant has broad concepts and broad experience, and those contacts can bring the library into touch with "state-of-the-art" information that it might not otherwise acquire.[26]

However, it should be noted that the use of external evaluators is not without its pitfalls. Evaluators tend to come with built-in prejudices and favorite solutions to organizational problems. They may seek to find problems that fit those solutions wherever they go, and, in general, outsiders tend to be more negative about situations than internal committees. This negativism can decrease the effectiveness of the overall evaluation effort. Another problem relates to the actual effect of an outsider coming into the organization. The outside evaluator represents a foreign element being introduced into the organization, and it is likely that some members of the library staff will view that person with suspicion. Much of the effectiveness of the process will rest squarely on the capacity of the consultant to overcome this suspicion and to work effectively with broad segments of the library staff.[27]

In general, it seems appropriate on most occasions for academic libraries to conduct their evaluations relying primarily on internal resources. Charging a committee under the chair of a librarian and including members from all segments of the library staff and various constituent groups outside of the library insures broad participation in the evaluation process. If the committee then feels the need for specific expertise, it might be wise to hire consultants to address the specific problems for which they are needed. In this way, the library can benefit from the best of both worlds.

But whether one chooses to rely on self-evaluation or on an outside expert, there are certain steps that should be followed to insure the effectiveness of the process. The need for establishing a relationship between the evaluator and the administration has already been discussed, so it seems most useful to say here only that the key to a successful evaluation may be the ability of the evaluator to establish a relationship with the library administration that will insure harmony and a nonthreatening atmosphere during the course of the evaluation, without forfeiting that person's credibility as an objective observer.[28]

Next the evaluator must make a diagnosis of the current situation within the organization. To do this, the person must first assemble information relating to the identity of the library, its environment, its folklore, its ideology, and its operations. This kind of data relates to what the library is, where it fits in the organizational structure of the university, its size, and its general organization. It is also useful at this time to look at the circumstances that have led to the initiation of the evaluation process. Information as to whether it was motivated internally or externally should be included, as should information as to how the results of the study are to used.[29]

Once this has been completed, information must be developed describing the structure of the library and the resources that are available to support its operations. Information about the formal organization of the library, its building and equipment, its financial support, and its staff should be included. It is also useful here to look at the communications network operating in the library and the informal structure of the library as it functions. Efforts should be made to trace the flow of information to see how it moves between the library administration and the staff; between the library and its users; and, most importantly, from the library to those responsible for funding its operation. This should include an inventory of those forces in and out of the library that exert influence in decision making and some study of various groups' perceptions of the operation. Information relating to the kinds of information that are available to the library, the mechanisms it has for acquiring that knowledge, and its capacity to get the information it needs through those devices is also critical.[30]

All of this relates to how a library operates internally, but a good evaluation also requires a thorough understanding of how the library fits into the context of the university. As a result, another information-gathering process must be used to see how it relates to its environment—that is, to its users, to those who provide its funding, and to those whose services compete with it for resources. Conditions that relate to the library's capacity to acquire and sustain support within the academic community should be included here. University-wide problems relating to retrenchment or the state of the economy or factors relating to the growth or decline of the funding base all should be discussed as part of this study. Another part of this has to do with the power structure both in the library and in the university as a whole. A thorough discussion of who exercises authority over the library and how the university power structure affects the library should be part of this consideration. Since the funding of the library depends in no small measure on its capacity to influence powers and pressure groups beyond itself, it is critical that it understand relationships in the broader university. In this way, it can identify those agencies that might reasonably support library initiatives.[31]

Once all of this information is collected, the evaluator must analyze the data and develop conclusions. Within the political context of the organization, that person should appraise the operations of the library, its impact on the community it serves, and the impact of that community on library operations. This should be done with an eye to identifying problems and developing alternative solutions to those problems. Once this is complete the evaluator should work with other members of the library staff and with the library administration to develop cost-benefit statements for each proposed solution. This can provide the basis for the administration's final analysis of the recommendations during the implementation stage of the process.[32]

After the diagnostic stage, it is imperative that the evaluation team work closely with the administration to implement the results of the evaluation where appropriate. The first part of this is the acquisition of the resources required to make the desired changes. This process actually begins as the alternative solutions are developed. Each should come with a price tag, and, as priority rankings are developed for the solutions, the relative cost-benefit effectiveness should be considered. Cost should include both the demand of the desired change on existing resources and new resources that might be required if it is implemented. As part of this process, an effort should also be made to assess the potential impact of the new service on library operations as a whole.[33]

At the point that the basic conclusions of the group have been developed, the evaluation team should meet with the library administration and work with it to find the necessary funds for implementation. This includes both internal negotiation for the shifting of library resources and assistance where possible in the director's negotiations with the university administration. This last step is a very delicate matter. On the one hand, the evaluator hopes to help the director get the funds needed for implementation, but, on the other, any inference that that person is trying to bypass the power structure may be ruinous to the process. The ultimate responsibility in this area rests with the library administration, and full implementation might take a long while. But somewhere early on, the evaluator and the library administration must determine what resources the library might reasonably expect to get to support change so that they might accurately assess the possiblity of implementing the various options. At this point, they should also determine how the evaluator can support the quest for those resources.[34]

From this point on, the process is in the hands of the library administration. While the actual diagnostic portion of the evaluator's work is done, the evaluation is not yet finished. Any evaluation is only as good as the portions of its recommendations that are actually implemented. Both the present health of the organization and the future capacity of the library to conduct evaluations depends on the willingness of the authorities to listen to assessments that have already been made. If the administrator chooses to ignore the recommendations of evaluators, few people will be willing to actively involve themselves in future efforts of this kind. As a result, it is incumbent on the library director to work with the group that was directly involved in the evaluation to choose which of the issues raised can reasonably be addressed, to work for the resources needed to address them, and to explain why other issues cannot or will not be dealt with at this time. In those areas where the solutions will be implemented, a priority list should be developed as to the order in which they will be addressed. After choosing the appropriate solutions from the lists offered by the people, efforts should be made to implement, validate, and incorporate those solutions into the standard operating procedures of the library.[35]

Once the solution to a problem is in place, the evaluation team can be of great help to the library administration in gaining acceptance for the change among both the library staff and library users. Instead of leaving the impression that one person is trying to impose a solution on the organization from the top, a perception can be developed that the solution was devised only after broad consultation. That perception can do much to gain acceptance for the measure and can help make the staff understand why the change took place. Then, a process of continuing evaluation of the results can lead to the routinization and integration of it into the normal procedures of the library. The successful implementation of specific changes can, in turn, assist in the development of faith in the evaluation process and lead to the development of a willingness to address organizational problems without the aid of a formal evaluation process. Success breeds success, and an understanding that one's work will have impact leaves an impression that people outside of the library hierarchy can contribute to the making of library policy, and that the evaluation process is worthwhile. This is the ultimate goal of any evaluation.[36]

The ideal evaluation process is an integrated one based on sound planning and understanding of the potential of evaluation in the particular situation in which the library finds itself. It should begin with the establishment of a good working relationship between the evaluators and the library administration and should include a method for acquiring all relevant data relating to the program being studied. Once this is completed the evaluator should assist in outlining and acquiring the resources required to implement various changes. The evaluation team can also be most helpful in getting the staff of the library to accept the changes that are put in place. Broad participation breeds a broad appreciation of the need for change, and this can enhance the willingness of people to accept specific innovations while whetting their appetite for more. The result should be better morale in the organization and an increased understanding of the mission of the library among the rank-and-file members of its staff.

One final word should be said about the ideal evaluation and its place in a library's operation. Evaluation is not or should not be an isolated event that takes place within the library every so often. Rather, it should be part of an integrated and continuing planning process carried out within the organization. H.R. Kells points out that much too often institutions are moved to look at themselves in a very formal and expensive way after which a few of the recommendations are implemented. Then the process stops, and the library proceeds about its business for a few years. Then the institution again requires an evaluation, and the process begins anew. Each time this happens, the library must start from scratch and develop new committees, new ground rules and new data collection procedures. And, since the skills learned in earlier processes have been ignored, it is likely that new skill levels will have to be developed. If, instead, the process is continued from evaluation through a planning mechanism to a second evaluation, much of the waste of the stop and start again approach can be avoided, and better information can be made available for decision making.[37]

While a discussion of an ideal evaluation is useful, no paper on the evaluation process would be complete without some comment on the kinds of evaluations that are being carried out within the library community. Libraries tend to use both outside consultants and inside evaluation teams at this time. In the 1930s and 1940s, one of the techniques that had a great vogue was the library survey. Some of these surveys were done in-house, but the more important and comprehensive ones were conducted by eminent librarians imported for the purpose. These consultants might address specific problems like inadequacies in the book collections, or they might address broad issues facing the library. The idea was that a library could bring in an expert who could then unearth problems within the organization with minimum of distress on day-to-day operations. A number of these surveys were conducted between 1935 and 1955 in major libraries throughout the United States, and they did have an impact on the management of library organizations. Wilson and Tauber contend that they did much to assist libraries to clarify their goals and objectives, to focus the attention of the university administration on the library and its problems, and to encourge the rationalization of library administration.[38] Ernst Erikson studied twenty of these surveys in 1958, and he came to similar conclusions. He found that 70 percent of the recommendations of the surveyors were actually implemented in host institutions.[39] Critics of the process charge that they were too bound up in a formula approach to evaluation for practical use, but few would argue that they have not been of some use.[40]

In more recent times, academic libraries have come to rely on consultants less for general studies of their organizations and more to meet specific information needs. Automation experts, experts on the new cataloging code, building consultants, and others are being hired regularly to meet specific needs. The process used in the general survey has largely been supplanted by self-study procedures modelled after Organizational Development programs. The most important of the recent developments in this area are the Management Review and Analysis Program (MRAP) and the Academic Library Development Program (ALDP). MRAP is a package developed by the Office of Management Studies of the Association of Research Libraries (OMS) working in conjunction with the management consulting firm of Booz, Allen, and Hamilton. It is designed to guide large university libraries through a systematic review of their management functions. This process grew out of a 1973 study of Columbia University's organization that combined elements of Organizational Development with the techniques of Action Research to develop a plan for library reorganization. From this study, OMS developed a highly structured manual designed to lead institutions with little experience or expertise in the use of these techniques through the process of evaluation with minimal outside assistance. In this way, the program hoped to minimize the cost of conducting a thorough analysis of library operations and to develop an evaluation program that could be used widely in the library community. This concept of assisted self-study was later adapted for use in smaller libraries as the ALDP. Reactions to this process have been mixed. Timothy Brown suggests that it should be understood when a process of this kind is initiated that MRAP advocates a particular management style and that it is expensive in terms of staff time and energy. Brown contends that it can only be effective when the library director and lower level managers are willing and competent to work with the kind of management structure that is likely to result. Success of the system depends entirely on the interpersonal skills, integrity, and cooperation of those people who actively participate in the process.[41]

As might be expected, the results that have come out of applications of MRAP have been mixed. Edward Johnson, Stuart Mann, and Carol Whiting found in their survey of ten MRAP participants that results at individual institutions varied widely. They discovered that, while an average of about 60 percent of the recommendations that emerged from these evaluations were implemented, the range of implementation went from a low of 10 percent to a high of 90. They found that there were wide differences of opinion both within individual libraries and between libraries as to the utility of the process. These three also discovered that there was little agreement anywhere as to what the process was supposed to accomplish or the degree to which it fulfilled the expectations of participants. In general, those who were less involved viewed it less favorably. In each case, the process led to some conflict, and this conflict made an overall assessment of the process difficult.[42]

This result is not surprising. Evaluations are highly individual affairs, and the success or failure of any application is dependent on a variety of local circumstances that do not generalize easily. Statistical measures applied to the results are often confusing. While it is clear that applications of this complex process has not been universally applauded, it has provided many people with experience in the analysis of library operations, has heightened the understanding of modern management techniques in the library community, and has led to some adjustments in library organizations.

Another kind of self-evaluation used in academic libraries are those that are undertaken as part of the accreditation processes through which every institution must pass. Specialized accreditation visits like those conducted in business schools, teacher education, and engineering generally require only a study of library collections relevant to their areas of interest. However, more formal work is required of law and medical libraries, and, when the regional associations conduct their decennial studies of institutions of higher education, the library tends to get substantial treatment. All of the accrediting associations devote a standard to the library, and many include a librarian on the visiting team that comes to campus as part of the process. While the degree to which this process is taken seriously varies widely from region to region and from institution to institution within each region, it is clear that an accreditation self-study can provide the impetus for a thorough review of library programs within the context of the university.[43]

The procedure under which the regional associations operate are similar in form. Every ten years institutions are required to undergo a formal review of their programs to retain their status as accredited institutions. When the time comes, the associations instruct the institution to conduct a self-study relating the goals and programs of the university to its standards. The effort expended on this study varies widely. At one institution, the university community might be divided into a dozen or more committees, each of which works to develop a portion of the final report. The result might be done in the president's office, and, while the result might be equally long, the impact of the process is likely to be very limited. The same kind of variation can be expected in that portion of the study that is devoted to the university library. At one institution, virtually every librarian may get a chance to contribute to the self-study process, and separate committees may be formed among library staff and general university faculty to consider the status of the university library. At another, the library director may write that portion of the self-study himself or have it written in his office, or the study of the library may be done in the university's research office with only minimal consultation with the library director and his staff. Once the self-study is completed, a visiting team is appointed by the regional agency to come to the campus to validate its results. The composition of this team varies. In the Southern Association, for instance, the team includes one member to evaluate each functional unit of the university, including a library director to study the library. In the North Central Association, the team is very small, and each of the team members must evaluate a number of functional areas. Librarians are seldom appointed to these teams. The visitation normally lasts three days, and, at the end of that period, a report is completed and forwarded to the headquarters of the association. That report then provides the basis for the continuation of the accreditation of an institution.[44]

The success or failure of the accreditation process to serve as an agent of change depends largely on the degree to which the self-study conforms to the evaluation process outlined above and to the theory of Organizational Development. Its success in this area varies widely from institution to institution, and it is clear that its standards cannot change this situation. Standards that are designed to apply to the University of Illinois and Monmouth College under one umbrella are not likely to be closely quantified or likely to define what is required to support a standard institution of higher education. But if one supports the idea that diversity is one of the major strengths among colleges and universities in the United States, then tightened controls may not be considered desirable or even useful. The accrediting agencies see themselves more as agents of change than enforcers of standards, and, in a more mature state, that may be precisely what most institutions of higher education need them to be. While they may disaccredit institutions that clearly are out of step with the mainstream of higher education, it is always understood that the vast majority of those institutions visited will retain their accreditation. As a result the best that can be hoped for is that an institution will look at itself honestly and then move to correct those problems it finds during that inspection.[45]

Accreditation is coming under increasing fire in recent months. As critics of higher education call for increased accountability in colleges and universities, the inconsistencies of this kind of evaluation have caused concern. However, as indicated earlier, evaluation processes are always likely to be inconsistent. While accreditation does not provide all of the answers, it does provide an opportunity for the library to examine itself within the context of the university as a whole. Even with its shortcomings, the process has, in the words of John Dale Russell "been responsible for enormous improvement in the quality of higher education in this country."[46]

An overall assessment of the evaluation process and the capacity of that process to develop the capacity of a library to adapt to changing situations is most difficult. It is easy enough to find in any institution positive effects from these processes, but it is just as possible to find evidence of their failures. The only thing that seems clear about evaluation as a whole is that it is an extremely complex process and that its success depends in large measure on whether the leadership of the organization to which the process is being applied understands it, is sympathetic to its purposes, and has the resources required to implement its recommendations. For evaluation to succeed, an openness in administrative style in the organization and a willingness to change is required for success, and these are often lacking in library administrations. It is clear that librarians and those who study libraries are not familiar enough with evaluative processes to make them work at peak effectiveness, but it is also true that the options available in the broader community of program evaluation are remarkably few. Further development in this area beyond an almost total reliance on Organizational Development and its offshoots is required if the library and its parent institution are to be truly accountable to their public. The movement away from the use of evaluation as a quality assurance device has been useful in times when academic institutions were expanding, but it is not yet clear whether this emphasis will serve the needs of higher education when it faces retrenchment. But even if the policy function requires strengthening in the future, the requirement for every organization to understand the need for the capacity to change will remain. And, as long as the requirements remain for developing this capacity and for providing mechanisms to assure the accountability of higher education, libraries will be called upon to evaluate themselves if they hope to compete in the academic setting.

NOTES AND REFERENCES

1. Eugene C. Olling, Charles W. Cole, "Methodologies and Instrumentation in Evaluations," *New Directions for Student Services* I (1978):36.

2. J. Victor Baldridge, "Organizational Change: the Human Relations Perspective versus the Political Systems Perspective," *Educational Researcher* I (1972):4–7.

3. David D. Dill and Charles P. Friedman, "An Analysis of Frameworks for Research on Innovation and Change in Higher Education," *Review of Educational Research* 49 (1979):411–18.

4. See Jerald Hage and Michael Aiken, *Social Change in Complex Organizations* (New York: Random House, 1970), and Gerald Zaltman, Robert Duncan, and Jonny Holbek, *Innovations and Organizations* (New York, 1973).

5. See E. M. Rogers, *Diffusion of Innovation* (Glencoe, Ill.: Free Press, 1962).

6. See J. Victor Baldridge, "Managerial Innovation: Rules for Successful Implementation," *Journal of Higher Education* 51 (1980):117–134, and Jack Lindquist, *Strategies for Change* (Berkeley, Cal.: Pacific Soundings Press, 1968).

7. Baldridge, "Managerial Innovation," p. 133.

8. See Ronald G. Havelock, *The Change Agents' Guide to Innovation in Education* (Englewood Cliffs, N.J.: Educational Technology Publications, 1973).

9. Ibid.

10. Egon Guba, "The Failure of Educational Evaluation," in *Evaluation of Education* (Englewood Cliffs, N.J.: Educational Technology Publications, 1973), pp. 1–9.

11. Joseph Wholey, *Evaluation: Promise and Performance* (Washington, D.C.: Urban Institute, 1979), pp. 49–76.

12. Ibid., p. 76.

13. Howard Davis and Susan Salasin, "The Utilization of Evaluation," in Elmer L. Struening and Marcia Guttentag, eds., *Handbook of Evaluation Research* 2 (Beverly Hills: Sage, 1975):621–666.

14. Sharon Studer, "Evaluative Need Assessments: Can They Make Evaluation Work?" *The Bureaucrat* 9 (1980):20.

15. See Dill and Friedman.

16. Ibid.

17. Ibid.

18. Havelock, pp. 43–63.

19. Ibid., p. 8.

20. Ibid., p. 9.

21. Ibid., p. 9.

22. Ibid., p. 9.

23. Ibid., p. 10.

24. Paul L. Dressel, "Accreditation and Institutional Self-Study," *North Central Association Quarterly* 46 (1971):286.

25. Havelock, p. 51.

26. Robert Perloff, "Evaluator Intervention: The Case for and Against," in his *Evaluator Interventions: Pros and Cons* (Beverly Hills: Sage, 1979), pp. 112–113.

27. Ibid., pp. 114–116.

28. Havelock, pp. 43–63.

29. Harry Levinson, *Organizational Diagnosis* (Cambridge: Harvard University Press, 1972), pp. 6666–92.

30. Ibid., pp. 95–169.

31. Ibid., pp. 172–247.

32. Ibid., pp. 352–365.

33. Peter H. Rossi, Howard E. Freeman, and Sonia R. Wright, *Evaluation: A Systematic Approach* (Beverly Hills: Sage, 1979), pp. 299–302.

34. Havelock, pp. 77–96.

35. Ibid., pp. 97–110.

36. Ibid., pp. 111–140.

37. H. R. Kells, *Self-Study Processes: A Guide for Postsecondary Institutions*, (Washington, D.C.: American Council on Education, 1980).

38. Louis Round Wilson and Maurice Tauber, *The University Library*, 2d ed. (New York: Columbia University Press, 1956), pp. 558–580.

39. Ernst W. Erikson, "College and University Survey, 1938–1952," Ph.D. dissertation, University of Illinois, 1958.

40.   Wilson, pp. 579–580.

41.   Michael K. Buckland, ed., The Management Review and Analysis Program, *Journal of Academic Librarianship* 1 (1976):4–13.

42.   Edward R. Johnson, Stuart Mann, and Carol Whiting, *An Assessment of the Management Review and Analysis Program (MRAP)* (University Park: Pennsylvania State University, 1977).

43.   Kenneth E. Young. "An Overview of the Accrediting Process," in Julie Carroll Virgo and David Alan Yuro, eds., *Libraries and Accreditation in Institutions of Higher Education* (Chicago: Association of College and Research Libraries, 1981), pp. 3–8.

44.   George M. Bailey, "Evaluation of Libraries in the Accrediting Process from the Standpoint of the Library," in Julie Carroll Virgo and David Alan Yuro, eds., *Libraries and Accreditation in Institutions of Higher Education* (Chicago: Association of Research Libraries, 1981), pp. 61–62.

45.   Dressel, pp. 283–284.

46.   John Dale Russell, "The Accrediting of Institutions of Higher Education," *Journal of Teacher Education* 1 (1950):83–93.

TOWARD A
RECONCEPTUALIZATION OF
COLLECTION DEVELOPMENT

Charles B. Osburn

INTRODUCTION

The library profession's view of collection development has undergone substantial change in recent years, and along with that transition the essential concepts embodied loosely by collection development are also evolving quite rapidly. For the purpose of this essay, collection development can be defined as a public service system, characterized by a process of decision making to determine the desirability of acquiring or retaining library materials. This definition will be analyzed elsewhere in the paper.

It is noteworthy that the term "collection development" is rather recent in the history of librarianship, having been in vogue only within the

Advances in Library Administration and Organization, volume 2, pages 175–198.
Copyright © 1983 by JAI Press Inc.
All rights of reproduction in any form reserved.
ISBN: 0-89232-214-4

past twenty years. Within the past ten of those years, moreover, the term has been modified to "collection management" in recognition of the full range of activities incorporated in the process and in recognition of new concepts attributable to the process. Clearly, the profession is now coming to grips with this aspect of its responsibilities, which evidently resembles the essence of the profession so closely that it was able to evolve with relatively little notice, almost as though taken for granted.

The literature of collection development, once so scant as to suggest that it was not an appropriate concern of librarianship, is now taking shape. Annual reviews of the literature and of activities are available (Magrill, 1980). Guidelines on a number of aspects of collection development are being promulgated through the American Library Association (Perkins). The national organization has taken the lead, followed by regional and local organizations, in mounting continuing education programs focused on collection development. Although a few books have been available on the selection function of collection development, it was not until 1980 that a manual was published (Stueart, 1980), in the form of a compendium of essays, each by a practitioner.

This flurry of activity during the past decade is an expression of the library profession's awareness of deep-rooted change in the making for libraries. Librarianship is in a quandary over the breadth and depth of events touching its profession now, as the future is absorbed at a great pace by the present. Among the chief concerns of collection development are many that the entire profession finds unsettling, and this can readily be interpreted as a sign that collection development is being judged central to library operations and pivotal in library/community relations. Indeed, it may well be that the single most difficult challenge to the field in the next five or ten years will reside in an adaptation to a greater scope of responsibilities.

Of immediate concern to collection development is the declining purchasing power of the acquisitions budget, and even if that problem should have subsided by the time the present paper is published, the cumulative problem of a dozen years will have to be addressed. Reconciling policy and goals for collection development with the fiscal realities of a dozen years then becomes a separate, but related problem. Yet, a myriad of changes not heretofore of evident relevance to collection development also now present themselves in a stark, uncompromising fashion. Along with the advancement of technology, especially in the area of communications, we must now also consider the notions and implications of a paperless society, as though the former did not constitute enough change on its own. Linked to these developments is the likelihood of powerful competition with other services or agencies in the rapidly growing information industry. What kinds of services will libraries provide in this environment and, therefore, which information sources will they "collect?'' In terms of collection development policy, how will these information sources mesh with others or replace others? What, in fact, will be the role of the book?

It seems that, almost simultaneously, other elements of essential change are emerging to place still more pressure on collection development. Of particular importance to research libraries, but also of general concern, is the heightened level of consciousness nationally, directed at the importance of preservation of the materials libraries determine to acquire and determine to retain. Related to all of these elements of change is the attention being given to an understanding of the appropriate roles to be assumed by the federal government and other organizations in the planning of library and information services and cooperation. In view of these weighty considerations for libraries, generally, and collection development, more specifically, it is both logical and fortunate, perhaps, that this age is also witnessing an increasingly intensive, broadening, and influential demand for the accountability of service agencies, and that this demand is coming from the public, not just from parent organization administrators. If those responsible for collection development fail to understand how this pressure applies to collection development, then libraries, in the larger sense, are sure to lose in the competition with other agencies and society, in consequence, will suffer a great loss.

Much is at stake in the directions that collection development will choose in the next few years. Indeed, it is critical that directions be chosen, not just followed without design, for they have direct bearing on the functions, goals, and mission of libraries. In that regard, it is especially noteworthy that the common basis for response to all the elements of change outlined above can be found in the inherent dynamism of a properly used collection development policy. That document is the symbolic nucleus of a system joining the information universe, the library, and the community.

This is not intended to be a comprehensive review of the literature of collection development. Instead, it is both an assessment of what seems to be the current dominant thinking about the role of collection development in a changing environment, and an effort to pave the way for a necessary rethinking of the basic concepts of collection development. An emphasis on large academic libraries is a bias of the author's own experience, but it also reflects emphases in the literature and in national developments. The broader concepts should be generally applicable.

THE ENVIRONMENT OF COLLECTION DEVELOPMENT

Traditionally, a chief contributor to the environment of collection development has been the publishing industry, with reference to books, journals, and newspapers, primarily. This is the sector that determines what will become selection decisions in libraries through both the price setting and quota setting policies of the industry it also determines the impact on acquisitions budgets. Little needs to be said about the so-called publication explosion of the past thirty-five years or about the tremendous rate of price increases of published materials in the past dozen years, because both are quite well within common knowledge these days. These events lead to the conclusion that society has a growing interest in information and, in fact, the idea that we live in an "information age" does stem from the concept of information as a commodity in great demand by diverse groups and individuals. One reason for this is the speed at which the conditions of life have been changing, as technology forces attention on efficiency and productivity, while always developing itself beyond the sociological capabilities of its full consumption or comprehension by society at any given time. The focus of society is less on the past, increasingly intensive on the future, with the present always slipping away. These characteristics of society, which is the collective library patron, have been treated here with sweeping generalizations, to be sure. But they do constitute a major environmental change to which collection development must adapt.

Technology must be considered at least for library purposes, not merely a product of its environment, but rather as a condition of the environment. That is because technology has so influenced the expectations of society that it is assumed that what is possible for the library to do, it should do, and whatever materials exist, the library should be able to provide. A key environmental factor for collection development, therefore, is a high level of public expectation.

It is this high level of expectation that has made way for an evolution in the basis of library operation and services that has accelerated, especially in the past four or five decades. That is, the evolution from a book-centered service to a journal-centered service to a technology-centered service. The suggestion here is not that books are excluded from the latter two eras or that books or journals will necessarily be excluded from the era of the technology-centered library, but rather that the emphasis is on one or the other as the evolution takes place. We have witnessed the growing importance of periodical literature and the reasons for that are clear: societal interest in current events (whether for scholarly or recreational purposes), societal interest in forecasting events based on current activity, and raised expectations for the likelihood of having this material because the means to provide it exist. The book is not supplanted in the journal-centered era, only its proportion of the total reading activity shrinks. This is an environmental factor of immense significance to collection development in the execution of policy.

It appears that we are, or will soon be, evolving into the era of the technology-centered library. This will mean the availability of a new, very broad range of information sources that may replace or duplicate others or that will be unique. Some may be competitive in the same format but offered by different vendors with some variations. The technology-centered library will not have to maintain its entire array of book format materials because necessary parts of them or even books in their entirety, may be easily retrievable in copy from some other library as a service of the technology. Because the public will have some familiarity with the power of technology and with the kinds of information in existence, their expectations for library service will be conditioned. These expectations will be factors in the environment of collection development, which, as we enter the technology-centered era of libraries, will be made extremely complex by the variety of materials and services available to meet the needs of the public, and by the range of options incorporated in the process of decision making.

The environment of collection development is defined ultimately by the community to be served by the individual library. Expectations, however they may derive, represent one major influence on the community's relationship to the library and collection development. The other form of environmental control exerted by the community is the stimulus that causes individuals in the community to have need of whatever materials and services might be available in the library. This is a question of the values and thought processes held by individuals and, collectively, by the community that stimulate interest in learning or reading for any reason. These values and thought processes change, and it is most important that collection development be sensitive to these changes and that policy be adapted to meet the needs stimulated by changing values and thought processes.

Although it never has been quite clear, there is a direct connection between the values and thought processes of the community as an environmental factor for collection development, and the idea of accountability of the library toward the community. Not only has this connection not been clear, it very likely has been obscured, purposely. The common scenario is that the community places its trust in the library to act in the community's best interests, yet does not inform the library about those interests. This is no great matter to the library, which has established its own professional standards of efficiency and effectiveness, of least importance among which would be a process to maintain surveillance over the interests and thought processes of the community.

As libraries move into an age conditioned by a thirst for information and raised expectations for service, it is logical that a dominant environmental factor for collection development will be that of accountability to the community. There already has been plenty of evidence that society is demanding more accountability from public, and even private, enterprises. This has largely been on the basis of costs. Beyond costs, however, there seem to be sufficient substantive reasons for the public to be even more demanding of libraries in the near future. The trust conferred upon libraries by the public will be tested as it never has been before.

THE FUNCTIONS AND ORGANIZATION OF COLLECTION DEVELOPMENT

Owing largely to the professionalization of librarianship, collection development has established itself as a distinguishable function in libraries, with its own distinguishable organization. This professionalization has also brought with it what could be termed an overlay of mystique, in conjunction with its own canon, derived primarily from within the confines of the collection development coterie. A sense of protectiveness is not unusual in professions, in delineating areas of competency and authority. Taking this trend a step further, however, the goal of maintaining a professional preserve evolved into a mechanism of defense against questioning from outside the designated collection development area, whether from elsewhere within the library or from outside the library. In some libraries, particularly large academic libraries, the trajectory of this professionally inspired movement led dangerously close to stasis in a function that should be the most dynamic of library enterprises. Perhaps because the sense of identity and common purpose among those responsible for collection development is a relatively recent turn in the events of librarianship, collection development is now beginning to look outward, in recognition that it is by no means disassociated from the whole library and the whole community.

In terms of its place within the organization, a constant nagging problem of collection development has been its projected image as a "soft" area. Measurable standards have been established for functions such as cataloging, binding, acquisitions, circulation, even reference. In the latter example, activities are measurable as hours of desk duty assigned per week and the experienced norms of numbers and categories of questions answered in the course of a month or a year. No similar standards for collection development exist; moreover, it is a function that has been regarded as one taking place behind the scenes, therefore, insignificant in visibility. It is worth noting in this connection that in many libraries the chief responsibility for collection development resides in the traditional technical services division, not in the traditional public service division of the library. Projecting the image of a soft area has meant for collection development that it is the activity that can be foregone or delayed when one of the more normalized or visible activities requires additional attention. As long as this situation obtains, it will be impossible for the larger organization, as well as for individual librarians, to set realizable goals and implementable priorities. Obviously, with the degree of change—at the heart of which will be collection development—libraries will experience in the next two decades, standards comprehensible to the general profession will have to be established for collection development as an organized activity. These will be discussed below.

It seems to be fairly well assumed in the profession of librarianship that the increased dependence upon technology in the library will bring about a substantial change in the configuration of staffing, overall. Although a precise description of likely change in staffing patterns would be highly speculative, if not pure guesswork at this time, it at least seems evident that the shift will be into the public service areas. Derek J. De Solla Price, long a student of the influence of technological change, observes that high technology does not merely do an old job better, "New products imply the generation of new markets that have not yet been perceived" (De Solla Price, 1979). He uses the word "markets" in a most liberal sense, however, because his examples suggest tasks that can be performed by increasingly sophisticated technology as well as the creation of functions in the organization that lead to a whole new enterprise and category of worker in the organization, the attraction of new categories of consumers of products and services, and the adoption of new habits among consumers. While we cannot now divine the best translation of these likely kinds of changes into specific library and library-related services, operations, or responsibilities, it is fairly safe to assume that these changes are ramifications of the role assumed by the library in bringing together the information universe and the community. Central to that role is collection development, whose functions and organization will have to be sensitive to and adaptable to change in the spheres it is charged to reconcile.

At the same time that collection development will be responsible for integrating new forms of information into the policy for development of resources, it will also bear a large part of the responsibility for determining which of the traditional materials must be preserved for posterity. The decision will be more than one of local impact, for it will require, in many instances, consultation of some larger policy on preservation, of regional or national scope. It is quite possible that the decisions about preservation will prove, in the long term, to be the most consequential for service to the community. Surely, as a larger proportion of the library information resources are represented in some format other than the traditional book, journal, or microform, the value of those traditional materials will be more greatly appreciated than ever before. The massive investment they have demanded cumulatively, not to mention their massive accumulation of knowledge and experience, already seems to be a more broadly shared concern among librarians and the informed public than ever before. How collection development will organize itself to determine which items need to be retained through preservation methods remains to be seen, but an obvious tool in arriving at these decisions will be the computer, which will facilitate communication about pertinent preservation decisions elsewhere in the nation.

It has been primarily within the past decade that collection development librarians have begun to sense keenly the connection among funding levels, purchasing power, expressed community needs, and selection decisions. This heightened awareness and the determination to gain control over a complex set of conditions have led to the understanding of collection development as a central management function. Collection development does seem now to be understood as a process of establishing priorities that will allow the most effective use of a budget in achieving predetermined goals, both long-term and short-term. Related to that function is the presentation of a request for a budget whose rationale is explained through commonly held expectations for the library and its community, in the context of knowledge of the relevant parts of the information universe. This already complex task will become even more so as the range of information resources broadens, of course, and as that expanding range of resources stimulates otherwise latent community interest. If it is logical that collection development should assume the responsibility for budget formulation on the bases of the kinds of information suggested as prerequisite, above, does it then not follow that those librarians are also the best equipped to condition the community, whence flows fiscal support, about the aspirations and limitations of the library? More will be said about this below.

ATTITUDES TOWARD AND WITHIN COLLECTION DEVELOPMENT

It is difficult to know whether a theory of collection development should be extractable from a theory of librarianship or whether the reverse should be true. No matter, for the profession is in need of both if it is to understand itself, present itself well to the public, and successfully meet the imminent challenge of change. A very strong argument could be made that the theory of librarianship does reside in an undiscovered theory of collection development, and that the tardiness of the profession to address collection development matters per se is directly responsible for its inability thus far to arrive at a satisfactory theory of librarianship. Although the present paper is not intended to advance a comprehensive theory for collection development, a few notions mentioned above do support the basis for theory: among them is the suggestion that collection development is central to library operations and pivotal in library/community relations. If this is a fundamental concept that could be embodied in a theory of collection development, then it will be important to note the value of less introspection than has been characteristic of collection development. Collection development must be a very outward looking process, and this requirement will most likely become even more evident in the future, as the nature of the universe of information changes, as internal potential for services expands, and as community expectations rise.

This trend runs counter to the traditional pattern of behavior of librarians within their organizations and communities, which is one of maintenance of a low profile. Subservience may be the word that best describes the spirit underlying the desire to maintain a low profile, and it probably derives from an inculcation of the concept of service in the profession, at a time when the primary library clientele represented a certain kind of elite concerned with self-betterment. What we are now able to surmise about the future indicates that libraries will be used for many other reasons because information is beginning to be viewed as, and used as, a commodity. Service no longer need be considered, indeed, no longer can be considered by librarians in the sense of subservience. While the self-image of librarians, and even the image perceived by the public, may be evolving slowly toward a better approximation of reality, success in the future will depend upon librarians' assumption of the role of information and service brokers rather than continuation in the role of maintainers of an intellectual utility. It is up to the collection development librarians, foremost, to lead in this movement toward the adoption of a new role and the establishment of a new image, since their processes are central internally and pivotal externally. If the role of information and service broker is not assumed by collection development librarians, it will be by other professions, and librarians will continue to be responsible only for maintenance of an intellectual utility, subordinate to the other group.

There has been much debate and much written about the evaluation of collections, which places the emphasis on methodology rather than on concern about purpose and expectation. Often, evaluation of this kind is impeded by a desire for perfection in methodology, a desire that probably is flawed by a strong sense of professionalism, sometimes misdirected. The desire for perfection also serves as a defensive *caveat*, of course. Already the attention to evaluation of collections, coming as late as it did in the history of librarianship, and in spite of its noble intentions, is becoming an anachronism. This is because the definition of collections must increasingly include in scope a range of information sources and services other than those traditionally considered part of the collection. The better word might simply be resources. Clearly, the collection development librarian must "know the collection," to cite one of the more unsettling platitudes of the collection development business. But this increasingly means having knowledge not just of the paper-based collection, but also of its interrelationship with other sources and services, making even more difficult the bases of comparison and measurement for purposes of evaluation.

More significant than collection or resources evaluation, now and in the future, is evaluation of the process of collection development and of specific performance within the process. Assuming that intelligent, conscientious librarians are involved in the process, a better understanding of collection development can surely be drawn from the monitoring and evaluation of a process that has been designed to achieve predetermined results. These results are more likely to be qualitative than quantitative, and the evaluation would reflect that feature. The process ought also be more understandable to the layman than would be the entire collection. Unfortunately, the design of a process for collection development presently is only in its earliest stage, because attention in collection development has most often been directed inward, toward the collection, rather than outward toward the community and the rest of the library.

This emphasis has evolved historically because the library is viewed as a great conservator force, and rightly so. Moreover, the conservator role has been espoused quite comfortably by the library profession, which traditionally has chosen to adopt a low profile, as observed previously. However, the justification for fulfilling a conservator role in libraries has become overshadowed, if not totally obscured, by a hollow desire to fulfill that role. The justification for conserving the products of humankind's intellect must surely be that of providing continuity for the stable development of the human race. This kind of continuity, which implies an active social role for the library, is even more essential to society as change occurs more and more rapidly. Consequently, the reasons behind the natural conservator role of libraries must now be emphasized so as to serve as the context in which collection development takes its place more aggressively in joining the library and the community.

GOALS OF COLLECTION DEVELOPMENT

Collection development took a giant step toward maturity when it recognized that, even in the largest of libraries, the collections cannot be expected to meet all needs. The overall goal, then, would be to select and retain materials against an established set of criteria, in the order of a plan. Once the decision was made, the ambivalence caused by a desire to meet daily, unanticipated needs and the conflicting desire to build collections, according to a preconceived notion of what a collection should be, came into play. This is the service versus collections syndrome, known most commonly in large academic libraries. Although a shift toward the idea of collection development as a service constitutes a major change in thinking, the concept of service as a goal remains ambiguous. To clarify it is to determine whom is to be served and how. Implicit in the clarification of the concept of service and its application in a given library setting is the development of a process. Again, it is the shift of emphasis from collection-oriented goals, eventually to process-oriented goals that will permit collection development to function most successfully in the future.

POLICY AND SELECTION CRITERIA

Working in close conjunction with process in collection development is policy for collection development. Recently, the design of policy has been a major issue within the profession, and appropriately so, because the resultant policy document holds great potential value in the process of collection development. While it is a safe bet that libraries for many years have maintained written statements of policy on a variety of library matters, it is singularly strange that attention to policy on the central matter of collection development had to wait so long. Among the characteristics of a policy statement are that it guides relatively predictable development of resources, it is an important instrument for training new collection development librarians, it assists in the design of a rational budget request and allocation, it becomes a central planning tool both in the library and in the community and, above all, it is an excellent basis for communications within the library and within the community. The process of creating and revising the policy can, of itself, be a most educational exercise for everyone involved, while the finished document can be a constant stimulus to the larger collection development process.

A policy does not relieve librarians of responsibility; on the contrary, it tends to place higher demands on librarians. For example, greater accountability, enhanced public relations and communications, and greater rationality in the development of collections should be direct results of the adoption of a vital collection development policy. In the most practical sense, a policy on collection development defines in local terms what is meant by selectivity, and it implies, therefore, if it does not make explicit, a definition of the collection development realm that is susceptible to cooperative programs. Given a level of local fiscal resources, one proceeds from an identification of a core collection of immediate need to the community and moves toward an identification of the next range of materials that can be provided through means other than local ownership. With the decreasing influence of the importance of ownership of materials in most libraries and the influence of the importance of establishing self-sufficiency, particularly in large academic libraries, collection development policy can serve as the instrument through which the integration of both nonbook information services and library cooperative programs can be achieved.

Essential to the rationality of collection development in the future will be the definition of core collection in terms and parameters that are commonly understood in the community. The purpose of developing, through policy, the definition of core collection is to enable the integration of local policy into a more general or complementary policy on collection development, established through a plan for regional or national cooperation. The core concept will have to embody not just the traditional book format materials, but also, increasingly in the future, it will have to refer to other information sources and services that become available through technology. To what extent technological advancement will lead to overlap in these kinds of services and those provided through cooperative library enterprises, and whether that will make any difference at all, remains to be seen. In any case, the policy of the cooperative will be informed by the needs expressed by member institutions through the medium of individual policies defining core collection; and core collection policy must be informed by an understanding of the values, habits, and expectations of the community. In that regard, the local core collection will probably comprise those elements that furnish the greatest daily service requirements of the community, plus those elements which historically have developed to create the individual identity of the library or to reflect an inherent aspect of continuity in the community.

The collection development policy that will have to emerge from the influx of technology-based information service joining with the need to establish a rational approach to cooperation will be immediately conducive to the integration of many media into our thinking about collection development and service. For example, the videodisc may help bridge the gulf that traditionally has separated book people and media people, because its format is a familiar one, while it also is capable of storing for easy retrieval a great variety of conventional, as well as innovative information.

This raises, again, the question of standards for collection development, which heretofore have been quantitative, if they have been in evidence at all. The basis of these quantitative standards has been local ownership, but this will have to become less important as the influence of technology as a medium for the location and retrieval of both information and documents becomes more forceful. Consequently, the basis for the invocation of qualitative standards can appropriately be assumed by collection development policy, for it is the documentary interpretation of the relationship between collection development performance and collection development standards. Again, this is a reference to the evaluation of collection development as a service, rather than simply to the evaluation of collections. In this new environment, it is most likely that, while the process of the collection development service will truly be the dynamic force behind policy, the implementation and maintenance of policy will be, at the same time, the driving agents of the process linking the community, the knowledge universe, and the library. The most meaningful standards, then, will be those that are applicable to the relationship between the process of collection development and the policy for collection development in terms of quality control.

Quality control of this type will probably have to take the form of a measurement of the capacity for service, rather than an evaluation of individual service. Similarly, evaluation will very likely be most productive if it is of the mechanisms for dialogue between library and community rather than of specific information sources acquired. If there are specific objects of quality control in this scheme, they would be a policy that is advocated by the community and implemented by the library, and a community that understands its participatory role in policy design.

THE COMMUNITY

It has always been somewhat of a platitude in collection development that the best guide to proper selection of books is to know one's community. Although this axiom has not been debated seriously, neither is there evidence to suggest that it has been heeded seriously, and it seems that a library's understanding of its community is going to be far more important, if not essential, to successful operations in the future. The overall record of collection development in this regard is one of independence, not of collaboration, and this has been a fairly successful mode, owing to reasonably adequate funding levels, to a naive sense that those who use libraries can manage on their own and communicate their wishes, and to the fact that alternative formats and substitute formats of information were very limited. It is now becoming clear that libraries must do more than just be responsive to a select clientele, they must become important to the community as a whole. Otherwise, our profession is told repeatedly, the library can become an anachronistic appendage to society, instead of the culturally vital social organ the profession would like it to be.

In a corporate setting, it is not uncommon for the business or industrial library to be whittled to bare bones one year, rebuilt and restaffed shortly later, only to experience the downside of the cycle again. There really are essentially only two differences between this kind of library and any other, except the private library, and they are the difference in size and scope of both library and community, and the question of utility or cost benefit applied by the community to the library in the corporate setting. While the latter has been the key difference, the other communities, whether academic or public, are becoming more conscious of benefits to be achieved as a result of costs, more conscious of priority establishment, and more conscious of community ownership and accountability to the community. Consequently, since, like the library in the corporate setting, other libraries depend upon their communities for support, the future of libraries does hinge very definitely on the priority and importance assigned to them by their respective communities. The divergence of library and community has been abetted almost systematically by the low profile maintained by librarianship, by the introspection and narrowness that accompanies professionalization, and by common belief in the goodness and necessity of libraries. Professions no longer go unchallenged by society, however, any more than traditional values go unquestioned. For these reasons, alone, each library will be better off for defining its community, trying to understand it, and demonstrating to it the value that can be expected of the library.

One element that will almost certainly begin to confuse the already complex relationship between library and community is the idea of information as a commodity. This concept will continue to be fostered by the abundance of information, the variety of its packages, the dependence and increasing premium placed upon it in a society whose most pronounced feature is change, and by the recognition that the development of a pricing structure for information seems to be an inevitability. It is true that the idea of charging library patrons for certain kinds of service is not at all new. What will be new, however, will be the great proportion of information services for which charges will be levied and the scope of subjects they will include. Moreover, the notion of information as a commodity suggests competition in an open marketplace, competition between the public sector and the private sector, and the risks of monopoly, of commodity control, and of failure in the marketplace. These are new concepts for libraries to comprehend, just as they are for the public, at least insofar as they refer to information and involve libraries.

At the present time, it is difficult, if not impossible, to determine how all of these elements of change will be sorted out in the future, and it seems unlikely that federal legislation, like a *deus ex machina*, will help clarify roles in a timely fashion. Rather, it would better be the public that determines the costs it can bear and the service patterns it expects, through a natural process. For their part in this natural process, librarians must swiftly adopt the understanding that electronic nonbook information media present a question only of format and that these media constitute a logical extension or richer mix of collection development activity. It is especially critical in the resolution of present uncertainties that libraries participate in the new brokerage of information to ensure the public of a full range of options in its determination of appropriate costs and use patterns. It is equally critical that libraries go about this in as ostensible a manner as possible so that their motives are not transparent to the public and their public image can be recast.

The time is ripe for a reassessment not only of services libraries can offer through collection development but, even more essentially, of the concepts of public, patron, clientele, and community as they relate to the goals of collection development. The terms patron and client refer to those who do make use of the library; these people are variables in library planning. The public and the community consist of all those who live or work within predetermined parameters of expectations for library service; these people constitute a nonvariable in library planning. Historically, the focus in library planning has been on the former group, those who take the initiative in demonstrating interest in the library, sometimes considered an elite within the community. Consequently, the library has often been associated with elitist strains in society and, more often than not, this has borne a pejorative connotation. A study of the etymology of the word "patron," in conjunction with an analysis of its traditional use as a name for one who avails oneself of library services would shed light on the evolution of this aspect of the library's image. Whether or not the elitist image of libraries is justified, or whether elitism is good or bad as a motivation for maintaining libraries will become irrelevant questions in the future, however, as information becomes more of a commodity in general demand by the public, brokered by the library.

Clearly, the entire community, not just the active clientele, will become an increasingly important consideration in the planning of collection development and related services in the future. With the goal of providing collections to support expanding services appropriate to the community and to earn the trust and support of the community, the library of the future will do well to integrate itself into the consciousness of the community. The recent history of libraries warns of the consequence of not accepting this challenge: Lower funding levels placed new restrictions on the development and maintenance of services, facilities, and collections, leaving library administration with a severe loss of flexibility; under these conditions the role of libraries begins to appear ambiguous both from within and from without, for the overall impact of success, and even of failure, diminishes in the community. The latent interdependency of library and community is described concisely by a learned layman, who advises, "the more serious the problems of knowledge and the library grow, the more depends on an effective spirit of understanding and collaboration between librarians and the users of knowledge, ultimately between the society and culture and the library profession" (Weintraub, 1980).

These insightful thoughts suggest that the roots of interdependence between library and community run very deep and that a natural infrastructure remains to be discovered. This would be a sociologically profound infrastructure whose emergence in history is only now in a preparatory stage, because the unprecented demand for information is only now beginning to converge with the unprecedented availability of information. That these developments will have an enormous impact on society seems a certainty, although the nature of the impact is open to speculation. Considering the depth of effect these information-generated changes will have on society and the key role that libraries can be expected to play, it does at least appear to be a safe bet that libraries cannot continue to rely on their traditional administrative approaches. No superficial public relations efforts, for example, will be adequate to uncover and gain control over the sociologically profound infrastructure that connects the community, the information or knowledge universe, and the library.

Consequently, the implications for change in library administration are penetrating, for a vastly new way of looking at planning and decision making will be required. The knowledge base of this new approach to administration would be a derivative of the community: motivations and goals of the community, with regard to information and intellectual stimulation; the topography of the relevant information universe; learning and information-seeking habits; and expectations relative to information, as well as absence of expectations. If the technical term "collection" is defined generically to include all information sources and services, as the developing mix seems to dictate, then collection development is the process that lies at the heart of this change. In summary, at question are an administrative knowledge base consisting largely of an understanding of a certain aspect of the sociology of the community, informing an administrative plan of action intended to keep that knowledge base current through a regularized interchange between library and community.

THE ROLE OF RESEARCH

It is true that the concepts of service and community have figured in the thought of library administration throughout the modern history of librarianship, but the concept of community as a chief determinant in managing library services, especially collection development, has not been emphasized. The shift from inward looking to outward looking administration is a major change of attitude. That the profession is amenable to this kind of change is becoming evident in developments such as the widespread discussion of and rudimentary participation in resource sharing and other cooperative programs; similarly, a trend toward attitudinal change in academic librarianship is suggested by the recent inception of a newsletter entitled *Library Issues: Briefings for Academic Officers, (Library Issues)* a purpose of which is to stimulate dialogue between the library and the community.

Beyond the change of attitude that needs to take place in library administration, and for which signs are beginning to be manifest, the methodology of library administration and collection development also requires revision. It seems somewhat ironic, in the midst of so much information and with the requirement of a master's degree for entrance into the profession, that librarianship has placed relatively so little importance on the value of research to management and planning. This situation may stem from the practice versus theory conflict that has divided the profession for at least a century. A likely resolution to the conflict will emerge from the implacement of technology in libraries in areas that have been especially labor intensive and repetitive in nature; but until then the practical rather than the theoretical will probably continue to dominate the educational program of librarians, and the role of research in library administration will probably continue to be unclear.

That is one possible scenario if librarians simply allow the course of events to flow as they are, but this cannot be the appropriate way to approach the profound changes that will affect the relationship of the library and the community as results of the new role of information in society. Instead, the time is ripe for the profession to adopt an approach to its work that is based on research, modelling, and planning. This would be a rather academic approach, in the sense that library administration would be both the consumer and the producer of research, while adapting research to development and planning. If library education cannot first produce the kinds of librarians who can subsequently influence change in management, then library management will suggest, through example, the kinds of librarians that need to be produced by the professional schools.

This is not to say that a rich base of research does not already exist, only that there is not much evidence that it is used significantly in library administration. It is possible that research in new areas should be undertaken, or that existing knowledge of areas outside of library science could profitably be applied to library administration. There is reason to believe that the profession is at least amenable to consideration of research in decision making and planning. This is demonstrable in the recent interest in library use and user studies within the profession, after hundreds—if not thousands—of such studies had been reported during the previous twenty years.

Observation was made earlier of the recent attention given by collection development librarians to the criterion of likely use in the design of collection development policy. It was noted that this new line of thinking (not new in all cases, to be sure) came about through the recognition that each library could not stand alone and that purchasing power may very possibly never be restored to former levels. Use and user studies appeared to hold the solution to the problem of materials selection posed by this new criterion in a new environment, and the fact that librarians' interests in engaging in use and user studies and applying them to the creation of policy constitutes a singularly important stage in the evolution of collection development. Analysis of the role of use and user studies seems to reveal that they hold a partial answer to the questions of collection development, not the complete answer. Although these studies do focus on at least a critical part of the community, limitations must be borne in mind.

Thus, the term "use" can be defined as some kind of recordable transaction connecting library material and a user; it does not mean that the material used is what was desired, or that information or enjoyment or any experience beyond the mere transaction took place. "Use" focuses on the collection as it stands. The term has no qualifications except those that can be assigned it under the precise conditions and parameters of the use study. It tells what was acted upon by a patron simply because it was there. With some minor exceptions, it tells little or nothing about what was desired but was not there. In the aggregate, "use" is easily skewed unless traced over a very long time; yet, ironically, its capacity to predict for purposes of selection is extremely limited. "Use" tends, therefore, to reflect a very static situation; it is a photographic representation of a very narrowly defined action.

The term "user" in this context reflects somewhat more dynamism, since it attempts at best to reflect change and variance in the user population. Depending upon the kind of user study conducted, ranging from a user-oriented analysis to circulation data to citation studies to a full-scale community survey, the predictive capacity varies. Squeezing the very most out of user studies holds the promise of informing library administration of habits of users and even of providing insight into motives of users. However, that promise can rarely be fulfilled, except in the most specific cases, because the activity under the microscope must be delineated so narrowly that it resembles a discrete phenomenon.

The problem is that there really is no single use or user study; there is rather a variety of kinds of use and kinds of user studies. The conventional use or user study is conducive to the syndrome of the self-fulfilling prophecy, particularly if policy decisions are guided by them. Moreover, the conventional use and user study sheds light on the small picture, rather than on the larger picture, so that it offers only a micro perspective on collection activity when planning more often requires a macro perspective. These studies tend to be one-shot efforts to *test* effectiveness when an ongoing process for *being* effective is desirable. While there is an important place for use and user studies in library administration, there is not yet a way of understanding the context in which they would be interpreted most appropriately. The result, therefore, is that conventional use and user studies tend to be employed in an *ad hoc* fashion in administration, and are subject either to being ignored or to being misused.

Use and user studies do provide a statistical element to the understanding of how and why information is related to the community, so it will be important for that kind of research to continue. But other areas are also fertile for research. Although there is a great deal in the literature about the development of networks and cooperative programs at several levels, most of this has to do with philosophy and design. What will be much needed as progress in these efforts is realized is research on the significance of networks and cooperative programs to the community and, especially, the influence they have on community attitude toward the library. The questions and hypotheses to be raised relative to this emerging dimension of librarianship are diverse, but research in these areas will help in making library service and community interests compatible. It is clear that networking and cooperative programs are becoming increasingly essential aspects of collection development.

In moving from the book-centered collection to the journal-centered collection and on to the technology-centered collection, librarianship is placing a colossal amount of faith in the community's ability to adapt readily to the precision demanded by technology, as well as to the power it harnesses as an information seeker. The profession's concern to date has largely focused on hardware, software, and its own ability to adapt to technology internally. Librarianship has not consulted outside itself in any truly substantial way, in spite of the fact that it will impose large added costs on its community and, at the same time, demand that the community learn new ways of approaching the collection. Since changes in the collection are essential for the community as well as for library operations, a great deal of research is needed—and as quickly as possible—on the impact of library technology on the community. The range of possibilities for research in this vast area seems almost boundless, for the steady influx of technology in libraries is pervasive and touches the heart of library service.

Research of most value to collection development and librarianship in dealing with change and in effecting the best possible service will shed light on the sociology of the community in its linkage with —or potential linkages with—the library and the universe of information and recorded expression. Studies exist of narrowly defined groups of library users, principally in a scholarly setting and principally as traditional user studies. There also exist analyses of the psychology of narrowly defined groups relative to libraries and information. However, considering the magnitude and nature of change likely in the near future, collection development policy and planning need to be supported by research on the library as a social institution. This means the systematic sociological analysis of the community and its relationship to the library as an integrated institution and of the library as it relates to the rest of the community. The nature of this kind of research can be refined through further definition of the role of collection development within the library and the community.

NEW CONCEPTS IN COLLECTION DEVELOPMENT

There are two concepts used earlier in the definition of collection development which bear further elaboration in connection with the establishment of an information base for collection development. First is the concept of collection development as a system. This means that collection development is a whole whose parts are movable but highly interdependent. The idea of system implies that collection development is not a specific action, but that it is dynamic, that it has a generating force or forces, and that anything put into or taken out of the system has some kind of impact on the system as a whole. Organically, the system is a sphere of influence that overlays a meaningful bond between specific functions of collection development and the related interests of the community, and between those specific functions and the rest of the library's services and operations. Collection development processes drive the system, both where it touches the community and where it touches other services and operations in the library.

The next concept incorporated in this definition of collection development is that of the decision making process, with special emphasis on the word "process." This process is the specific element of energy that drives the collection development system, for it both informs and is informed by the community about the relationship between goals and needs, and informs and is informed by other library operations and services about goals and parameters. The word "process" means that information becomes knowledge through experience, and that this is layered or made cumulative, always providing context for subsequent cycles of the process. Process is, in itself, a learning experience that should translate from a continuous testing of policy, plans, operations, and services against a constant flow of information about the community. In a narrow sense, the end of a cycle in the decision-making process of collection development is achieved with the selection or weeding of certain materials, but in a broader sense that decision regenerates the collection development system.

As service organizations, libraries traditionally have characterized their responsibilities in terms of responsiveness to needs. How these needs are identified and whether all needs are expressed have not usually been the kinds of concerns that have been translated into management action. In fact, the motive of responsiveness in the development of library collections has led to the adoption of a passive role for libraries in their community, even as, in many instances, professional zeal may have fostered a kind of isolated active role internally in the library. But collection development in the future will be able to cope successfully with its environment only if it adopts an active, even an aggressive, role in the community. Whereas librarianship frequently has taken a strong professional lead in matters of a technical nature, it must now do so in matters of a sociological nature. That the library is a social institution will be more recognizable in the next decades than it has been for several decades, so the profession will do well to recognize the inherent qualities of collection development that make of it a sociological system and make that system work well. Then, degree of responsiveness can be considered a valid standard, measurable against attributes of the collection development process.

Fortunately, there are tested methods for developing a process to bring together the library and the community in an appropriate way, and they need only be adapted. Marketing, as it is conceived in the business world, incorporates many activities and concepts that can be of great value in effecting the kinds of administrative change necessary in the future. Marketing aims at satisfying the user, thereby achieving organizational goals; marketing research establishes the overall size and structure of the market, identifies user characteristics, assesses needs of the users, and interprets trends in the market; marketing strategies include the development of overall plans to maximize impact on the market in both the short- and the long-term, decisions on which products and services to offer, and the establishment of standards and of measures of performance. These concepts and activities of marketing are outlined in any general textbook on marketing, but the concepts are broadened somewhat when applied to a nonprofit organization. For example, "marketing is the effective management by an organization of its exchange relations with its various markets and publics" (Kotler, 1975). Here, the definition refers not just to users, but to the entire community, and, of particular interest to the management of a system, it also incorporates as a goal bringing about "voluntary exchanges of values" (Kotler, 1975 p. 6). Marketing is a creative management function whose strategies and goals have been codified. They can be transported to and adapted to the collection development system to the advantage of both library and community.

A similar, yet different, set of principles to guide the collection development system can be found in intelligence activity. In the sense intended here, intelligence means information gathering for strategic purposes and planning. It is an old military activity that is particularly applicable to library administration for several reasons: Intelligence is an offensive maneuver that is most effective when unobtrusive; it applies to a community whose patterns of behavior have an impact on the organization; it assumes that an understanding of the community's patterns of behavior and motivation are essential to planning and to the determination of strategic offensive moves. Similar to military intelligence, library administration deals with a complex community over which it has no authority and only indirect influence, yet to which it must respond effectively in an anticipatory mode.

Fundamental to an intelligence function for collection development is an understanding of the sociology of recorded human expression and communication. This is the study of the interrelationships of the recorded universe, parts of society, and society generally; and the effects of one on the others in a system. It is historical, descriptive, analytical, and projective. It has to do with the motivation and production of recorded expression and communication, the reasons and ways of its transmission, the parameters and organization of the system and its parts. It analyzes the ways in which the system develops and evolves. It examines the past in order to understand the present and uses this knowledge to plan the future.

CONCLUSION

It is by now abundantly evident that various forces for change are beginning to give new direction to librarianship, and that change will soon permeate librarianship even to its core. At the very time when the introduction of advanced technology is forcing reorganization and reallocation in libraries, the demand for accountability and the expectations placed by society on all public institutions are leading libraries to reassess their role in society and their proper mode of administration. Because collection development quite naturally represents the essence of librarianship, it occupies the nuclear position in these considerations of change and thus is the appropriate basis for collaboration between library and community as the means of programming the best future for library service. However, the realization of a collaborative relationship is contingent upon the reconceptualization of collection development as a communications process driving an integral system of library, information universe, and community. It is in a context such as this that research and theory will be able to flourish most productively.

REFERENCES

Churchman, C. West, *The Systems Approach and Its Enemies*. New York: Basic Books, 1979.

"Collection Management," *The ALA Yearbook*. Chicago: American Library Association, 1976.

Crickman, Robin D., "The Emerging Information Professional." *Library Trends* 28 (Fall): 311–327, 1979.

De Solla Price, Derek J., "Happiness is a Warm Librarian." In Lancaster, F. Wildred, ed. *The Role of the Library in an Electronic Society. Proceedings of the 1979 Clinic on Library Applications of Data Processing.* Urbana: University of Illinois Graduate School of Library Science. P. 8.

Featheringham, T. R. "Paperless Publishing and Potential Institutional Change." *Scholarly Publishing* 13 (October):19–30, 1981.

Hammer, Donald P., ed. *The Information Age: Its Development, Its Impact.* Metuchen, N.J.: Scarecrow Press, 1976.

Harrison, Helen P. "Non-Book Materials: A Decade of Development." *Journal of Documentation* 35 (September 1979): 207–248.

Hills, Philip, ed. *The Future of the Printed Word. The Impact and the Implications of the New Communications Technology.* Westport, Conn.: Greenwood Press, 1980.

Josey, E. J., ed. *The Information Society: Issues and Answers.* American Library Association's Presidential Commission for the 1977 Detroit Annual Conference. Phoenix: Oryx Press, 1978.

Kotler, Philip. *Marketing for Nonprofit Organizations.* Englewood Cliffs, N.J.: Prentice-Hall, p. x, 1975.

Lancaster, F. Wilfrid, ed. *The Role of the Library in an Electronic Society. Proceedings of the 1979 Clinic on Library Applications of Data Processing.* Urbana: University of Illinois Graduate School of Library Science, 1980.

Library Issues: Briefings for Academic Officers. Edited by Richard M. Dougherty. Ann Arbor: Mountainside Publishing, bimonthly, 1980.

Magrill, Rose Mary, "Collection Development and Preservation." *Library Resources and Technical Services* 24 (Summer) 1980:247–273; 25 (July–September):244–266, 1981.

Montagnes, Ian, "Perspectives on the New Technology." *Scholarly Publishing* 12 (April): 219–229,1981.

Osburn, Charles B. "Marketing the Serials Aspects of Collection Development." In *Serials Collection Development: Choices and Strategies*, Lee , Sul H., ed. Ann Arbor: Pierian Press, 1981. Pp. 9–17.

Perkins, David L., ed. *Guidelines for Collection Development.* Chicago: American Library Association, 1979. Other sets of guidelines also are being prepared by the Resources and Technical Resources Division of the American Library Association.

Rochell, Carlton C., ed. *An Information Agenda for the 1980's. Proceedings of a Colloquium, June 17–18, 1980.* Chicago: American Library Association, 1981.

Scholarly Communication. The Report of the National Enquiry. Baltimore: The Johns Hopkins University Press, 1979.

Shera, Jesse H. "Sociological Relationships of Information Science." *Journal of the American Society for Information Science* 22 (March, 1971):76–80.

Shera, Jesse H., and Cleveland, Donald B. "History and Foundations of Information Science." *Annual Review of Information Science and Technology* 12:249–275.

Singleton, Alan. "The Electronic Journal and Its Relatives." *Scholarly Publishing* 13 (October):3–18, 1981.

Smith, David. *Systems Thinking in Library and Information Management.* New York: Saur, 1980.

Stueart, Robert D., and Miller, George B., Jr., eds. *Collection Development in Libraries: A Treatise*. 2 vols. Greenwich, Conn.: JAI Press, 1980.

Svenonius, Elaine, and Witthus, Rutherford. "Information Science as a Profession." *Annual Review of Information Science and Technology* 16:292–316, 1981.

Swanson, Don R., "Evolution, Libraries and National Information Policy." *Library Quarterly* 50 (January):76–93, 1980.

Weintraub, Karl J., "The Humanistic Scholar and the Library." *Library Quarterly* 50 (January):34, 1981.

STRATEGIC AND LONG RANGE
PLANNING IN LIBRARIES AND
INFORMATION CENTERS

Michael E. D. Koenig and Leonard Kerson

ABSTRACT

This chapter reviews the topic of long range and strategic planning in the context of libraries and information centers. It develops the thesis that with the emerging developments in technology a major change has taken place in the nature of long range planning for libraries. For the first time, the technology allows real choices among alternatives, and so for the first time libraries in fact really need to implement strategic long range planning in the fundamental sense of its being a tool to choose among alternatives.

The chapter attempts to serve as a primer to the methodology and the literature of strategic and long range planning, and in particular to discuss those methodologies as they pertain to libraries and information centers. The literature relating specifically to library long range planning is reviewed.

Advances in Library Administration and Organization, volume 2, pages 199–258.
Copyright © 1983 by JAI Press Inc.
All rights of reproduction in any form reserved.
ISBN: 0-89232-214-4

INTRODUCTION

This chapter will attempt to be not only a review of the library strategic and long range planning literature and an entry into the long range planning literature on a broader scale, as well as a primer to long range planning methodology, it will also attempt to make a prognosis of sorts about how long range planning should develop on the context of libraries and information centers. Henceforth the phrase "strategic and long range planning" will be abbreviated to "long range planning." This essay will not attempt, however, to be a prescriptive how-to article in library long range planning.

In a recent article in *Library Journal*, (Koenig, 1982) Koenig argues that in the relatively recent past, essentially within the last decade, the nature of librarianship or information management has undergone a radical and profound change. So dramatic is this change, that the word "seachange" which Drucker (1980) has recently repopularized[1] springs to mind as an apt description. That change is is, of course, the impact of computer-based information processing technology. Now, instead of trying to control an information explosion characterized by doubling periods of fifteen years with a print technology whose rate of growth was substantially slower, some twenty-four years, we have at our disposal a technology whose rate of growth is stunningly faster. The number of units that can be integrated into one chip has been growing at a rate even faster than the two-year doubling period predicted by Moore's Law (Yasaki, 1981). The next generation of super computers, the Cray-2 generation, reportedly will achieve an increase in capability equivalent to more than three doubling periods, an increase which will have been achieved in approximately eight years (Johnson, 1982; 1981). While no similar bench marks exist for software, it is clear that capability here too is doubling at a rate far in excess of every fifteen years. Very simply, the effect will be that of an information controllability explosion. The information explosion will not have gone away, it is simply that the power to manipulate the problem will be doubling in capability far faster than the problem. Instead of playing catch-up ball, we will be in the far more enjoyable position of designing and evaluating future strategies and alternatives. Instead of living in a professional culture almost devoid of the opportunity for meaningful long range planning, we will be operating in a professional culture and environment where our decisions, even if made by default, will determine future consequences. In short, we are at the beginning of a future where anything other than serious and continued attention to long range planning will be irresponsible.

One of the significant effects of this technique is that the whole armamentaria of long range planning techniques will be appropriate to the library/information community. Since the multiplicity of alternatives will be provided and shaped by the technology, all of the more quantitative techniques of technological forecasting will be appropriate. Equally important will be the more intuitive techniques of forecasting and planning. Human factors, including of course the political, will be central in building possible scenarios and choosing among the alternatives.

This is a very different future from the library planning of the past, which might be described as strategic positioning in the terminology of business long range planning. Most of the library planning described in the literature is basically some variation of a self-study or self-evaluation program, which consists of assessing the library's offering or services in light of the community's needs. To describe this as positioning rather than planning is not to denigrate it. It is a cybernetic, feedback-based, responsiveness to the libraries' context and user community that is eminently worthwhile. The point remains, however, that for the most part it is essentially a corrective procedure, what might be described as reactive course control; it is not proactive planning for a future environment that may differ in very significant ways from the present. Since the planning process is a continuum, the distinction is of course not a black and white one. It is, in Ackoff's (1973) terminology, "reactivist" behavior, or what Davis (1980) has termed "coping." Self-evaluation planning in addition to reacting to discrepancies between the library and its surroundings, can of course be extended to include analysis of the tendencies of the library and its surroundings, and to estimate future congruence and to plan for it. For example, the demographic changes of a public library's community can be extrapolated into the future, the library services can be planned based on that extrapolation. Many of the self-evaluation studies described here very consciously undertake such analysis. While this is indeed planning for the future, it still remains a very different sort of planning from that which the library world will now have to undertake.

What is Long Range Planning?

Steiner's (1969) definition of strategic planning, "The process of determing the major objectives of an organization and the policies and strategies that will govern the acquisition, use, and disposition of resources to achieve those objectives," reflects concerns introduced in almost all discussions of the nature of long range planning. It is an ongoing process that continuously informs decision making, taking into account the broadest, most fundamental goals of the organization. The key question asked is "What business are we in?" and the answer is largely the responsibility of top-level management. These basic, organization-wide goals are advanced by allocation of resources through policies and programs whose objectives are narrower and the focus of short range or tactical planning. Measuring the results of decision making is essential, so that alternative strategies in pursuit of stated goals can be followed when necessary, or modification of those goals to achieve or reestablish organizational relevance to the environment can occur. Long range planning properly implemented is continual and cybernetic in nature.

Social organizations practicing continuous planning cycles parallel living organisms, and this relationship is explored by systems theory (see Miller, 1978). The history and development of the organization's "brain," its management function, monitors internal structures and processes as well as environmental factors to which the organization must adapt to survive, to establish an equilibrium. Planning can be viewed as the process which consciously directs movement from one equilibrium to another, incorporating in organizations higher aims than that of maintaining a stable relationship with the environment. Such self-stabilization is sometimes referred to as dynamic conservation in organizations, and just as higher organisms exhibit goal-seeking behavior, organizations, too, should seek to do more than merely survive. The planning process is the key to more purposeful behavior. One can formulate definitions of long range planning *ad infinitum*, (see Bell and Kreusch, 1976) but the essential concepts are those of selection among alternatives and of the ongoing feedback based cybernetic notions of planning.

Long Range Planning as Systems Analysis

One of the most fundamental precepts of long range planning is that long range planning is, in effect, merely an application of systems analysis. What is perhaps most striking is that this profound truth is so little mentioned. Indeed specific equating of the two is conspicuous by its absence. This may be because the identity is so obvious that it does not need stating, or, as the authors suspect, because the bulk of the general long range planning literature, as opposed to that discussing specific methodologies, is directed toward administration and towards executives, and the authors fear that the elaboration, or even the recognition of the identity would be impolitic. Systems analysis is, or at least its perception is that of, the niggling analysis of small details, the tactical analysis of how many terminals are needed for an online catalog, for example. Long range planning on the other hand is not tactical; it is strategic; it represents the larger questions of the positioning and the orientation of the whole organization. Furthermore, systems analysis for a whole complex of reasons that deserves an essay in its own right, is perceived as requiring a level of mathematical skill that few administrators and decision makers possess.[2]

Therefore, the identification of long range planning as applied systems analysis in the context of an examination of appropriate courses of action given one's expectations for the future is not a common one. The tool seems too limited and tactical for the strategic purpose at hand, and even if it were appropriate, it seems too demandingly mathematical to seriously contemplate. And in any case, "everyone knows" that we can't pin down the future with mathematical precision.

In fact, however, the previous description of long range planning as, in effect, future oriented systems analysis, albeit systems in the macro sense, is perfectly appropriate. Both long range planning and systems analysis are concerned with precisely the same thing—the selection of alternatives. The identity of systems analysis with the selection of alternatives is beyond the scope of this article, but the reader is referred to Bickner (1978) for an excellent discussion. Long range planning, it can be argued, is precisely the analysis of the set of alternatives from which we must choose when contemplating the future, and the consequent selection of the appropriate alternative. In fact that definition of long range planning, is also in effect a definition of multiple scenario analysis. This, in turn, is the point we make elsewhere—that multiple scenario analysis is not a technique of long range planning, it is long range planning, and other techniques are therefore not competitors of multiple scenario analysis, but techniques for accomplishing multiple scenario analysis. Dick Levin (1981) has put it very directly: "That's so basic and so important that I'll say it again. It's not a plan if it doesn't illuminate and choose strategic alternatives for the organization."

The consequences of this identification of long range planning and systems analysis for the implementation of long range planning is important. While long range planning generally is not nearly so mathematically based as the practice of system analysis (much less the reputation), the same sort of mind set is appropriate to both—an analytical mind set. When evaluating alternatives, one must weigh pluses and minuses, benefits and benefits foregone (costs). There is a tendency to perceive long range planning as a qualitative process and systems analysis as a quantitative one. Neither characterization is correct. What is to be avoided however is the acceptance of a mindset that dichotomizes qualitative and quantitative. In real world decision making or alternative selection, only some aspects can be quantified; the balance must be treated qualitatively. The more of those always numerous factors that can be quantified however, the better we are likely to do in our qualitative judgements when weighing the thereby reduced balance of factors. This view, which comes with the territory in systems analysis and is the essence of good systems analysis, is also the essence of good long range planning.

The paragraphs previously mentioned could be rewritten just as logically by substituting the phrase cost analysis or cost/benefits analysis[3] for
systems analysis. This holds because cost analysis is applied systems
analysis (although some might reverse the equation to imply that systems
analysis instead is a subset of cost analysis). The consequences of these
identities is that those persons undertaking long range planning should be
as familiar with certain basic concepts of economic and systems analytic
decision making as are cost analysts or systems analysts. Those concepts
are:

1. cost as benefit foregone
2. present value
3. opportunity cost
4. sunk cost
5. externalities

The reader is referred to Bickner (1978) for discussion of points 1,2,4
and 5 and to Koenig (1980) for discussion of points 2,3,4 and 5. Points
2,3, and 4 will be discussed briefly in this paper. All five points are
basically common sense conceptual ways of analyzing alternatives. None
requires any sophisticated mathematical skills. They are, in effect, tools
of logic that help in avoiding errors of analysis, just as knowing of the
error of false syllogisms helps in avoiding that error of analysis. They are,
in that regard, qualitative humanistic tools rather than quantitative ones.

The danger of ignoring the essential identity of long range planning and
systems analysis is that the perceptions of long range planning as a
qualitative process, in contrast to quantitative techniques such as systems
analysis or cost analysis, encourages the non-use of tools of logical thinking that have developed within the areas of systems and cost analysis.
Ideally, one of the first steps in any long range planning process would be
a seminar series for the long range planning participants that is devoted to
the analytical processes of systems and cost analysis.

METHODOLOGIES

Forecasting

Since long range planning by definition involves the analysis of the
"futurity" of different alternatives, the perception or prediction of what
that future holds, which is the process of forecasting, is generally regarded as an essential and constituent part of long range planning and will
be so treated in this paper. However, the point cannot be made too
strongly that forecasting is not long range planning, it is merely a part of

it. It is easy to lose sight of this point amid the profusion of literature on the various methodologies of forecasting, which we will call

- Crystal Ball Techniques
- Morphological Analysis
- Modeling Techniques
- Extrapolatory Techniques

The classification is merely one of several ways of looking at what is a very mixed bag of techniques. There are other equally logical ways by which the various forecasting techniques might be categorized.

Crystal Ball Techniques

As the name connotes, these techniques attempt to forecast the future in an intuitive, relatively nonquantitative, nonformal fashion. (The future predicted, however, may have to be described in a quantitative fashion.) There have evolved, however, several concepts and methodologies to make this intuitive process somewhat more tractable, and hopefully somewhat more effective.

Decomposition

One of the techniques is that of *Decomposition*: that is, rather than trying to forecast, for example, the size of a market or a level of demand *per se*, one attempts to decompose what is to be predicted into, if possible, its constituent parts. For example, if we were to try to predict the number of online bibliographic searches to be conducted in the United States in 1986, we might just guess at a number, but we might have more confidence in our results if we tried to decompose the intended result into some set of constituent parts. One set might be:

> How many scientists/researchers/professionals will there be in the U.S.? and how many searches per scientist/researcher/professional? How many students will there be? and how many searches per student? What will the overall adult population be? and how many non-job related searches will there be per person?

Such a decomposition can of course be extended further. One might well want to make further distinctions in the class of scientist/researcher/professional. The assumptions that such techniques are advantageous is so intuitively attractive and convincing that relatively little empirical testing of the notion has been done. Armstrong, Denniston, and Gordon (1975) tested the techniques in reverse, asking the subjects to make estimates back in time (so that the correct answer could be confirmed without waiting to see what the future held) about questions such as:

1. How many high school dropouts were there in 1969?
2. How many packs of Polaroid color film were used in the United States in 1970?

Respondents were asked the questions boldly, as above, and in a decomposed format. The decomposed format for question 2 is below:

1. How many people were living in the United States in 1970?
2. What was the average size of a family?
3. What percentage of families owned cameras?
4. Of those families owning cameras, what percentage owned Polaroid cameras?
5. What was the average number of packs of film used per Polaroid camera owner?
6. What percentage of Polaroid film sales were color film?

The decomposed versions of the questions yielded better results in all cases.

Amalgamation

Another technique, which is referred to as *Amalgamation*, is simply the notion of taking refuge in the safety of numbers. That is, the amalgamated result (typically an average) of a number of judges is likely to be better than the result obtained by using just one judge. Not only does amalgamation provide the opportunity to improve validity by letting the biases of different judges cancel each other, it also has the potential to improve reliability. That is, if an individual makes the same judgement more than once, the amalgamation of those results will typically be superior to the majority of those individual judgements. There is an extensive literature on amalgamations, even amalgamations of the literature, (Armstrong, 1975; Lorge, Fox, Davitz, Brenner, 1958; Zagone, 1967) and one can say with some confidence that amalgamation should be used where possible. It is virtually always better than the majority of components (individual predictions) from which it is derived, and it is sometimes better than the best component. Furthermore, it is particularly useful when uncertainty is high, which of course is the typical situation for long range planning.

Despite the very well documented advantage of amalgamation, there still frequently exists an intuitive reluctance to believe that it is likely to be superior to that of one very well chosen judge. In other words, there is a very plausible argument that in order to amalgamate, you need to broaden the pool of judges, and that almost inevitably in so doing, you must lower the average quality or level of expertise of the judge, and that therefore the quality of the amalgamated judgement will be inferior. While the above sounds plausible, it supposes that we can identify expertise, and that the quality of judging is proportional to expertise. Neither assumption appears to be warranted, particularly the later. Armstrong has assembled convincing evidence that the quality of prediction improves with increased expertise only up to a certain level, and that the relationship is relatively random beyond that level (Armstrong, 1978). In other words, forecasters should have some expertise in the field in which forecasts are desired, but a modicum of expertise appears to be just as effective, in terms of forecasting skills, as a high level of expertise. Or, as Armstrong puts it, "use the least expensive experts."

Given the point above, it becomes much easier to accept the utility of amalgamation. To quote a cliché, "the best is often the enemy of the better." In an attempt to get the best possible estimate or forecast, we are in danger of foregoing the better—the use of an amalgamated forecast.

Consensus Techniques

There is a variety of methods for assembling a panel of experts in order to arrive at some sort of consensus prediction. The most common of these is the *Delphi* Technique. This methodology, first developed at the Rand Corporation, consists of some number of rounds of sequential individual interrogations of a panel of experts. The key concepts are "anonymity" and "iterativity." Anonymity means that the experts are queried individually, not as part of an assembled group. There is no face-to-face contact. This means each person can react openly, candidly and honestly, without regard to peer group pressure. The iterative aspect is that after each round the group's responses are fed back to each individual as information for the next round. The moderator typically will ask the "outliers," those whose response is markedly different from the bulk of the group, to explain or elucidate their thinking. This between-rounds information is stripped of any identifiers that would link individual respondents with particular responses. In such fashion it is hoped that reactions to the responses of other experts will be based purely on the information content, not on status, interpersonal skills, and so on.

Delphi studies have traditionally been accomplished by means of printed questionnaires delivered and collected by mail. It is of course a truism, but an important one, that questionnaire design is very important. Questionnaires must be very carefully thought out and reviewed to avoid biasing responses in some particular direction. The logical review questions to ask of the questionnaire components is: What unexamined assumptions lie behind the questions?

With the advent of computer conferencing and teleconferencing, there is obviously an opportunity to implement Delphi studies with less inconvenience, and with prompter round-to-round response than by mail. There is already a sizeable literature on the human factors of computer conferencing beginning to emerge, and some of the results are quite supportive of the assumptions underlying the Delphi technique, particularly the avoidance of face-to-face groups. When comparing problem solving by face-to-face groups with computer conferencing, the correlation between appropriate technical skills and the assumption of group leadership seems to be higher for computer conferencing. Similarly perhaps, women more often assume leadership roles in a computer conferencing context (Hiltz and Turoff, 1978). A reasonable interpretation of both cases is that with computer conferencing, skills of social dominance are less important and the quality of the contribution is more important than in the face-to-face situations.

The reported use of Delphi techniques in the library literature have been relatively common. The most ambitious was a study undertaken by the Public Library research group of the (British) Library Association in 1937–1974. The results were of rather motherhood and apple pie sort: for example, predictions of greater use of automation, continuing price increases for books, more use of audio-visual materials (Kennington, 1977).

In considering Delphi techniques, one of the points that is frequently raised is that a Delphi result is apt to represent more of a consensus about what the panel hopes to see achieved, rather than a hard-headed evaluation of what is truly likely to transpire. An example of that might be the Delphi prediction in 1969 of high quality portable microform readers and the replacement of most professional journals with microform within fifteen years (Bernstein, 1969). Plainly that has not happened, and probably now never will. Microform technology has for the most part been leapfrogged by Moore's Law and the decreasing cost of electronic storage. The point of course is that no amount of desire for high quality portable microform devices, the famous cuddly microfiche reader, made them happen. What combination of lack of market, lack of appropriate technology, and lack of effort in the required direction by those qualified to address the problem produced the "failure," is a matter of conjecture. What is now ironic is that telecommunications and computer technology, with flat screen devices and infra red transmission to replace wires will apparently soon be able to offer a display device far cuddlier than the dreams of the microform proponents.

A very interesting predictive problem now is the degree to which computers will be able to recognize and process speech input. Like the cuddly microfiche reader, this will have a major impact on librarianship if it comes about, and like the cuddly microfiche reader, it is devoutly desired by many. Some differences are that there is perceived to be a vast market to be opened by such a capability (the market for the executive work station, given such a capability, is huge compared to the market for word processing), and this has resulted in an attention to the problem which the cuddly microfiche reader never received. The point of course is that to some modest degree (and that degree is the subject of much debate) technology can be driven. In forecasting, one must distinguish between how fast it is being driven (voice recognition) and how fast we hope it is being driven (the cuddly microfiche reader). The failure to make such distinctions seems to be a very typical problem with the Delphi technique. These failures of good intention seem to be far more important than the procedural problems so often mentioned in the literature of the Delphi technique. Those procedural criticisms are summarized in works by Dyer (1979) and Fischer (1978), and in the interest of parsimony, the interested reader is referred there.

The specific example above of microform technology, does, however, illustrate the potentially great utility of long range planning. The date of the study mentioned, 1969, roughly coincides with the advent of large-scale integration (the etching of many circuit components into one chip). In 1969, unless one were very well informed as to the whereabouts of the cutting edge of technology, and very prescient to boot, one could hardly be expected to be aware of the speed with which storage costs might be expected to fall. Just a few years later though, Moore's Law had been coined and publicized, and an awareness of that phenomenon and a healthy respect for the power of an exponential doubling, particularly when the doubling period is of the order of two years, made it very clear that microforms were unlikely ever to be more than an interim technology, whose role would be comparable to that of the iron lung in the campaign to conquer polio, to borrow an example from Lewis Thomas (1974). That is, of course, not to say that microform would not be useful in the interim, but simply that long range plans could be made in a much sounder fashion once the nature of microform as interim technology was apparent. The beauty of a pattern of exponential growth, is that if we can have confidence that it will continue (in this case, Moore's Law has already held up for five more doubling periods since its promulgation; in fact the doubling period has been slightly faster than two years, and with gallium arsenide in the wings waiting to replace silicon, and with bio-chip technology behind that, it gives every indication of holding up for at least as long in the future) (Yanchinski, 1982) then we can, as in this case, recognize interim technologies well before the interim period is over, and avoid the problem of making too great a commitment to that technology. Needless to say, exponential growth does not always continue unabated. One need only remember the enthusiasm, also of the late 1960s, for the exponential growth of air cargo. The price of fuel has done in that exponential growth.

The name E-T-E for Estimate-Talk-Estimate has been coined for a simpler spinoff of the Delphi technique. In E-T-E, the experts assemble face to face, make a round of estimates, then talk about their estimates and the reasoning behind them, then each makes an estimate again, and like Delphi, continue cycling until a consensus is reached, or until opinions no longer seem to be in flux. The advantage of such a procedure is speed and simplicity; the disadvantage is of course the extraneous interpersonal factors that are allowed to enter into the process. This can be somewhat mitigated by a strong and impartial moderator who enforces a period of "brainstorming" like rules during the talk phase. The basic rules of brainstorming are typically:

- consider any idea, opinion, alternative, regardless of apparent feasibility, frivolity, and so on
- no criticism of another's idea is allowed
- ideas are to be encouraged or supported, particularly unusual ones.

In other words, a free-form period is set up during which criticism is not allowed. After this period, the moderator may then summarize some of the ideas, disassociating them as much as possible from individuals, before allowing discussion of feasibility.

Scenario Development and Multiple Scenario Analysis

Among the various crystal ball techniques, the concept of *Multiple Scenario Development Analysis* is certainly the most important. Indeed, it may well be questioned whether multiple scenario analysis should be included under the rubric of forecasting, for multiple scenario analysis is, in a larger sense, long range planning itself; all of the other techniques of forecasting can be regarded as techniques helpful for devising scenarios. Even when only one future scenario is specifically recognized, one can maintain that this is merely a "degenerate" version of multiple scenario analysis in which all but one possible scenario has been dismissed consciously or unconsciously as too unlikely to warrant attention. The authors have chosen to treat multiple scenario under forecasting to preserve conventional terminals but work to make the point strongly that ultimately multiple scenario analysis is not a type of forecasting, but is long range planning, for which forecasting is merely a tool. Symptomatic of this identity is that almost everyone's prescription for a straightforward "do it yourself" method of long range planning is in fact a version of multiple scenario analysis. (If it is not, mistrust it immediately.)

The basic concept behind multiple scenario analysis is simply that of taking a set of possible assumptions about the future and then developing scenarios based on those various assumptions. From these scenarios, one can select a reasonable course for future action. Simple enough, but in that word "selection" alone is buried rather a good deal of subtlety.

Examined more closely, multiple scenario analysis can be broken down into five major steps. (There are almost as many prescriptions for multiple scenario analysis as there are writers on the subject. The authors have seen prescriptions that vary from four steps to sixteen.) The first step is that of identification and definition. What are the objectives of the organization? What factors or events are likely to impact the organization? What range of values is likely or even possible for those functions?

The second step is that of assessing the probabilities of those factors that have the potential to exert a significant impact on one's future. These factors in turn may have interrelated probabilities. For example, we might lay out some of the probabilities that might impact library and information systems in a fashion like that below:

EVENT	PROBABILITY
1. Cost effective Voice Data Input by 1985	.8
2. Inexpensive Satellite to Rooftop Communications	.6
3. Major Breakthrough in Fibre Optics	.6
4. PTT Imposition of Major Restrictions on data transfer	.3
5. International Funding Program for 3rd World Information Provision	.2

Going one step further, and essaying probabilities of one event given the occurrence of another:

Conditional Probability of i
Given Event j

Event i	Event j	1	2	3	4	5
1. Voice Data Input		1	.8	.8	.8	.8
2. Satellite Communications		.6	1	.6	.6	.6
3. Fibre Optics		.6	.4	1	.8	.6
4. PTT Restrictions		.2	.5	.2	1	.1
5. 3rd World Funding		.4	.2	.1	.2	.1

Given probabilities such as the above, there are computer programs available to assess the bounds of higher order probabilities. (What for example is the probability of event 4 given events 2 and 3?) This particular phase of multiple scenario analysis is in fact an application of cross impact analysis (Sarin, 1978)—that is, what is likely to be the effect of one development upon the likelihood of another?

The third step is to compute the probabilities of the various possible scenario bases, and to choose the scenarios that will be developed. Even the relatively circumscribed list of factors above leads to the possibility of some thirty-two scenarios, so clearly some selectivity is required. An algorithmic selection of possible scenarios on the basis of probability or likelihood of occurrence is straightforward enough, but frequently one desires to develop at least some scenarios on the basis of sensitivity. In other words, let's not just develop scenarios on the basis of likelihood, let's also examine those scenarios to which the organization would be most sensitive, those that would have the greatest effect on the organization. A term long used for scenario planning on such a basis is contingency planning. Contingencies are, of course, not always worst case scenarios: they can occur at the other end of the spectrum as well. Planning for the disastrous, in contrast to the fortuitous contingency, may be more demanding, but it frequently serves the organization well, as having a scenario for a major setback may help very much in case a minor one develops.

The fourth step is to develop the chosen scenarios. Given the set of assumptions upon which the scenario is based, how will the future develop, and what is the logical course of action for the organization to chart through that future? Each scenario may not necessarily result in just one logical course of action. There may well be more than one. Indeed the process of scenario development may well reveal new factors that should be factored back into the selection of scenarios.

The final step, based on the scenarios developed is to rank the likely alternative courses of action for the organization. In step one, the likely major or strategies decisions to be made in the future were identified, or at least a partial list was developed. As other likely decisions reveal themselves in the planning process, particularly in scenario writing, that list presumably was extended. These alternative courses of action are to that degree in accord with it. The next step is to rank those alternatives overall, across the scenarios. What is being looked for are those alternatives that have the greatest ''resilience'' or ''robustness.'' The appropriate alternative to select is one that not only is appropriate for the most likely scenario, but is also not inappropriate for other likely scenarios. The most appropriate alternative for the most likely scenario is not necessarily the alternative of choice if it lacks resilience or if it is decidedly inappropriate for other reasonably likely scenarios. Another notion here is correctability—how correctable or modifiable is an alternative if a different future from the one envisioned unfolds?

As a first pass, the alternatives can be ranked on the basis of estimated utility—the sum of the estimated utility of each alternative in each scenario (the utility of an alternative in a scenario might be rated on a scale of +5 to −5, plus 5 meaning the alternative is very appropriate, to −5 meaning that it would be very inappropriate, perhaps disastrous), times the probability of that scenario. Ultimately, for the reasons outlined in the section on risk attitude, the selection of alternatives must be a qualitative one: Which alternative course of action performs best across likely future scenarios without unduly exposing the organization to unacceptable risk? A good tutorial article on multiple scenario analysis is that by Nair and Jurin (Nair 1979).

Morphological Analysis

The term Morphological Analysis has been coined to describe what is essentially just a systematic way of assembling a large checklist of possibilities or alternatives for design or for the future. A morphological analysis consists of five basic steps:

- defining and formulating the problem as explicitly as possible.
- identifying and characterizing all parameters.
- building a multidimensional matrix (a morphological box) from those parameters.
- examining all solutions (each cell in the morphological box is a potential solution).
- analyzing the best solutions.

For example, we might be concerned with the problem of how best to deliver information to the library patron, and we identify three parameters: that of display mechanism, that of number of locations, and that of intermediation. If we build a matrix of those parameters and the alternatives within each parameter, we might arrive at something like Figure 1. We have deliberately limited the parameters to three, so that the matrix, the morphological box, is only three dimensions and can easily be represented in two dimensions. Although we cannot easily spatially visualize a matrix of more than three dimensions, there is no reason that the analysis of a real life problem need be limited to three parameters or three dimensions. The concept indeed is of a morphological box in n-space, where n the number of dimensions is limited only by the complexity of the problem. What results is a complex checklist of possible alternatives or scenarios to investigate. The formal approach of deliberating all possibilities presumably helps us to avoid overlooking unconventional but possibly effective solutions or outcomes.

When the number of parameters and alternatives gets large, then the morphological box can become very large and unwieldy. At that point,

Figure 1. Sample Morphological Box

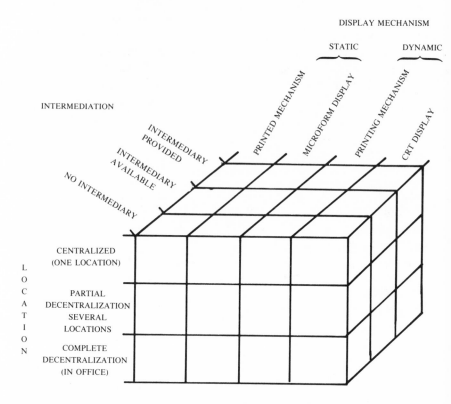

computer programs can manipulate the morphological box as an n-dimensional matrix, and just as one can calculate the distance from any cell to any other in a three-dimensional box, the same can be done in n-dimensional space. Using this capability, known feasible solutions can be entered, and other cells can be ranked by their closeness to those known feasible solutions, thus suggesting an order of examination of the other cells roughly in order of their likely feasibility.

Morphological analysis was developed by a very successful Swiss astrophysicist and aeronautical engineer, Fritz Zwicky, and he has promoted the notion vigorously (Zwicky, 1969; Wills et al., 1972). While documented successful cases of vigorous morphological analyses are rare, to say the least, the idea is probably very useful if for no other reason than to force the examination of what are the parameters and the alternatives available in any decision space.

Extrapolatory Techniques

There are a number of extrapolatory techniques used to project a trend forward in time into the future. There is a great deal of mathematical jargon that has developed around these techniques that tends to obscure them and make them seem much more formidable than they are in reality. To put it very simply, there are two fundamental techniques, drawing a straightline and fitting it to data on conventional graph paper, and drawing a straightline and fitting it to data on semi-log graph paper. There are of course sophisticated variations on these techniques, such as mathematically dealing with seasonal fluctuations, for example, and we will discuss these below, but in reality most of those enhancements and sophistications are defensible and utilitarian only for the relatively short term, not for the time frames involved in long range planning.

Exponential Smoothing

Perhaps the most basic concept in extrapolatory analysis is that of the *Moving Average*. Instead of predicting next month's performance, circulation, or number of online searches, or whatever, by last month's, we simply use the average of the last several months. That is the, forecast quantity FQ for time t+1 (the upcoming time period) equals the quantity of time t (the most recent), the quantity for time t−1 (the next to most recent period), etc. all divided by N, where N equals as many time periods as we choose to use. If we choose 4 time periods, for example, then:

$$FQ_{t+1} = \frac{Q_t + Q_{t-1} + Q_{t-2} + Q_{t-3}}{4} \tag{1}$$

The adjective moving comes simply from the fact that we calculate an average and move it along with time. As we complete each time period, that time becomes time t, the quantity for that period Q+, and we then predict for the next period, time t+1. Of course in reality, we are often in the midst of a time period, for example a month, and we wish to provide estimates for next month and the most recent figures to work with are last month's so, perforce, our equation become in reality:

$$FQ_{t+1} = \frac{Q_{t-1} + Q_{t-2} + Q_{t-3} + Q_{t-4}}{4} \tag{2}$$

Such a prediction surrounded by some "confidence intervals" frequently becomes the basis for reporting by exception. For example, each month's circulation is predicted by a moving average, and if in fact the circulation for a branch deviates from its prediction by more than some percentage, say 10%, then that fact is immediately brought to the attention of the director or head of public services, rather than simply being incorporated into a routine low priority report.

The moving average approach is still rather simplistic—it simply says that our prediction of the future is that it will be like the average of the several most recent time periods. The moving average does not capture trends, up, down, or cyclical. The next logical improvement is simply to weight the components of the moving average in a fashion to give more emphasis to the most recent time periods. If there is a trend up or down, then giving more weight to the level of last month's performance than to the level of performance three or four months ago will clearly provide a better forecast. For example we might modify the first equation above to look like:

$$FQ_{t+1} = \frac{4Q_t + 3Q_{t-1} + 2Q_{t-2} + 1Q_{t-3}}{10} \tag{3}$$

We have simply weighted the most recent time periods more heavily, and the divisor N, has simply become the sum of the weights, in this case 10, rather than simply the number of time periods used to make the forecast. Again, our choice of four time periods is arbitrary, just as is our choice of the various weights.

The weighted moving average above is functionally the equivalent of what is known as exponential smoothing. Indeed, if we use weights that proceed in a geometric fashion rather than an arithmetic fashion, that is, weights that vary by a fixed proportion (weight 1 is to weight 2, as weight 2 is to weight 3, etc.) rather than varying by a fixed quantity (the result of subtracting weight 2 from weight 1, is the same as the result of subtracting weight 3 from weight 2 etc.), we have arrived at exponential smoothing. An example of a weighted moving average that is also exponential smoothing might be:

$$FQ_{t+1} = \frac{8Q_t + 4Q_{t-1} + 2Q_{t-2} + 1Q_{t-3}}{15} \tag{4}$$

If we were to carry the number of periods on indefinitely the formula above would approach as its limit:

$$FQ_{t+1} = \frac{8Q_t + 4Q_{t-1} + 2Q_{t-2} + 1Q_{t-3} + 1/2Q_{t-4} + 1/4Q_{t-5}\cdots}{16} \tag{5}$$

Functionally this formula does not differ very much from the one above, since the importance of those older time periods becomes vanishingly small. The point of introducing it is to show that if we write it with a separate weight for each part Q, it becomes:

$$FQ_{t+1} = 1/2Q_t + 1/4Q_{t-1} + 1/8Q_{t-2} + 1/16Q_{t-3} + 1/32Q_{t-4}\cdots \tag{6}$$

The formula for exponential smoothing is usually written as:

$$FQ_{t+1} = aQ_t + a(1-a)Q_{t-1} + a(1-a)^2Q_{t-2} + a(1-a)^3Q_{t-3}\ldots \qquad (7)$$

Where a is a constant which lies in the range between 0 and 1.

It is relatively easy to see that Eq. 6 above is simply one particular version of the more general Eq. 7, a version in which (a) equals 1/2. An (a) of 1/2 is in fact a rather large (a) to use in practice, but it was used here because it is the (a) with which it is easiest to demonstrate the essential identity of Eq. 4 through 7.

It is from the equation in form 7 that the name "exponential smoothing" derives, as the weights vary simply by the exponent of the $(1-a)$ term. This is even clearer if we take advantage of the facts that any quantity with an exponent of zero equals one, and that any quantity with an exponent of one simply equals itself, and write the equation in the form:

$$FQ_{t+1} = a(1-a)^0Q_t + a(1-a)^1Q_{t-1} + a(1-a)^2Q_{t-2} + a(1-a)^3Q_{t-3}\ldots] \qquad (8)$$

Note however that we are simply using an exponential formula to smooth the sort of data that can be plotted on conventional graph paper, data that is relatively static. We are not smoothing data that are growing exponentially, the sort of data that must be plotted on semi-log paper. Exponential smoothing then, confusingly enough, has nothing to do with exponential growth, the sort of growth, like the information explosion of Moore's Law, that can be characterized by a doubling period.

There is a valid reason however for introducing the complexities of Eq. 7 and 8. That reason is that from those equations one can derive a much more elegant, and more importantly, a much simpler formula. The formula is:

new forecast = old forecast + a(latest observation − old forecast)
or

$$FQ_{t+1} = FQ + a(Q_t - FQ_t) \qquad (9)$$

The formula is not only very much simpler computationally, but it is also very much simpler from a data keeping and data accessioning point of view. Nothing is needed but the most recent data for quantities and forecasts. The disadvantage to the formula is that there is nothing intuitively very plausible or convincing about it as one looks at it. It is only the identity with formulas 7 and 8 that provide that plausibility. That of course is the reason for introducing formula 9 via formulas 7 and 8. This derivation is set out in more detail in Makower and Williamson (1967).

At this point, we still do not have much more than the ability to project relatively static data patterns into the future. Two extensions must be added. The first concerns seasonality. Data may fluctuate in a cyclical pattern, and while that pattern is typically seasonal, other cyclicalities are possible. Seasonality is normally calculated as the relationship between a period (typically a month or a quarter) and the moving average prediction for that month. For example, May book circulation might typically be 125% of the moving average forecast for May, while July book circulation might be 85% of the moving average forecast for July. Seasonality can also be expressed arithmetically rather than multiplicatively; for example, the seasonal factor for May might be an increase of 6,000 units. Seasonality can also be calculated by regression techniques using dummy variables for the time periods. In practice, this does not seem to have any advantage over the moving average proportionality approach, and the latter is far simpler and more intuitive. In any case computer programs to calculate seasonality or to deseasonalize data are available in most computer centers. (Be careful in use of deseasonalized data. As the remark attributed to Elliot Trudeau points out: "deseasonalized, the weather in Canada is just like Hawaii.") Most of these are descendants of the Census XII program developed by the Bureau of the Census. (See Armstrong, 1978.)

The second extension is the calculation of trends, and in the context of long range planning, this is far more important than seasonality. Like seasonality, trends can be calculated either additively (arithmetic growth or decline) or multiplicatively (geometric or exponential growth or decline). If we choose to treat the trend, let's call it growth, arithmetically, and if we wish to smooth our estimate of growth (which is after all logical, we should be just as chary, probably even more chary, of making our estimate of growth on just the most recent data, as we were of making our estimate of basic volume of operations on just the most recent data) then we come to the formula:

$$G_{t+1} = G_t + \beta(\underbrace{FQ_t - FQ_{t-1}}_{\text{Growth of base forecast}} - G_t) \tag{10}$$

where G is the arithmetic growth factor and β is another constant that like (a) above must lie in the range between 0 and 1. If we think of the growth of the base forecast ($FQ_t - FQ_{t-1}$) as one term, GF, then the equation can be written as:

$$G_{t+1} = G_t + \beta(GF - G_t) \tag{11}$$

This is very similar to Eq. 9, the exponentially smoothed base forecast.

If we choose to regard the growth in multiplicative terms, and to smooth it, the equivalent to Eq. 10 is:

$$G_{t+1} = G_t + \beta \left(\frac{FQ_t - G_t}{FQ_{t-1}} \right) \tag{12}$$

If we think of FQ_t/FQ_{t-1} as the growth of the base forecast (GF) then Eq. 12 also simplifies to Eq. 11.

The only disadvantages to applying the smoothing equation such as 9 (base forecast) or 11 (trend forecast) to make a forecast is that one must have previous forecasts to use as input. For Eq. 9, we must step back to Eq. 7 for that purpose. Equation 11 can be bookstrapped in similar fashion. The appropriate formula is:

$$G_{t+1} = \beta GF_t + \beta(1-\beta)GF_{t-1} + \beta(1-\beta)^2 GF_{t-2} + \beta(1-\beta)^3 GF_{t-3} \ldots \tag{13}$$

In such a fashion, one can extrapolate trends forward in time. First the base forecast is made, then a cyclicality/seasonality correction is made, then the trend/growth correction is applied. So far, the method has only been discussed in terms of projecting one time period forward, but there is of course nothing to prevent its being carried on as many times as are necessary to arrive at the desired time horizon.

A rule of thumb that has been suggested in terms of how many periods of historical data are needed to project a given number of periods into the future is that the number of periods of historical data needed is four times the square root of the number of periods to be forecast; that is, if HD equals historical data (in periods) and TH equals time horizon (in periods), $HD = 4\sqrt{TH}$ (Armstrong, 1978). Another question is what size (a) or (β) to use. A rule of thumb for (a) is that $a = \frac{2}{HD + 1}$. In general a higher (a) is more appropriate in unstable situations, and a lower (a) in more stable situations or if there is doubt about the accuracy or consistency of measurement of the data. Most computer packages for forecasting will have some capability of determining what would have been the optimal (a) or (β) for past forecasts, with the assumption that that will be optimal in the future. In other words, since Q_t, Q_{t-1}, etc. are known, the program can act as if Q_t were unknown, try to predict it, and see which parameters worked best, then step back one, attempt to predict Q_{t-1}, see if those parameters still look good, and so on. In any case, the experimental evidence seems to be that exponentially smoothed forecasts are not particularly sensitive to the choice of these parameters (Armstrong, 1978).

The authors have spent some time in elaborating on the mathematical foundation of exponential smoothing as a technique of extrapolatory forecasting for several reasons. First, it is a technique of extrapolatory forecasting that is relatively straightforward, and can be comprehended and applied with mathematical skills no more complex than standard arithmetic and algebra. It can be done anywhere with paper, pencil, and primitive pocket calculator. Access to a computer is not required. Yet despite this basic simplicity, the authors have almost never seen it set forth in a fashion that does not assume that anyone taking the trouble to read about extrapolatory techniques is quite comfortable with higher mathematics. Secondly, the other more trendily bandied about extrapolatory techniques, while mathematically more complex—they cannot readily be done with primitive pocket calculator—are simply doing exactly the same three basic steps of base analysis, cyclicality analysis and trend analysis. If one understands exponential smoothing, one can ask the right questions about the other techniques and not be "snowed" by terminology. Furthermore, there seems in fact to be no evidence that any of the other extrapolatory techniques work any better, and indeed there seems to be some evidence to the contrary (see Armstrong, 1978; Kang and Rouse, 1980).

Regression Techniques. There are a variety of techniques, some very colorfully named, based on the statistical properties of regression techniques. The classic visual portrayal of regression is a graph like that below,

Figure Two.   Sample Regression Relationship (Hypothetical Data)

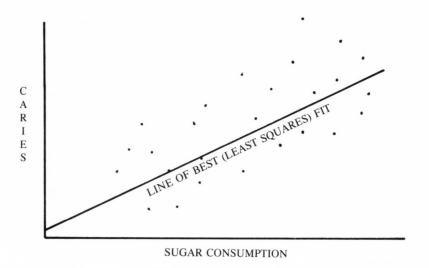

SUGAR CONSUMPTION

showing the variables that tend to vary together in a consistent and linear fashion. A line that "fits" the data best is expressed in the fashion of Y = a + bx (a being the point at which the line would cross the y axis, and b being the slope). Best fit is defined as the line such that the sum of the squares of the distance from the individual data points to the line is the least possible. The y variable might be caries, and the x sugar consumption. Equally well, the y variable might be online searches and the x variable time; and the result is an extrapolatory predictive technique.

When regression techniques are used in such a fashion, with the past values of some quantity as the predictor variables and the future values of that quantity as the criterion variables, it is termed auto regression—the past values of a quantity over time being used to derive a regression relationship that can be projected to forecast future values of that quantity.

If auto regression is combined with the use of moving averages the technique is called ARMA—auto regression moving average. The use of moving average figures rather than raw data serves to smooth the data, and the auto regressive techniques serve to provide the trend component of the analysis. Cyclicality can be handled in the same fashion as for exponential smoothing. The limitation of ARMA techniques is that regression analysis is capable of handling variables only in a linear additive fashion. Multiplicative or exponential growth can be handled only by the creation of logarithmic or exponential variables which are linear in their parameters. This restriction adds a good deal of complexity to regression-based techniques.

Although it cannot be so clearly demonstrated visually, regression techniques can be used to predict a criterion variable based on more than one predictor variable. Here the formula is of the sort $Y = a + b_1x_1 + x_2b_2 + b_3x_3 \ldots$ where we have used three predictor variables, x_1, x_2, and x_3. Miriam Drake has used just such techniques to predict the total operating costs of a university library (Drake, 1976). The resulting formula was:

Total Operating Cost* = .557 + .014x(volumes held) + .814x(volumes added)
+ .132x(professional staff)

*in $100,000

From such a formula, one could predict future operating costs by applying the formula to ARMA projections of the individual components. Indeed, there are computer routines to do precisely that, and they and the concept are known as MARMA techniques—Multivariate Auto Regression Moving Average. MARMA therefore suffers from the same limitations as does ARMA; the components can only grow additively, not exponentially (that is, they can only grow additively as analyzed by the technique; of course, that is not to say that they are so constrained in reality), and consequently the predictor variable is similarly constrained.

It is perhaps instructive and salutary to note that Drake points out that the carefully constructed formula had very limited predictive utility. The change in the economic climate, particularly the rapid increase in book prices soon rendered the formula and the predictions out of date and inadequate.

There are in addition further refinements of regression techniques. Probably the best known is called Box-Jenkins after the names of its two originators (Box and Jenkins, 1976). It is based on the concept of trend analysis by creating a new series based on the differences between successive forecasts and corresponding actual performance, and then determining what is needed to reduce the auto correlations of this series to stationarity (the absence of time-varying properties). The method is flexible, but requires a great deal of subjective input from the analyst, as well as a high degree of mathematical sophistication.

Another and similar regression-based variation is Adaptive Filtering (Makridakis and Wheelwright, 1979; 1978), which, like Box-Jenkins, expresses forecasts as functions of past values, but which optimizes the parameter through a steepest descent nonlinear least squares approach. Methodologically it is somewhat simpler than Box-Jenkins, but it still requires a substantial degree of mathematical expertise for implementation and evaluation (like Box-Jenkins by means of the auto-correlation of residuals).

Despite some of the mathematical elegancies of these variations, there is very little evidence that they contribute any real utility. A typical result is that reported in an article by Kang and Rouse (1980) on the subject of forecasting demands for library network services. They used Box-Jenkins methodology, adaptive filtering, and vanilla-flavored linear regression techniques. The latter was noticeably more accurate than either of the more complex methods. Armstrong (1978) in reviewing the literature, found only one case in which Box-Jenkins outperformed simpler methods.

The upshot of this review is that BFE (Bold Freehand Extrapolation) is probably as effective in forecasting, at least for the time frame in which we are interested, as the glamorous mathematical techniques. The bells and whistles of methodologies such as MARMA, Box-Jenkins, or Adaptive Filtering are essentially subtle ways of recognizing and correcting for fluctuations, such as seasonality, that are important only in the relatively short term. In the longer term, there is simply too much variability in the data, too much interconnectedness with other events for such refinements to be anything more than an irrelevancy (Twiss, 1979).

It is the authors' contention that for long range planning, two pads of graph paper, one conventional, and one semi-log are just as effective, if used wisely, as any of the variety of techniques described above. Probably even the caveat "if used wisely" is unnecessary, as the mathematical techniques can be just as foolishly abused.* For shorter-term

---

*That is not to say, of course, that wise use is not important, indeed essential.

forecasts, exponential smoothing appears to be more comprehensive, easier to use, and more often correct than the ARMA/MARMA techniques and their derivatives. Readers who question this conclusion, who take an "if there is smoke there must be fire" attitude toward Box-Jenkins and Adaptive Filtering are encouraged to read Armstrong, who is arguably the most experienced forecaster in the business today, who has come to virtually the same conclusions, and who has marshalled an impressive array of results and examples to support them (Armstrong, 1978). The discussion of extrapolatory techniques in a library context at this time results in a strange irony. Although there have been the classic discussions of the rate of growth of the literature and of libraries, the work of Rider (1944), and Price (1963) being the prime examples, extrapolative techniques have been relatively little used in library planning. Yet we are now leaving an era when the library world was so ordered, regular, and predictable, that era when extrapolative analysis was so appropriate. Librarians and information officers in this newer, much more chaotic world are correctly perceiving the need for greater planning. The recent triple issue of the *Journal of Library Administration* (1981) devoted to planning is an indicator of that trend. The danger is that librarians in their new-found enthusiasm for planning may seize upon extrapolatory analysis, using it and relying upon it where it is not really appropriate. Extrapolatory analysis will of course continue to be useful in charting the outlines of the capability of the technology with which we have to deal, but the alternatives within the technology, and therefore the course of actions of a library, will probably be much too complex to be manipulated in any straightforward extrapolatory fashion.

Modeling Techniques

Simulation and role playing. Simulation in the form of role playing, as a method of predicting the actions or the outcomes of actions of others is a useful technique, particularly when there is a conflict situation or when it is difficult to get an honest statement of intentions. The actions that people arrive at in real life are frequently rather different from what those people would have predicted they would do under those circumstances. By the use of simulations and role playing, it is possible to arrive at future scenarios that may more realistically reveal intentions than can more conventional approaches. For example, in role playing, simulation respondents were asked simply to predict what actions Upjohn executives would take, having recently learned that one of the company's major products, Panalba, was apparently discovered to produce very severe side-effects. These same respondents were then immersed in a role-playing situation in which they took the part of Upjohn executives. Intriguingly, while their response to the question of "What would you do if?" was to take the drug off the market, their response in the role-playing situation turned out to be precisely that which the Upjohn executives in fact did, to leave the drug on the market, and resist government attempts to remove it (Armstrong, 1977)

What this suggests in the arena of libraries and information services, is that simulation/role-playing techniques might be very useful techniques for librarians for example, to use in predicting the future actions of other major participants on the information scene—bibliographic utilities, data base vendors, telecommunication companies, and so on.

These are precisely the areas, or more accurately the participants, among whom there are conflicting interests and from whom it is difficult to get an accurate read-out on intentions. That of course is not a value judgement, but merely the observation that some parts of the information scene are, for intrinsic reasons, more characterized by unpredictability and real and potential conflicts of interest than are others. The authors have neither seen nor heard of evidence that such role playing is under-way, but they suggest that if not, it might be very useful for groups such as ARL or LITA to experiment with the technique. It might indeed shed some interesting light on what to expect next.

At a somewhat more local level, some reported use has been made of simulation/role playing. Townley et al. report the use of a structured role playing tool called LIPS, Library Information Planning Simulator, to simulate the library service planning for a local community (Townley et al, 1978). They report that one of the more interesting and consistent results was that those taking the role of librarians 'indicated a primary interest in school library applications, and less interest in making their facilities responsive to the total needs of the community," at least as perceived by other participants in the simulation. There seems to be a message in these results that librarians might take to heart. At the very least the experiment deserves to be replicated on a larger scale. The tool itself is an offshoot, indeed, a version of a tool called Policy Negotiations developed by the University of Michigan, which is available from the University of Michigan Extension Gaming Service, Ann Arbor, Michigan, 48109, for $5. Even if not used as a predicting/planning device, it could serve as a very useful adjunct to case study techniques in teaching library administration.

There are a number of basic ground rules for role playing/simulation. Give the players time to prepare, and make sure that they do indeed bone up on their history, and that they read for their roles. If the player knows that Harvard pulled out of the Yale, Harvard, New York Public Library joint depository scheme, and that Harvard withdrew support from the Yale, Harvard, Columbia joint medical library project, that player might well play Harvard's role in the Research Libraries Group with more con-viction and authority. Similarly, the use of props helps lend an air of authenticity and conviction. If you are going to play the role of a tele-communications company, dress in a three-piece suit, not blue jeans. If you are going to assemble a group of people to make simulated board room decisions, get an appropriately pompous sort of room to assemble in, and get someone to take orders for coffee and to serve it: don't use the staff lounge and its coin-op drink machines. In short, the rules in implementing role playing/simulation are to make it as realistic, both in terms of the context from which the players are arriving, and in terms of the props, as possible. A quick run through or rehearsal on the cheap, with a more full-blown show to follow is a poor economy. It is too likely that the "performance" will simply follow the pattern of the rehearsal, without the spontaneity and the conviction that might lead to new insights.

Econometric techniques. Modeling techniques in which the model used is a mathematical one are called *Econometric Techniques* in the jargon of forecasting. Many of the models used by forecasters, however, are very much simpler than what an econometrician would regard as econometric techniques. The basic constituent of econometric techniques is that there be some element of causality, rather than simply an extrapolation. For this reason, econometric techniques are intuitively attractive. Suppose, for example, that one were attempting to predict the number of online searches performed in an institution. One might posit the following relationships: The quantity of online searching is

- inversely proportional to price—the higher the charge, the less the business.
- a function of funding support—the greater the funding support being received by the community (perhaps a university) the more use is made of online searching.
- a function of the number of data bases—the more there is to search, the more searching will be done.
- an inverse function of frustration, the longer the wait, the less use.
- a function of experience—the more people there are who have done or had done for them an online search, the more searching will be done.

From this one might arrive at a simple model of the form:

$$\frac{OLS_{T+1}}{OLS_T} = \frac{1/P_{T+1}}{1/P_T} \times \frac{F_{T+1}}{F_T} \times \frac{\sqrt{\#DB_{T+1}}}{\sqrt{\#DB_T}} \times \frac{1/LnQ_{T+1}}{1/LnQ_T} \times \frac{\sqrt{U_{T+1}}}{\sqrt{U_T}}$$

where OLS = the number of online searches performed in a period, P = the average price/search as of the beginning of the period,

F = the amount of funding in place at the beginning of the period, #DB = the number of data bases available, Q = Queue time, the length of time from requesting the opportunity to do or have done a search and the accomplishment of it, as of the beginning of the period (L_nQ = the natural logarithm of Q), and U = the number of users as of the beginning of the period. The model is expressed as a simple ratio relationship, rather than as a more conventional formula, simply to illustrate the point that such a model (and the one illustrated above is not trivial by forecasting standards) could be worked out without the aid of sophisticated mathematics or computer programs. The model can be incremented forward period by period on the basis of last period's searching was to the variables as next period's searching is to the update of these variables. Of course we need to predict how the variables themselves will change. What has been the trend in the pricing of online searching? What is the prospect for funding support? How rapidly has the number of data bases been increasing? Does that seem to be following any patterned progression? How long will the queue time be? What are our plans for more active support of online searching? How many users will there be?

The ratio relationship above is of course a formula in the conventional sense if we choose to regard $\dfrac{OLS_{T+1}}{OLS_T}$ simply as a growth ratio, or correspondingly we can solve for the predicted level of online searching:

$$OLS_{T+1} = \left(\frac{1/P_{T+1}}{1/P_T} \times \frac{F_{T+1}}{F_T} \times \frac{\sqrt{\#DB_{T+1}}}{\sqrt{\#DB_T}} \times \frac{1/LnQ_{T+1}}{1/LnQ_T} \times \frac{\sqrt{V_{T+1}}}{\sqrt{V_T}} \right) OLS_T$$

What we can also do is to try to derive a formula, which we have verified based on more history than just two periods. We can take this formula, for example, and see how well it would have worked in the past, and used those results to refine it further. There are mathematical techniques to facilitate this process, but they are beyond the scope of this chapter. (Note, since ours is a relatively straightforward multiplicative model, and since by taking the logarithms to the base e, 10, or whatever of those variables, we could reduce the relationship to one that is linear in its parameters, we could have used regression techniques to develop our model. Our model indeed looks not too dissimilar from Drake's formula (1976) except that we posit that our variables interact more directly than simply additively. The point is that the distinctions between extrapolatory and econometric techniques is a porous one. Regression, basically thought of as an extrapolatory technique, can be thought of as an econometric modeling technique as well.)

The use of econometric techniques in the long range planning literature related to libraries and information handling is very limited to say the least. The only uses that the authors are aware of, are those such as

Buckland's study (1975) of circulation policies, that are micro in focus and that are clearly operations research in intent, rather than, constituting long range planning.

On a far larger scale, econometric techniques have been used to model the future of the world. The famous or infamous *Limits to Growth* study by Meadows (1974) is based on such a model, and it in turn is based on the "industrial dynamics" econometric methodology of Jay Forester at MIT. The Limits to Growth model has generated much controversy, and many challenges to its assumptions. One of the advantages to modelling, of course, is that it challenges assumptions, and it tends to reveal which assumptions are critical. The name for that process is *Sensitivity Analysis*: To what assumptions are our projections sensitive? Another advantage of econometric modeling is that it can deal with interdependencies. The simple model above illustrates this to a very limited degree, in that it at least treats the interrelationship of its variables multiplicatively rather than simply additively. More complex models can of course model much more complex relationships and interdependencies.

Evaluation of Alternatives

Since long range planning is ultimately the evaluation of and selection among a set of alternatives, the decision making techniques used to select from among the alternatives are of fundamental importance to long range planning. One must keep in mind that there are two different sets of alternatives involved in long range planning. The first is the set of likely future alternatives for the environment. Given those alternatives, the second set of alternatives is the set of alternative programs of action that the library or whatever agency is the subject of the planning may carry out. Some of these techniques have already been covered in the discussion of multiple scenario analysis.

Programmatic Analysis

Another fundamental concept to long range planning and its relevant decision analysis is that of *Programmatic Analysis*, that is, the analysis of the undertakings or organization in terms of their programs, what is being accomplished, why, for whom, and what resources are being expended for that purpose. To put it simply, this approach focuses on for what purpose the resources are being expended, rather than simply to whom the check is being written. At the operational level this concept is reflected in the movement from line item budgeting to program budgeting, particularly PPBS, Program Planning and Budgeting System, and ZBB, Zero Base Budgeting. In actual practice, PPBS and ZBB are usually implemented as operational planning systems, rather than as long range planning. A program budgeting system within the organization, including either PPBS or ZBB, is the most appropriate basis for, and a great facilitator of the interfacing of operational planning and long range planning. Again, program budgeting is beyond the scope of this article, but it fortunately has been well covered in the library literature. The reader is referred to Raffel and Shisko (1969) for the classic example of program analysis in a library context, and to Koenig (1980) for a discussion and examples of program budgeting in the library context.

Decision Trees

A basic technique in the evaluation of alternatives is that of the *Decision Tree* in which events and their associated probabilities and costs are laid out. Their probabilities and costs are then "folded back" to the decision points to arrive at an expected costs for each alternative. To illustrate with a simple example, assume the alternatives between leasing for five years and purchasing a piece of equipment are being evaluated. The lease cost includes maintenance and the purchase price does not. For purposes of simplicity, we will assume no scrap value after five years, and that all dollars have been discounted to their present value. Below is laid out a decision tree that includes estimates of the probabilities of various maintenance costs if the machine is purchased.

BUY/LEASE DECISION TREE

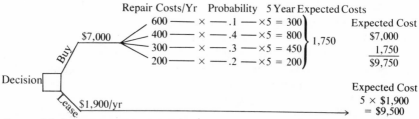

By multiplying probabilities by cost, we arrive at an estimated (expected value) five-year repair cost of $1,750. Then we can fold that information back to conclude that the best expectation is that the lease cost is approximately $250 less over the five-year period than the purchase cost. What has been computed is the expected value of the repair cost, and then of the two alternatives.

Risk Attitude

Too often, the mathematically correct expected value is taken at face value as the answer when comparing alternatives. What has been ignored is the *Risk Attitude*. The importance of risk attitude in selecting alternatives can be illustrated by the following hypothetical situation. If given a choice between Game 1 where one has a 50% chance of winning $20 (and suffers no losses) and Game 2 where one has an 80% chance of winning $10 (and suffering no losses), most people would recognize that the expected value of Game 1 is .5 × $20 or $10, and Game 2 is .8 × $10 or $8, and that Game 1 is in fact more attractive. Now, however, if we posit games 1A and 2A where the probabilities remain the same, but the pots are raised to $10,000,000 and $5,000,000 the responses might be very different. The expected value of Game 1A is .5 × $10,000,000 or $5,000,000, while Game 2A is "merely" .8 × $5,000,000 or $4,000,000. To the corporate planner for IBM, Game 1A is still probably preferable, an expected value of $5,000,000 versus the $4,000,000 of Game 2A. But certainly we as individuals would prefer an 80% shot at $5,000,000 to a 50% shot at $10,000,000. The *Utility* of those two outcomes is not the same as the expected value in this case, because of our risk attitude, that we would gladly give up the chance for a few million we have never seen, to significantly decrease our chance of not winning big at all. The point of course is that expected value and decision trees are tools, not answers. Their results must be evaluated in terms of the organization's risk attitude.

In the process of building scenarios, identifying the variables pertinent to each, and in assessing the probabilities of those variables and ultimately of the outcomes, what we have accomplished is commonly termed *Risk Analysis* for those alternatives.

Monte Carlo Methodology.   One of the techniques that is commonly used in risk analysis, with one of the more colorful names, is *Monte Carlo Methodology*. What this means simply is that we use a random process to simulate some event. For example, we may be evaluating the alternative of providing free on-line searching in our library in the future. How many terminals, support staff, and so on will be needed to provide a defined acceptable level of service? If we have some idea about the nature of online users, the types of search they request, and the varying amounts of time those searches require, we could literally simulate the likely future situation by creating cards that represented certain types of demand, making the quality of these cards proportional to the distribution of these types of demand, and then drawing those cards randomly, but in conjunction with known or expected time fluctuations to simulate the arrival and effect of demand for service. Hence the name Monte Carlo. If these random drawings are repeated enough, we arrive (assuming we have started with good data and assumptions) at a good representation of how demand is likely to distribute itself. Of course we might do this more easily via computer, and we would probably take advantage of some of the capabilities of queuing theory as well.

One of the realizations that Monte Carlo techniques produce is that probabilities are freqently best expressed not simply as point estimates, .5 or .3 for example, but as distributions.

Decision Analysis.   A more sophisticated risk analysis that takes this into consideration has been dubbed *Decision Analysis*. In decision analysis, the intent is to arive at a *Cost Lottery* for the different alternative programs for accomplishing some objective. In a cost lottery, one compares the probability distributions of the costs involved in each of the alternatives. For example, suppose we were attempting to evaluate different alternatives for document delivery. They might look something like that below:

DOCUMENT DELIVERY COST LOTTERY

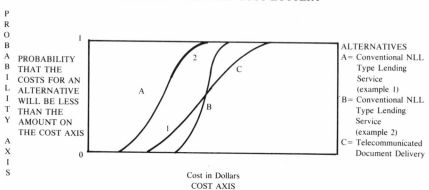

Cost in Dollars
COST AXIS

Suppose for the purpose of discussion that curve A represents a conventional NLL type National Periodicals Center, and that C represents online telecommunicated delivery. In all cases that curve A is to the left, the less expensive end of the lottery, of C, and therefore stochastically (probabilistically) dominates C. In fact, however, if we wound up at point 1 on curve C rather than point 2 on curve A we would have been far better in choosing the online system. What is even more likely, is a situation like curves B & C, where B represents the NPC, and C again represents telecommunication-based delivery system. The costs involved in one alternative (B) are much better known than for the other alternative (C), and so there is less variation in its probability distribution. On the other hand, alternative C has the potential to be much more economical, but if things do not fall into place, it could be much more expensive.

The utility of such a presentation is that it leads to a further round of analysis and that is the basis of decision analysis. The logical questions that result from viewing such a presentation are: What are the factors on which the great variation of costs for alternative C depends? In other words, what are the factors to which alternative C is sensitive (sensitivity analysis)? And then, what information can be gathered (and at what cost) to reduce that uncertainty? Those questions are the basis of decision analysis, the steps of which may be graphed as follows (Menke, 1977):

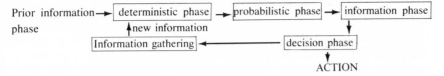

- deterministic phase: the analysis, decomposition and structuring of the problem.
- probabilistic phase: the assessing of uncertainties, and the assignment of probability distributions.
- information phase: estimating the value/cost of gathering new information to reduce uncertainty. (This is the concept that distinguishes decision analysis from other techniques.)
- decision phase: the decision to gather more information, or to select a course of action.

From the probability distribution, one can estimate an expected value of perfect information (EVPI). For example, to return to our first case of curves A and C, clearly one would choose curve A, yet there is still the possibility that we might wind up at point 2 on Curve A when we could have wound up at point 1 curve C. The magnitude of those differences times the probability of their happening is the expected value of perfect information. While we will never have perfect information, if we have a rough idea of the expense of achieving merely better information to reduce uncertainty somewhat, one can similarly make an estimate of the expected value of that less than perfect information. (Milliken and Morrison, 1973) This for librarians and information professionals should make decision analysis an intriguing concept; it is one of the few places that one can quantify in a meaningful sense the value of information.

In summary, decision analysis investigates the robustness of different alternatives that is, it examines not just point probability estimates, but probability distributions) and their sensitivity to different assumptions, and then examines the cost effectiveness of gathering more information to reduce the uncertainties, where appropriate, associated with particular alternatives. Even though some of the mathematical techniques of determining the value of further information are beyond the scope of this chapter, the idea is a powerful one, and if kept consciously raised as a mental flag in a long range planning exercise, leads analysis logically in the direction of "Where do we want to go next in this study?" (Bunn and Thomas, 1977).

Goal programming is a relatively new technique for the selection among alternatives (Ignizio, 1978; Lee, 1972). It is basically a generalized resource allocation and program planning tool which is best described as a multiple goal extension of linear programming. Goal programming therefore cannot easily be described without assuming a knowledge of the fundamentals of linear programming.

In linear programming, the solution to a series of constraints is found which best satisfies one objective function. For example, if one has a machine shop capable of producing products A, B, and C, and if the profit on product A is $40, B is $30 and C is $20, the objective function for a week's production might be to maximize $(A \times \$40) + (B \times \$30) + (C \times \$20)$. One might have constraints such as product A requires 3 hours of machine X's time, B 2½ hours, and C 1 hour, and if there are 80 hours of time on machine x available, then $80 = (3 \times A) + (2\frac{1}{2} \times B) + (1 \times C)$. There would be similar constraints for other processes, raw materials, labor, and so on. Linear programming is then a methodology to "solve" such constraints to produce a maximum or minimum value of a desired objective function, such as the one above. There are numerous good explanations of linear programming. The book by Makower and Williamson (1967) contains a particularly good, brief explanation.

In goal programming, the concept is extended to functionally include multiple objective functions. Although a detailed description of the procedure is beyond the scope of this essay, an examination of the goals used by Mott, Lee and McGeehan (1978) in a program analysis of a documentation center might be instructive. Those objectives were:

1. To provide an adequate total staff (at least 95% of last year's staff, but no more than 110%).
2. To provide a balanced revenue, 85% divided to current revenues, and 15% oriented to new development effort.
3. To avoid allocation of staff to projects of low utility to users.
4. To provide desired levels of staffing to meet five information service goals (delineated separately).
5. To provide at least minimal staff to each proposed project.
6. To provide an adequate ratio of administrative and support staff to service staff.
7. To minimize costs.

From the objectives and from data about the costs and expected utilities of various projects, the various constraints and an objective function were defined. To implement the process, it is necessary to prioritize the different goals (objectives). Given the potentially conflicting goals, the solution does not necessarily satisfy all goals (whence the necessity to specify priorities). When some goals are not obtained, different solutions can be created by assigning new priorities. In effect this procedure asks how high a comparative priority a marginal goal must have before it is important enough to be accomplished in the overall scheme of things. The Mott, Lee and McGeehan article is a good example of such a process in action.

Goal programming has for the most part been used for short term planning, but the methodology can be extended to greater time horizons. It has the potential of being a very powerful analytic tool in environments in which there are multiple and potentially conflicting goals and objectives. It very definitely should be of interest to library long range planners.

Economic Fundamentals of Alternatives Analysis

The conceptual similarities between systems analysis and long range planning become even clearer when one examines the economic fundamentals underlying them. They are both, in essence, techniques for the determination of appropriate *Investment Decisions*. Although the term investment decision conjures up images of coupon clippers and Wall Street gunslingers, it is in fact a far broader concept than that. A dictionary definition of "invest" is "to spend or utilize (time, money or effort) for future advantage or benefit." Whenever we propose spending some resource—time, money, or effort—for some future advantage or benefit, we are advocating an investment decision. That definition as it stands, prefaced by a phrase like "the analysis of alternatives concerning the expenditure or utilization of . . ." is in effect an excellent definition of systems analysis. If we simply move it forward in time, by inserting the word future—"the analysis of future alternatives . . ."—we arrive at a definition of long range planning.

Investment Decisions and Present Value. There are two trends at work that increasingly make it important to think of long range planning in terms of its being an investment decision. The first trend (already mentioned) (Koenig, 1982) is the increasing impact of modern technology, communications technology, data processing (teleinformatics as it has been termed) upon library operations. Investment decision is inherent in the nature of technological change. In the expectation of future savings or efficiencies, we implement a more modern technology. That implementation, however, requires the time, money, or effort that constitutes an investment. Long gone are the days when a library existed from year to year with only very minor changes in its operating procedures.

The second trend, one with which we are all too familiar, is the trend toward continued high inflation. A natural result of this trend is the need for more convincing justifications for investment decisions and more sophisticated presentations of those justifications. An investment of $500,000, for example, with a savings or benefit of $100,000 a year, is a relatively attractive venture whose attractiveness is clear in a period of low inflation. In a period of high inflation, it is not at all clear that such an investment is a wise one. Simply dividing the investment by the yearly savings to arrive at the simple pay-back period is not a very helpful tool for making that decision.

The result of inflation is that, in any analysis that takes place over any length of time, the dollar cannot be regarded as a constant unit. The dollar two years from now will be a very different creature from today's dollar. This difference, this lack of dollar commensurability, must be explicitly taken into account. Introducing and investing in technology necessitates looking at most of our new ventures as investment decisions whose effects over a period of time must be analyzed. The joint result of these two trends is that in order to prepare any planning document, it is necessary to know how to deal with dollars as they vary with time.

The conventional technique for dealing with the changing value of nominal monies (for example, the dollar) is the concept of *Net Present Value*. Even in an inflation-free economy dollars are not constant in value over time. If somehow one could be guaranteed that a dollar in future time would have the same purchasing power as a dollar today, one would still not be indifferent as to the choice between that future dollar and a dollar today. The pressure of inflation in the economy merely influences the need for discount, it does not cause it. The point is that in comparing alternatives that have been characterized by dollars, one must reduce those dollars to a common denominator. The conventional procedure is to discount future dollars to their present value. This technique will not be covered here, both because it is too fundamental, and because adequate coverage is not practical within the size constraints of this review. Net present value is, however, adequately described elsewhere within the library literature (Koenig, 1980), although one cannot help observing that awareness of net present value concepts is not nearly as widespread in the information community as it might be (Koenig, 1971). A general prescriptive that the authors wish to emphasize strongly is that one should have acquired a familiarity and an ease with the concept of and the calculation of net present value before undertaking long range planning.

Sunk Cost and Opportunity Cost.   There are two other economics concepts that are absolutely fundamental in alternatives analysis. Both are remarkably simple notions. The first concept is *Sunk Cost*, which describes basically anything that has already been spent, and that is irretrievable. (If it can be retrieved, that retrievability is a future event, and should be treated as a future event.) The consequence of the concept is starkly simple. Sunk cost is irrelevant. All decision making is ultimately no more than the analysis of "Where am I now, what are my alternatives, what benefits will I receive and what costs will I incur?" What has already been spent is beside the point.

This does not mean that data based on past information is not useful and that we cannot use such data to predict or extrapolate into the future, indeed, much of what follows will be addressed to techniques for doing precisely that. What it does mean is that the only rationally legitimate input in a decision process is our current state of affairs and our expectations for the future. The past illuminates the present and helps predict the future, but it should never enter directly into a decision. Any argument or statement such as, "We have spent over \$X,000 on this system and all that money will be wasted if we don't make it operational" is completely false logic. If one has invested money and effort in a computerized circulation control system and is now evaluating whether to continue that effort or purchase a commercially available system, the amount already spent is useful only in predicting how much more may have to be spent to make the system operational. For decision making purposes the only valid factors are: (1) how much more will it cost to make our system operational? and (2) what will the benefits be? The term "sunk" is colorful but legitimately and usefully so. What we have spent is gone, sunk. Forget about it, it is for precisely this reason that net present value methodology addresses only present and future costs. Nowhere, and very deliberately so, is there any inclusion of past costs.

The second concept is that of *Opportunity Cost*, which is a somewhat more subtle but equally valuable concept for the decision maker or analyst. The definition of opportunity costs are "those costs involved in the opportunities foregone in the pursuit of the alternative that has been chosen." Without an example, this definition sounds like jibberish, but at least the centrality of choice between alternatives is apparent. The classic economic example is that of a company which is contemplating building a factory on a plot of land it owns on the edge of town for the purpose of building new, improved widgets. The company calculates all its costs involved in this proposed new venture, its likely sales and revenues, then makes a decision as to whether or not to go ahead with the plan. That sounds logical enough. What in fact, however, the company is considering are two different alternatives—to build or not to build the factory. If the company does not build the factory, then it has another opportunity facing it. It can lease that piece of land it owns, or perhaps sell it to a supermarket chain. In any case, that land represents opportunities to do something other than build a factory on it or let it lie fallow. Those costs are the opportunity costs foregone by the decision to build a factory, and those costs should be explicitly included in any decision making process. It can easily be demonstrated that in many cases, the ignoring of the opportunity costs would result in the wrong decision.

The ramifications for long range planning for libraries and information centers are obvious. In the past, the range of alternatives was typically so limited that few opportunity costs presented themselves. Now, with a far broader range of opportunities and technologies, there may be opportunities to use facilities or resources already in hand for purposes other than what they have been routinely used for in the past. Those opportunities must be explicitly recognized to avoid the opportunity cost error. This sort of recognition is not something that librarians or information officers have had to arrive at with any frequency in the past, and is not yet the routine element of the culture of decision making in the profession that it must be in the future.

The importance of opportunity cost enters for yet another reason—the unusual handling characteristics of information as an economic good. Information as a commodity or good, behaves with a flexibility and dupli-catability, all enhanced by the computer age of course, that makes it quite unlike any other good, and, the point here, presents a large number of opportunities. Information can be exchanged, bartered, and so on without its loss to the owner, and this enormously enlarges the event horizon, the number of opportunities to be considered. Thus for two reasons, the concept of opportunity cost will be increasingly important to the library/ information community (Koenig, 1978).

REVIEW OF LIBRARY PLANNING LITERATURE AND APPLICATION

General

Library literature of recent years reveals that long range planning is a relatively new concern in the profession. A variety of authors have dealt with the question of the nature and premises of long range planning, borrowing heavily from the business management literature of long range planning, strategic planning, and systems analysis. It is useful to consider the emphases of such writers, as it is to them that many in librarianship will turn for understanding of such planning.

Several general works on library management treat planning, both strategic and tactical. Evans (1976) sees planning as being of eight types, relating to objectives, policies, procedures, rules, programs, budgets, grand strategies and competitive strategies. Although the uninitiated may need more explanation than he provides in understanding the interrela-tionship among these, and in judging time frames for each, he provides good library management examples. Rizzo (1980) focuses his discussion on the importance of establishing organization mission and objectives and places considerable value on an MBO approach. Stueart (Stueart, Robert and Eastlick, 1981) of the three, makes clearest the distinctions between strategic and tactical planning, asserting the primacy of objective and goal formulation in the long range planning process and acknowledging the confusion in the literature among the terms mission, goals, objectives, and so forth, an acknowledgement anyone reading more than one author will appreciate.

Academic Libraries

Although long range planning for different types of libraries presents some considerations peculiar to each, many concerns articulated in the literature of one type can be generalized meaningfully to all. Such is the case with Davis's article (1980), which relates to academic libraries. He sees library administration as yet to take a proactive approach to planning, wherein mastery of the relationship between an organization and its environment and codetermination of the future are sought. Librarians, he says, have a long-standing tradition of coping. His advice to begin working backward from desirable future outcomes to immediate requirements is classic MBO. He advocates stakeholder planning, the participation by all groups who have an interest in the library, and urges confidence in risk taking based on knowledge of where the library wants to go and how it will get there. A key component of his conceptualization of planning is that of adjustment in organizational structure for a more productive interface with the environment.

McClure (1978), also writing about academic libraries, has much to say of more general interest. He considers planning within the paradigm of an open system: the environment—political, social, and economic—interacts with the organization, resources flowing between the two. He stresses needs assessment as vital to goal and objective identification. Each objective is translated into several programs. Evaluation, both formative, which is ongoing, modifies the system, and addresses strategic concerns and summative, which follows an operation and is product-oriented, is required. Summative evaluation provides feedback to the primary philosophy stage of his model.

Elsewhere, McClure (1980) explores the question of information vital to the planning process. Going beyond user surveys, he documents the existence of a classic two-stage, gatekeeper like (in T.J. Allen's Terminology (1969)) pattern of information flow within library administration. He points out the utility of locating and using these "information-rich" individuals within the library organization and recommends the following: the establishment of the position of information resources manager, the education of employees in information evaluation, reducing automatic response situations for individuals, avoiding reliance on favorite sources who yield a narrow view, encouraging internally produced information, and evaluating librarians in their ability to handle information related to library goals (McClure, 1978). Contributions such as this to the literature give focus to theoretical considerations in planning, but, as McClure himself admits, detailed procedures are lacking.

A frequently referred to approach to long range planning is that of Bell and Kreusch, who attempt to develop a conceptual model of comprehensive planning based on the experience of developing a new Health Affairs Library at East Carolina University, Greenville, North Carolina.

While offering insights into the process of incorporating the parent institution's goals into plans for the library, the article disappoints in failing to specify what data contributed to decision making strategy selection. "The third alternative was selected, because it was believed that such a comprehensive facility would best serve the needs of the Division in the sense of collection and service capabilities."

The questions of how those needs were determined and how each alternative (without our now dwelling on what the alternatives were) was weighed—with what units of which scale—remain unanswered and are critical. The "how-we-did-it" article can be heartening as well as instructive, but to be of real value, contributions to the literature of library planning must not shy away from describing the tools of planning.

An important contributor to thinking about long range planning for libraries has been Webster (1978), who also identified strategic planning information as both a vital and insufficiently attended to need in academic libraries. Two others are allocation of resources and the analysis and forecasting of library environments. As director of the Association of Research Libraries' Office of Management Studies, he has been associated with increased interest in planning in member libraries. In part responding to the demand for accountability and sound management in an atmosphere of fiscal retrenchment, OMS developed the Management Review and Analysis Program and made this assisted self-study approach available in 1973. The information needs for MRAP belong to the action research tradition, which is one of MRAP's bases, the other being organizational development, which emphasizes interpersonal dynamics while focusing on implementing planned change within an improved organizational climate. Several projects preceded MRAP, the most significant being the study of Columbia University's Libraries' organization and staffing, undertaken by ARL with a Council of Library Resources grant and employing the firm of Booz, Allen, and Hamilton as primary investigator. (See Booz, Allen, and Hamilton, 1973.)

While not a planning process per se, MRAP requires the large library to address fundamental questions that are the essence of a long range planning effort, those of mission, goals and objectives, and the internal organization structure through which it perceives and negotiates its internal and external environments. Webster (1974) described it as involving a systematic investigation of the top management functions of a research library. Over what he says is a nine-month period, the study team composed of library staff and task forces investigates planning and control, organizational development, and personnel with a view toward attaining service objectives. The 400-page manual originally developed was conceived of as a starting point, with each library being expected to address its own situation taking into account local concerns. Central to the success of the program is top management commitment to continuing self-analysis.

A 1977 study by Johnson of MRAP's impact on participating libraries revealed general satisfaction of goals for MRAP set forth in the 1973 OMS annual report. However, differences in perception of the value of MRAP by different strata of library management were observed, as was considerable concern about MRAP's cost in terms of staff time and energy. While most libraries would benefit from needs assessment, environmental analysis, evaluation of management climate, and clarification of goals and objectives, Johnson suggests such studies need not be undertaken with the time pressures of a full-scale MRAP, and once done might lead to the conclusion that a given library does not need MRAP at all.

In 1979 OMS redesigned MRAP so that libraries could undertake smaller-scale studies using any or all of eight program modules in management functions, incorporating it into the more extensive Academic Library Program. Included also is the Academic Library Development Program (ALDP) (Morein et al., 1977) for libraries with staffs of more than twenty and fewer than fifty which had been developed at the University of North Carolina at Charlotte, with support from the Council on Library Resources. ADLP has been modularized, allowing participating libraries to do full-scale or selected self-study.

A third program, Planning Program for Small Academic Libraries (Association of Research Libraries, 1980), for institutions with staffs under twenty, become available in 1979 as part of the Academic Library Program and has been used by more than twenty libraries to date, with support for piloting the program coming from the Lilly Foundation of Indianapolis, Indiana. Some specific objectives are:

> To create within the library a more positive approach to change, one which focuses on anticipating needed changes and on promoting constructive approaches to these changes.

> To increase the library's problem-solving capabilities, and to expand its abilities to deal more effectively with an increasingly dynamic and complex environment (p. 17).

In discussing specific libraries where the Planning Program has been applied, Webster and Sitts (1981) describe a situation where a distinguished private college's library had the benefits of an energetic director, a sizeable budget for collection developing, and an already embarked upon renovation and enlargement of the physical facility; yet the following questions and concerns needed attention:

> What should the future character of the library be like? What is the best way of managing the library's collections to reflect the changing interests of the college? How can the teaching faculty be encouraged to make better use of the library? What

improvements could be made in allocation and selection procedures to assure the best
use of limited acquisition funds? How can a talented library staff more actively relate
to teaching faculty and manage the collections? What should the philosophy of library
growth and development be for the next 5 to 10 years, particularly in regard to
technology, institutional cooperation, nature of the collection, and character of
library services offered? (p. 131).

The Planning Program, which Webster and Sitts say addresses all these
questions systematically, is comprehensive, including long and short
range planning. It employs a model in which library purposes and activities are divided into four domains—policy, users, service delivery, and
management. The policy domain includes those concerns most clearly
identifiable as elements of long range planning, namely decisions about
formulation of mission and institutional priorities, allocation of resources,
and general orientation of the parent organization. Self-study in this
domain enhances the library's awareness of its environment and the
values that shape it. In the user domain, librarians recognize the need to
understand users belonging to diverse client groups, which is as pressing a
need as that of understanding the nature of the information users require.
The service delivery domain is that of library operations, wherein service
capabilities which bring user and resources together are strengthened.
The management domain coordinates the library's life in the other domains, including achieving harmony between library goals and the college
or university's goals. The success of the Planning Program derives from
the development of high levels of knowledge and information, a large
number of strategies for dealing with problems, clear understanding of
issues and decision, and increased motivation of individuals who have
identified problems and solutions to seek tangible results.

Apart from OMS assisted self-study, many university libraries have
developed long range plans, often in the context of total university planning. Throughout the country there was what has been termed "Mission
Madness," as goal setting, five-year planning, and mission articulation
preoccupied administrators of institutions of higher education in the
1970s. Much of this activity parallelled the "bottoms-up" planning style
that OMS's approach used. That is, lower-level supervisors' plans were
transmitted upwards through the organizational hierarchy, thereby
maximizing commitment to change by the very people who would implement it. Increased recognition of evaluation research and its emphasis
on the cyclical nature of planning promises that parent institutions and
their libraries will continue to benefit from self-study and the resultant
planning process.

Many universities and even smaller colleges have planning offices. The
aforementioned Booz, Allen, Hamilton study of Columbia University's
Libraries recommended such an office within the library. The American

Management Association's Center for Planning assisted Cornell to develop a long range plan for its libraries, and the library director reported that a key concern was the provision for continuous planning within the management program (Kaser, 1973). Another major comprehensive study which emphasized continuous, systematic planning was the University of Michigan's.

Public Libraries

In the area of public library comprehensive planning, the needs of individual libraries and systems have resulted in a major development, the PLA *Planning Process* (Palmour, 1980), published in April 1980. The history of the manual is worthy of a brief summary, as it highlights the progress in librarianship towards recognition of the importance of comprehensive planning, a recognition which, as indicated earlier, lagged greatly behind that by for-profit organizations.

The Council on Library Resources and the National Endowment for the Humanities undertook the support of a project in the early 1970s, the proposed Public Library Goals Feasibility Study, which considered whether a new Public Library Inquiry would be necessary to give clearer direction to the Public Library movement. The final report of that study, *A Strategy for Public Library Change* (Martin, 1972), contained recommendations which ultimately were not carried out, but it did pinpoint neglected important concerns, concerns *A Planning Process* now treats. *Strategy* did mention librarians' failure to formulate objectives and it did identify critical skills of a sort that now are developed in *A Planning Process*. Importantly, *Strategy* also recognized a need that a concurrent PLA project, the measurement of effectiveness of Public Libraries Study being done at Bureau of Library and Information Science Research at Rutgers, promised to satisfy.

The study had roots in the mid-1960s and PLA's interest then in accrediting public libraries. The need to measure effectiveness of service was articulated, and practical methods of data collection related to performance output were described in *Performance Measures for Public Libraries* (DeProspo, 1973), an interim and ultimately the only report to emanate from the Rutgers study, which was never completed. *A Planning Process* did not emerge for several years after *Strategy* and *Performance Measures*, but these two reports contributed to dissatisfaction with PLA's *Minimum Standards for Public Library Service, 1966*, and the PLA standards committee decided a new approach was necessary, focusing on the needs of the community rather than the needs of the individual library. The PLA contracted with King Research for the design of planning procedures, which would address the challenges of providing tools for analysis of a library's situation, setting of objectives, making decisions, and evaluating achievements. Vernon E. Palmour was the principal investigator, and his methodology was based on that which he and Marcia Bellassai had developed for the 1975 Planning Study of the Baltimore County Public Library.

The introduction to PLA's *A Planning Process* emphasizes that indeed planning is a process and that what is sought is not a finished plan but rather a dynamic commitment to the continuous cycles of planning. As laid out in the manual, the steps of the first cycle contain no surprises for anyone familiar with planning literature in general. They are:

1. Assessing community library needs.
2. Evaluating current library services and resources.
3. Determining the role of the public library in its community.
4. Setting goals, objectives and priorities.
5. Developing and evaluating strategies for change.
6. Implementing the plan.

A series of secondary one-year cycles calls for monitoring and evaluating progress toward goals, with community needs continuing to inform and drive library priorities. A new primary cycle is initiated in five years.

The manual's recommendations are just that—recommendations. When the effort to complete the initial cycle is beyond the library's resources, aspects of that cycle can be deferred. Flexibility of the process is advanced as one of its virtues. Central to planning, of course, is management of data, an information management system that determines what information is needed, coordinates collection, and takes responsibility for analysis and dissemination. This function is aided by the manual's sample instruments for staff, citizen, and student user surveys, tables for assessing services, and also sample goal and objective statements.

A project sponsored by the British Research and Development Department dovetailed with Palmour's work, and two British libraries were included as test sites for the PLA manual. The British project, Benefit Assessment for Systems Change (BASYC) (Morris, 1979a) is a cost-effective modeling technique, which allows participative planning by asking stake-holder groups to identify goals the library will achieve. Strategies evolve and groups register the extent to which they perceive each goal being advanced by each strategy. Strategies are modified and one is finally selected as satisfying interests of diverse groups. The ultimate decision maker may use or reject this final consensus strategy. The implementation of this strategy can be done in the same participatory style as that of the study of alternatives.

Discussion of *A Planning Process* will doubtlessly continue to appear in public library literature, one systematic case study of the planning process in progress being undertaken currently at Columbia University's School of Library Service. Reports of the two British trials have appeared. At the Borough Library of Islington (London), it was observed that information made available through the process enhanced decision making throughout the organization (Morris, 1979b). At the Sheffield Library, the process was deemed very ambitious and expensive in terms of high-ranking staff time, although the possible usefulness for smaller, localized programs was seen. (See Dyson, 1980.)

The North Carolina State Library, recognizing its own need for community analysis to justify increased funding in an atmosphere of accountability, undertook implementation of such analysis at the level of sixty-nine local systems using a methodology devised by Greer. It concluded that doing the analysis and evaluating current library resources were easier than developing a long range plan and therefore the agency eagerly awaited the PLA manual. In comparing the Greer and PLA approaches, they conclude that the former's methodology is more rigorous in assessing community and library environment, evaluation of current library services and resources, and in determination of public library role in the community, whereas the PLA manual places greater emphasis on the cyclic nature of planning and the need to evaluate and update goals, objectives, and priorities. Suggestions for improving the next edition of the PLA manual include the request for a more exhaustive definition of long range planning, taking into account the assessment of strategies as appropriate to desired objectives. Also, discussion of management techniques such as PERT and CPM has been found wanting; the library is asking for the tools that planners in industry use (McKay, 1980).

Other recent writings on *A Planning Process* seek both to clarify its value for the participating library and to provide guidance around predictable pitfalls. Hagwood (1981) suggests a training cycle as a useful precursor to the manual's primary cycle. In the training cycle a small-scale problem is treated using all the suggested steps in the manual, thereby extending the primary cycle to three steps: training; thinking, wherein the real problem in all its complexity is considered, and which may take months for the five-year plan; and measuring, which corresponds to the manual's primary cycle per se. Elsewhere he does a good job of relating the planning process to the systems analysis and design approach, describing the library as a human activity system whose viability depends on agreement of purposes by participants. Its subsystems are of three levels of purpose: to perform quotation tasks, to check resources and monitor effectiveness in fulfilling purposes, and to monitor the system's overall response to changes in environment and to make adjustments. The higher levels require information flowing upward from the lower. The planning committee, at level three, adapts the system's stated function to changes in needs of the community and selects strategies for satisfying them.

Bellassai (1981) sees that factors contributing to the value of the planning process are also potential sources of problems. The broad-based representative planning committee represents the participative, stakeholder aproach to planning, which much library literature advocates. However, the role of each member must be made clear as must be the understanding of which matters are finally the library director's province. She also points out that data collection tends to slow momentum, causing dropouts among community representatives. Also, a deluge of collected data represents an information overload for the committee. The data coordinator, who refines and presents information meaningfully, is therefore, a key person.

Lynch (1981) reports that the public library community has not completely turned its back on the questions of standards; indeed, the absence of national standards and their neglect in the *Planning Process* are a matter of considerable concern. At this point, the PLA Board has accepted a recommendation that "once a sizeable group of public libraries have used this process, PLA intends to examine the results and assess the need to produce guidelines which would assist local libraries in planning." The Goals, Guidelines and Standards for Public Libraries Committee plans to promote consistent measurement of library output by preparing, reviewing, and publishing a manual on performance measures for public libraries and encouraging libraries to use measurements with help from state library agencies, library schools, publications, and so forth. Regardless of developments in national standards, however, PLA has taken a great step forward by focusing library attention on local service needs through *A Planning Process*. In the current economic and political climate in America, such planning is clearly a local concern.

The PLA *A Planning Process* is the most significant contribution to comprehensive public library planning in library literature, but it is not the only one. Against a background of planning in the public sector and its relation to the public library, Goldberg has (1976) developed a model that explicitly utilizes systems thinking, although his main concern is program planning. His PIES (Planning, Implementation and Evaluation System) model emphasized the strategic orientation of PPBS, wherein planning, programming and implementation are complementary operations. If the budgeting aspect becomes too large because of concern with efficiency, strategic planning, and, therefore, effectiveness suffer. The PIES model has two phases, planning and implementation. The system's orientation along a means-end continuum finds planning at the ends pole, with the formulation of service goals and setting objectives establishing the strategic planning orientation. Selecting program strategy and designing the program precede his conception of task management orientation, the steps of transition from planning to action, monitoring, and summative evaluation.

Other contributions to the literature have been useful. The incorporating of demographic projections by regional planning boards is developed by Kunz (1976),who sees such data used in planning other local facilities. Greer (1978) provides a framework for actually manipulating library applicable data derived from census figures, incorporating inferences for service from aggregate characteristics of communities. Martin (1976) in describing the value of user survey in planning, underscores the need for sound research methodology in implementing user studies and says studies of use and nonuse must span total communicating systems in a community, of which the library is but one element. Articles such as these clarify and supplement the contributions of *A Planning Process* and should not be neglected by library managers seeking to plan effectively.

School Libraries and Media Centers

In the school media center field, the major contributions to planning literature have come from James Liesener (1976), whose concerns regarding the failure of standards to address systematically the objectives formulation, resource allocation, and evaluation related to programs led him to develop very clear, documented relationships between inputs, processing, and output costs. Again, while the emphasis is on program planning, his approach incorporates elements common to most comprehensive planning systems and includes fundamental goals and objectives of embedding institutions as consideration in program design. His conceptualization of the media program is as a basic system model which differentiates program components and reflects the specific relationship among them. This model also clarifies means-ends distinctions, which were not previously delineated in media program literature. That is, relationships between system inputs and outputs were not understood.

His system calls for effective participation by various stake-holder groups throughout the planning process, which he sees as having nine steps:

1. Definition of program output alternatives.
2. Survey of perceptions of current services.
3. Determination of service preferences and priorities in relation to local needs.
4. Assessment of resource and operational requirements of services.
5. Determination of costs of preferred services and/or current services.

6. Calculation of program capability.
7. Communication of preferred services currently feasible to total client group.
8. Reallocation of resources and implementation of changes in operations to provide the range and level of services selected.
9. Periodic evaluation of services offered and documentation of changing needs.

Liesener provides model instruments and techniques for implementation of these steps, and he encourages the media specialist by saying that school administrators are generally supportive of such a systematic management approach. However, he does remark that the greatest obstacle to success for such a program is the media specialist's failure to adopt a proactive posture.

Very little has appeared in the literature on long range planning in the special library environment. This does not connote lack of interest, but rather a different kind of interest. The special library typically must conduct long range planning as a component of a larger organization. Furthermore, that organization, typically a corporation, can change directions and objectives with a speed that is quite unlike what is characteristic of the environment of academia or public libraries. For that reason, and because of the lack of long-term archival roles for the library providing some sort of stability and predictability despite changes in the present organization, formal long range planning by special libraries, which is not part of a larger organizational process, is unlikely to be very productive. One result of this embedded context nature of special libraries is that very little appears about them in the literature of long range planning. The long range planning process is taken more for granted, and what has been written tends to emanate either from the planning (facilitation) department or from consultants who have been involved with a specific project. Such literature tends to pay, as yet, scant attention to library and information center planning, and frankly, because of the nature of corporate confidentiality, tends to be rather desanitized of anything but methodology.

The special librarian then should be armed with a knowledge of the various methodologies of long range planning, in order to successfully cope with whatever long range planning methodology might be adopted by the present organization. Indeed, the Special Libraries Association has a continuing education workshop devoted to just that purpose. [4] The methodology section of this chapter can also be viewed as devoted to precisely that need, although of course it is designed to be broadly applicable to librarians and information officers in general.

Just emerging in the corporate environment is a concept closely relating to long range planning called enterprise analysis (Parker, 1982). It is outside the nominal scope of this article, but it will be mentioned briefly because the authors expect it to have major impact upon librarians, particularly special librarians. Enterprise analysis is a loosely defined concept that has emerged form the disciplines of data processing and MIS (Management Information Systems). It refers to the notion of finding out what the organization or enterprise is all about, and what that enterprise's information requirements are or will be (long range planning) with the intent that automated information systems may be designed that will be responsive to the enterprise's needs. At this point, enterprise analysis and LRP are only very loosely linked in the literature, but a stronger future linkage seems inevitable. Part of the reason for this lack of linkage is terminological. Much of the work on enterprise analysis has originated with IBM, and the term has been coined by IBM. It will not be surprising therefore if some non-IBM terminology is soon instituted for enterprise analysis in the management literature, and the linkage with long range planning becomes more evident and better articulated.

The importance of enterprise analysis to librarians and information officers is its focus upon the identification of information requirements, a process in which the skills of the librarian or information officer should be central. What is striking to a librarian is that the work that is emerging in the process of elucidating information requirements for enterprise analysis makes no mention whatsoever of the rich library literature concerning the reference interview, which is ultimately the same process. Here is a topic—the role of the librarian in enterprise analysis—that also deserves an article in its own right.

The term enterprise analysis has in fact been coined to generally describe a variety of information analysis techniques that have sprung up to fill a void, namely, to answer the question "How do we know the requirements around which to design an information system?" There is not sufficient scope within the context of this article to describe these techniques in detail, but some will be mentioned briefly so as not to frustrate the reader who is interested in pursuing the topic.

- Strategy Set Transformation—is a term for the top-down analysis of macro-information requirements derived from an analysis of specific organizations objectives and strategies. In other words, given long range planning and the strategies it produces, what information requirements result (King, 1978)?
- Critical Factor Analysis—consists essentially of asking users to define the critical factors, the factors critical to success, in performing their functions or in making their decisions. From those factors can be derived information systems requirements (Rockart, 1979).

- Process Analysis—consists of trying to define the key processes to an organization, and from that to identify the information and information system requirements. An increasingly well-known process analysis package is BSP (Business Systems Planning) developed by IBM (1981).
- Decision Analysis—(note the term is used here in a different context than elsewhere in this article) is a three-stage process of (1) identifying and describing key decisions, (2) defining the decision algorithm or process—how is the decision made, and (3) defining the information needs elucidated by the decision process (Ackoff, 1967; Munro and Davis, 1977).
- Input/output/process analysis—is the process of defining systems in terms of inputs and outputs, and the consequent information requirements. There are at least two major packaged input/output/ process analysis systems, ISAC (Information Systems work and Analysis of Changes) developed by the Karolinska Institute and the University of Stockholm (Lundeberg et al., 1981), and ADS (Accurately Defined Systems) developed by NCR (Lynch, 1969). Data flow diagrams are the basic technology of impact output analysis.
- Stage assessment—is the concept of describing an organization's position and charting its future development along the life cycle of automated information system development posited by R. Nolan (1979), and from that positing certain kinds of present and future information needs. Nolan's D.P. life cycle concept has had enormous influence upon line management, supervision of data processing, and his work should be read by anyone interfacing with D.P. or about D.P. at a senior level.

What all of these processes or techniques have in common is the concept of information requirements determination. What is now fascinating is the convergence of long range planning and enterprise analysis around the concept of the data dictionary/directory (Sakamoto and Ball, 1982), the tool which is also increasingly seen as the heart of data processing and data administration. The data dictionary/directory is basically a classic library function, but a function which has arisen in data processing, not in the library or information center. The impact of this for librarianship will be addressed in future articles. The fundamental point to be made however, is that the combination of information needs assessment and the classification of those needs and of what information is on hand, both of which are functions that the librarian is perhaps best equipped of all contenders to cope with, are increasingly being regarded as of central importance to the organization.

Strategic Data Bases

An interesting tie-in between the special library and long range planning is the concept of the strategic data base. As is frequently pointed out, most vigorously by King and Cleland (1977), strategic or long range planning is a very information-dependent exercise. Furthermore, it is or should be a continuous cyclical process. The logical extension of these premises is that the long range planning team or process should be supported with appropriate ongoing strategic data bases or, as King has more recently referred to it, as "a planning information subsystem" to the planning system (King, 1981). King and Cleland identify five such strategic databases (SDB):

1. Strength and Weakness SDB (a candid and concise statement of the most significant strengths and weaknesses of an organization).
2. Business and Industry Criteria SDB (requirements for successful performance in the enterprise area of operations).
3. Competitive SDB (strengths and weaknesses of the competition, and what their strategies are likely to be).
4. Environmental Opportunities and Risks SDB (what can happen in the environment: regulation, new technology, new markets, etc).
5. Management Viewpoints and Values SDB (strategic objectives and constraints and risk attitudes, social responsibility, etc.).

Given such requirements, it is certainly logical for the corporate library or information center to be an active participant in the creation of these SDBs, and therefore in the corporate long range planning process. Such involvement is a golden opportunity to achieve a position of greater centrality in the organization. Such participation also requires a knowledge of the terminology of long range planning, which is one of the major reasons for the relatively extensive discussions of methodology in this article. Despite the author's skepticism about the utility of Box-Jenkins methodology, for example, it may be important to know the name. There is, however, little evidence that such involvement takes place with any frequency. The authors believe that this is an opportunity that should be taken advantage of more aggressively and intend to publish further on this topic. This topic has however been addressed recently in the library environment. M.K. Brown (1981), apparently unaware of the business literature, has produced an article on precisely the topic of gathering information for long range planning in libraries, and had delineated the SDB concept specifically in the library context.

Review

Just how much long range planning is being done by libraries is hard to assess. ALA's Office for Research has been trying to keep track of the use of *A Planning Process*, and despite questions about the accuracy of their data, at the end of 1980 they concluded that, "however you measure size, libraries of all sizes are using *A Planning Process*." A study by Moore (1981) looks at long range planning in Missouri libraries. Its conclusions are interesting, but because of sample size they cannot be generalized beyond that state. The study found:

1. a substantial minority of libraries were engaged in some form of long range planning;
2. long range planning in libraries is more operations-oriented, that is, concerned with budgeting over a period of five years, than strategy-oriented;
3. the use of long range planning is affected by organizational factors, namely library size and network affiliation, and by the director's educational level.

Moore's sample was stratified, representing academic, public and special libraries. He says, "For those small libraries serving a limited clientele, long range planning is probably not necessary or particularly desirable since such libraries operate within a limited range of goals and alternative actions."

There is one area which clearly has seen widely practiced long range planning, and while the focus of this paper has been the individual library or system, the planning of state library agencies must be mentioned. The Library Services and Construction Act requires that each of the fifty-seven state and territorial library administrative agencies submit annual updating of a basic long range plan in which a state's goals, objectives, and priorities, as well as activities for defined time periods are specified. Such long range planning includes multitype library cooperation, and LSCA Title III in particular provides impetus for the networking and cooperation which figure prominently in the present and the future of statewide plans.

Serial literature provides the business community with a stream of new perspectives in long range planning, focusing either on the larger process or particular details. As library managers become more sophisticated about planning, such literature should be part of their professional reading. Recent articles from serials like *Long Range Planning, Managerial Planning,* the *Harvard Business Review,* and so on while written for industrial managers, can be examined with the library in mind. A sampling is included here in the hope that more exhaustive forays by library managers into this sort of planning literature will follow.

If librarian-managers enter more actively into the strategic planning process, they will do well to consider the dangers that Berry (1981) presents. If forecasts on which objectives are based prove inaccurate, the objectives must be reevaluated and not remain the target, despite the new input. He says strategic planning often stops with the assignment of objectives and resumes with measuring accomplishment against them. One can easily see this happening in an organizational environment where the flame of planning and MBO has been recently lit and perhaps is being tended by a tenderfoot rather than an eagle scout. Berry says the development of objectives should be top-down, with negotiations allowed.

Naylor (1979) says this more emphatically. He stresses that strategic planning is the business of the chief executive officer and also of line managers. "He or she who controls the strategic planning process controls the company" (Naylor, 1979, p. 4.). It must be done by those with responsibility for achieving goals. Operating managers, at the head of divisions of functional departments, must also do strategic planning. In a sense he is opposing a point made by Moran (1978), who feels that cooperative planning for libraries should be the responsibility of the occupant of a position created for that purpose, an individual with no other responsibilities. If Moran is right about the problems in gaining staff acceptance of the library's having to share resources, perhaps Naylor is right. Who but the very top officer has clout enough to implement plans for cooperation? Certainly, a newcomer to the organization or even a veteran with what is perceived as a fancy new title may not. Naylor also stresses the need for control of information in the planning process, as does library literature, but he warns against allowing the management information system department or function to control the planning process by, for example, controlling computer software used. As librarians, who may not have to deal with an MIS department per se, we very clearly recognize the power residing in information control and are sensitive to the manipulation of data in different ways for different purposes. Clearly, the strategic planning process is one in which that professionally whetted awareness should be put to good use.

Irwin (1978) believes strategic planning is still in its infancy and is least likely to encounter resistance from chief executive officers who see long range planning as their job, and from people who have participated in a well-structured planning program. He touches on one point that merits further discussion for librarians. In answering skeptics who say planning is not feasible in the face of unavailable or unreliable data, he says such conditions make decision making riskier, but are not to be avoided, and he urges caution in use of computer models because faulty data can result in strategic plans that have little bearing on reality.

Tenaciously held attachment to the belief in the library as an educational institution may result in goal conflict. According to Sawyer (1980), dealing with this requires recognition of two different goal levels. The first is beyond compromise, wedded intrinsically to a value system. The second is that of expedient goals, those which negotiate contingencies and are a way to advance general goals at a given moment. A greater goal for libraries can be general life enhancement of clients, taking the view that if the latter are happily and safely occupied, the library is making its contribution and can, with clear conscience, provide Harlequin romances and not promote Jane Austen. Alternatively, and this is perhaps more likely, the mission (and this term seems more appropriate in this discussion than "goal") of educating can still be retained, with the goal of providing popular-taste material pursued in the furtive hope of aiming sights higher, once the client gets used to the library and libraries.

PRESCRIPTIVES

Although this chapter is not intended to be a how-to article on long range planning, there are several basic aspects that the authors feel strongly should be mentioned in any review work in the field that may well be consulted in how-to mode.

Long Range Planning Must Be Supported Wholeheartedly by Management

This point is obvious but too often ignored. Without top management commitment, long range planning becomes an arid, counterproductive exercise. Without top management commitment, middle management effort can too easily be seen as artificial, time-consuming, and worthless; in short it can be morale sapping. Belief in the commitment to implementation likewise enforces a realities hardened analysis. For people to take long range planning seriously, and therefore to do a good job of it, they must have confidence that it is in fact a prelude to implementation. Some of DeProspo's (1981) comments on the realities of planning zero in on this point nicely.

Long Range Planning Is Not Done by a Person or a Department

Long range planners or long range planning departments do not do (or should not do) long range planning—they facilitate it: long range planning is ultimately a decision making process, a solution among alternatives. That function is best done by that management who will be responsible for implementing it. To do otherwise is to risk lack of commitment as we have said before. The long range planner or long range planning department helps in the preparation and development of alternatives, and in providing tools and mechanisms for decision-makers to use in making the appropriate decisions.

Long Range Planning Is a Cyclical Process

Far too easily lost in the variety of methodologies is the point that long range planning is not, or should not be, a one-time process. Long range planning should be an ongoing cyclical cybernetic (feedback) phenomenon. The notions of multiple scenario analysis and of strategic data bases are important in focusing on this concept. As the environment, the technology, the users needs, and so forth change, the scenarios should change accordingly, and the strategic data bases should change accordingly. As they change, then perhaps our decisions (long range planning is a choice among alternatives) should change. Clearly not only should scenarios and data bases be updated, but decisions should be reviewed frequently. A recent example of such a change is the decision of Columbia University Libraries not to develop a microform catalog, but to move toward online. This decision was probably abetted by the King Research Report (Wiederkehr, 1980) on the future of the catalogue, which was funded by the Council on Library Resources. It illustrates perfectly, however, how long range plans may well need to change in the face of a changing environment.

Long Range Planning Requires Unfreezing

Long range planning is a major ongoing effort that requires participation from many staff members who may never have been involved in strategic decision making before. They are apt to be skeptical (another reason for top management commitment and involvement) and cautious, and induction into a strategic decision making modality may be threatening. It may well require a different way of thinking than heretofore exercised (see Long Range Planning as Systems Analysis, above). For those reasons, the implementation of a long range planning process may well require a process of unfreezing, and the appointment of a suitable person to act as facilitator and change agent. Indeed this function is one of the most important for a long range planning officer or department to perform. This function is important of course not only in implementing long range planning, but also for helping to implement some of those changes that long range planning inevitably brings about. The staff involvement and unfreezing process are discussed by Henley (1981), and Zweizig and McClure (1981) in terms of various issues of staff involvement and training for planning.

CONCLUDING REMARKS

This chapter is not intended to be a how-to article for library long range planning. Rather it has attempted to be a source for the literature (including the how-to literature) of strategic and long range planning, particularly as it applies to libraries and information centers. The authors however have not attempted to avoid expressing some strong opinions not only on the necessity of long range planning, but on how it should be conducted. The nature of technology is changing the library world to a radical degree. No longer can our planning be reactive catch-up coping. Now we are faced with what strategic and long range planning is all about—the delineation of and the selection among alternatives. The opportunities furthermore are more than simply that of exercising choice; long range planning provides, as well, the opportunity to shape those alternatives, to shape the future. If we do not take advantage of these opportunities, however, our future will of necessity be shaped for us.

NOTES

1.   Taken of course from Shakespeare's *The Tempest*.

2.   Among those reasons of course is that peer recognition among systems analysts and operations researchers is based on publication, which in turn is most easily achieved by demonstrating mathematical complexity and novelty (even if at the expense of relevance or utility). Similarly, the desire of systems analysts to retain the secrets of the guild and exclude outsiders by cloaking common sense in the garb of offputtingly recondite mathematics is also at work.

3.   Since cost is benefit foregone, the phrase cost/benefit analysis is essentially redundant, and although in common use, will not be used further here.

4.   Continuing Education Course CE 226 "Strategic Planning for Library Managers."

REFERENCES

Ackoff, R.L., "Management Misinformation Systems." *Management Science* 14(4):B147–B157, 1967.

———, "Planning in the Systems Age." *Sankyhn: The Indian Journal of Statistics*, Series B 35, Part 2, 1973.

Allen, Thomas J., and S.I. Cohen, "Information Flow in Research and Development Laboratories." *Administrative Science Quarterly* 14(1):12–19, 1969.

Armstrong, J. Scott, "Social Irresponsibility in Management." *Journal of Business Research* 5:135–213, 1977.

———, *Long-Range Forecasting, From Crystal Ball to Computer*. New York: John Wiley & Sons, 1978.

Armstrong, J. Scott, W.B. Denniston, and M.M. Gordon, "The Use of the Decomposition Principle in Making Judgements." *Organizational Behavior and Human Performance* 14:257–263, 1975.

Association of Research Libraries, Office of Management Studies, *Planning Program for Small Academic Libraries: An Assisted Self-Study Manual*. Washington, D.C.: Association of Research Libraries, 1980.

Bell, JoAnn, and R.B. Kreusch, "Comprehensive Planning for Libraries." *Long Range Planning* 9(5):48–56, 1976.

Bellassai, Marcia Courtney, "Public Library Planning and the ALA/PLA Process: What's in it for your Library?" *Journal of Library Administration* 2(2,3,4), 1981.

Bernstein, G., "A Fifteen Year Forecast of Information Processing Technology." Report prepared by the Research and Development Division, Naval Supply Systems Command. Management Information Services, Detroit, Michigan, 1969.

Berry, Waldron, "Beyond Strategic Planning." *Managerial Planning* 29(5):12–15, 1981.

Bickner, R.E., "Concepts of Economic Cost." In Donald W. King (ed.), *Key Papers in the Design and Evaluation of Information Systems*. White Plains, N.Y.: Knowledge Industry Publications, 1978.

Booz, Allen and Hamilton, Inc., *Organization and Staffing of the Libraries of Columbia University*. Westport, Conn.: Redgrave Information Resources Corp., 1973.

Box, G.E.P., and C.M. Jenkins, *Time Series Analysis, Forecasting and Control*. San Francisco: Holden-Day, 1976.

Brown, Maryann Kevin, "Information for Planning." *Journal of Library Administration* 2(2,3,4), 1981.

Brown, Robert G., "Less Risk in Inventory Estimates." *Harvard Business Review* 37(July/August):104–116, 1959.

Buckland, Michael H., *Book Availability and the Library User*. New York: Pergamon Press Inc., 1975.

Bunn, Derek, and Howard Thomas, "Decision Analysis and Strategic Policy Formulation." *Long Range Planning* 10(6):23–30, 1977.

Business Systems Planning-Information Systems Planning Guide, Application Manual GE20-0527-3, Third Edition, IBM Corporation, 1981.

Davis, Peter, "Libraries at the Turning Point: Issues in Proactive Planning." *Journal of Library Administration* 1(2):11–24, 1980.

DeProspo, Ernest R., "The Evaluative Component of Planning: An Opinion Essay." *Journal of Library Administration* 2(2,3,4), 1981.

DeProspo, Ernest, et al., *Performance Measures for Public Libraries*. Chicago: American Library Association, 1973.

Drake, Miriam, "Forecasting Academic Library Growth." *College and Research Libraries* 37(1):53–59, 1976.

Drucker, Peter, *Managing in Turbulent Times*. New York: Harper & Row, 1980.

Dyer, Esther R., "The Delphi Technique in Library Research." *Library Research* 1:41–52, 1979.

Dyson, C., *A Planning Process for Public Libraries*. BLR & DD Report 5541, March 1980.

Evans, G. Edward, *Management Techniques for Librarians*. New York: Academic Press, 1976.

Fischer, Russell G., "The Delphi-Method: A Description, Review and Criticism." *Journal of Academic Librarianship* 4(2):64–70, 1978.

Goldberg, Robert L., *A Systems Approach to Library Program Development*. Metuchen, N.J.: Scarecrow Press, 1976.

Greer, Roger C., *Community Census Data for Library Planning*. Denver: Community Analysis Associates, 1978.

Hagwood, John, "You Too Can Be a Library Planner." *Public Libraries* 20(1):19–22, 1981.

Henley, James S., "Staff Participation in Planning: Developing Effective Group Processes." *Journal of Library Administration* 2(2,3,4), 1981.

Hiltz, S.R., and M. Turoff, "Electronic Networks: The Social Dynamics of a New Communications System." Paper presented to the American Sociology Association Seminar on Social Networks, San Francisco, 1978.

Ignizio, James P., "A Review of Goal Programming: A Tool for Multiobjective Analysis." *Journal of the Operational Research Society* 2(11):1109–1119, 1978.

Irwin, Patrick H., "Who Really Believes in Strategic Planning?" *Managerial Planning* 27(3):6–9, 1978.

Johnson, Edward, et al., *An Assessment of the Impact of the Management Review and Analysis Program.* University Park: Pennsylvania State University, 1977.

Johnson, Jan, "Supercomputers: Counting on the CDC 205." *Datamation* 27(11):71–79, 1981.

———, "Supercomputers: Seymour Leaves Cray." *Datamation* 28(1):52–61, 1982.

Journal of Library Administration, 2(2,3,4), 1981.

Kang, Jong H., and William B. Rouse, "Approaches to Forecasting Demands for Library Network Services." *Journal of American Society for Information Science* 31(4):256–263, 1980.

Kaser, David, *Report from the Director of the University Libraries, 1972/73.* Ithaca, N.Y.: Cornell University Libraries, 1973.

Kennington, Don, "Long Range Planning for Public Libraries—A Delphi Study." *Long Range Planning* 10(2):73–78, 1977.

King, William R., "Strategic Planning for Management Information Systems." *M.I.S. Quarterly* 2(1):27–37, 1978.

———, "Strategic Planning for Public Service Institutions: What Can Be Learned from Business." *Journal of Library Administration* 2(2,3,4), 1981.

King, William R., and David I. Cleland, "Infomation for More Effective Strategic Planning." *Long Range Planning* 10(1):59–64, 1977.

Koenig, M.E.D., "Special Features of Knowledge as Commodity." In "Economics of Knowledge and Information," by A. Anker, B. Griffith, M. Koenig, and D. Samples. *Journal of Information* 2(3):135–142, 1978.

———, *Budgeting Techniques for Libraries and Information Centers.* New York: New York Special Libraries Association, 1980.

———, "The Information Controllability Explosion." *Library Journal* 107(19);2052–2054, 1 Nov. 1982.

Koenig, M.E.D., A.C. Findlay, J. Cushman, and J. Detmer, "SCOPE: A Cost Analysis of an Automated Serials Record System." *Journal of Library Automation* 4(3):129–140, 1971.

Kunz, Arthur H., "The Use of Data Gathering Instruments in Library Planning." *Library Trends* 24(3):459–471, 1976.

Lee, Sang M., *Goal Programming for Decision Analysis.* Philadelphia: Auerbach Publishers, Inc., 1972.

Levin, Dick, *The Executive's Illustrated Primer of Long-Range Planning.* Englewood Cliffs, N.J.: Prentice-Hall, 1981.

Liesener, James W., *A Systematic Approach for Planning Media Programs.* Chicago: American Library Association, 1976.

Lorge, Irving, D. Fox, J. Davitz, and M. Brenner, "A Survey of Studies Contrasting the Quality of Group Performance and Individual Performance, 1920–1957." *Psychological Bulletin* 55:337–372, 1958.

Lundeberg, M., G. Goldkuhl, and A. Nilsson, *Information Systems Development, A Systems Approach.* Engelwood Cliffs, N.J.: Prentice-Hall, 1981.

Lynch, H.J., "ADS: A Technique in Systems Documentation." *Data Base* 1(1):6–18, 1969.

Lynch, Mary Jo, "The Public Library Association and Public Library Programming." *Journal of Library Administration* 2(2,3,4), 1981.

Makower, M.S., and E. Williamson, *Operational Research, Problems, Techniques and Exercises.* London: Teach Yourself Books, 1967.

Makridakis, S., and S.C. Wheelwright (eds.), *Forecasting Methods and Applications*. New York: John Wiley & Sons, 1978.

———, *Forecasting*, Volume 12, Studies in Management Science, Robert E. Machol (ed.). Amsterdam: North Holland Publishing Co., 1979.

Martin, Allie Beth, *A Strategy for Public Library Goals Feasibility Study*. Chicago: American Library Association, 1972.

Martin, Lowell A., "User Studies and Library Planning." *Library Trends* 24(3):483–496, 1976.

*McClure, Charles R., "The Planning Process: Strategies for Action." *College & Research Libraries* 39(6):456–466, 1978a. (orig. ref. 56)

*———, "The Information Rich Employee and Information for Decision Making: Review and Comments." *Information Processing and Management* 14:381–394, 1978b. (orig. ref. 59)

———, "Planning for Library Effectiveness: The Role of Information Resources Management." *Journal of Library Administration* 1(3):4–16, 1980.

McKay, David N., "A State Agency View of PLA's New Planning Process." *Public Libraries* 19(4):115–117, 1980.

Meadows, Donella H., et al., *The Limits to Growth*. New York: Universe Books, 1974.

Menke, Michael M., "Strategic Planning in an Age of Uncertainty." *Long Range Planning* 12(August):27–34, 1977.

Miller, James Grier, *Living Systems*. New York: McGraw-Hill, 1978.

Milliken, J.G., and E.J. Morrison, "Management Methods from Aerospace." *Harvard Business Review* 51(March–April):6–13, 1973.

Moore, Gary, "Library Long Range Planning: A Survey of Current Practices." *Library Research* 3(2):155–165, 1981.

Moran, Robert F., "Library Cooperation and Change." *College & Research Libraries* 39(4):6–9, 1978.

Morein, P. Grady, et al., "The Academic Library Development Program." *College & Research Libraries* 38(1):37–45, 1977.

*Morris, W.E.M., "Benefit Assessment for Systems Change in Libraries and Information Services: A Research Project in the Public Libraries Field." *Journal of Librarianship* 2(1):15–23, 1979a (orig. ref. 73)

*———, *ALA Planning Process for Public Libraries—U.K. Test*. BLR & DD Report 5540, November, 1979b. (orig. ref. 74)

Mott, Thomas H., Jr., Sang M. Lee, and Thomas J. McGeehan, "A Goal Programming Model for Information Science Service Planning." American Society for Information Science 1978 Midyear Meeting. (Extended abstract available from Mott, Dean, Graduate School of Library and Information Science, Rutgers University.)

Munro, M.C., and B. Davis, "Determining Management Information Needs—A Comparison of Methods." *M.I.S. Quarterly* 1(2):55–67, 1977.

Nair, Keshavan, and Rakesh K. Jarin, "Generating Future Scenarios—Their Use in Strategic Planning." *Long Range Planning* 12(1):56–61, 1979.

Naylor, Thomas H., "Organizing for Strategic Planning." *Managerial Planning* 28(1):3–17, 1979.

Nolan, R.L., "Managing the Crisis in Data Processing." *Harvard Business Review* 57(2):115–126, 1979.

Palmour, Vernon E., et al., *A Planning Process for Public Libraries*. Chicago: American Library Association, 1980.

Parker, M.M., "Enterprise Information Analysis: Cost-Benefit Analysis and the Data Managed System." *IBM Systems Journal* 21(1):108–123, 1982. (Note: The entire issue is devoted to Enterprise analysis and contains five very thought-provoking articles.)

Price, D.J.D., *Little Science, Big Science*. New York: Columbia University Press. 1963.
Public Library Association, *Minimum Standards for Public Library Systems*. Chicago: American Library Association, 1966.
Raffel, Jeffrey A., and Robert Shisko, *Systematic Analysis of University Libraries: An Application of Cost Benefit Analysis to the M.I.T. Libraries*. Cambridge, Mass.: M.I.T. University Press, 1969.
Rider, Fremont, *The Scholar and the Future of the Research Library*. New York: Hadham Press, 1944.
Rizzo, John B., *Management for Librarians*. Westport, Conn.: Greenwood Press, 1980.
Rockart, J.F., "Critical Success Factors." *Harvard Business Review* 57(2):81–91, 1979.
Sakamoto, J.G., and F.W. Ball, "Supporting Business Systems Planning Studies with DB/DC Data Dictionary." *IBM Systems Journal* 21(1):54–80, 1982.
Sarin, R.K., "A Sequential Approach to Cross Impact Analysis." *Futures* 10(1):53–62, 1978.
Sawyer, George C., "The Hazards of Goal Conflict in Strategic Planning." *Managerial Planning* 28(6):11–14, 1980.
Steiner, George, *Top Management Planning*. New York: Macmillan, 1969, p. 34.
Stueart, Robert D., and John Taylor Eastlick, *Library Management*, 2d. ed. Littleton, Colo.: Libraries Unlimited, 1981.
Thomas, Lewis, *The Lives of a Cell: Notes of a Biology Watcher*. New York: Viking Press, 1974.
Townley, Charles T., Theresa Anderson, and Russell J. Stambaugh, Jr., "Policy Negotiations: Simulation as a Tool in Long Range Planning." *Special Libraries* 69(3):89–93, 1978.
Twiss, Brian C., "Recent Trends in Long Range Planning Forecasting for Technology-Based Organizations—Book Review Article." *Long Range Planning* 12(2):120–124, 1979.
Webster, Duane E., "The Management Review and Analysis Program: An Assisted Self-Study to Secure Constructive Change in the Management of Research Libraries." *College & Research Libraries* 35(2):114–125, 1974.
————, "Improving Library Performance: Quantitative Approaches to Library Planning." In Nancy Fjallbrant and Kerstin McCarthy (eds.), *Developing Library Effectiveness for the Next Decade*. Goteborg, Sweden: IATUL, 1978.
Webster, Duane E., and Maxine K. Sitts, "A Planning Program for the Small Academic Library: The PPSAL." *Journal of Library Administration* 2(2,3,4), 1981.
Wiederkehr, Robert R.V., *Alternatives for Future Library Catalogs: A Cost Model*. Rockville, Md.: King Research Inc., 1980.
Wills, Gordon, with Richard Wilson, Neil Manning, and Roger Hildenbrandt, Technological Forecasting, The Art and its Managerial Implications. London: Penguin Books, 1972.
Yanchinski, Stephanie, "And Now—the Biochip." *New Scientist* 93(1288):68–71, 1982.
Yasaki, Edward K., "Supercomputers: Highbrow Hardware." *Datamation* 27(6):55–63, 1981.
Zagone, Robert B., *Social Psychology, An Experimental Approach*. Belmont, Calif.: Brookes/Cole Publishing Co., 1967.
Zweizig, Douglas L., and Charles R. McClure, "Issues in Training Practitioners for Library Planning." *Journal of Library Administration* 2(2,3,4), 1981.
Zwicky, Fritz, *Discovery, Invention, Research through the Morphological Approach*. New York: Macmillan, 1969.

PROJECT MANAGEMENT:
AN EFFECTIVE PROBLEM-SOLVING APPROACH

Robert L. White

ABSTRACT

A problem-solving model for libraries utilizing a project management approach is described. This approach not only serves to improve the quality of information available for solving problems but also enhances staff support for those decisions. The criteria for appointing such groups and ensuring their effectiveness as well as the benefits and problems of this approach to library management are also discussed.

Advances in Library Administration and Organization, volume 2, pages 259–270.
Copyright © 1983 by JAI Press Inc.
All rights of reproduction in any form reserved.
ISBN: 0-89232-214-4

I. INTRODUCTION

One of the recurring themes in the management literature for the last two decades has been the desirability of increasing the involvement of subordinates ("nonmanagers") in the decision making and problem-solving functions of the organization. Administrators can no longer depend solely on traditional or authoritative methods of management. The complexity of today's organizations and libraries requires that administrators delegate more problem-solving responsibilities to those individuals situated where the work is being done.[1] The opportunity for non managers to contribute to the solution of organizational problems helps to increase the overall level of cooperation and general acceptance of decisions. In addition, it tends to improve the effectiveness of information gathering and assessment within the organization.

II. PROBLEM SOLVING AND STAFF INVOLVEMENT

Human capital in the form of a highly motivated and well-trained work force is more vital to the success and effectiveness of an organization than physical facilities, the latest equipment, or a new system.[2] American administrators have tended to take their employees for granted and have concentrated too much on technological solutions to problems.[3] Productivity cannot be improved simply by using a technical approach that throws more hardware or a new process into the work place. Real gains in productivity can be realized not just through increased physical effort but also by greater coordination and wider employee involvement in managing the organization.[4] Today a greater proportion of employees expect and are demanding to be consulted. They want to exercise some influence on the management system within their organizations.[5]

Likert reports that the use of participative or group management tends to promote higher productivity, reduces costs, and improves problem solving within an organization. In addition, administrators who employ teamwork and collaborative supervision techniques tend to encourage the development of employees with higher performance goals.[6]

The effectiveness of a decision is generally influenced by the quality of information available and the degree to which a solution is accepted by subordinates. The low effectiveness of a solution might be due to not utilizing or collecting key bits of information regarding a problem. In addition, a solution might be lower in effectiveness due to the resistance and opposition from those individuals assigned to implement it.[7] Administrators often overlook the fact that individuals are generally willing to accept change if they are given a chance to be involved in the problem-solving process.[8]

Ouchi has observed that American managers, in comparison with their Japanese counterparts, are very quick to make decisions. However, the implementation of those decisions tends to be much slower because more often than not key individuals are not given an opportunity to influence the final outcome. Consequently, those same employees who were not involved in making the decision have little interest or motivation in ensuring its successful implementation. The Japanese tend to spend more time reaching consensus on a proposed solution, and this is usually translated into a shorter implementation period since acceptance is built into the process and has already been obtained.[9]

III. LIBRARY ENVIRONMENT: PROBLEM SOLVING

A new generation of librarians has entered the profession and they have brought with them different experiences and attitudes. Those same librarians, many of whom have entered middle management positions, want a greater role in determining the direction of their respective libraries. The librarians of the 1980s expect to be involved in the management of their libraries. Library administrators may not feel completely comfortable with these attitudes, but to ignore them would not seem prudent for several reasons. First, it is generally acknowledged that the complexity of today's organizations has made it exceedingly more difficult for one person or coterie of individuals to effectively manage without increased staff involvement. Secondly, a well-trained professional and support staff can become even more motivated and supportive by providing them the opportunity to be genuinely involved in the solving of organizational problems.

There has been a trend toward more cooperative management and peer review in libraries, with academic libraries being the most noticeable example. It is becoming increasingly clear that for library managers to be effective there must be a greater sharing of power with subordinates in directing today's libraries and information centers.

Likert and Bennis have discussed the characteristics of group problem solving. Both concur that a cooperative or group approach provides a mechanism for helping to develop the full potential of subordinates, utilizes the diverse skills of the staff, allows for a collaboration of specialists in analyzing problems, provides for a wider perspective, and is most effective when organized around problems to be solved.[10] The rationale for appointing a committee or group is to assist in solving organizational problems.[11]

Standing committees are not foreign to libraries. However, the appointment and functioning of temporary project groups warrants further discussion as to the benefits and problems with this particular management approach. Bennis's model of project management provides a useful starting point.

IV. PROJECT MANAGEMENT

Bennis has described and discussed project management as an effective method of solving organizational problems.[12] Project teams are assembled and organized around clearly identified and specific problems. Individuals are appointed to serve on a project team based on their appropriate training and experience as they relate to the problem at hand. Very often a multidisciplinary approach to problem solving is required and this necessitates appointing individuals with the appropriate experience or educational background (e.g., marketing, engineering, statistics, systems analysis, production, etc.). In addition, a project director is usually appointed to coordinate the work of the team, assign responsibilities to members, and ensure the progress of the group in accomplishing the assigned task. The work milieu of the project team is one of collegiality whereby each member of the team is treated as an equal with a particular area of expertise to contribute. Decisions within the team tend to be made cooperatively with deference paid to individuals with the appropriate technical background. When the work of the project team is completed, a report with recommendations is submitted to management for review and decision. After the team has issued its report, the group is dissolved and the individuals return to their respective departments within the organization. What is appealing about Bennis's project management model is its emphasis on utilizing organizational expertise in a nontraditional or cooperative setting to address a specific problem on an ad hoc or provisional basis.

V. LIBRARY PROJECT MANAGEMENT

The concept of project management as applied to libraries is a useful approach to library problem solving. Library administrators must be willing to take a definite risk in order for project management to work. An administrator may find that a group has conscientiously analyzed a problem area and presented recommendations contrary to the "conventional wisdom" of the library organization.

There is an explicit obligation by the library administrator to evaluate group recommendations and findings seriously as to their anticipated effectiveness and outcome. It is absolutely essential and crucial that the library decision maker willingly forego and reserve a final judgement until receiving the report and analysis of available alternatives. Serious morale problems can ensue if library staff members perceive a group assignment as merely an inconsequential organization exercise. The enthusiasm and motivation of future groups appointed to investigate organization problems will be impaired if reports and recommendations are routinely received and promptly forgotten. Library administrators should provide and allow for a fair hearing and consideration of recommended alternatives with the aim of improving the effectiveness of library problem solving.

Vroom and Yetton present a model of leadership styles which incorporate group and individual problem situations, and acceptable decision methods to address those problems. The analysis of which decision method to utilize depends on the nature of the problem (group or individual), on quality (information available to the decision maker), and subjective factors (likelihood of acceptance of decision by subordinates). The application of the appropriate decision method is dependent on an analysis of the problem situation by the manager.[13]

In some instances the appointment of a group may not be appropriate if there is only a need for technical information. In this case, it might be more effective to consult with library staff members individually rather than creating a project or work group. If the problem involves not merely the need for technical information but also acceptance and support from the library staff, then the appointment of a group would be more appropriate and effective. Many problems require quick resolution, and there is not adequate time for extensive library staff participation and involvement. There are, however, basic questions regarding the future development and direction of an organization which require an orderly gathering and evaluation of information. It is this type of question or problem that seems well suited to a group problem-solving technique. Of course, staff resources will limit the number of policies, programs, or problems that can be fully investigated and evaluated at any one time.

VI. ESTABLISHING PROJECT GROUPS

The library administrator should first seriously question whether a project group is really required and if a different problem-solving approach might not be more appropriate (e.g., manager makes decision after consulting with staff members individually, delegate responsibility to single individual, etc.) If it is decided that a group would be beneficial, the following should be developed and documented: a clear, concise, and specific charge to the project group; clear and precise objectives; and clearly stated responsibilities. A general time frame that is realistic and flexible for completing the group's assignment should be established. It is certainly not fair to expect a group to discuss and evaluate an issue adequately when an unrealistic target date or deadline is set for the completion of the group's assignment.

The composition of the project group should be clearly delineated and the coordinator of the group and other members identified in the written charge of responsibilities. Selection to serve on a group should be based on expertise or interest in the assigned or identified problem area. An additional and important factor in selecting the membership of an appointed group is the consideration of the departments within the library that have an interest in the particular problem area. In addition, the size of the project group should be kept to manageable proportions (i.e., three to five individuals). Too large a group can unnecessarily delay and inhibit the progress of completing the assigned task.

The type of product or output desired from the project group should be specified (e.g., list of recommendations, comprehensive analysis, brief report, oral presentation). Lastly, the following should be clearly indentified and communicated to the project group: individual(s) to receive the group's report, stated procedures for reviewing and evaluating the work group's recommendations or finding, and who the final decision maker(s) will be.

VII. SUCCESSFUL PROJECT GROUPS

There are some basic practices, based on experience, that can help enhance the effectiveness and functioning of library project groups. In a library with an established structure of standing committees, there may be a problem in establishing an agreeable work group meeting schedule and calendar that does not conflict with existing committee assignments. One approach that can work quite well is to distribute blank monthly calendars to each group member and request an indication as to available dates and times to meet. Not only does this facilitate the planning of meeting dates but it also helps ensure the maximum attendance by group members. After a set of agreeable meeting dates and times have been selected by the project group coordinator, based on the returned calendars, a memorandum should be sent to each group member announcing the established meeting schedule with dates, times, and locations of the meetings listed.

To help facilitate the smooth running of scheduled meetings, an agenda with a listing of items for discussion should be distributed and received by the group members prior to every meeting. This can also serve as an opportunity to remind individuals regarding the date, time, and place of the meeting.

It is the responsibility of the group coordinator to provide a framework for group problem solving. The project group needs to select a problem-solving method to assist the group in its assignment. Problem-solving or analytical methodologies abound (e.g., systems approach, policy analysis, program evaluation, rational decision making, management consulting approach). These methodologies share the following common elements: problem definition, information gathering, analysis of alternative, making recommendation(s), and presenting a report.

A variation of the problem-solving methodologies as described by Likert and Hatry et al. will be outlined briefly.[14] The problem-solving process can be delineated in terms of five main steps or elements:

1. Definition of Problem. A definition of the library problem under investigation and a needs assessment should be conducted. The scope of the problem should be discussed, the library's client groups or service populations described, and an indication as to the severity of the problem area should be discussed.

2. Criteria for Problem Solution. The criteria, conditions, or requirements which the solution should meet, need to be developed. The criteria should be carefully considered since they are utilized to compare and evaluate the considered alternatives. In addition, the dollar cost should be utilized as a criterion for evaluating any proposed alternative.

3. Possible Alternatives and Information Gathering. The major characteristics and details of the "alternate ways" of attempting to meet the listed criteria and solve the defined problem should be described. For the most part, it is realistic to consider no more than five or six alternatives for in-depth analytical purposes. The "cost" of each proposed alternative must be estimated. The types of costs that should be considered are improvement costs, operating costs, opportunity costs, and associated costs. The "effectiveness" of each alternative should be estimated against the established criteria or requirements.

4. Comparison and Evaluation of Alternatives. A presentation should be made comparing the "assets and liabilities" of the alternatives based on their costs and effects. Display formats such as tables and charts are very instructive in presenting this type of information. The major "uncertainties" and "assumptions" involved with each alternative should be clearly presented. The "feasibility of implementing" the various options or alternatives should also be considered when conducting an evaluation. Any special requirements needed for implementation should be documented.

5. Recommended Alternative and Report. The evaluation and report findings with the recommended alternative should be documented in such a way that it allows individuals reading the analysis to understand and evaluate the findings and recommendations for action. In addition, a tentative time schedule for implementing the desired alternative should also be presented.

What is important is that there is some understanding and agreement on the procedures to be followed regardless of the particular problem-solving methodology.

To encourage group participation and discussion it is important to provide a common starting point. Prior to the meeting of the group, the coordinator should conduct a review of the literature. Sources of information should be available to group members for their review and study. In addition, a selective bibliography should be provided to each member of the group. In this way, each individual will be able to bring a basic and common level of knowledge to the group's discussions and deliberations.

The possiblity of released time for group members, for a portion of their regularly assigned duties, should be seriously considered. By releasing individuals from regular duties, a more complete or full contribution to the temporary group assignment can be made. The consideration of this action is highly dependent on the magnitude of the assignment and the importance that the library administrator attaches to the problem.

It addition to structural concerns, the social dynamics of the project group require consideration. It is important that the group coordinator not inhibit the desire of the group members to express their views and opinions. The rationale behind the project group concept is to provide a vehicle from which staff members can analyze problems and contribute toward library planning. Open and frank discussions of all major points should be promoted and expected. In addition, the coordinator should encourage every group member to participate in the discussions and every member should be given due respect as to viewpoints or perspectives expressed. Each individual must be willing to compromise and perhaps most importantly, retain a sense of humor, purpose, and balanced perspective. After the project group has completed its study, findings and recommendations should be presented to the library administration or designated decision-making body.

VIII.   BENEFITS

The library organization can derive distinct benefits from this problem-solving approach. A major benefit is that this concept does not create an additional permanent layer of organizational bureaucracy. Many organizations, including libraries, find they are captives of permanent standing committees that tend to perpetuate themselves. The use of temporary special purpose groups to investigate particular library problems is a very effective method for gathering and analyzing information. By creating groups to attack specific issues, the library administrator retains greater flexibility in marshalling the library staff's analytical resources and capabilities. New groups can be created as problems arise that demand investigation. There is something exciting and energizing about bringing a new combination of library staff members together to investigate a problem and contribute to its resolution because of their prior experience, education, or special interest.

There is a real opportunity to encourage an overall library perspective with the staff through the creation of project groups. All too often library staff members from different departments are myopic in their perspective. They tend not to see the library organization as a set of interdependent parts that function totally as an operational entity. By appointing individuals from various sections of the library with different but interrelated skills and experiences, the library manager will be in a position to encourage a clearer understanding and appreciation for the interdependence of the library organization. Furthermore, involvement of the library staff tends to enhance acceptance of the final decision.

It is only natural to take a dim view of a decision that has been made without consultation or consideration for those affected by it. John Adams has described this desire by an individual to be recognized and involved as the "passion for distinction":

> A desire to be observed, considered, esteemed, praised, beloved, and admired by his fellows is one of the earliest, as well as keenest dispositions discovered in the heart of man . . . wherever men, women, or children are to be found . . . every individual is seen to be strongly actuated by a desire to be seen, heard, talked of, approved and respected, by the people about him and within his knowledge.[15]

The process is important! Library staff want to participate, cooperate, and contribute their ideas if only given the opportunity to do so. They will give a library administrator the benefit of the doubt on most major decisions, if only the time were taken to consult and confer with the individuals who are responsible for performing the work in the organization. Not only is it desirable for library administrators to effectively solve problems, but it is also important that those same solutions be fairly derived after due consultation.

Project groups can greatly improve organizational problem solving by actively soliciting different perspectives and viewpoints. Few of us have the capability or the endurance to develop and maintain a level of expertise in all facets of librarianship, information science, data processing, administration, personnel, planning, and so on. Quite simply we have lost (or perhaps never had) an ability to be intimately familiar with every operational detail of the library and its organizational and functional complexity. The library organization, librarianship, and information technology have all changed to the extent that libraries, once run more casually, can no longer afford a passive and closed administrative style. Bennis states that a more open or democratic approach to social organization is not only more efficient and adaptive but it also promotes the "ability to survive and prosper" in a change-oriented environment.[16] We can no longer just react to problems. What is required is an active problem-solving approach. This can be encouraged and promoted by actively involving staff members in the problem-solving process within the library organization. Staff consultation and participation are necessary components for active and effective problem solving in today's libraries.

IX. POTENTIAL PITFALLS

While project management as applied to libraries has its benefits, there are some potential pitfalls and problems that can be encountered with this process. There should be a clear reporting and review procedure for handling the reports, findings, and recommendations of project groups. The review procedures and the identification of the ultimate decision makers(s) should be clearly described in the charge to the project group. Nothing is more frustrating than to undergo the hard work of reaching a workable solution and having the group's findings flounder on the waves of library administrative indecision and uncertainty. It should be made clear as to who should review the group's report and make a final determination as to its recommendations.

Tannenbaum and Schmidt warn that it is important for the administrator to be forthright and extremely clear in communicating the extent to which authority is being reserved and exactly what problem-solving responsibilities are being delegated to subordinates. What needs to be communicated is the role the subordinates are to play in the resolution of a problem, whether it be information gathering, analysis, making a decision, or implementing a recommended solution. If this is not clearly understood by all the parties involved, the end result could very well be confusion and resentment.[17]

The size of the library staff can be an important factor. In a larger library system, it may be possible to provide staff members with released time from a portion of regular departmental assignments in order to meet the obligations of the project group. If group members are not given adequate time to prepare for the assignment, the group's decisions and recommendations may be of somewhat lower quality. However, providing released time may create a real hardship in libraries with a relatively small number of staff members. In addition, if too many committees or project groups have been appointed, the staff in a small library may be spread too thin as far as responsibilities and workload.

It is undesirable to overutilize the same library staff members for project group assignments to the exclusion of other qualified individuals. It is more productive to rotate group assignments in order to allow as many individuals as possible the opportunity to participate. Some staff members will always seem more qualified for work group assignments, but a concerted effort should be made to vary group appointments and ensure fair representation (i.e., professional and support staff, library departments, departmental or branch libraries). Overutilizing specific individuals as project group members may promote the routinization of work assignments for the participants with a resultant loss in group creativity and spontaneity. In addition, one loses the benefit of getting a wider group of staff with a varied viewpoint.

Lastly, if the recommendations and reports of previous work groups have been routinely disregarded, one can assume that staff motivation to participate on future work groups will be severely depressed. This is not meant to imply that work group reports are sacrosanct. There should be however, explicit commitment on the part of the library manager to consider and evaluate the group's recommendations seriously. If this cannot be done, then the library manager should consider foregoing the appointment of project groups.

X. CONCLUSION

The complexity of today's library problems requires a multidisciplinary approach to problem solving. Present and future library problems can be effectively resolved by tapping the enthusiasm and motivation of library staff members for consultation and participation in project groups. In some cases, the project group concept may be hampered because of staff size limitations and the availability of in-house expertise. However, it can be an effective problem-solving technique in medium and larger size libraries.

Library decision makers should not utilize this approach to rationalize *a priori* decisions. If this is attempted, the library administrator will find that it will create staff morale problems and lessen the future prospects for effective group problem solving.

NOTES

1. Keith Davis, "Evolving Model of Organizational Behavior," in *Organizational Behavior: A Book of Readings*, ed. Keith Davis (New York: McGraw-Hill, 1974), p. 15.

2. Rensis Likert, The Human Organization: Its Management and Value (New York: McGraw-Hill, 1967), p. 114.

3. William G. Ouchi, *Theory Z: How American Business Can Meet the Japanese Challenge* (Reading, Mass.: Addison-Wesley Publishing Company, 1981), p. 4.

4. Ouchi, pp. 190 and 268.

5. Robert Tannenbaum and Warren Schmidt, "How to Choose a Leadership Pattern," *Harvard Business Review*, 51, 3 (1973):166.

6. Likert, *The Human Organization*, pp. 44–47; 63.

7. Norman R. F. Maier, *Problem-solving Discussions and Conferences: Leadership Methods and Skills* (New York: McGraw-Hill, 1963), pp. 3–5; Victor H. Vroom and Philip W. Yetton, *Leadership and Decision-Making* (Pittsburgh: University of Pittsburgh Press, 1973), pp. 20–27.

8. Leo Moore, "Too Much Management, Too Little Change," *Harvard Business Review*, 34, 1 (1956):41–44.

9. Ouchi, pp. 43–47.

10. Rensis Likert, *New Patterns of Management* (New York: McGraw-Hill, 1961); Warren G. Bennis, "Beyond Bureaucracy: Will Organization Men Fit the New Organizations," in *Tomorrow's Organizations: Challenges and Strategies*, ed. Jong S. Jun and William B. Storm (Glenview, Ill.: Scott, Foreman, and Co., 1973), pp. 70–76.

11. Likert, *New Patterns of Management*, p. 173.

12. Bennis, "Beyond Bureaucracy," pp. 70–76.

13. Vroom and Yetton, pp. 30–31.

14. Likert, *New Patterns of Management*, p. 175; Harry Hatry et al., *Program Analysis for State and Local Governments* (Washington, D.C.: Urban Institute, 1976).

15. John Adams, "Discourses on Davila; A Series of Papers on Political History," in *The Works of John Adams*, Vol. VI. (Boston: Little and Brown, 1851), pp. 232–33.

16. Warren G. Bennis, *Changing Organizations* (New York: McGraw-Hill, 1966), pp. 16–32.

17. Tannenbaum and Schmidt, 170.

REFERENCES

Adams, John, "Discourses on Davila; A Series of Papers on Political History." In *The Works of John Adams*. Vol. VI. Boston: Little and Brown: 221–403, 1851.

Bennis, Warren G., "Beyond Bureaucracy: Will Organization Men Fit the New Organizations." In *Tomorrow's Organizations: Challenges and Strategies*, edited by Jon S. Jun and William B. Storm. Glenview, Ill.: Scott, Foreman and Co., 1973. Pp. 70–76.

———, *Changing Organizations*. New York: McGraw-Hill, 1966.

Davis, Keith, "Evolving Models of Organizational Behavior." In *Organizational Behavior: A Book of Readings*, edited by Keith Davis. New York: McGraw-Hill: 3–15, 1974.

Likert, Rensis, *The Human Organization: Its Management and Value*. New York: McGraw-Hill, 1967.

———, *New Patterns of Management*. New York: McGraw-Hill, 1961.

Maier, Norman R. F. *Problem-Solving Discussions and Conferences: Leadership Methods and Skills*. New York: McGraw-Hill, 1963.

Moore, Leo. "Too Much Management, Too Little Change." *Harvard Business Review*, 34, 1:41–48, 1956.

Ouchi, William G. *Theory Z: How American Business Can Meet the Japanese Challenge*. Reading, Mass.: Addison-Wesley Publishing Company, 1981.

Tannenbaum, Robert, and Schmidt, Warren. "How to Choose a Leadership Pattern." *Harvard Business Review*, 51, 3:162–80, 1973.

Vroom, Victor H., and Yetton, Philip W. *Leadership and Decision-Making*. Pittsburgh: University of Pittsburgh Press, 1973.

A PRELIMINARY AND SELECTIVE SURVEY OF TWO COLLECTIONS OF JUVENILIA IN FLORIDA

Michele M. Reid

INTRODUCTION

In view of the amount of material available for study, research in the field of librarianship concerning the investigation and handling of nineteenth-century American juvenile literature is extremely limited. There is particularly a lack of research regarding the specific holdings of rare juvenile collections in various institutions in the United States. This is because most of the items are not accessed through a card catalog or similar finding tool. Secondary bibliographical sources are often inaccurate and make a first-hand review of the materials a necessity. This problem is particularly evident in Florida, where few researchers are aware of the exhaustive collections of nineteenth-century juvenilia that are housed at

Advances in Library Administration and Organization, volume 2, pages 271–356.
Copyright © 1983 by JAI Press Inc.
All rights of reproduction in any form reserved.
ISBN: 0-89232-214-4

the University of South Florida at Tampa and the University of Florida at Gainesville. There is a need to gather information about the holdings of these and other Florida collections by means of established data gathering tools. The resultant data can thus be used in making a critical evaluation and comparison of the holdings in these collections, and result in the formation of a Union List of nineteenth-century American juvenilia for the selected Florida institutions. The results of the study could serve as a preliminary approach to the establishment of a comprehensive Union List of all rare juveniles in Florida. If similar studies could be undertaken in other states, complete bibliographic control and access to rare American children's books would eventually be established on a national scale.

Because of the resources and manpower that would be required for the Floridian study, this researcher undertook a preliminary investigation of the holdings in Tampa and Gainesville of ten selected nineteenth century authors. This study would prove useful in the planning of the larger study of nineteenth-century juvenile holdings and the formulation of a Union List for all or selected Florida institutions. It is also significant for the bibliographies it supplies for the ten selected authors, most of whose works and contributions to juvenile literature are little known or appreciated.

RELATED LITERATURE

Dissertations and Theses

Only one study could be located that dealt specifically with nineteenth-century juvenile holdings in American institutions. Smith[1] developed a Union List of what she defined as "landmark" titles held by fifteen Great Lakes institutions as part of her critical and historical evaluation of juvenile titles printed in English during the years 1658–1865. Her time span is broader than that of this study, but she limits the number of titles included to 123.

Cropper outlined juvenile literature from the Norman conquest through the late nineteenth century. Also included are critical subject essays, among which those on Jacob Abbott, author of the Rollo books, and the Stratemeyer Syndicate, which produced many girls' and boys' series books, would seem pertinent for background information.[2]

Two surveys of themes recurrent in American juveniles were done by Shaw[3] and by Lee.[4] Shaw considers titles published from 1850 to 1964. Lee covers the period 1744 to 1850 and includes English publications as well.

Pfau searched for original American editions of juveniles or American or foreign reprints published in 1848.[5]

Research on Individual Authors

Research has been done on individual authors of the period being covered, most notably on Lydia Maria Child, Catharine Maria Sedgwick, and Mary Howitt. Taylor[6] and Lamberton[7] did studies on Lydia Maria Child, and biographical treatments on this authoress were produced by Baer[8] and Meltzer.[9] Baer and Meltzer also provide excellent bibliographies of works by Child herself and of secondary sources. Gidez's study of the works of Catharine Maria Sedgwick included "the first complete bibliography of Miss Sedgwick's works."[10] Welsh did a general study of Sedgwick and included bibliographies of foreign translations and of her periodical publications.[11] A classic source for other material on Sedgwick is *Life and Letters*, edited by Dewey,[12] while Foster points to further articles and studies on Sedgwick.[13] Mention should also be made of Woodring's bibliographical notes on Mary Howitt. Although no general bibliography of Mary Howitt has been published, this list serves as a valuable supplement to entries of her works made under her name in such sources as the *Dictionary of National Biography*.[14]

Bibliographies

The most valuable sources for the study of nineteenth-century juveniles are the bibliographies of Blanck and Welch. Blanck's outstanding classic, *Peter Parley to Penrod: A Bibliographical Description of the Best-Loved American Juvenile Books*,[15] includes those titles he considered "milestones" in juvenile reading from 1827 to 1926. It is a chronological listing of 113 titles, described in full bibliographic detail, with a list of 43 additional "borderline" selections following the main body of the work. His definition of "milestones" accords with Smith's definition of "landmark" titles.[16] Blanck is also the compiler of the *Bibliography of American Literature*.[17] Here he excludes those writers who wrote primarily for juveniles (e.g., Arthur, Abbott, Alger), but he includes others who wrote both adult and juvenile materials (e.g., Child). Since many popular writers did venture at least occasionally into the realm of juveniles, he can be a valuable resource. Welch's *A Bibliography of American Children's Books Printed Prior to 1821*[18] is also outstanding in the field and includes holdings from the foremost institutional and private collections. The American Antiquarian Society, the Pierpont Morgan Library, and the Library of Congress are among those represented. Welch's twenty-six-page "Chronological History of American Children's Books" provides an invaluable overview to the periods covered.

Other bibliographies that are also helpful are Wead,[19] Foley,[20] and *First Books By American Authors, 1765–1964*, published by the Seven Gables Bookshop.[21] In addition, the traditional general bibliographical sources are invaluable; these include Wright,[22] Sabin,[23] Thompson,[24] Evans,[25] Shaw-Shoemaker,[26] Roorbach,[27] Shoemaker,[28] and Kelly.[29]

Catalogs and Collections

Related to the bibliographies, the catalogs of both institutions and booksellers are indispensible for a study of juvenile literature of this period. Foremost is Rosenbach's *Early American Children's Books*,[30] which contains bibliographical descriptions and facsimiles of books in his private collection. The books included were published in America between 1682 and 1836. This is the most well-known and comprehensive work on this period of juvenile Americana, and includes an often-quoted introduction and valuable annotations. The Rosenbach Collection is now housed at the Free Library of Philadelphia. In 1975, the Free Library issued a companion volume to Rosenbach entitled *A Checklist of Children's Books, 1837–1876.*[31] It serves as a catalog to those holdings in the collection that fall between the given chronological parameters.

In addition to the catalog of Rosenbach's private collection, the sales catalogs of the Rosenbach Company are valuable sources of information, especially bibliographic, for American juvenilia. They have been reissued as a ten-volume set, grouped into subject categories. Volumes 1 through 3 concern Americana.[32]

The Osborne Collection of Early Children's Books, 1566–1910,[33] although limited to English books, is useful for tracing those titles which were popular in America and later reprinted by American presses. Volume 2 of this catalog was published in 1975, but the researcher was unable to examine it.

The Pierpont Morgan Library produced a catalog for its 1954 exhibition of children's literature that attempts to represent all important American, English, or European works that have had an influence upon later American publications.[34] The materials were gathered from many significant institutional and private collections, and the bibliographic notes made for each entry are reliable. This library later published *Early Children's Books and Their Illustration,*[35] which contains a selection of 225 "milestones" in children's literature dating from the third century to the beginning of the twentieth.

Another exhibition catalog worthy of note is from the National Book League in London, and entitled *Children's Books of Yesterday and Today.*[36] There are 1,001 entries with a section devoted to American works.

Among the dealers' catalogs available, Schatzki's *Children's Books Old and Rare,*[37] is typical. Headings include "Juvenile Fiction" and "Books About Children's Books."

Other general catalogs that are known to all, but that are nevertheless valuable for the material they contain on early juveniles, include H.W. Wilson Company's *Children's Catalog*,[38] the British Museum's *General Catalogue of Printed Books*,[39] and the various Library of Congress catalogs.

Of the many articles describing the holdings of the various famous collections, Allen[40] deals with the American Antiquarian Society, and Egoff[41] with the Osborne Collection. "When Rare Books are Children's Treasures"[42] lists and describes a number of well-known subject collections, and an entire issue of *Wilson Library Bulletin*[43] is devoted to the discussion of the various research libraries in the United States that are active in the field of children's literature.

In June of 1981, after the Baldwin Library's card catalog had been examined for this study, G.K. Hall published *The Index to the Baldwin Library*.[44] This work reproduces the Library's card catalog in book form. It also contains an index to short stories and fairy tales in the collection.

Collections of Nineteenth-Century Literature

Andrew Tuer and other bibliophiles compiled collections of nineteenth-century material (and earlier), thus preserving some titles that otherwise would not be known today. In addition, works like *Pages and Pictures From Forgotten Children's Books*,[45] *Stories From Old Fashioned Children's Books*[46] and *1000 Quaint Cuts*[47] provide an overview and introduction to the literature, emphasizing as they do its enormous variety. Of similar value is James's *Children's Books of Yesterday*.[48]

General Introductory Histories

Many works give a general overview of early juvenile literature. Authorities of this type include Darton,[49] Adams,[50] Meigs,[51] and Thwaite.[52] Others of some merit include Currie,[53] Field,[54] Moore,[55] Hollowell,[56] Moses,[57] Hart,[58] and Arbuthnot.[59] For a similar treatment of children's illustrators, Mahoney's is the classic work.[60]

Targ's *Bibliophile in the Nursery: A Bookman's Treasury of Collector's Lore on Old and Rare Children's Books*[61] provides a miscellany of vignettes, background and historical pieces, bibliographical pieces, and essays. Tassin's article in *Cambridge History of American Literature*,[62] Saucier,[63] and Burnite[64] provide further introductory material.

Analysis and Criticism

Heading the list of critics of children's literature is Hazard, who treats searingly the moralistic women writers of juveniles of this period and examines Irving, Hawthorne, and Twain in his analysis of American writers. Hazard believes the classics of the literature are those that children prefer, and that they are the best judges of what reading material they like.[65]

Green emphasizes English authors, some of which had great influence in America: Maria Edgeworth, Charles and Mary Lamb, Catherine Sinclair, and others. His period of coverage is 1800 to 1964, so he includes many classics that are beyond the range of this study. His work is scholarly yet readable, and is important since he treats some of the works not mentioned in Hazard.[66]

Of works of narrower scope, *A Century of Children's Books* by Barry has been the standard text for more than half a century.[67] The section on poetical works for children is particularly noteworthy, according to Smith,[68] Barry examines titles published in English between 1700 and 1825.

Equally important and limited to American children's books from 1747 to 1840 is *Forgotten Books of the American Nursery: A History of the American Story Book* by Halsey. Included are English books popular in the United States, but the emphasis is on the slow development of genuinely American works. Progress is traced from the staid, didactic stories of Puritan days to the beginning of a literature for enjoyment in the first half of the nineteenth century.[69]

Kiefer covers roughly the same time period as Halsey does in her *American Children Through Their Books, 1700–1835*, but is more interested in tracing the changing status of the child in American society as revealed in the juvenile literature of the time than on the literature itself.[70] Another similar sociological examination was made by MacLeod.[71] This study, however, is concerned with a later time period. Both works are valuable for their extensive bibliographies of both primary and secondary source materials.

Two collections of papers and lectures should be mentioned as important in providing background in juvenile literary criticism. The first, *Society and Children's Literature*[72] includes papers presented on research, social history, and children's literature at a symposium sponsored by Simmons College and the ALA's Committee on National Planning for Special Collections of the Children's Services Division. Pertinent selections include Henne's "American Society as Reflected in Children's Literature," and Heaney's "In for a Penny, In for a Pound," a discussion of "penny dreadfuls." The second, *The Hewins Lectures, 1947–1962*,[73] includes Haviland's "The Travelogue Storybook of the Nineteenth Century," and Jordan's "From Rollo to Tom Sawyer" (also in book form with other selections as *From Rollo to Tom Sawyer and other Papers,*)[74] both of which have proven valuable to this study.

Grade's essay on the value and originality of American juvenile writers of the nineteenth century should be mentioned as a brief analytical study of children's literature.[75] Cadogan and Craig's look at girls' fiction, 1839–1975, adds an interesting feminist perspective to that area of juvenilia.[76]

In addition to the above critical and analytical studies, the researcher found the following works of supplementary value. Ash[77] and Field[78] provide brief descriptions of institutional collections in the United States and Canada. Ash is more general, covering all special and subject collections, while Field describes only collections in the field of children's literature.

Hart,[79] Allibone,[80] and *Yesterday's Authors of Books for Children*[81] provide information on the sometimes quite illusive authors of juveniles, who frequently enjoyed writing under numerous pseudonyms.

Summary

It is evident from this survey of the related literature that although little has been written comparing the holdings of various institutions in the field of nineteenth-century American juveniles, or of the means by which this might be accomplished, much has been written concerning the works themselves, their historical context, and the famous collections to which some belong. The body of writings that exists in connection with these last topics is so numerous that it would be impossible within the scope of this survey to review all the titles that would be uncovered. In view of this, an attempt has been made to present those titles which were considered particularly relevant to this study and also those that were considered representative works in the realm of historical, critical, and analytical studies. For more exhaustive listings of such titles, the reader is urged to consult the following bibliographies.

Elva Smith provides historical outlines for each period of children's literature, which are followed by extensive bibliographies for each topic.[82] To supplement Smith, whose work was published in 1937, Haviland,[83] Leif,[84] and Pellowski[85] are recommended. Also, a general introductory bibliography by Stalloman has appeared in *Peabody Journal of Education*.[86]

METHODOLOGY

Definitions

A *Union Catalog* or *List* is defined by Wynar as "a catalog that lists, completely or in part, the holdings of more than one library or collection."[87]

American nineteenth-century juvenile literature will include those items described by Welch as

> narrative books written in English, designed for children under fifteen years of age. They should be the type of book read at leisure for pleasure. The book must have been originally written for children or abridged for them from an adult version.[88]

In general, only imaginative works by the ten authors listed in this study are included, in the form of books, chapbooks, toy books, pamphlets, and tracts. Articles appearing in magazines, gift books, or annuals edited or written by the ten authors are not included. In very few cases, other types of works that are edited by an author are included. Books that are entirely comprised of poetry, educational treatises, or books on child-rearing are not included. Holographs are not included, nor are facsimile editions. Fictionalized treatments on travel and books dealing with natural history or science, however, are included, as well as books on manners intended for children.

It is recognized that some titles may be classified as either juvenile or adult books. If there was any doubt concerning these borderline items they were included in the study.

In the bibliographies given for each individual author, only the first locatable American edition of a title is given. In the holdings lists of the two institutions, all American editions held of a title are given.

Collections Investigated

The two collections included in the study are the Baldwin Collection of the University of Florida at Gainesville and the one contained in the Special Collections Department of the University of South Florida at Tampa. They are the largest collections of nineteenth-century juveniles in the state and therefore represent the major proportion of Florida holdings. (The collection at Florida State University at Tallahassee is devoted to poetical works, which are not being treated in the present investigation.)

The Baldwin Collection contains approximately 40,000 British and American children's books in English published before 1900. All titles are cataloged by main entry (by author, if determinable, and, if not, by title). Access by subject, editor, or translator is also possible. No classification is attempted, and shelf arrangement is generally alphabetical by main entry.

The Special Collections Department of the University of South Florida Library contains the Harry K. Hudson Collection of American Boys' Books in Series of approximately 5,000 volumes, and a companion collection of American Girls Books in Series of approximately 1,000 volumes.

Both are uncataloged, but accessed through indexing systems. In addition, there are about 500 chapbooks and 400 miniature juveniles, along with approximately 5,000 additional juveniles contained in the American Literature Collection, some of which have been cataloged according to Library of Congress Classification. There are also some 8,000 dime novels.

The selection of the ten authors whose titles were sought in the two collections was done in the following manner. Since the researcher was primarily interested in girls' books, it was determined that the authors be limited to female writers, because they wrote the majority of girls' books. Authors were chosen who were active during the years 1800 through 1850. These dates are approximate, however, since few author's dates correspond exactly to that ideal time period. So, Priscilla Wakefield is included here, although the first American edition of her *Mental Improvement* appeared in 1799. The writings of Lydia Maria Child are also examined, although she published until her death in 1880. The majority of her books for children, however, were produced from 1824 to 1856. In addition, the period of 1800 to 1850 was chosen because the number of authors active during those years was minimal, and the number of titles each produced is of manageable size. (Only Mary Sherwood could be considered a voluminous author, of the ten chosen). After about 1850 the number of writers and the output of juvenile titles increased tremendously. Choosing the time span of 1800 to 1850, therefore, makes the number of titles involved in the bibliographies of reasonable size. Also, little bibliographical study has been devoted to this time period as opposed to the latter half of the century.

After searching unsuccessfully for a total of ten American authors suitable for the study, it was deemed necessary to include British writers popular in America in the list. During the first half of the nineteenth century, British books were extremely popular with American audiences and they were imitated in the productions of American writers. Five British authors meeting the parameters of the study were chosen: Barbara Hofland, Mary Howitt, Mary Butt Sherwood, Catherine Sinclair,[89] and Priscilla Wakefield. The American authors chosen were: Lydia Maria Child, Mary Hughs,[90] Eliza Leslie, Elizabeth Phelps, and Catharine Sedgwick.

Compilation of Author Bibliographies

Before the holdings information for the Baldwin Collection and the University of South Florida Special Collections Department collection could be gathered, bibliographies of each of the ten authors listed in the study were compiled. All verifiable juvenile titles published in America by each of the ten authors needed to be identified in order to discover the extent of the two institutions' holdings.

Information for the brief description about each author appearing at the beginning of each bibliography was gathered from various biographical sources. These sources appear in abbreviated form at the end of the description. (The key to abbreviations used, giving the citation for each source, is given in the appendix.) These biographical sources also provided bibliographic information, along with those bibliographies previously mentioned in the literature review. Each title was verified using at least one of these sources and recorded on 3" by 5" cards. The following bibliographic information is given for each title:

1. author's name
2. title
3. place of publication
4. publisher
5. date of publication
6. explanatory or descriptive notes
7. source of the above information (see the appendix for the list of abbreviations and short titles for the sources), and the number of the entry in the source (if applicable).

Any special problems involved with any individual entries are explained with the particular entry.

Compilation of Holdings List

If a copy of a title in the author bibliographies is held by the Baldwin Collection or the University of South Florida Collection, the collation for that individual copy is given immediately under the title entry. In this case, the title is not repeated, but the imprint is given again. Other editions of the title held then follow in chronological order. For each of these editions, "Reprint ed." is used, followed by enough of the title to indicate if it differs from the first or earlier editions. The imprint and collation is then given for each entry.

For all the holdings entries, the letter B (for Baldwin Collection) or S (for University of South Florida Collection) appears in the left margin, indicating which institution holds the copy. The LC call number is given in the right margin for any cataloged University of South Florida materials.

LYDIA MARIA CHILD (1802–1880) was the author of the poem, "On Thanksgiving Day" (1857), which is known to almost every American child. It begins with the famous line, "Over the river and through the wood, / To grandfather's house we'll go." She also established the first monthly for children in America, the *Juvenile Miscellany*, the success of which, however, was daunted by her abolitionist activities. She produced the first antislavery book in 1833, entitled *Appeal in Favor of that Class of Americans Called Africans*. She was also a pioneer for women's rights. Her works, although didactic in character, were popular in her day, and her stories appeared in gift books, annuals, and magazines such as *Atlantic Monthly*.

ALL, AP, AMB, ANAU, BIB, BIO, CA, CY, DIC AM, DIC EN, DIC LIT, DIC NA, EV, NC, RE

BIOGRAPHICAL SKETCHES OF GREAT AND GOOD MEN, DESIGNED FOR THE AMUSEMENT AND INSTRUC-TION OF YOUNG PERSONS.
Boston: Putnam & Hunt; Philadelphia: Ash, 1828.
Mansell
Blanck 3097

THE CHILDREN'S GEMS. THE BROTHER AND SISTER: AND OTHER STORIES.
Philadelphia: New Church Book Store, 1852.
Anon. attributed to Mrs. Child by the NY State Library—Blanck
Blanck 3173

B   Reprint ed.: THE BROTHER AND SISTER, AND OTHER STORIES.
Philadelphia: T. Ellwood Zell, 1864 [c1852].
64 p.: plates; 15 cm.

EMILY PARKER: OR, IMPULSE, NOT PRINCIPLE. IN-TENDED FOR YOUNG PERSONS.
Boston: Bowles and Dearborn, 1827.
Blanck 3091
Shoe 28455

EVENINGS IN NEW ENGLAND. INTENDED FOR JUVE-NILE AMUSEMENT AND INSTRUCTION.
Boston: Cummings, Hilliard, 1824.
Blanck 3088

FACT AND FICTION: A COLLECTION OF STORIES . . .
NY: C.S. Francis; Boston: J.H. Francis, 1846.
Blanck 3155
Wright 517
Mansell

FIRST SETTLERS OF NEW ENGLAND: OR, THE CON-
QUEST OF THE PEQUODS, NARRAGANSETS AND
POKANOKETS: AS RELATED BY A MOTHER TO HER
CHILDREN, AND DESIGNED FOR THE INSTRUCTION
OF YOUTH.
Boston: Munroe and Francis; NY: C.S. Francis, 1829.
Blanck 3100
Shaw 32668
Sabin 12714
Mansell

B   ———.
Boston: Munroe and Francis, 1829.
283 p.: frontis.; 17.5 cm.

FLOWERS FOR CHILDREN . . .Ser. 1. FOR CHILDREN
EIGHT OR NINE YEARS OLD . . .
NY: C.S. Francis; Boston: J.H. Francis, 1844.
Blanck-P
Blanck 3149
Mansell

B   ———.
NY: C.S. Francis, etc., 1844.
190 p.: frontis.; 15.5 cm.

FLOWERS FOR CHILDREN . . .Ser. 2. FOR CHILDREN FROM
FOUR TO SIX YEARS OLD . . .
NY: C.S. Francis; Boston; J.H. Francis, 1845.
Blanck-P
Blanck 3151
Mansell

B   ———.
NY: C.S. Francis, etc., 1845.
178 p.: frontis.; 15.5 cm.

B   Reprint ed., FLOWERS . . . Series 2.
NY: C.S. Francis, etc., 1855.

B   Reprint ed., LITTLE JANE, ILLUSTRATED.
Boston: Lothrop, [18—].
Unpaged plates; 15.5 cm.
"Reprinted from Flowers for Children . . . II. For Children
from Four to Six Years Old, 1845"—Blanck
Blanck 3217

FLOWERS FOR CHILDREN . . .Series 3. FOR CHILDREN OF
ELEVEN AND TWELVE YEARS OF AGE . . .
NY: C.S. Francis; Boston: H.H. Francis, 1847.
Blanck-P
Blanck 3157
Mansell

B   Reprint ed., FLOWERS . . . Series 3.
NY: C.S. Francis, etc., 1850.
184 p.: frontis.; 15.5 cm.

B   Reprint ed., FLOWERS . . .
NY: C.S. Francis, etc.
Ser. 1, 1846, and Ser. 3, 1847 (Bound together).
190, 184 p.: frontispieces; 15 cm.

[Note: Baer (see note 8) and Meltzer (see note 9) record the following:
FLOWERS FOR CHILDREN. (Series I and II)
NY: C.S. Francis, 1844.
and
————. (Series III)
NY: C.S. Francis, 1846.

This is earlier than the entries in Blanck. Maybe this is due to a difference
in copyright and publishing dates. I still prefer Blanck, however.]

B   Reprint ed., FLOWERS FOR CHILDREN . . .
Boston: Crosby, Nichols, Lee, 1861.
3 parts in one.
190, 178, 184 p.; ill., frontis.; 18 cm.
Half-title.
LITTLE GIRL'S OWN BOOK . . .
Boston: Carter, Hendee, and Babcock, 1831.
Blanck 3108
Mansell

B   Reprint ed., LITTLE GIRL'S OWN BOOK . . .
NY: C. Austin, [c1833]
288 p.: ill., col. frontis; 14.5 cm.
Inscribed 1852.

B   ————.
Inscribed 1866.
MAGICIAN'S SHOWBOX, AND OTHER STORIES.
Boston: Tickner and Fields, 1856.
Mrs. Child served as editor. The author was Mrs. Caroline
Tappan.—Blanck
Blanck 3182
Mansell

NEW FLOWER FOR CHILDREN . . . FOR CHILDREN
FROM EIGHT TO TWELVE YEARS OLD . . .
NY: C.S. Francis, 1856.
Blanck 3182
Mansell

B   Reprint ed. NEW FLOWER FOR CHILDREN . . .
Boston: Crosby, Nichols, Lee, 1861, [c1855]
311 p.: ill.; 18 cm.
half title

B   Reprint ed., BOY'S HEAVEN AND OTHER STORIES.
Boston: Lothrop; Dover, N.H.: Day, [18–]
p. 13–160 only: 15 cm.
half title
"Reprinted from A NEW FLOWER FOR CHILDREN"—
Blanck
Blanck 3206

RAINBOWS FOR CHILDREN.
NY: C.S. Francis; Boston: J.H. Francis, 1848, [c1847]
Edited by Mrs. Child, Author: Mrs. Caroline Tappan—Blanck
Blanck 3161
Free
Mansell

B   ——.
NY: C.S. Francis; Boston: J.H. Francis, 1848, [c1847]
170 p.: plates; 18 cm.

B   Reprint ed., RAINBOWS FOR CHILDREN.
NY: J. Miller, [18–]
170 p.: plates; 18 cm.

S   Reprint ed., RAINBOWS . . .
Boston: Ticknor and Fields, 1867, [c1847]
169 p., [1] p.: ill.; 19 cm.
Added t.p., engraved.
Authorship attributed to Caroline Tappan by Editor.

B   Reprint ed., RAINBOWS . . .
Boston: Ticknor and Fields, 1868.
170 p.: plates; 18 cm.

ROSE MARIAN AND THE FLOWER FAIRIES. ADAPTED
FROM THE GERMAN LEGEND.
NY: C.S. Francis; Boston: J.H. Francis, 1850.
"Copyright notice dated 1839; in error for 1849? . . .
No earlier printing found. The above was deposited for
copyright Dec. 27, 1849."—Blanck
Blanck 3166

B   Reprint ed., ROSE MARIAN . . .
        Boston: Crosby & Ainsworth; NY: Felt, 1865, [c1839]
        46 p.: plates; 18 cm.
        YOUTH'S SKETCH BOOK.
        Boston: Lilly, Wait, 1834.
        Blanck 3120

Note: The following are probably reprint editions of stories previously published in other collections, but the researcher was unable to verify this fact.

B   THE MAN WHO KILLED HIS NEIGHBOURS.
        S.l.: s.n., [18–]
        32 p.; 10 cm.
        chapbook

B   NEVER THROW STONES.
        Boston: Lothrop, [18–]
        unpaged: plates; 15 cm.
        Inscribed 1881

B   YOUNG ARTIST. ILLUSTRATED.
        Boston: Lothrop, [18–]
        unpaged: plates; 15.5 cm.

    BARBARA WREAKS HOOLE HOFLAND (1770–1844) was a British writer whose novels and moral tales for children were popular in America. She is best known for the *Son of a Genius* and the *Captives in India*. Her other works are in the typical didactic style of the period. Her many adult publications, reprint story collections, (unless held by the institutions studied) and British editions for which no American counterparts were found are not included here.

ALL, DNB

        ADELAIDE; OR, THE INTREPID DAUGHTER: A TALE . . .
        Boston: Munroe and Francis, [1834]
        Mansell
B   ———.
        Boston: Munroe and Francis, [18–]
        192 p.: frontis.; 15 cm.

B   AFFECTIONATE BROTHERS: A TALE.
        NY: Gilley, 1816.
        Welch 601.1
        Shaw 37855
        Mansell

B   Reprint ed., AFFECTIONATE . . .
          Boston: Munroe and Francis, 1831.
          119 p.: frontis; 15.5 cm.

B   Reprint ed., AFFECTIONATE . . .
          NY: C.S. Francis; Boston: J.H. Francis, 1853.
          150 p. 10 p. cat.: frontis.; 15.5 cm.

B   Reprint ed., AFFECTIONATE . . .
          Boston: Chase and Nichols, 1863.
          150 p: frontis.; 15.5 cm.

B   Reprint ed., AFFECTIONATE . . .
          Philadelphia: Porter & Coates, [18—]
          150 p.: col. frontis.; 16 cm.

B   Reprint ed., AFFECTIONATE . . .
          Philadelphia: Porter & Coates, [18—]
          Inscribed 1879.
          Copy bound upside down.

S   Reprint ed., AFFECTIONATE . . .
          Philadelphia: Porter & Coates, [18—]
          150 p.: col. frontis.

B   Reprint collection, HOME TALES: INCLUDING THE AF-
          FECTIONATE BROTHERS; THE SISTERS; THE BLIND
          FARMER AND HIS CHILDREN.
          NY: C.S. Francis; Boston: J.H. Francis, 1851.
          150, 192, 159 p., 5 p. cat.: plates; 16 cm.

          ALFRED CAMPBELL, THE YOUNG PILGRIM: CON-
          CERNING TRAVELS IN EGYPT AND THE HOLY
          LAND.
          Boston: Munroe and Francis, [18—]
          Mansell

B   ———.
          Boston: Munroe and Frances, [18—]
          216 p.: plates; 15.5 cm.

          ALICIA AND HER AUNT: OR, THINK BEFORE YOU
          SPEAK. A TALE FOR YOUNG PERSONS. NEW
          EDITION.
          NY: Gilley, 1830.
          Mansell

B   ———.
          NY: Gilley, 1830.
          175 p., 4 p. cat.: frontis.; 15 cm.

S   Reprint ed., ALICIA AND HER AUNT . . .
          NY: C.S. Francis, 1859.
          [1] p. cat., 144 p.

B   Reprint ed., ALICIA AND HER AUNT . . . A NEW ED., REV.
    Philadelphia: Porter & Coates, [18—]
    144 p: col. frontis.; 16 cm.

    BEATRICE: A TALE FOUNDED ON FACTS.
    NY: Harper, 1830.
    2 vols.
    Mansell

    BLIND FARMER, AND HIS CHILDREN . . .
    NY: Gilley, 1817.
Also published by
    Albany: Websters & Skinners, 1817.
    Welch 602.1, 602.2
    Shaw 41066
    Mansell

B   ———.
    Albany: Websters & Skinners, 1817.
    120 p.; 14.5 × 8.5 cm.
    printed buff paper over boards.

B   Reprint ed., BLIND . . .
    Boston: Nichols, 1868.
    159 p.: frontis.; 15.5 cm.

B   Reprint ed., BLIND . . .
    Philadelphia: Porter & Coates, [18—]
    159 p.: col. frontis.; 16 cm.

    . . . THE CAPTIVES IN INDIA, A TALE. METROPOLITAN
    ED.
    Washington: Green, 1835.
    Mansell

    DAUGHTER OF A GENIUS: A TALE FOR YOUTH.
    Boston: Munroe and Francis, 1824.
    Shoe 16563
    Mansell

B   ———.
    Boston: Munroe and Francis, 1824.
    192 p.: frontis.; 15.5 cm.

B   Reprint ed., DAUGHTER . . .
    Boston: Munroe and Francis, [18—]
    192 p.: frontis.; 15.5 cm.

S   Reprint ed., DAUGHTER . . . 2D ED.
    Boston: Munroe and Francis; NY: C.S. Francis, [1830]
    ix, 192 p.: engraved frontis.
    1830 inscribed in book

B   Reprint ed., DAUGHTER . . . A NEW EDITION, REVISED.
         Boston: Chase and Nichols, 1865.
         159 p.: frontis.; 15.5 cm.
B   Reprint ed., DAUGHTER . . . A NEW EDITION, REVISED.
         Philadelphia: Porter & Coates, [18—]
         159 p.: col. frontis.; 16 cm

ELIZABETH AND HER THREE BEGGAR BOYS.
         NY: Dean, 1838.
         Mansell

ELLEN, THE TEACHER. A TALE FOR YOUTH.
         NY: Gilley, 1815.
         2 vols.
         Welch 603.1
         Shaw 34930
         Mansell
B   ———.
         NY: Gilley, 1815.
         vol. 2
         93 p.; 14.5 × 9 cm.

B   Reprint ed., ELLEN . . .
         NY: Gilley. 1819.
         189 p: frontis 14.5 × 8.5 cm.

         Welch 603.2

B   Reprint ed., ELLEN . . . A NEW EDITION, REVISED.
         Philadelphia: Porter & Coates.
         157 p.: col. frontis.; 16 cm.

ENERGY: A TALE.
         Boston: Carter and Mussey, 1844.
         Mansell
B   ———.
         Boston: Carter and Mussey, 1844.
         176 p.: ill.; 16.5 cm.
B   Reprint ed., ENERGY . . .
         Boston: Strong and Broadhead. 1849.
         176 p.: frontis.; 16.5 cm.

FAREWELL TALES
         NY: Dean, [1840?]
         Mansell
Also published by
         Boston: Roberts, [184?]
         Mansell

B ———.
    Boston: Munroe and Francis, 1842.
    216 p.: plates; 14.5 cm.
    half-title

B Reprint ed., FAREWELL . . .
    Boston: Munroe and Francis, 1845.
    216 p.: plates; 14.5 cm.

B Reprint ed., FAREWELL . . .
    NY and Boston: C.S. Francis, 1857.
    216 p.: plates; 15 cm.

    GOOD GRANDMOTHER AND HER OFFSPRING: A TALE.
    NY: J. Eastburn, 1817.
    Welch 604
    Shaw 41067
    Mansell

B ———.
    NY: J. Eastburn, 1817.
    170 p.; 15.5 cm.
    paper bound

B Reprint ed., GOOD . . .
    Boston: Simpkins, 1821.
    139 p.: frontis.; 15.5 cm.

B Reprint ed., GOOD . . .
    Newburyport: Tilton, 1833.
    121 p.: frontis.; 15.5 cm

B Reprint ed., GOOD . . . A NEW EDITION, REVISED.
    Boston: Chase and Nichols, 1863.
    150 p.: frontis.; 15.5 cm.

B Reprint ed., GOOD . . . A NEW EDITION, REVISED.
    Philadelphia: Porter & Coate, [18—]
    150 p.: col. frontis.; 15.5 cm.

    HELPLESS ORPHANS, AND OTHER STORIES.
    Boston: Shepard, Clark & Brown, [1840]
    Mansell

B ———.
    Boston: Shepard, Clark & Brown, [1840]
    176 p.; 15.5 cm.
    preface dated 1840.

HISTORY OF A CLERGYMAN'S WIDOW AND HER YOUNG
FAMILY.
Boston: Munroe and Francis, [182?]
Also published by
NY: Gilley, 1830.
Mansell

B   Reprint ed., THE CLERGYMAN'S WIDOW . . . A NEW AND
REVISED EDITION.
Philadelphia: Porter & Coates, [18—]
183 p: col frontis.

HISTORY OF A MERCHANT'S WIDOW AND HER YOUNG
FAMILY.
NY: Gilley, 1830.
Mansell

B   ————.
NY: Gilley, 1830.
178 p.; 14 cm.
Also published as
THE MERCHANT'S WIDOW, AND HER FAMILY.
Boston: Munroe and Francis, [182?]
Mansell

B   Reprint ed., THE MERCHANT'S WIDOW . . . A NEW AND
REVISED EDITION.
NY: C.S. Francis; Boston: J. H. Francis, [18—]
178 p.: frontis.; 15 cm.

HISTORY OF AN OFFICER'S WIDOW, AND HER YOUNG
FAMILY.
NY: Gilley, 1815.
Welch 605
Shaw 34931
Mansell

B   Reprint ed., THE OFFICER'S WIDOW . . . A NEW AND
REVISED EDITION.
Philadelphia: Porter & Coates, [18—]
184 p.: col. frontis.; 16 cm.

B   Reprint ed., THE OFFICER'S WIDOW . . . A NEW AND
REVISED . . .
Boston: Chase and Nichols, 1863.
184 p.: frontis.; 16 cm.

B   Reprint ed., THE OFFICER'S . . .
NY: C.S. Francis; Boston: J.H. Francis, [18—]
184 p.: frontis.; 15.5 cm.

B   Reprint collection, DOMESTIC TALES: BEING THE HIS-
     TORIES OF THE OFFICER'S, MERCHANT'S, AND
     CLERGYMAN'S WIDOWS, AND THEIR YOUNG
     FAMILIES.
     NY: C.S. Francis; Boston: J.H. Francis, 1850.
     184, 183 p.: plates; 16.5 cm.
     half-title

INTEGRITY, A TALE.
     Philadelphia: Small, 1823.
     Mansell

IWANOWNA, OR THE MAID OF MAOSCOW, A NOVEL.
     Philadelphia: Carey, 1815.
     Shaw 34932
     Mansell

LITTLE   MANUEL,   THE   CAPTIVE   BOY.   A   TRUE
     STORY . . .
     Boston: Edmunds, [1831?]
     Mansell

MATILDA: OR, THE BARBADOES GIRL, A TALE FOR
     YOUNG PEOPLE.
     Philadelphia: Carey, 1817.
     Welch 606
     Shaw 41068
     Sabin 32413
     Mansell

B   Reprint ed., BARBADOES GIRL. A TALE FOR YOUNG
     PEOPLE. A NEW EDITION, REVISED.
     NY: C.S. Francis; Boston: Crosby, Nichols, 1852.
     176 p.; 15.5 cm.

B   Reprint ed., BARBADOES GIRL, A NEW EDITION,
     REVISED.
     Boston: Chase and Nichols, 1863.
     176 p.: frontis.; 15.5 cm.

B   MODERATION. A TALE.
     Boston: Peirce, 1848.
     148 p.: frontis.; 17 cm.
     Baldwin

RICH BOYS AND POOR BOYS, AND OTHER TALES.
     Boston: Bowles, 1836.
     Mansell

SELF-DENIAL, A TALE.
NY: s.n., 1828.
Mansell
B   Reprint ed., SELF . . .
Boston: Carter and Mussey, 1845.
154 p.: 17 cm.
B   Reprint ed., SELF . . .
Boston: Peirce, 1848.
154 p.: frontis.; 17 cm.

SISTERS. A DOMESTIC TALE.
Hartford: Sheldon & Goodwin, 1815.
Welch 607
Shaw 34934
Mansell
B   ———.
Hartford: Sheldon & Goodwin, 1815.
212 p.: frontis.; 15 cm.
B   Reprint ed., SISTERS . . . NEW EDITION.
NY: Burgess, 1831.
166 p.: frontis; 15 cm.
half-title
B   Reprint ed., SISTERS . . .
NY: C.S. Francis; Boston: J.H. Francis, 1851.
192 p.: frontis.; 15.5 cm.
B   Reprint ed., SISTERS . . .
Boston: Chase and Nichols, 1863.
192 p.: frontis.; 16 cm.

SON OF A GENIUS: A TALE, FOR THE USE OF YOUTH.
NY: Eastburn, Kirk, 1814.
Note in Rosenbach (#565)—originally published in 1812.
Welch 608.1
Shaw 31737, 32819
Mansell
B   ———.
NY: Eastburn, Kirk, 1814.
251 p.: ill.; 16 cm.
B   Reprint ed., SON . . . SECOND AMERICAN EDITION.
NY: Bliss, 1818.
251 p.: ill.; 14 cm.
Welch 608.2
B   Reprint ed., SON . . .
Boston: Well, 1826
216 p.; 15 cm.

B   Reprint ed., SON . . . NEW AND IMPROVED EDITION.
NY: Harper, 1832.
213 p.: ill., frontis.; 16 cm.
half-title

B   Reprint ed., SON . . .
Hudson, Ohio: Sawyer, Ingersoll, 1852.
216 p.; 16 cm.

B   Reprint ed., SON OF A GENIUS. A TALE FOR YOUTH.
NY: C.S. Francis, 1858.
210 p., 14 p. cat.: frontis.; 15 cm.

B   Reprint ed., SON . . .
Boston: Chase and Nichols, 1863.
210 p.: frontis.; 15.5 cm.

B   Reprint ed., SON . . .
Philadelphia: Porter and Coates, [18—]
210 p.: col. frontis.; 16 cm.

B   Reprint Collection, STORIES OF GENIUS: FOR THE YOUNG.
INCLUDING THE SON OF A GENIUS; THE DAUGHTER
OF A GENIUS: AND ALICIA AND HER AUNT.
NY: C.S. Francis, 1855.
210, 159, 144 p.: frontis.; 16 cm.
half-title

STOLEN BOY. A STORY . . .
NY: Gilley, 1830
Mansell

B   Reprint Collection, TALES OF CLAIRMONT CASTLE. CON-
TAINING THE WOODVILLE FAMILY, THE FRANKS,
SIR FRANCIS VANHESON, THE WHITE LIE, THE
PEDIGREE, THE SPRING GUN, THE FUGITIVE.
Philadelphia: Ash, [18—]
185 p.: frontis.; 15 cm.

THEODORE: OR, THE CRUSADERS. A TALE FOR YOUTH.
Boston: Munroe and Francis, 1824.
Shoe 16564
Mansell

B   ———.
Boston: Munroe and Francis, 1824.
180 p.: plates; 18.5 cm.

UNLOVED ONE: A DOMESTIC STORY.
NY: Harper, 1844

WILLIAM AND HIS UNCLE BEN: A TALE DESIGNED FOR
THE USE OF YOUNG PEOPLE.
NY: Gilley, [1865]
Mansell

YOUNG CADET: OR, HENRY DELAMORE'S VOYAGE TO
INDIA . . .
NY: Roorbach, 1829.
Shoe 33576
Mansell

B   Reprint edition, YOUNG . . . NEW EDITION.
Philadelphia: Anners, [18—]
206 p.: frontis.; 16 cm.

YOUNG CRUSOE: OR, THE SHIPWRECKED BOY . . . NEW
ED.
NY: Harper, 1833.
Mansell

YOUNG PILGRIM, OR ALFRED CAMPBELL'S RETURN TO
THE EAST . . .
NY: Roorbach, 1828.
Shoe 33577
Mansell

B   ———.
NY: Roorbach, 1828.
211 p.: 18.5 cm.

B   Reprint ed., YOUNG . . . NEW EDITION . . .
Philadelphia: Kay, 1831.
211 p.: plates; 15 cm.

MARY BOTHAM HOWITT (1799–1888) was a British writer and poet,
who also translated the novels of Frederika Bremer and the tales of Hans
Christian Andersen into English. (Her translations, however, are not
included in this bibliography.) She wrote charming books for children on
her own or together with her husband William. Among the gift books she
is associated with are the *Hyacinth* and the *Dial of Love*.

ALL, ALLSUP, BIB, BIO, BRIT, CA, DIC EN, EV, NEW

(Please note: some reprints may have been included in the following
bibliography, due to the lack of bibliographical references available for
study.)

ALICE FRANKLIN. A TALE. ANOTHER PART OF "SOW-
ING AND REAPING."
NY: D. Appleton; Philadelphia: G. Appleton, 1843.
Mansell
Baldwin

B ———.
NY: D. Appleton; Philadelphia: G. Appleton, 1843.
174 p., 16 p. cat.: frontis.; 15.1 cm.
half-title

ANGEL UNAWARES, AND OTHER STORIES.
NY: Miller, 1865.
Free
Kelly
Mansell

B ———.
NY: Miller, 1865.
291 p.: plates, frontis.; 18.5 cm.
half-title

ARTIST-WIFE, AND OTHER TALES.
NY: Stringer & Townsend, 1853.
Roorbach
Mansell

AUTHOR'S DAUGHTER.
NY: Harper, 1845.
Roorbach
Mansell

BRIGHT DAYS: OR, HERBERT AND MEGGY.
Boston: Lothrop, [1847]
Mansell

CHARMING STORIES FOR YOUNG FOLKS.
NY: Knox, [18—]
Mansell

B CHARMING STORIES FOR YOUNG FOLKS. ILLUS-
TRATED.
NY: Hurst, [18—]
260 p., 2 p. cat.: ill.; 18.5 cm.

CHILDHOOD OF MARY LEESON.
Boston: Crosby, Nichols, 1848.
Free
Mansell

B   ———.
        Boston: Crosby, Nichols, 1848.
        143 p.: frontis.; 16 cm.
B   Reprint ed., CHILDHOOD . . .
        Boston: Crosby, Nichols, [18—]
        143 p.: frontis.; 16 cm.
        half-title
        Inscribed 1866

CHILDREN'S YEAR . . .
    Philadelphia: Lea and Blanchard, 1848.
    Mansell
B   ———.
        Philadelphia: Lea and Blanchard, 1848.
        179 p., 4 p. cat.; plates; 18 cm.
B   Reprint ed., CHILDREN'S . . .
        Boston: Lothrop, [18—]
        257 p.: frontis.; 18.5 cm.

CHILD'S DELIGHT: OR, THE THREE WISHES AND OTHER
ENTERTAINING STORIES.
    NY: Miller, [18—]

CHRISTMAS TREE: A BOOK OF STORIES.
    NY: C.S. Francis, 1852.
    Free
    Mansell
S   Reprint ed., CHRISTMAS . . .
        NY: C.S. Francis; Boston: J.H. Francis. 1855.
        160 p.: ill.

B   COUNTRY SKETCHES.
        NY: Colby, 1853.
        128 p.: plates; 15 cm.
        Baldwin
B   Reprint ed., COUNTRY . . .
        NY: Sheldon, Lamport & Blakeman, 1855.
        128 p.: plates; 15 cm.

FAVORITE SCHOLAR . . .
    NY: C.S. Francis; Boston: J.H. Francis, 1844.
    Mansell
B   ———.
        NY: C.S. Francis; Boston: J.H. Francis, 1844.
        175 p., 6 p. cat.: plates; 15 cm.

B   FIRESIDE TALES.
     NY: C.S. Francis; Boston: J.H. Francis, 1855.
     160 p.; 15 cm.
     Baldwin

B   Reprint ed. FIRESIDE . . .
     Boston: Roberts Brothers, [18—]
     160 p.; 15.5 cm.

     GABRIEL: A STORY OF WICHNOR WOOD . . .
     NY: Collins and Brother, 1850.
     Roorbach
     Mansell

B   ———.
     NY: Collins and Brother, 1850.
     230 p.: frontis.; 16 cm.

     Also,

B   GABRIEL . . .
     NY: Robert B. Collins, 1850.
     230 p.: frontis.; 15.5 cm.

B   HONEST GABRIEL: OR THE REWARD OF PERSEVER-
     ANCE.
     Philadelphia: Perkinpine & Higgins, [18—]
     216 p., 32 p. cat.: frontis.; 17.5 cm.
     Baldwin

     HOPE ON! HOPE EVER!, OR, THE BOYHOOD OF FELIX
     LAW.
     Boston: Munroe, 1840.
     Mansell

B   Reprint ed., HOPE . . .
     NY: Appleton, 1841.
     212 p.: frontis.; 15 cm.
     half-title

B   Reprint ed., HOPE . . .
     NY: Appleton, 1843.
     212 p., 16 p. cat.: frontis.; 15 cm.
     half-title

B   Reprint ed., HOPE . . .
     NY: Appleton, 1863.
     212 p.: frontis. ; 15.5 cm.
     half-title

S   Reprint ed., HOPE . . .
        Philadelphia: Davis, Porter & Coates, 1867.
        225 p.
        With John Howitt.
        JACK AND HARRY: OR, PICTURES FOR THE YOUNG.
        Boston: J.E. Tilton, 1859.
        Mansell

B   ———
        Boston: J.E. Tilton, 1859.
        72 p.: ill.; 23 cm.

        LILLIESLEA, OR LOST AND FOUND. A STORY FOR THE
        YOUNG.
        NY: Boutledge, [18—]
        Mansell

        LITTLE COIN, MUCH CARE: OR, HOW POOR MEN LIVE. A
        TALE FOR YOUNG PERSONS.
        NY: Appleton, 1842.
        Mansell

B   ———.
        NY: Appleton, 1842.
        171 p., 16 p. cat.: frontis.; 15 cm.
        half-title

S   Reprint ed., LITTLE . . .   PR
        NY: Appleton, 1845.   4809
        171 p.; frontis.; 16 cm.   .H2
        added t.p.   L5

B   Reprint ed., LITTLE . . .
        NY: Appleton, 1863.
        171 p.: frontis.; 16 cm.
        half-title

        With John Howitt.
        LITTLE DICK AND THE ANGEL.
        Boston: Tilton, [1869?]
        Mansell

        . . . THE   LITTLE   PEACEMAKER . . . FOLLOWED   BY
        PRINCE HEMPSEED ON HIS TRAVELS: AND WILLIAM
        AND HIS TEACHER.
        NY: Cassell, Petter, Galpin, [1885]
        Mansell

B   same as above? . . . THE LITTLE . . .
        London and NY: Cassell, Petter, Galpin, [18—]
        97 p., 16 p. cat.: plates; 17.5 cm.

LOVE AND MONEY: AN EVERY-DAY TALE.
NY: Appleton, 1844.
Mansell

B ———.
NY: Appleton, 1844.
173 p.: frontis.; 15 cm.
half-title

B Reprint ed., LOVE . . .
NY: Appleton, 1863.
173 p.: frontis. 16 cm.

MIDSUMMER FLOWERS. FOR THE YOUNG.
Philadelphia; Lindsay & Blakiston, 1854.
Free
Mansell

B ———.
Philadelphia: Lindsay & Blakiston, 1854.
226 p., 6 p. cat.: plates; 19.5 cm.
half-title

MY JUVENILE DAYS, AND OTHER TALES.
NY: D. Appleton; Philadelphia: G.S. Appleton, 1850.
Mansell
Baldwin

B ———.
NY: D. Appleton; Philadelphia: G.S. Appleton, 1850.
176, 178, 184 p., 6 p. cat.: frontis.; 16 cm.
half-titles

B MY OWN STORY: OR, THE AUTOBIOGRAPHY OF A CHILD.
NY: D. Appleton; Philadelphia: G.S. Appleton, 1844.
176 p., 18 p. cat.: frontis.; 15 cm.
half-title
Baldwin

B Reprint ed., MY OWN . . .
NY: D. Appleton; Philadelphia: G.S. Appleton, 1850.
176 p., 3 p. cat.: frontis.; 15.5 cm.
half-title

B Reprint ed., MY OWN . . .
NY: D. Appleton, 1851.
176 p., 4 p. cat.: frontis.; 15.5 cm.
half-title

S Reprint ed., MY OWN . . .   PR
NY: D. Appleton, 1858.   4809.H2
176 p.: ill.; 16 cm.   Z5
added t.p. engraved   1858

B   Reprint ed., MY OWN . . .
         NY: D. Appleton, 1863.
         173 p.: frotnis.; 15.5 cm.
         half-title

         MY UNCLE THE CLOCKMAKER: A TALE.
         NY: D. Appleton; Philadelphia: G.S. Appleton, 1845.
         Free
         Baldwin
         Mansell

B   ———.
         NY: D. Appleton; Philadelphia: G.S. Appleton, 1845.
         180 p. 16 p. cat.: frontis.; 15 cm.

B   Reprint ed., MY . . .
         NY: D. Appleton, [18—]
         177 p.: frontis.; 16 cm.

         NEW BOOK OF STORIES FOR THE YOUNG.
         Philadelphia: T.K. Collins, Jr., 1850.
         Roorbach

         NEW STORY BOOK. ILLUSTRATED.
         NY: Miller. 1866.
         Mansell

B   ———.
         NY: Miller, 1866.
         226 p., 2 p. cat.: plates; 18.5 cm.
         half-title

         NO SENSE LIKE COMMON SENSE: OR, SOME PASSAGES
         IN THE LIFE OF CHARLES MIDDLETON, ESQ.
         NY: D. Appleton, 1843
         Mansell

S   ———.   PR
         NY: D. Appleton, 1843.   4809
         176 p.: ill.; 15 cm.   .H2
         added t.p., engraved   N6

B   ———.
         NY: D. Appleton; Philadelphia: G.S. Appleton, 1843.
         176 p., 16 p. cat.: frontis.; 15.5 cm.
         half-title

B   Reprint ed., NO . . .
         NY: D. Appleton, etc., 1863.
         176 p.: frontis.; 16 cm.
         half-title

OUR COUSIN IN OHIO: FROM THE DIARY OF AN AMERICAN MOTHER.
NY: Collins and Brother, 1849.
Free
Mansell
Sabin 33373

S ———.
NY: Collins, 1849.
viii, 251 p., [1] p. cat.

B ———.
NY: Collins and Brother, 1849.
251 p.: ill.; 16.5 cm.

PETER DRAKE'S DREAM, AND OTHER STORIES.
NY: Miller, 1865.
Mansell
Kelly

B Reprint ed.?, PETER . . .
NY: Miller, 1866.
280 p., 6 p. cat.: plates; 18.5 cm.
half-title

PETER PARLEY'S FABLE OF THE SPIDER AND FLY.
Boston: Carter and Hendee, 1830.
Mansell

PICTURE BOOK FOR THE YOUNG . . .
Philadelphia: Lippincott, 1856.
Mansell

B Reprint ed., PICTURE . . .
Philadelphia: Lippincott, 1862.
56 p.: plates; 18 cm.

PLEASANT LIFE.
NY: Nelson, [187–]
Mansell

POETICAL TALES FOR GOOD BOYS AND GIRLS.
Worcester. (Mass.): Livermore, 1847.

B Reprint ed., POETICAL . . .
Boston: E. Livermore, 1854.
62 p.: 14 cm.

POPULAR MORAL TALES FOR THE YOUNG . . .
NY: D. Appleton: Philadelphia: G.S. Appleton, 1850.

RAG-BAG: A COLLECTION OF STORIES.
Philadelphia: Lindsay & Blakiston, [186?]
Mansell

SADDLER MULLERS WENDEL, WITH OTHER TALES.
Boston: Crosby, Nichols, Lee, 1852.
Roorbach

B   ———.
Boston: Crosby and Nichols, [18—]
70 p.: ill., frontis.; 19.5 cm.
half-title

B   ———.
Boston: Crosby, etc., [18—]
70 p.: ill., frontis.; 21.5 cm.

B   SKETCHES OF NATURAL HISTORY.
Boston: Weeks, Jordan, 1839.
198 p.: ill.; 16 cm.
Baldwin
Also, published by

B   Boston: Carter, 1839
216 p.: ill.; 14.5 cm.
Baldwin

SONGS AND STORIES, FOR MOTHER'S DARLING.
Philadelphia: Lippincott, Grambo, 1854.
Mansell

SOWING AND REAPING: OR, WHAT WILL COME OF IT.
Boston: Munroe, 1840.

B   Reprint ed., SOWING . . .
NY: D. Appleton, 1841.
170 p.: frontis.; 15.5 cm.
half-title

B   Reprint ed., SOWING . . .
NY: D. Appleton: Philadelphia: G.S. Appleton, 1843.
170 p.: frontis.; 15.5 cm.
half-title

B   Reprint ed., SOWING . . .
NY: D. Appleton, 1863.
170 p.: frontis.; 16 cm.
half-title

STORIES FROM THE REFORMATION. FOR THE ENTER-
TAINMENT AND INSTRUCTION OF YOUTH.
NY: C.S. Francis, 1857.
Mansell.

STORYBOOK: WITH ILLUSTRATIONS.
NY: C.S. Francis; Boston: J.H. Francis, 1850.
Baldwin
Mansell

B   ———.
NY: C.S. Francis, etc., 1850.
3 × 160 p., 7 p. cat.: plates; 16 cm.

B   STORY OF A GENIUS: OR COLA MONTI. FIRST AMERI-
CAN EDITION.
NY: D. Appleton, 1863.
180 p.: frontis.; 16 cm.
Baldwin

STRIVE AND THRIVE, A TALE.
Boston: Munroe, 1840.

B   Reprint ed., STRIVE . . .
Boston: Munroe, 1841.
175 p.: frontis.; 16.5 cm.
half-title

B   Reprint ed., STRIVE . . .
New Haven: Babcock, 1841.
179 p.: frontis.; 15.5 cm.

B   Reprint ed., STRIVE . . .
NY: D. Appleton, 1841.
175 p.: frontis.; 15.5 cm.
half-title

S   Reprint ed., STRIVE . . .
NY: D. Appleton, 1841.
[2] p. cat., 175 p.: ill.
engraved frontispiece and t.p.

B   Reprint ed., STRIVE . . .
NY: D. Appleton, 1843.

B   Reprint ed., STRIVE . . .
NY: D. Appleton, 1863.
175 p.: frontis.; 16 cm.
half-title

TALES IN PROSE: FOR THE YOUNG.
Boston: Weeks, Jordan, 1839.
Mansell

B   Reprint? TALES . . .
Boston: Weeks, Jordan, [18—]
183 p.: frontis.; 16 cm.

B Reprint ed., TALES . . .
   NY: Harper, 1847.
   183 p., 16 p. cat.: frontis.; 16 cm.

B THE TURTLE DOVE: AND OTHER STORIES.
   NY: C.S. Francis; Boston: J. H. Francis, 1850.
   160 p.: 15.5 cm.
   half-title
   Baldwin

   TWO APPRENTICES. A TALE FOR YOUTH.
   NY: D. Appleton, 1845.
   Mansell

B Reprint ed., TWO . . .
   NY: D. Appleton, 1849.
   179 p.: frontis.; 15.5 cm.
   half-title

B Reprint ed., TWO . . .
   NY: D. Appleton, 1863.
   175 p.: frontis.; 16 cm.
   half-title

   WHICH IS WISER; OR, PEOPLE ABROAD, A TALE FOR
   YOUTH.
   NY: D. Appleton, 1842.
   Mansell

B ———.
   NY: D. Appleton, 1842.
   184 p.: frontis.; 15 cm.
   half-title

B Reprint ed., WHICH . . .
   NY: D. Appleton; Philadelphia: G.S. Appleton, 1843.
   184 p., 16 p. cat.: frontis.; 15.5 cm.
   half-title

S Reprint ed., WHICH . . .
   NY: Appleton, 1849.
   184 p.
   engraved t.p.

B Reprint ed., WHICH . . .
   NY: D. Appleton, 1863.
   184 p.: frontis.; 16 cm.
   half-title

   WHO SHALL BE GREATEST?
   Boston: Munroe, 1841.
   Mansell

B   ——.
> Boston: Munroe, 1841.
> 242 p.: frontis.; 16 cm.
> half-title
> Also published by

B   NY: D. Appleton, 1841.
> 178 p.: frontis.; 15.5 cm.
> half-title
> Baldwin

B   Reprint ed., WHO . . .
> NY: D. Appleton, Philadelphia: G.S. Appleton, 1843.
> 178 p., 16 p. cat.: frontis.; 15.5 cm.

B   Reprint ed., WHO . . .
> NY: D. Appleton, 1863.
> 178 p.: frontis.; 16 cm.
> half-title

WOOD LEIGHTON: OR, A YEAR IN THE COUNTRY.
> Philadelphia: Carey, Lea & Blanchard, 1837.
> 3 vols.
> Mansell

WORK AND WAGES: OR, LIFE IN SERVICE. A CONTINU-
ATION OF "LITTLE COIN, MUCH CARE."
> NY: D. Appleton; Philadelphia: G.S. Appleton, 1843.
> Mansell

B   ——.
> NY: D. Appleton, 1843.
> 178 p., 16 p. cat.: frontis.; 15.5 cm.

S   Reprint ed., WORK . . .
> NY: Appleton, 1856.
> 178 p., 2 p. cat.: ill., engraved frontis. and t.p.

B   Reprint ed., WORK . . .
> NY: D. Appleton, 1863.
> 178 p.: frontis.; 16 cm.

MARY ROBSON HUGHS was an English native who immigrated to Philadelphia in 1818, where she ran a school for young ladies until 1839. She wrote under the pseudonym of "Aunt Mary" and is known for her various moral Aunt Mary's tales for children. She was greatly influenced by the work of Maria Edgeworth.

ALL, MEB

(Please note: some of the stories later were published and republished in various forms and in various groupings. Reprints have been avoided, but may inevitably have slipped in. Also, there are many British publications that are not included in this group, because no American edition was found for these titles.)

AUNT MARY'S STORIES FOR CHILDREN . . .
  Boston: Phillips, Sampson, [184?].
  Mansell
B Reprint ed., AUNT . . .
  Boston: Phillips, Sampson, 1850.
  143 p.: plates; 15.5 cm.
S Reprint ed., AUNT . . .   PZ
  NY: G. Leavitt, 1868.   6.H88
  143 p.: ill.; 16 cm.   Au

AUNT MARY'S TALES FOR BOYS AND GIRLS.
  Philadelphia: Lindsay & Blakiston, 1851.
  Roorbach
B Reprint ed., AUNT . . .
  Philadelphia: Lindsay & Blakiston, 1860.
  4 × 64, 58, 58, 60, 72, 63, 64 p., 8 p. cat.: frontis.; 15.5 cm.

AUNT MARY'S TALES, FOR THE ENTERTAINMENT AND
  IMPROVEMENT OF LITTLE BOYS . . . FIRST AMER-
  ICAN FROM THE THIRD LONDON ED.
  NY: Bliss, 1817.
  Shaw 41093
  Welch 619
  Rosenbach 552
B Reprint ed.? AUNT . . .
  NY: Bliss, [18—]
  174 p.: frontis.; 14.5 × 8.5 cm.

B Reprint ed., AUNT . . . SECOND AMERICAN FROM THE
  THIRD LONDON EDITION.
  NY: Roorbach, 1827.
  174 p.: frontis.; 14 cm.

AUNT MARY'S TALES, FOR THE ENTERTAINMENT AND
  IMPROVEMENT OF LITTLE GIRLS . . . FIRST AMER-
  ICAN FROM THE THIRD LONDON EDITION.
  NY: Bliss, 1817.
  Welch 620
  Shaw 41094

B   ———.
      NY: Bliss 1817
      168 p.: frontis.; 14 × 8.5 cm.

BUDS AND BLOSSOMS FOR THE YOUNG.
      Philadelphia: Lindsay & Blakiston, 1848.
      Mansell
      Baldwin

B   ———.
      Philadelphia: Lindsay & Blakiston, 1848.
      205 p.: plates; 18 cm.
      half-title

B   Reprint ed., BUDS . . .
      Philadelphia: Lindsay & Blakiston, 1854.
      205 p.: plates; 18 cm.
      half-title

COUSINS: A MORAL TALE . . .
      Philadelphia: Small, 1826.
      "Published in England by Darton under title 'The Alchemist'
      (1818)."
      Shoe 24909
      Wright 1240a

B   DAISY . . .   (Gift book?)
      NY: Sheldon, Blakeman, 1856 [c1855]
      94 p.: frontis.; 12 cm.

B   Reprint ed., DAISY . . .
      NY: Sheldon, Blakeman, 1864.
      94 p.: plates; 15 cm.

B   Reprint ed., DAISY . . .
      NY: Sheldon, Blakeman, [18—]
      94 p.: plates; 15 cm.

EDWARD THE SUNDAY SCHOLAR, A SKETCH FROM
      REAL LIFE . . .
      Boston: Munroe and Francis, 1825.
      Shoe 20973
      Mansell

B   ———.
      Boston: Munroe and Francis, 1825.
      44, 20 p.: 19 cm.

EMMA MORTIMER: A MORAL TALE.
Philadelphia: T. Ash, [1829]
Shoe 39045
Wright 1240B
Mansell

S ——.   PS
Philadelphia: T. Ash, [1829]   2044
249 p.: 17 cm.   .H28
                                                                                 E4

FAMILY DIALOGUES: OR, SUNDAY WELL-SPENT.
Philadelphia: Pr. by Rakestrau, for the Tract and Book
Society of the Evangelical Church of St. John, 1828.
Shoe 33605

FRANK WORTHY: OR, THE ORPHAN AND HIS BENE-
FACTOR. FOR LITTLE BOYS AND LITTLE GIRLS.
Philadelphia: Lindsay & Blakiston, [1849]
Mansell
Roorbach

B ——.
Philadelphia: Lindsay & Blakiston, 1849.
72 p.: col. frontis.; 15 cm.

S ——.   PZ
Philadelphia: Lindsay & Blakiston, 1849.   6
72 p.: ill.; 16 cm.   .H88
                                                                                 Fr

B Reprint ed.? FRANK . . .
NY: J. Miller, [c1849]
72, 58, 64 p.: frontis.; 15 cm.
Also: May Morning; The Young Artist
half-title

B Reprint ed.? FRANK . . .
Philadelphia: Lindsay & Blakiston, [c1849]

GENEROSITY: OR, SYBELLA AND FLORIENCE, FOR
LITTLE BOYS AND LITTLE GIRLS.
Philadelphia: Lindsay & Blakiston, [1849]

B ——.
Philadelphia: Lindsay & Blakiston, 1850.
64 p.: col frontis.; 15 cm.

B Reprint ed.?
GENEROSITY
NY: J. Miller, [18—]
64 p.: frontis.; 15 cm.

GIPSY FORTUNE-TELLER: OR, THE TROUBADOUR. FOR
LITTLE BOYS AND LITTLE GIRLS.
  Philadelphia: Lindsay & Blakiston, 1849.
  Free
  Roorbach
  Mansell
B Reprint ed.? GIPSY . . .
  Philadelphia: Lindsay & Blakiston, [c1849]
  64 p.: col. frontis.; 15 cm.

HENRY GOODWIN: OR, THE CONTENTED MAN.
  Boston: Wells & Lilly, 1819.
Also published in
  Philadelphia, 1819.
  Shaw 48287-8

HOLIDAYS IN THE COUNTRY: OR, VANITY DISAP-
POINTED. FOR LITTLE BOYS AND LITTLE GIRLS.
  Philadelphia: Lindsay & Blakiston, [1849?]
  Mansell
B ———.
  Philadelphia: Lindsay & Blakiston, 1850.
  64 p.: col. frontis.; 15 cm.
B Reprint ed? HOLIDAYS . . .
  NY: J. Miller, [18—]
  64 p.: frontis.; 15 cm.

IVY WREATH . . .
  Philadelphia: Lindsay & Blakiston, [c1849]
  Free
  Mansell
B ———.
  Philadelphia: Lindsay & Blakiston, [c1849]
  175 p.: plates, col. half title; 18.5 cm.

B JESSAMINE . . .   (Gift book?)
  NY: Sheldon, 1864, [c1855]
  95 p.: plates; 15 cm.
  Baldwin

JULIA ORMOND: OR, THE NEW SETTLEMENT.
  NY: Dunigan, 1846.
  Mansell
  Wright 1240c

KEEPSAKE STORIES
  Philadelphia: Anners, [1841]
  Mansell

B   LILLY . . .   (Gift book?)
       NY: Sheldon, 1864 [c1853]
       96 p.: plates; 15 cm.
       Baldwin

       LISSIE LINDON AND HER MOCKINGBIRD.
       Philadelphia: Lindsay & Blakiston, 1849.
       Mansell
       Roorbach

       LITTLE ADVENTURER. A TALE. FOUNDED ON FACT.
       Philadelphia: Small, 1827.
       Mansell
B   Reprint ed. LITTLE . . .
       Philadelphia: Lindsay & Blakiston, 1849.
       63 p.: col. frontis.; 15.5 cm.

       MAY MORNING: OR, A VISIT TO THE COUNTRY. FOR
       LITTLE BOYS AND LITTLE GIRLS.
       Philadelphia: Lindsay & Blakiston, 1849.
       Roorbach
       Mansell
B   ———.
       Philadelphia: Lindsay & Blakiston, 1849.
       58 p., 80. cat.: col. frontis.; 15 cm.
B   Reprint ed., MAY MORNING.
       NY: J. Miller, [18—]
       48 p.: frontis.; 15 cm.
       Inscribed 1868

       METAMORPHOSES: OR EFFECTS OF EDUCATION. A
       TALE.
       Philadelphia: Small, 1820.
       Welch 621
       Shoe 1695
       Mansell
B   ———.
       Philadelphia: Small, 1820.
       268 p.: frontis.; 14.5 × 8.5 cm.

       MOTHER'S BIRTH-DAY: OR, THE BROKEN VASE. FOR
       LITTLE BOYS AND LITTLE GIRLS.
       Philadelphia: Lindsay & Blakiston, 1849.
       Roorbach
       Mansell

B   Reprint ed.? MOTHER'S BIRTH-DAY.
       NY: J. Miller, [c1849]
       60 p.: frontis.; 15 cm.

       ORNAMENTS DISCOVERED: A STORY, IN TWO PARTS.
       NY: Gilley, 1817.
       Mansell
       Welch 622
       Shaw 41095

B   ———.
       NY: Gilley, 1817.
       180 p.: 14 × 8.5 cm.

S   Reprint ed., ORNAMENTS . . .
       NY: Harper, 1855.
       194 p.

       PLEASING AND INSTRUCTIVE STORIES FOR YOUNG
       CHILDREN.
       Philadelphia: Ash & Anners, [c1838]
       Free
       Mansell

B   ———.
       Philadelphia: Ash & Anners, [c1838]
       96 p.: plates; 14 cm.

S   Reprint ed.? PLEASING . . .   PZ
       Philadelphia: T. Ash, [18—]   6
       105 p.: ill.; 15 cm   .H88
       P1

       PROUD GIRL HUMBLED, OR, THE TWO SCHOOLMATES.
       FOR LITTLE BOYS AND LITTLE GIRLS.
       Philadelphia: Lindsay & Blakiston, [1849]
       Mansell

B   same? PROUD . . .
       Philadelphia: Lindsay & Blakiston, [c1849]
       58 p.: col. frontis.; 15 cm.

B   Reprint ed? PROUD . . .
       NY: J. Miller, [c1849]
       58 p.: frontis.; 15 cm.

B   Reprint ed., PROUD . . .
       NY: Alden, 1869.
       58 p.: frontis.; 15 cm.

       ROSE . . .   (Gift book?)
       NY: Sheldon, Blakeman, 1856.
       Mansell

S, B ——.
> NY: Sheldon, Blakeman, 1856, [c1853]
> 95 p.: plates; 12.5 cm.

B   Reprint ed., ROSE . . .
> NY: Sheldon, Blakeman, 1864.
> 95 p.: plates; 15.5 cm.

STORIES FOR CHILDREN, CHIEFLY CONFINED TO WORDS OF TWO SYLLABLES.
> Philadelphia: Small, 1820.
> Welch 623
> Shoe 1696
> Mansell

B   ——.
> Philadelphia: Small, 1820.
> 238 p.: 14.5 × 9 cm.

B   TULIP . . .   (Gift book?)
> NY: Sheldon, Blakeman, 1856.
> 98 p.: 11.5 cm.

B   Reprint ed., TULIP . . .
> NY: Sheldon, Blakeman, 1859.
> 96 p.: plates; 15 cm.

B   Reprint ed., TULIP . . .
> NY: Sheldon, Blakeman, 1864.
> 96 p.: plates; 15 cm.

YOUNG ARTIST: OR, SELF-CONQUEST. FOR LITTLE BOYS AND FOR LITTLE GIRLS.
> Philadelphia: Lindsay & Blakiston, [1849?]
> Mansell

B   YOUNG ARTIST.
> NY: J. Miller, [1849]
> 64 p.: frontis.; 15 cm.

B   Reprint ed.? YOUNG ARTIST.
> Philadelphia: Lindsay & Blakiston, [c1849]
> 64 p.: col. frontis.: 15 cm.

B   Reprint ed.? YOUNG ARTIST.
> NY: Allen, 1869, [c1849]
> 64 p.: frontis; 15 cm.

B   Reprint ed.? YOUNG ARTIST: OR, SELF-CONQUEST . . .
> Philadelphia: Lindsay & Blakiston, [18—]
> 64 p.: col frontis.; 15 cm.

YOUNG SAILOR: OR, PERSEVERANCE REWARDED. FOR
LITTLE BOYS AND LITTLE GIRLS.
Philadelphia: Lindsay & Blakiston, [1849?]
Mansell

B ———.
Philadelphia: Lindsay & Blakiston, 1850.
63 p.: col frontis.; 15 cm.

TWIN BROTHERS: OR, LUCK AND GOOD CONDUCT.
Boston: Wells and Lilly, 1820
Welch 624
Shoe 1697

TWO SCHOOLS: A MORAL TALE.
Baltimore; F. Lucas, Jr., [1835]
Note: also published
Philadelphia: Ash, 1836.
Mansell
Wright 1240c,d

VILLAGE DIALOGUES.
Boston: Well & Lilly, 1820.

WILLIAM'S RETURN: OR, GOOD NEWS FOR COTTAGERS.
2d ED.
Boston: Munroe & Francis, Bowers, 1817
Shaw 41096

ELIZA LESLIE (1787–1858), a native of Philadelphia, is known as a
writer of cookbooks and books on home economics. She also wrote short
stories and juveniles. Her short stories appeared in *Godey's Lady's Book*
and *Graham's Magazine*. She edited an annual entitled the *Gift*, and the
juvenile souvenir, the *Violet*. She is perhaps best known for the *American
Girl's Book* (1831) and *Pencil Sketches*, a three-volume series published
from 1833 to 1837.

AMB, AMAU, CY

ALTHEA VERNON: OR, THE EMBROIDERED HANDKER-
CHIEF. TO WHICH IS ADDED, HENRIETTA HARRI-
SON: OR, THE BLUE COTTON UMBRELLA.
Philadelphia: Lea & Blanchard, 1838.
Roorbach
Wright 1648
Mansell
BM

AMERICAN GIRL'S BOOK: OR, OCCUPATION FOR PLAY
HOURS.
Boston: Munroe & Francis: NY: C.S. Francis, 1831.
Roorbach
Bruntjen 7943
Mansell

B   ———. FOURTH EDITION.
Boston: Munroe & Francis; NY: C.S. Francis, 1846.
383 p.: frontis.; 14.5 cm.

B   ———. SIXTEENTH EDITION.
NY: Allen Brothers, 1869.
383 p.: ill. half title, frontis.; 16 cm.

B   ———. SIXTEENTH EDITION.
NY: Allen Brothers, 1869.
383, 309 p.: ill., frontis.; 15.5 cm.
Also: Hints for happy hours: or, amusement for all ages.
On Spine: Enlarged.
half title.

B   ———. SIXTEENTH EDITION.
NY: R. Worthington, 1881.
383 p.: plates; 18.5 cm.

B   AMERICAN GIRL'S BOOK.
NY: C.S. Francis, [1855?]
382, 309 p. cat.: ill., frontis.; 15.5 cm.
Also: Hints for happy hours; Or, amusement for all ages.
On spine: Enlarged.
Inscribed 1855.

B   GIRL'S OWN BOOK: OR, OCCUPATION FOR PLAY
HOURS . . .
Boston: De Wolfe, Fiske, [1895?]
383 p.: ill.; 19.5 cm.
Inscribed 1895.

ATLANTIC TALES: OR, PICTURES OF YOUTH.
Boston: Munroe & Francis; NY: C.S. Francis, 1833.
Mansell
Bruntjen 19732

BIRTH-DAY STORIES.
Philadelphia: Anners, [1840]
Mansell

KITTY'S RELATIONS, AND OTHER PENCIL SKETCHES.
Philadelphia: Carey & Hart, 1847.
Mansell

Wright 1650
Roorbach
BM

MAID OF CANAL STREET, AND THE BLOXHAMS.
Philadelphia: A. Hart, 1851.
Wright 1510
Roorbach
Also contains Barclay Compton; or, the Sailor's Return

PENCIL SKETCHES: OR, OUTLINES OF CHARACTER AND
MANNERS.
Philadelphia: Carey, Lea & Blanchard, 1833–37.
3 vols. (1st series, 1833;
2d series, 1835;
3rd series, 1837)
Sabin 40203
Bruntjen 19733
Wright 1655
BM

S   ———.   PS
    Philadelphia: Carey, etc., 1833–37.   2244
    vol. 1 only.   L5P4
    274 p.; 19 × 11 cm.   v.1

S   ———.   PS
    Series 2 and 3 (2 vols. in 1)   2244
    Philadelphia: Carey, etc., 1834–37.   L5P4
    281 p., [5] p., 283 p.   v.2 + 3

S   Reprint ed., PENCIL SKETCHES.
    Philadelphia: Hart, 1852.
    not available for examination

STORIES FOR ADELAIDE . . .
    Philadelphia: Ash, [1829]
    Mansell
    Shoe 39274

B   Reprint ed., STORIES . . .
    Philadelphia: Anners, [c1843]
    108 p.: plates; 15.5 cm.

B   Reprint ed.? STORIES FOR ADELAIDE . . . A SECOND
    BOOK FOR HER LITTLE FRIENDS.
    Philadelphia: Hazard, 1856.
    128 p.: plates; 14.5 cm.

STORIES FOR EMMA . . .
    Boston: Munroe & Francis; NY: C.S. Francis, 1829.
    Shoe 39275

STORIES FOR HELEN . . .
Philadelphia: H. Anners, [1845]
Mansell
Roorbach

B   Reprint or same? STORIES FOR HELEN . . .
Philadelphia: H. Anners, [c1845]
140 p.: frontis.; 15.5 cm.

STORIES FOR SUMMER DAYS AND WINTER NIGHTS.
Philadelphia: H.F. Anners, [18—]
Roorbach

B   Reprint ed.? STORIES . . .
NY: Kiggins & Kellogg, [c1853]
173 p.: 16 cm.

STORIES FOR YOUNG PEOPLE.
Philadelphia: H.F. Anners, [18—]

YOUNG AMERICANS: OR, SKETCHES OF A SEA-VOYAGE,
AND A SHORT VISIT TO EUROPE . . .
Boston: Munroe & Francis; NY: C.S. Francis, 1829.
Shoe 39276
Mansell

B   ——.
Boston: Munroe & Francis, etc., 1829.
281 p., 2 p. cat.; 15 cm.

YOUNG LADIES' MENTOR: OR, EXTRACTS IN PROSE
AND VERSE, FOR THE PROMOTION OF VIRTUE AND
MORALITY.
Philadelphia: J. Johnson, 1803.
Mansell
Welch 751
Shaw 4518

B   ——.
Philadelphia: J. Johnson, 1803.
viii, 9–155 p.; 16.5 cm.

YOUNG REVOLUTIONISTS: CONTAINING THE STORIES
OF RUSSEL AND SIDNEY; AND CHASE LORING.
TALES OF THE AMERICAN REVOLUTION.
NY: C.S. Francis; Boston: J.H. Francis, 1845.
Mansell
Roorbach

S, B   Reprint ed., YOUNG REVOLUTIONISTS: OR RUSSEL
AND SIDNEY AND CHASE LORING . . . SECOND EDI-
TION . . .

Philadelphia: Hazard, 1853.
187 p.: plates; 17.5 cm.

WONDERFUL TRAVELS . . .
Boston: Munroe & Francis, 1832.
Mansell
Bruntjen 13383

ELIZABETH STUART PHELPS (1815–1852) was a New England writer known for her slightly fictionalized autobiographical works (*Sunny Side*, 1851; *A Peep at Number Five*, 1852; and *Angel Over the Right Shoulder*, 1852). She often wrote under the pseudonym of "H. Trusta." Her daughter, Elizabeth Stuart Phelps Ward, carried on in her mother's literary footsteps as a writer of popular light fiction and juveniles (such as the Tiny series).

ALL, AMB, AMAU, CY, DIC AM, DIC NA, OX AM, RE

ANGEL OVER THE RIGHT SHOULDER, OR, THE BEGINNING OF THE NEW YEAR.
Andover: Draper; Boston: Jewett, 1852.
Mansell
Wright 1883

B　———.
Andover: Draper, etc., 1852.
29 p.: frontis.; 15.5 cm.

KITTY BROWN AND HER CITY COUSINS.
Philadelphia: American Sunday School Union, [1852].
Mansell
Roorbach

B　———.
Philadelphia: American Sunday School Union, [c1852].
94 p.: plates; 15.5 cm.

KITTY BROWN AND HER LITTLE SCHOOL.
Philadelphia: American Sunday School Union, [c1852].
Mansell
Roorbach

B　———
Philadelphia: American Sunday School Union, [c1852].
107 p.: ill., frontis.; 15.5 cm.

KITTY BROWN BEGINNING TO THINK.
Philadelphia: American Sunday School Union, [1853].

B　———.
Philadelphia: American Sunday School Union, [c1853].
153 p.: plates; 15.5 cm.

LAST LEAF FROM SUNNY SIDE.
Boston: Phillips, Sampson, 1853.
Allibone
Wright 1884
Sabin 61373
Mansell

LITTLE KITTY BROWN AND HER BIBLE VERSES . . .
Philadelphia: Amer. Sunday Sch. Union, [1851]
Mansell

B   ———.
Philadelphia: Amer. Sunday Sch. Union, [c1851]
94 p.: plates; 15.5 cm.

LITTLE MARY: OR, TALKS AND TALES FOR CHILDREN.
Boston: Phillips, Sampson, 1854, [c1853?]
Allibone
Mansell
Roorbach

B   ———.
Boston: Phillips, Sampson, 1854, [c1853]
186 p., 3 p. cat.: ill.; 17.5 cm.

A PEEP AT "NUMBER FIVE": OR, A CHAPTER IN THE
LIFE OF A CITY PASTOR.
Boston: Phillips, Sampson, 1851.
Allibone
Sabin 61374
Roorbach
Mansell

B   Reprint ed., A PEEP . . . TENTH THOUSAND.
Boston: Phillips, Sampson, 1852.
296 p.: frontis.; 16.5 cm.

B   Reprint ed., A PEEP . . . THIRTIETH THOUSAND.
Boston: Phillips, Sampson, 1858.
296 p., 4 p. cat.: frontis.; 16.5 cm.

SUNNY SIDE: OR, THE COUNTRY MINISTER'S WIFE.
Andover: Draper, 1851.
Wright 1886
Allibone
Sabin 61375
Mansell

TELL-TALE: OR, HOME SECRETS TOLD BY OLD
TRAVELLERS.
Boston: Phillips, Sampson, 1853, [c1852?]

Sabin 61376
Allibone
Wright 1887
Roorbach

S ———. PS
    Boston: Phillips, Sampson, 1853. 2557
    263 p.: 4 plates, (incl. frontis.); 16 cm. .P4
     T4
B Reprint ed., TELL-TALE: OR, HOME SECRETS. SIXTEENTH
    THOUSAND.
    NY: Sheldon, 1863, [c1852].
    262 p.; 16 cm.

CATHARINE MARIA SEDGWICK (1789–1867) was a popular New England authoress whose novels were admired by Bryant and Hawthorne. Her books were also translated and widely read in Europe. In all her works she exalts the simple virtues of domestic life. She was an ardent Unitarian, and many of her works for children were designed as Sunday School books.

ALL, AMB, AMAU, AP, DAB, DIC AM, DIC EN, DIC LIT, DIC NA, NC

B BEATITUDES.
    Boston: Bowles and Dearborn, 1828.
    144 p.: frontis.; 14.5 cm.
    Baldwin

    BOY OF MOUNT RHIGI . . .
    Boston: Crosby and Nichols, 1847.
    Mansell
B Reprint ed., BOY . . .
    Boston: Peirce, 1848 [c1847]
    252 p.: frontis.; 17 cm.
    half-title

    CITY CLERK AND HIS SISTER, AND OTHER
    STORIES . . .
    Philadelphia: Hazard, 1851.
    Mansell
    Roorbach
B Reprint ed., CITY . . .
    Philadelphia: Hazard, 1853.
    91 p.: frontis; 14.5 cm.

B   Reprint ed., CHARLIE HATHAWAY: OR, THE CITY
           CLERK . . .
           NY: Allen Brothers, 1869.
           91, 64 p.: ill., frontis.; 15 cm.

CLARENCE: OR, A TALE OF OUR OWN TIMES.
           Philadelphia: Carey & Lea, 1830.
           2 vols.
           Cooper, 3434
           Sabin 78769
           Mansell
           Wright 2339
           BM

DEFORMED BOY.
           Brookfield: E. & G. Merriam, 1826.
           Mansell
B   ———.
           Brookfield: E & G. Merriam, 1826
           36 p.; 13.5 cm.

FACTS AND FANCIES FOR SCHOOL-DAY READING, A
           SEQUEL TO "MORALS OF MANNERS."
           NY: Wiley & Putnam, 1848, [c1847]
           LITWRIAM
           Sabin 78770
           BM
           Mansell
           Baldwin
B   ———.
           NY: Wiley, etc., 1848, [c1847]
           208 p. (incomplete): plates; 15 cm.
S   Reprint ed., FACTS . . .
           NY: Putnam, 1873.
           216 p.

HOPE LESLIE: OR, EARLY TIMES IN THE MASSACHU-
           SETTS.
           NY: White, Gallaher, & White, 1827.
           2 vols.
           Sabin 78775
           Shoe 30564
           Wright 2348
           Mansell

S   Reprint ed., HOPE . . .   PS
        NY: Harper, 1842   2798
        2 vols.   .H63
        18 cm.   1842

        LESSONS WITHOUT BOOKS . . .
        Boston: Bowles, 1830.
        2 vols.
        Cooper 3435
        Mansell

        THE LINWOODS: OR, "SIXTY YEARS SINCE" IN
        AMERICA.
        NY: Harper, 1835.
        2 vols.
        Sabin 78784
        BM
        Wright 2350
        Roorbach
        Mansell

        LIVE AND LET LIVE: OR, DOMESTIC SERVICE ILLUS-
        TRATED.
        NY: Harper, 1837.
        Sabin 78786
        Wright 2351
        Roorbach
        Mansell

B   LOUISA AND HER COUSINS: A SEQUEL TO "LESSONS
        WITHOUT BOOKS." . . .
        Boston: Bowles, 1831.
        321 p.: frontis.; 15 cm.
        Baldwin

        A LOVE TOKEN FOR CHILDREN. DESIGNED FOR SUN-
        DAY-SCHOOL LIBRARIES . . .   (Gift book?)
        NY: Harper, [1837]
        Roorbach
        Sabin 78788
        Mansell

B   Reprint ed.?, A LOVE . . .
        NY: Harper, 1838, [c1837]
        142 p., 18 p. cat.; 15.5 cm.

MARRIED OR SINGLE? A NOVEL.
NY: Harper, 1857.
2 vols.
Sabin 78790
Mansell

MARY HOLLIS. AN ORIGINAL TALE.
NY: NY Unitarian Book Society, 1822.
Shoe 10217
Wright 2354
Mansell

MEANS AND ENDS, OR SELF TRAINING.
Boston: Marsh, Capen, Lyon & Webb, 1839.
Sabin 78792
Mansell

B   MEANS . . . SECOND EDITION.
NY: Harper, 1842.
278 p., 1 p. cat.

S   MEANS . . . SECOND EDITION.
NY: Harper, 1843.
278 p., 12 p. cat.

MORALS OF MANNERS: OR, HINTS FOR OUR YOUNG
PEOPLE.
NY: Wiley and Putnam, 1846.
Baldwin
Mansell
Sabin 78795
Free
Roorbach

B   ———.
NY: Wiley, etc., 1846.
63 p.: frontis.; 14.5 cm.

B   Reprint ed., MORALS . . .
NY: G. Putnam, [c1846]
63 p.: frontis; 15 cm.

B   MORALS . . . NEW EDITION. REVISED
NY: G.P. Putnam, 1854.
63 p.; 15 cm.

MYSTERIOUS STORY-BOOK: OR, THE GOOD STEP-
MOTHER. BY WHOM?
NY: Appleton, 1856.
Mansell
BM

A NEW ENGLAND TALE: OR, SKETCHES OF NEW-
ENGLAND CHARACTER AND MANNERS.
NY: Bliss & White, 1822.
Wright 2357
Sabin 78796
Shoe 10218
Mansell

S   ———.   PS
NY: Bliss & White, 1822.   2798
vii, [5], 282 p.; 19.5 cm.   .N4
                                      1822

PLEASANT SUNDAYS.
Boston: Bowles, 1832.
"Attributed by Roorbach to C.M. Sedgwick"
Mansell

POOR RICH MAN, AND THE RICH POOR MAN.
NY: Harper, 1836.
Wright 2358
Sabin 78798
Roorbach
Mansell

S   ———.   PS
NY: Harper, 1836.   2798
2 p., 1, [7]–186 p., 12 p. cat.; 16 cm.   .P6
                                      1836

B   Reprint ed., POOR . . .
NY: Harper, 1840, [c1836]
186 p.: 16 cm.

REDWOOD: A TALE . . .
NY: Bliss & White, 1824.
2 vols.
Sabin 78800
Shoe 17936
Mansell
BM
Wright 2366

SKETCH OF MARY DYRE.
Boston: s.n., 1831.
Mansell
Bruntjen 9145

STORIES FOR YOUNG PERSONS . . .
   NY: Harper, [1840]
   Roorbach
   Sabin 78802

B   Reprint ed. STORIES . . .
   NY: Harper, 1841, [c1840]
   185 p.; 16 cm.

STORIES OF THE SPANISH CONQUESTS IN AMERICA.
DESIGNED FOR THE USE OF CHILDREN.
   Boston: Bowles, 1830.
   3 vols.
   Cooper 3436

B   ———.
   Boston: Bowles, 1830.
   vol. 1
   237 p.: frontis.; 15 cm.

TALES AND SKETCHES.
   Philadelphia: Carey, Lea & Blanchard, 1835.
   Sabin 78804
   Roorbach
   Wright 2368

TALES AND SKETCHES. SECOND SERIES . . .
   NY: Harper, 1844.
   Wright 2369
   Mansell
   BM   "Cover title: Wilton Harvey and other tales"

TALES OF CITY LIFE. I. THE CITY CLERK. II. LIFE IS
   SWEET.
   Philadelphia: Hazard and Mitchell, 1850.
   Wright 2370
   Mansell

THE TRAVELLERS. A TALE. DESIGNED FOR YOUNG
   PEOPLE.
   NY: Bliss & White, 1825.
   Wright 2371
   Mansell
   Sabin 78806, 96483
   Shoe 22233
   BM

B   ———.
   NY: Bliss & White, 1825.
   171 p.; 14 cm.

MARY MARTHA BUTT SHERWOOD (1775–1851) was a prolific English writer of religious tracts, the most famous of which is the *History of Little Henry and His Bearer*. *Little Henry* was the first missionary book for children, having been written during Mrs. Sherwood's stay in India. Her other well-known work is the three-part *History of the Fairchild Family*, which was extremely popular in its day. It is a moral didactic work, intended to terrify sinful young readers into obedience and instill "proper behaviour' and "good habits." It had a great influence on writers of juvenile works in England and America.

ALL, BIO, BRIT, CA, DIC EN, EV, NEW, OX EN, WW

(Please note: Of the numerous titles by Mrs. Sherwood that were located, many could be found with only English imprints; they are not included below.)

B   ALLEN CRANE, THE GOLD SEEKER.
> Troy, NY: Merriam, Moore.
> unpaged: ill.; 14 cm.
> Baldwin

THE AYAH AND THE LADY. AN INDIAN STORY . . .
> Boston: S.T. Armstrong and Crocker & Brewster; NY:
> J.P. Haven, 1822.
> Mansell
> Shoe 10259

B   Reprint ed., THE AYAH . . .
> NY: Roorbach, 1828.
> 86 p.; 14.5 cm.

THE BABES IN THE WOOD OF THE NEW WORLD.
> NY: M. Day, 1831.
> Mansell

THE BLESSED FAMILY.
> Boston: S.T. Armstrong, 1832.
> Shoe 14107
> Mansell

THE BLIND MAN AND LITTLE GEORGE.
> Boston: S.T. Armstrong, 1823.
> Mansell
> Shoe 14108

B   ———.
> Boston: S.T. Armstrong, 1823.
> 15 p.; 14.5 cm.

THE BROKEN HYACINTH, OR, ELLEN AND SOPHIA . . .
Philadelphia: American Sunday School Union, 1828.
Mansell
Shoe 35177

B ———.
Philadelphia: Amer. Sunday Sch. Union, 1828.
106 p., 2 p. cat.; 14 cm.

B Reprint ed., THE BROKEN . . .
Philadelphia: Amer. Sunday Sch. Union, 1828.
106 p.; 14.5 cm.

THE BUSY BEE.
[Andover: Printed for the New England Tract Society by
Flagg and Gould, 1821]
Mansell
also published by
Portland: Hyde, 1822.
Mansell

CHARLES LORRAINE: OR, THE YOUNG SOLDIER:
DRAWN FROM SCENES OF REAL LIFE.
Boston: S.T. Armstrong and Crocker & Brewster, 1823.
Shoe 14109
Mansell

B THE CHILD IS BUT A CHILD.
Providence: Weeden and Peek, [18—]
14 p.: ill.; 14.5 cm.
Baldwin

THE CHILDREN OF THE HARTZ MOUNTAINS . . .
Philadelphia: Amer. Sunday Sch. Union, [1826]
also under title: The little beggars
Shoe 26072

B Reprint ed.? THE CHILDREN . . . OR, THE LITTLE
BEGGARS.
Philadelphia: Amer. Sunday Sch. Union, [18—]
36 p.; 14.5 cm.

CLARA STEPHENS: OR, THE WHITE ROSE . . .
Philadelphia: Amer. Sunday Sch. Union, 1827.
BM
Mansell

CLEVER STORIES FOR CLEVER BOYS AND GIRLS . . .
Philadelphia: Appleton, 1845.
Free
Roorbach

B   Reprint ed., CLEVER . . .
      Philadelphia: Appleton, etc., 1846.
      3 × 64 p., 4 p. cat: ill., frontis.: 14.5 cm.
B   Reprint ed., CLEVER . . .
      Philadelphia: Appleton, etc., 1847.
      3 × 64 p., 4 p. cat.: ill., frontis.; 14.5 cm.

COMMON ERRORS.
      Philadelphia: Latimer, 1833.
      Containing: Common errors; Edward Mansfield; The ball and
      the funeral.
      Mansell
      Bruntjen 21189

THE DRY GROUND.
      New Haven: S. Babcock, Sidney's Press, 1833.
      Mansell
      Bruntjen 21190

DUTY IS SAFETY: OR, TROUBLESOME TOM.
      Philadelphia: G.S. Appleton; NY: D. Appleton, 1847.
      Mansell.
B   Reprint ed., DUTY . . .
      Philadelphia: G.S. Appleton, etc., 1850.
      64 p., 16 p. cat.: ill., frontis.; 14.5 cm.

EASY QUESTIONS.
      New Haven: S. Babcock, Sidney's Press, 1830.
      Cooper 3470
B   ———.
      New Haven: S. Babcock, Sidney's Press, 1830.
      17 p.: frontis.; 10.5 cm.
B   EASY QUESTIONS FOR A LITTLE CHILD . . .
      NY: General Protestant Episcopal SS Union, 1854.
      40 p.; 105.cm.
      chapbook

EDWARD MANSFIELD, A NARRATIVE OF FACTS.
      Salem: Whipple and Laurence, 1827.
      Shoe 30591:
      Mansell

ERMINA: OR, THE SECOND PART OF JULIANA OAKLEY.
      Philadelphia: Amer. Sunday Sch. Union, 1827.
      BM
      Shoe 30592
      Mansell

THE ERRAND-BOY.
>   Boston: Lincoln & Edmand, [1821]
>   "Cover dated 1821"-LC note.
>   Mansell
>   Shoe 6786

B   Reprint ed., THE ERRAND-BOY.
>   Philadelphia: Amer. Sunday Sch. Union, 1825.
>   34 p., 2 p. cat.: frontis.; 13.5 cm.
>   chapbook

B   Reprint ed., THE ERRAND-BOY.
>   Philadelphia: Amer. Sunday Sch. Union, 1827.
>   36 p.: frontis.; 14 cm.
>   Series V. No. 132 chapbook

B   Reprint ed., THE ERRAND-BOY.
>   Philadelphia: Amer. Sunday Sch. Union, 1830.
>   34 p.: frontis.; 13.5 cm.

S   Reprint ed., THE ERRAND-BOY.
>   Philadelphia: Amer. Sunday Sch. Union, [1828?]
>   34 p.: ill. (frontis.) woodcut: 9 × 14.2 cm.
>   IX Series. no. 902

B   Reprint ed., THE ERRAND BOY . . . ALSO: MEMOIR OF
>   JUDE CAIN, WHO DIED IN LIVERPOOL, FEBRUARY 3,
>   1829 . . .
>   Philadelphia: Amer. Sunday Sch. Union, 1830.
>   34 p., 16 p.: frontis.; 15 cm.
>   Baldwin

THE FATHER'S EYE.
>   NY: J.S. Taylor, 1847.
>   Mansell

THE FLOWERS OF THE FOREST.
>   Philadelphia: Latimer, 1833.
>   Mansell
>   Bruntjen 21191
>   Also published under the title: Lily of the Valley.

B   Reprint ed., THE FLOWERS . . .
>   NY: Sunday Sch. Union of Methodist Episcopal Church,
>   1852.
>   79 p.: ill.; 15 cm.

LILY OF THE VALLEY.
>   NY: J.S. Taylor, 1836.
>   Roorbach

B   LILY . . . 2d ed.
       NY: J.S. Taylor, 1837.
       123 p., 20 p. cat.; 15.5 cm.

B   LILY . . . 3rd ED.
       NY: J. Taylor, 1838.
       101 p.: frontis.; 15.5 cm.

B   LILY . . . 3rd ED.
       NY: Dodd, 1840.
       101 p.: frontis.; 15.5 cm.

B   LILY . . . 6th ED.
       NY: Baker & Scribner, 1846.
       101 p., 16 p. cat.; 15.5 cm.

       THE GIPSY BABES: A TALE OF THE LAST CENTURY . . .
       Philadelphia: Amer. Sunday Sch. Union, 1827.
       Mansell
       Shoe 30593
       Also published under title: The two gipsy babes . . .

B   ———.
       Philadelphia: Amer. Sunday Sch. Union, 1827.
       54 p.: frontis.; 13.5 cm.
       Series VI, No 169

B   Reprint ed., THE TWO GIPSY BABES . . . REV. ED.
       Philadelphia: Amer. Sunday Sch. Union, 1829.
       36 p.: frontis.; 14.5 cm.

B   GOLDEN CLUE: OR, ADVENTURES OF A PILGRIM IN SEARCH OF THE PATH TO SALVATION . . .
       Boston: J. Loring, 1831.
       108 p.: frontis.; 15 cm.
       Baldwin
       Roorbach

       THE GOVERNESS: OR, THE YOUNG FEMALE ACADEMY . . .
       NY: Printed for O.D. Cooke, Hartford, J & J Harper, pr., 1827.
       Also under title: The governess: or, the little female academy
       Mansell
       Shoe 30594

THE HAPPY CHOICE: OR, POTTERS' COMMON.
Philadelphia: Amer. Sunday Sch. Union, [1825?]
Shoe 22270
Also published:
Philadelphia: Amer. Sunday Sch. Union, 1830 [dated ed.]
BM
Mansell
Appeared also under title: The potters' common.

B   THE POTTER'S COMMON . . . NEW AND IMPROVED
EDITION.
NY: Carlton and Porter, [18—]
254 p., 2 p. cat.: ill.; 15.5 cm.

THE HEDGE OF THORNS.
NY: Wood, 1820.
Welch 1193.1, 1193.2
Shoe 3204
Mansell
Also published by
Philadelphia: Sunday and Adult Sch. Union, 1820.
Welch 1193.3
Shoe 3205

B   Reprint ed., THE HEDGE . . .
Boston: Lincoln & Edmands, 1821.
52 p., incl. printed paper covers: 1 plate; 13.5 cm.

S   Reprint ed., THE HEDGE . . .
Boston: Lincoln & Edmands, 1821.
50 p.: ill. (frontis.) woodcut; 8.8 cm. × 14 cm.

THE HINDOO TRAVELLER SEARCHING FOR THE TRUE
RELIGION, AND FINDING IT IN CHRIST . . .
Boston: J. Loring, [1828]
rev. Boston ed.
Mansell

THE HISTORY OF EMILY AND HER BROTHERS.
Philadelphia: Sunday and Adult Sch. Union, 1819.
Welch 1194.1
Shaw 49411

B   Reprint ed., THE HISTORY . . .
Boston: S.T. Armstrong and Crocker & Brewster, 1821.
24 p.; 12.5 cm.

HISTORY OF GEORGE DESMOND, FOUNDED ON
FACTS . . .
Boston: S.T. Armstrong and Crocker and Brewster, 1822.
Mansell: M. Sherwood supposed author.

HISTORY OF HENRY FAIRCHILD, AND CHARLES TRUE-
MAN.
    Phila: Sunday and Adult Sch. Union, 1819.
    Mansell
B   Reprint ed., HISTORY . . .
    Boston: S.T. Armstrong and Crocker & Brewster, 1821.
    36 p.; 14.5 cm.
B   Reprint ed., HISTORY . . .
    Boston: S.T. Armstrong, etc., 1821.
    36 p.; 14 cm.

THE HISTORY OF HENRY MILNER, A LITTLE BOY WHO
WAS NOT BROUGHT UP ACCORDING TO THE
FASHIONS OF THIS WORLD . . .
    Burlington, N.J.: D. Allison, 1823.
    Mansell
    Shoe 14110
B   Reprint ed., THE HISTORY . . .
    Phila: Half-Price Bookstore, 1824.
    191 p.: frontis.; 14.5 cm.

HISTORY OF JOHN MARTEN, A SEQUEL TO THE LIFE OF
HENRY MILNER.
    NY: Harper, 1846.
    Roorbach
    Mansell

B   HISTORY OF LITTLE EMILY AND HER MOTHER.
    (title page missing.)
    Also: The two sisters, Eighth ed., 1826
    the ayah and the lady, Eighth ed, 1824
    Julian Percival, 1826
    Stories 2
    66, 34, 94, 26, 70, 35 p.: frontispieces; 13.5 cm.

THE HISTORY OF LITTLE GEORGE AND HIS PENNY.
    Portland, (ME.): Wm. Hyde, 1820.
    Welch 1195
    Shoe 3207
B   Reprint ed., THE HISTORY . . .
    Boston: Lincoln & Edmands, 1821.
    24 p.: frontis.; 12.5 cm.

LITTLE GEORGE AND HIS PENNY.
    Newburyport: W & J Gilman, 1820.
    Welch 1198
    Shoe 3212

B ———.
       Newburyport: W & J Gilman, 1820.
       12 p.: ill.; 13.5 × 7.5 cm.

       THE HISTORY OF LITTLE HENRY AND HIS BEARER.
       FROM THE SECOND LONDON EDITION.
       Andover (Mass.): Mark Newman, 1817
       Note in Welch: originally pub. anon. in 1814.
       Welch 1196.1
       Shaw 41051, 42109
       Baldwin

B ———.
       Andover: Mark Newman, 1817
       86 p.: frontis.; 14 cm.

B   Reprint ed., THE HISTORY . . . SECOND AMERICAN FROM
       THE SECOND LONDON EDITION.
       Hartford: Hudson, 1817.
       36 .; 16 cm.

B   Reprint ed., THE HISTORY . . .
       Boston: Lincoln & Edmands, 1818.
       36 p.: ill.; 14.5 × 9 cm.
       Welch 1196.5

B   Reprint ed., THE HISTORY . . .
       Hartford: Goodwin, 1820.
       32 p.: ill.; 10.5 × 6.5 cm.
       Welch 1196.18

B   Reprint ed. . . .
       Hartford: Goodwin, 1822.
       52 p.; 14 cm.

B   Reprint ed. . . .
       NY: Methodist Episcopal Church, 1828.
       p. 1–44; 13.5 cm.
       On cover: 1827

S   Reprint ed. . . .
       Phila: Amer. Sunday Sch. Union, [c1830]
       69 p.; frontis.
       Frontispiece by Gilbert.

B   Reprint ed. . . .
       Philadelphia: Amer. Sunday Sch. Union, [18—]
       69 p.; frontis.; 15 cm.

S   Reprint ed. . . .
       NY: Amer. Tract Society, [18—]
       No. 107

B   Reprint ed., THIRD AMERICAN EDITION.
      Catskill; N. Elliott, 1818.
      54 p.: 14 × 9 cm.
      Welch 1196.6

B   Reprint ed. . . . THE HISTORY . . . FROM THE EIGHTH
      LONDON EDITION.
      NY: E.B. Gould, 1817.
      84 p.: frontis.; 14 × 8.5 cm.

B   Reprint ed. . . . FROM THE EIGHTH LONDON EDITION.
      NY: J.C. Trotten, 1819.
      60 p.: 14.5 cm.
      Welch 1196.14

B   Reprint ed., LITTLE HENRY AND HIS BEARER. A REVISED
      EDITION.
      NY: General Protestant Episcopal Sunday Sch. Union, 1863.
      69 p.; 15.5 cm.
      half-title

B   Reprint ed., LITTLE HENRY AND HIS BEARER BOOSY.
      NY: Nilson, [18—]
      64 p.: col. frontis.; 14.5 cm.

HISTORY OF LUCY CLAIRE, AS RELATED BY A
CLERGYMAN, BEING INTENDED FOR THE USE OF
YOUNG WOMEN.
      Hartford: Robinson, 1828.
      Shoe 35180
      Mansell

B   ———.
      Hartford: Robinson, 1828.
      108 p.: frontis.; 14.5 cm.

THE HISTORY OF MARY SAUNDERS.
      Boston: S.T. Armstrong and Crocker & Brewster, 1823.
      Shoe 14111

B   ———.
      Boston: S.T. Armstrong, etc., 1823.
      16 p.; 14 cm.
      On cover: 1825.

HISTORY OF MASTER HENRY, A PLEASING NARRATIVE
      FOR THE YOUNG.   (Reprint ed?)
      Boston: Dayton and Wentworth, 1855.
      6 parts in 1 vol.
      Mansell

THE HISTORY OF SUSAN GRAY, AS RELATED BY A
CLERGYMAN . . .
  Phila: Bacon, 1825.
  Shoe 22271
  Mansell
B   Reprint ed., THE HISTORY . . .
  Phila: Bacon, 1827.
  144 p.: frontis.; 14 cm.
Also published by:
  Portland: Shirley & Edwards, 1825.
  Shoe 22272
  Mansell

THE HISTORY OF THE FAIRCHILD FAMILY: OR, THE
CHILD'S MANUAL . . .
  NY: Haven, Carvill, Bliss, Collins and Hannay, Collins, 1828.
  (Pr. by Sleight and George, Jamaica).
  2 vol. in 1
  Shoe 35182
Also published by:
  NY: Burgess, Jun., 1828.
  "First American from 9th London ed."

THE HISTORY OF THEOPHILUS AND SOPHIA. FIRST AM.
ED.
  Andover: M. Newman, 1820.
  Welch 1197
  Shoe 3210
B   ———.
  Andover: M. Newman, 1820.
  51 p.; 14.5 × 9 cm.
S   Reprint ed., THE HISTORY . . .
  [Philadelphia]: Amer. Tract Soc., [18—]
  32 p.: ill.
  Bound with: Memoir of David Acheson Jr. #5
  #7

HOME
  New Haven: S. Babcock, Sidney's Press, 1833.
  Mansell
  Bruntjen 21192

THE IMPROVED BOY . . .
  New Haven: S. Babcock, Sidney's Press, 1830.
  Shoe 3473
  Mansell

THE INFANT'S PROGRESS FROM THE VALLEY OF DE-
STRUCTION TO EVER-LASTING GLORY.
> Boston: S.T. Armstrong and Crocker & Brewster, 1821.
> "1st American ed."
> Shoe 6790
> Mansell

B   Reprint ed., THE INFANT'S . . .
> Philadelphia: Amer. Sunday Sch. Union, 1829.
> 197 p.: frontis.; 14 cm.

B   Reprint ed., THE INFANT'S . . .
> NY: Carter, 1851.
> 359 p.: frontis.; 17.5 cm.
> half-title

THE IRON CAGE . . .
> NY: General Protestant Episcopal Sunday Sch. Union, 1842.
> Mansell

JACK THE SAILORBOY.
> Phila: G.S. Appleton; NY: D. Appleton, 1846.
> Mansell
> Baldwin
> Roorbach

B   ———.
> Phila: G.S. Appleton, etc., 1846.
> 64 p.: ill., frontis.; 14.5 cm.

JULIAN PERCIVAL. FIRST AM. ED.
> Salem: Whipple & Lawrence, 1827.
> Shoe 30597
> Rosenbach 703
> Mansell

B   ———.
> Salem: Whipple & Lawrence, 1827.
> 36 p.: frontis.; 14.5 cm.

JULIANA OAKLEY . . . 1st AMERICAN ED.
> NY: Morgan, Wilder, Campbell, 1825.
> Shoe 22275
> Mansell
> Also published by:
> JULIANA OAKLEY. A TALE.
> Boston: Crocker & Brewster; NY: J.P. Haven, 1825.
> Shoe 22273

Also published by:
   JULIANA OAKLEY . . .
   Hartford: O.D. Cooke, 1825.
   Shoe 22274
   Mansell
Also published by:
   JULIANA OAKLEY . . .
   Philadelphia: Amer. Sunday School Union, 1825.
   Shoe 22276

B   Reprint ed.? JULIANA OAKLEY . . .
   NY: Carton & Porter, Sunday Sch. Union, [18—]
   96 p.: plates; 15 cm.

B   JULIANA . . . 2d Ed.
   Philadelphia: Amer. Sunday School Union, 1827.
   88 p.: frontis.; 14 cm.

B   JULIANA . . . 2d Ed.
   Philadelphia: Amer. Sunday School Union, 1827.
   88 p.; 15.5 cm.
   #10

THE LADY IN THE ARBOUR . . .
   New Haven: S. Babcock, Sidney's Press, 1833.
   Mansell

THE LADY OF THE MANOR . . .
   Phila: Towar & Hogan, stereotyped by L. Johnson, 1820.
   1 vol.
   Shoe 3211
Also published by:
   NY: Bliss & White, 1825–29.
   7 vols.
   Shoe 22277
   Mansell
Also published by:
   NY: Wood [and others]; Boston: Richarson & Lord; Phila:
   Gregg, Towar & Hogan, 1826.
   7? vol.
   Mansell
Also published by:
   Bridgeport: Sherman, 1828.
   Mansell

THE LAST DAYS OF BOOSY: OR, SEQUEL TO LITTLE
   HENRY AND HIS BEARER . . .
   Phila: Amer. Sunday Sch. Union, [ca. 1840]
   Mansell

Also published by:
   Phila: Smith, [c1843]
   Mansell

LET ME TAKE CARE OF MYSELF.
   Providence: Weeden and Peek, [18—]
   Mansell

LITTLE ROBERT AND THE OWL.
   Boston: S.T. Armstrong and Crocker & Brewster, 1824.
   Shoe 17971
   Mansell

B ———.
   Boston: S.T. Armstrong, etc., 1824.
   20 p.; 14.5 cm.

B Reprint ed., LITTLE . . .
   Wendell, Mass.: Metcalf, 1830.
   24 p.: ill.; 14.5 cm.

THE LITTLE WOODMAN, AND HIS DOG CAESAR.
   Phila: Amer. Sunday Sch. Union, 1827.
   Mansell
Also published by:
   Phila: Amer. Sunday Sch. Union, [1826]
   Shoe 26076

B Reprint ed.? THE LITTLE . . .
   Phila: Amer. Sunday Sch. Union, [18—]
   36 p.: frontis; 14 cm.
   V Series no. 148.

THE LOFTY AND THE LOWLY WAY.
   NY: J.S. Taylor, 1839.
   Mansell
   Baldwin

B ———.
   NY: J.S. Taylor, 1839.
   99 p., 8 p. cat.; 15.5 cm.

B Reprint ed., THE LOFTY . . .
   NY: Dodd, 1840
   99 p.; 15.5 cm.

B MARTIN CROOK, THE WIDOW'S SON . . .   (Gift book?)
   Phila: Fisher & Bro.; Balt.: Fisher & Dennison,, [18—]
   191 p.; 5.5 cm.
   On spine: The child's keepsake
   Baldwin

S MARY ANNE.
  NY: Lane & Scott, 1849.
  45 p.: frontis.
  University of South Florida See also THE RED BOOK . . .

 MARY GRANT: OR, THE SECRET FAULT.
  Phila: Amer. Sunday Sch. Union, 1827.
  "Obedience to Parents" included
  BM
  Mansell
B Reprint ed.? MARY . . .
  Phila: Amer. Sunday Sch. Union, [18—].
  72 p.: ill., frontis.; 15 cm.

 MARGARET GREEN.
  Portsmouth: Miller, 1824.
  Shoe 17972

 MASTER HENRY'S RABBIT: THE BEES: AND THE FAITH-
  FUL DOG.
  Troy, NY: Merriam & Moore, [ca. 1850]
  Mansell

 THE MAY-BEE, TO WHICH IS ADDED THE WISHING
  CAP . . .
  Boston: S.T. Armstrong and Crocker & Brewster, 1823.
  Shoe 14112
 Also published:
  The MAY-BEE.
  NY: AM Tract Society, [1820?]
  BM
B Same as above?
  THE MAY-BEE
  NY: NY Tract Society, [18—]
  Series II no. XXIV chapbook
  16 p. ; 10.5 cm

 MEMOIRS OF SERGEANT DALE, HIS DAUGHTER, AND
  THE ORPHAN MARY.
  Boston: S.T. Armstrong and Crocker and Brewster, 1821.
  1st Am. from 11th London ed.
  Shoe 6791
B Reprint ed.? MEMOIRS . . .
  Phila: Amer. Sunday Sch. Union, [18—]
  86 p.; 15.5 cm.
  Leatherbound
  #76

B   Reprint ed.? MEMOIRS . . .
     86 p.: frontis.; 15 cm.
     Inscribed 1845.

     THE MILLENNIUM: OR TWELVE STORIES, DESIGNED TO
     EXPLAIN TO YOUNG BIBLE READERS, THE SCRIP-
     TURE PROPHECIES . . .
     NY: Leavitt; Boston: Crocker & Brewster, 1829.
     Mansell
     Shoe 40411

     Reprint Collection
B   NARRATIVES OF LITTLE HENRY AND HIS BEARER: THE
     AMIABLE LOUISA: AND ANN ELIZA WILLIAMS.
     NY: Am Tract Society, [18—]
     61, 17, 25 p.: plates; 16 cm.

     THE ORPHAN BOY.
     Boston: S.T. Armstrong and Crocker and Brewster, 1821.
     Mansell
B   ———.
     Boston: S.T. Armstrong, etc., 1821.
     36 p.; 14 cm.

S   Reprint ed., THE ORPHAN . . .
     Boston: Lincoln & Edwards, 1822.
     32 p. (of 34)
     lacks final leaf and wraps
     chapbook

     THE ORPHANS OF NORMANDY: OR FLORENTIN AND
     LUCIE. FIRST AMERICAN EDITION.
     Hartford: D.F. Robinson, 1827.
     Shoe 30603
B   THE ORPHANS . . . SECOND AMERICAN EDITION.
     Hartford: D.F. Robinson, 1828.
     108 p.; 14.5 cm

     THE PILGRIM OF INDIA ON HIS JOURNEY TO MOUNT
     ZION . . .
     Boston: J. Loring, [c1828]
     rev. Boston ed.
     Am. ed. of The Indian Pilgrim . . . , orig. Brit. ed of 1818.
     Shoe 35187

     THE PINK TIPPIT: OR, THE CONTRAST IN SABBATH
     SCHOLARS DISPLAYED.
     Boston: J. Loring, [1825?]
     Mansell

B   same as above?
         THE PINK . . .
         Boston: J. Loring, [18—]
         104 p.; 15.5 cm.

         PROCRASTINATION: OR, THE EVIL OF DELAY. 2d ed.
         (earliest ed. found)
         NY: General Protestant Episcopal Sunday Sch. Union, 1829.
         Mansell
         Shoe 40412

         PRIMER: OR, FIRST BOOK FOR CHILDREN.
         Hartford: Huntington, 1828.
         Mansell
         Shoe 35188

         THE NUN. FIRST AMERICAN FROM THE LONDON
         EDITION.
         Princeton: Moore Baker, 1834.
         Mansell

         THE ORANGE GROVE.
         NY: General Protestant Episcopal Sunday Sch. Union, 1842.
         Mansell

         QUESTIONS FOR CHILDREN, WITH ANSWERS FROM
         SCRIPTURE.
         New Haven: S. Babcock, Sidney's Press, 1831.
         Mansell
         Bruntjen 9182

         THE RE-CAPTURED NEGRO . . .
         Boston: S.T. Armstrong and Crocker & Brewster, 1821.
         Shoe 6792
         Mansel
         Also published as
         DAZEE: OR, THE RE-CAPTURED NEGRO.
         Newburysport: W & J Gilman, 1822.
         Mansell
         Shoe 10260

         THE RED BOOK, AND MARY ANNE . . . 1ST AMERICAN
         FROM 2D LONDON ED.
         NY: Pendleton and Hill, 1831.
         Mansell
B   Reprint ed., THE RED BOOK.
         NY: Carlton & Phillips, 1851.
         45 p., 2p. cat.; 14 cm.   see MARY ANNE.

RELIGIOUS FASHION, OR, THE HISTORY OF ANNA . . .
> Phila: Amer. Sunday Sch. Union, [1827].
> BM
> Shoe 30604a
> Mansell

B ———.
> Phila: Amer. Sunday Sch. Union, [1827].
> 138 p., 6 p. cat.; 14 cm.

B THE ROSE, A FAIRY TALE.
> Boston: S.T. Armstrong and Crocker & Brewster; NY:
> J. Haven, 1824.
> 16 p.; 14.5 cm.
> Baldwin

ROXABEL.
> NY: Harper, 1831.
> 3 vols.
> Roorbach
> Bruntjen 9183
> Mansell

A RUSTIC EXCURSION FOR TARRY-AT-HOME TRAV-
ELLERS. A SERIES OF INTERESTING TALES, HAV-
ING A STRICTLY MORAL TENDENCY, AND DESIGNED
FOR THE INSTRUCTION OF CHILDREN.
> Balt: J.S. Horton, 1836.
> Mansell

SCRIPTURE PRINTS, WITH EXPLANATIONS IN THE
FORM OF FAMILIAR DIALOGUES . . .
> NY: Pendleton and Hill, 1832.
> Could also be under title: Conversations on the Bible . . .
> Mansell
> Bruntjen 4702

SHANTY THE BLACKSMITH, A TALE OF OTHER TIMES.
> NY: J.S. Taylor, 1839.
> Mansell

B ———.
> NY: J.S. Taylor, 1839.
> 198 p.: plates; 16 cm.

B Reprint ed., SHANTY . . .
> NY: Dodd, 1840.
> 198 p.: plates; 15.5 cm.

B Reprint ed., SHANTY . . .
> Phila: Gihon, Fairchild, 1841.
> 142 p.; 15 cm.

S, B   Reprint ed., SHANTY . . .
        NY: J. Taylor, 1847.
        198 p.; 16 cm.

        THE SHEPHERD OF THE PYRENEES.
        Phila: Amer. Sunday Sch. Union, [1827 or 8?]
        Mansell
        Shoe 22278

        Please note: reprint ed. of THE HISTORY OF THEOPHILUS
        AND SOPHIA, which see.

B   same as above?
        THE SHEPHERD . . .
        Phila: Amer. Sunday Sch. Union, [18—]
        54 p.: frontis.; 14.5 cm.

B   Reprint ed?
        THE SHEPHERD . . .
        Phila: Amer. Sunday Sch. Union, [18—]
        54 p.: frontis.; 14 cm.
        XI series, no. 110.

        SOCIAL TALES FOR THE YOUNG.
        Phila: J. Whetham, 1835.
        Mansell

        As reviser.
        SPANISH DAUGHTER. BY THE REV. GEORGE BUTT
        . . . REV. AND COR. BY HIS DAUGHTER, MRS. SHER-
        WOOD . . .
        Boston: S.T. Armstrong and Crocker & Brewster; NY: J.P.
        Haven, 1824.
        BM
        Mansell
        Roorback

        STORIES EXPLANATORY OF THE CHURCH CATE-
        CHISM . . .
        Balt.: Prot. Episc. Tract Society of Balt., 1823.
        Shoe 14114
        Mansell
        Also published by:
        Burlington, NJ: D. Allison, 1823.
        Shoe 14115
        Also published by
        Phila: E. Bacon, 1823.
        Shoe 14116

same as above TITLE?
STORIES FOR SUNDAYS ILLUSTRATING THE CATE-
CHISM . . .
Phila: Lippincott, 1869.
Mansell
Free
Roorbach

SUSANNAH: OR, THE THREE GUARDIANS . . .
Phila: Amer. Sunday Sch. Union, 1829.
BM
Mansell
Shoe 40413

THINK BEFORE YOU ACT.
Phila: G.S. Appleton, NY: D. Appleton, 1846.
Mansell
Roorbach

B   Reprint ed., THINK . . .
Phila: G.S. Appleton, etc., 1847.
64 p.: ill., frontis.; 14.5 cm.

B   Reprint ed., THINK . . .
Phila: G.. Appleton, etc., 1850.
64 p., 16 p. cat.: ill., frontis.; 14.5 cm.

S   Reprint ed., THINK . . .
Phila: G.S. Appleton, etc., 1851.
64 p., 16 p. cat.: ill., frontis.
2 copies: one bound in green; one in red

B   Reprint ed., THINK . . .
NY: R. Carter, 1853.
64 p., 16 p. cat.: ill, frontis.; 15 cm.

A TINY FOOTFALL WITHIN THE GOLDEN GATE. (Reprint
ed.?)
NY: Prot. Episc. Soc., 1869.
Mansell

THE TWO FAWNS . . .
New Haven: S. Babcock, 1833.
Mansell
Bruntjen 21195

THE TWO SISTERS.
Phila: Amer. Sunday and Adult Sch. Union, 1820.
1st American ed.
Welch 1199
Shoe 3213

B   Reprint ed. THE TWO . . .
       Phila: Amer. Tract Society, [18—]
       12 p.; 17.5 cm.
       #127

     VICTORIA.
       Phila: Whetham, 1833.
       Mansell
       Bruntjen 21196

B   ———.
       Phila: Whetham, 1833.
       272 p.; 15.5 cm.

     THE VIOLET LEAF.
       Newark: B. Olds, 1835.
       Mansell

B   ———.
       Newark: B. Olds, 1835.
       58 p.: frontis.; 10.5 cm.

     THE WISH: OR, LITTLE CHARLES . . .
       Phila: Amer. Sunday Sch. Union, 1827.
       BM

     THE WISHING CAP.
       Newburyport: W & J Gilman, 1820.
       Welch 1200.2
       Shoe 3214
       Also published by:
       Portland (Me): W. Hyde, 1820.

B   ———.
       Portland: W. Hyde, 1820.
       29 p.: ill.; 10.5 × 7 cm.
       Welch 1200.2
       Shoe 3215

B   Reprint ed., THE WISHING . . .
       NY: M. Day, 1832.
       24 p.: frontis.; 14 cm.

B   Reprint ed., THE WISHING . . .
       NY: M. Day, 1833.
       p. 1–17: ill.; 12.5 cm.

B   Reprint ed., THE WISHING . . .
       NY: Am. Tract Soc, [18—]
       16 p.: ill., frontis.; 11 cm.
       chapbook

B   Reprint ed., THE WISHING . . .
       NY: Am. Tract Soc., [18—]
       16 p.: ill.; 10.5 cm.
       Series II., No. 25

Note: Baldwin Collection also has THE WORKS.
       NY: Harper, 1834.
       423 p.:20 cm.
       vol. 5

CATHERINE SINCLAIR (1800–1864) wrote one of the milestones of juvenile literature, *Holiday House*, in 1839. This work, directed against the moral, didactic books for children that were the norm for this time, was an early example of the movement toward the establishment of a purely imaginative juvenile literature which would come to fruition at midcentury. Miss Sinclair also wrote *Charlie Seymour* and *Frank Vansittart* for young readers, as well as a series of hieroglyphic picture-letters in 1861. She wrote short stories and articles about Scotland and its people, and produced two popular novels.

ALL, BIO, BRIT, DIC EN, NEW, OX EN, TT, WW

(Please note: only two of Miss Sinclair's books were found with American imprints, the rest having mainly only British publishers, as was the case of *Frank Vansittart.*)

B   CHARLIE SEYMOUR: OR, THE GOOD AUNT AND THE
       BAD AUNT. A SUNDAY STORY.
       NY: Betts and Anstice, 1832.
       176 p.; 15 cm.
       Baldwin

B   Reprint ed., CHARLIE . . .
       NY: R. Carter, 1842.
       176 p., 3p. cat.; 15.5 cm.

       HOLIDAY HOUSE.
       NY: Carter, 1839.
       Mansell

B   HOLIDAY HOUSE: A SERIES OF TALES.
       NY: Carter, 1853.
       318 p., 12 p. cat.: plates; 17.5 cm.

PRISCILLA WAKEFIELD (1750–1832) was a British philanthropist and one of the earliest promoters of savings banks in England. She is best known for her books for children on travel and natural history. Her most well known work, entitled the *Juvenile Travellers* (London, Darton & Harvey, 1801) describes an imaginary tour through Europe. A Quaker, she published a memoir of William Penn in 1817.

ALL, BRIT

(Please note: Most of Mrs. Wakefield's most well-known works are not found below, since only the British editions of the books were located. They include the following:

AN INTRODUCTION TO THE NATURAL HISTORY AND CLASSIFICATION OF INSECTS (1816);
EXCURSIONS IN NORTH AMERICA . . . (1806);
THE JUVENILE TRAVELLERS . . . (1801);
LEISURE HOURS (1794);
PERAMBULATIONS IN LONDON . . . (1809);
THE TRAVELLER IN AFRICA . . . (1814);
THE TRAVELLER IN ASIA . . . (1817).

All the above were published in London, by Darton and Harvey.)

A BRIEF MEMOIR OF WILLIAM PENN. COMPILED FOR THE USE OF YOUNG PERSONS.
 Phila: Peirce, 1818.
 Mansell
 Welch 1394.1
B Reprint ed., A BRIEF . . .
 NY: M. Day, 1821.
 54 p.: frontis.; 14.5 cm.
B A BRIEF . . . 2nd Ed.
 NY: M. Day, 1833.
 231 p.: frontis.; 15 cm.

DOMESTIC RECREATION: OR, DIALOGUES ILLUSTRA-TIVE OF NATURAL AND SCIENTIFIC SUBJECTS.
 Phila: J. Johnson, 1805.
 Mansell
 Welch 1395
 Rosenbach 311
 Shaw 9679
B ————.
 Phila: J. Johnson, 1805.
 182 p.: 6 plates; 15 × 9.5 cm.

A FAMILY TOUR THROUGH THE BRITISH EMPIRE
. . . PARTICULARLY ADAPTED TO THE AMUSEMENT
AND INSTRUCTION OF YOUTH.
Phila: J. Johnson, 1804.
Mansell
BM
Welch 1396
Shaw 7683

B   ———.
Phila: J. Johnson, 1804.
354 p.: 17.5 × 10 cm.

INSTINCT DISPLAYED . . . FIRST AMERICAN FROM THE
SECOND LONDON EDITION.
Boston: Cummings, Hilliard, Swan, 1816.
Mansell
Welch 1397
Shaw 39695

B   ———.
Boston: Cummings, etc., 1816.
335 p.: 15.5 × 8.5 cm.

AN INTRODUCTION TO BOTANY. 1st Amer. and 5th
LONDON ED . . .
Boston: Belcher & Burdett, 1811.
Mansell
Shaw 24351
Also published by: AN INTRODUCTION . . . 5th ED.
Phila: Kimber & Conrad, 1807.
Mansell
Also published by: AN INTRODUCTION TO BOTANY.
Phila: Kimber and Conrad, 1811.
Mansell
Shaw 24352

JUVENILE ANECDOTES, FOUNDED ON FACTS. COL-
LECTED FOR THE AMUSEMENT OF CHILDREN.
Phila: Johnson & Warner, 1809.
Rosenbach 408
Welch 1398
Shaw 19127
Mansell
Contains: "33 moral stories of English children"—Rosenbach

MENTAL IMPROVEMENT: OR THE BEAUTIES AND
WONDERS OF NATURE AND ART. FIRST AMERICAN,
FROM THE THIRD LONDON EDITION.
New Bedford: C. Greene, 1799.
Mansell
Welch 1399.1
Evans 36664

B   ——.

New Bedford: C. Greene, 1799.
264 p.; 18 × 11 cm.

SKETCHES OF HUMAN MANNERS . . . FIRST AMERICAN
EDITION.
Phila: Johnson & Warner, 1811.
Welch 1400
Sabin 100984
Shaw 34353
Mansell

B   ——.

Phila: Johnson & Warner, 1811.
252 p.; 14.5 × 8.5 cm.

SUMMARY OF FINDINGS

The holdings lists indicate that the Baldwin Collection has practically all
the titles listed for Barbara Hofland, Mary Howitt, and Mary Hughs. For
Catherine Sinclair, both of the American titles listed are contained in the
Baldwin Collection, which also has many of her British titles. Of the
remaining authors, all are well represented by substantial holdings.

The University of South Florida Collection, although small in comparison with that of the Baldwin Collection, has an appreciable number of
titles by Mary Howitt (9 titles). Barbara Hofland (3 titles), Mary Hughs (4
titles), Eliza Leslie (4 titles), Catharine Sedgwick (4 titles), and Mary
Sherwood (9 titles), are fairly well represented. Only one title each by
Lydia Maria Child and Elizabeth Phelps is held in the collection, and
Catherine Sinclair and Priscilla Wakefield are not represented there by
any American editions.

CONCLUDING REMARKS

It can be argued that the sample of ten particular authors for this study
does not accurately reflect the total holdings and strengths of the two
collections that were examined. Similarly, the limiting of the author bibli-

ographies to American imprints left out much material published by the British authors (Catherine Sinclair, Priscilla Wakefield, and Mary Sherwood in particular), which might have been located. The exclusion of magazines, gift books, annuals, and poetical works from the scope of this study also resulted in the omission of much material since almost all of the authors investigated produced items in these categories.

The limited number and quality of source materials and bibliographical aids available to the researcher made the analysis of some titles difficult. This is particularly evident in the problem of reprint editions that was mentioned in most of the bibliographies. It was also difficult to determine whether many publications were juveniles or material clearly meant for adult readers. The result of this last point is the inclusion of many titles some might consider not part of children's literature.

It is hoped that the results of this investigation, despite its limitations, will encourage further needed study in this area of bibliographic research. As has been said, the present state of bibliographic organization of nine-teenth-century juveniles in American collections falls far short of allowing them to be properly accessed or appreciated.

ACKNOWLEDGEMENTS

Thanks are due to Dr. Alice Smith and Mr. J.B. Dobkin of the University of South Florida for whom this survey was originally prepared as a student assignment, and to the staff of the Baldwin Library who cordially allowed me access to their catalog while I prepared the assignment.

NOTES AND REFERENCES

1. Alice M. Smith, *Significant encounters: A Critical and Historical Evaluation of Landmarks in the Development of Imaginative Literature Printed in English for Children and Youth, 1658–1865; And Their Availability in Fifteen Selected Great Lakes Area Collections* (Ed.D. dissertation, Wayne State University, 1966; Ann Arbor, Mich.: University Microfilms, 67-10,492, 1980).

2. Abstract of "Syllabus for Teaching History of Children's Literature with Papers on Certain Highlights in Both England and America," by M.B. Cropper (A.M.L.S. thesis, University of Michigan, 1950), in *Library Literature*, 1949–1951 (New York: Wilson), p. 154.

3. Abstract of "An Historical Survey of Themes Recurrent in Selected Children's Books Published in America Since 1850," by Jean D. Shaw (Ed.D. dissertation, Temple University, 1966), in *Dissertation Abstracts* 28A, pt. 1, July–September (Ann Arbor, Mich.: University Microfilms, 1967) p. 1059-A.

4. Abstract of "A Comparative Thematic Categorical Survey of Children's Publications in England and America From 1744 to 1850," by Elaine J. Lee, (Ed.D. dissertation, Temple University, 1976), in *Resources in Education* (Washington, D.C.: GPO, April, 1977).

5. Abstract of "Children's Literature Published in the United States During the Year 1848," by E. Pfau (A.M. thesis, University of Chicago, 1951), in Library literature, 1952–1954 (New York: Wilson), p. 150.

6. Abstract of "An Interpretive Study of Lydia Maria Child," by Lloyd C. Taylor (Ph.D. dissertation, Lehigh University, 1956), in Dissertation Abstracts 16, November–December (Ann Arbor, Mich.: University Microfilms, 1956), p. 2443.

7. Citation of "A Biography of Lydia Maria Child," by Bernice G. Lamberton (Ph.D. dissertation, University of Maryland, 1953), in Doctoral Dissertations Accepted by American Universities, 1951–1952 19 (New York: Kraus Reprint Corp., 1964), p. 258.

8. Helene G. Baer, The Heart is Like Heaven: The Life of Lydia Maria Child (Phila: University of Pennsylvania Press, 1964).

9. Milton Meltzer, Tongue of Flame: The Life of Lydia Maria Child (New York: Crowell, 1965).

10. Abstract of "A Study of the Works of Catharine Maria Sedgwick," by Richard B. Gidez (Ph.D. dissertation, Ohio State University, 1958), in Dissertation Abstracts 19, July–October (Ann Arbor: University Microfilms, 1958), p. 797.

11. Sister Mary M. Welsh, Catharine Maria Sedgwick: Her Position in the Literature and Thought of Her Time Up to 1860 (Washington: Catholic University of America, 1937). (Cited in Foster, pp. 160, 163).

12. Lydia Maria Child, Life and Letters. ed. Mary E. Dewey (New York: Harper, 1871).

13. Edward H. Foster, Catharine Maria Sedgwick (NY: Twayne, 1974).

14. Carl R. Woodring, "William and Mary Howitt: Bibliographical Notes," Harvard Library Bulletin 5 (Spring 1951): 251–55.

15. Jacob Blanck, Peter Parley to Penrod: A Bibliographical Description of the Best-Loved American Juvenile Books (NY: Bowker, 1938).

16. Smith, p. 28.

17. Jacob Blanck, comp., Bibliography of American Literature, 6 vols. (New Haven: Yale University Press, 1955–1979).

18. D'Alté Welch, A Bibliography of American Children's Books Printed Prior to 1821 (Worcester, Mass.: American Antiquarian Society, 1972).

19. Katherine H. Wead, comp., A List of Series and Sequels for Juvenile Readers, 2d ed., rev. and enl. (Boston: Faxon, 1923).

20. P.K. Foley, American Authors, 1795–1895 (Kennebunkport: Milford House, Inc., 1969).

21. First Books By American Authors, 1765–1964 (NY: Seven Gables Bookshop, 1975).

22. Lyle H. Wright, American Fiction, 1774–1850 2d rev. ed. (San Marino: Huntington Library, 1969), and his American Fiction, 1851–1875 (San Marino: Huntington Library, 1957).

23. Joseph Sabin, Bibliotheca Americana . . . (NY: Sabin, 1869–1892; Bibliographical Society of America, 1928–36).

24. Lawrence S. Thompson, The New Sabin (Troy, NY: Whitston, 1974–80).

25. Charles Evans, American Bibliography . . . , Vol. 13 (Worcester: American Antiquarian Society, 1955; reprint ed., NY: P. Smith, 1962).

26. Ralph R. Shaw and Richard H. Shoemaker, American Bibliography: A Preliminary Checklist for 1801–1819 (NY: Scarecrow, 1958–1963).

27. Orville H. Roorbach, Bibliotheca Americana (Metuchen: Mini-print, 1967).

28. Richard S. Shoemaker, et al. A Checklist of American Imprints 1820–1833 (Metuchen: Scarecrow, 1964–1979).

29. James Kelly, American Catalogue of Books . . . (Metuchen: Mini-print, 1967).

30. Abraham S.W. Rosenbach, Early American Children's Books with Bibliographical Descriptions of the Books in His Private Collection (Portland, Me.: Southworth Press, 1933).

31. Free Library of Philadelphia, Special Collections Central Children's Department, *A Checklist of Children's Books, 1837–1876* (Phila: The Library, 1975).

32. Rosenbach Company, *The Collected Catalogues of Dr. A.S.W. Rosenbach, 1904–51*, vols. 1–3 (NY: Arno, 1968).

33. Judith St. John, comp., *The Osborne Collection of Early Children's Books, 1566–1910*, with an introduction by Edgar Osborne (Toronto: Toronto Public Library, 1958).

34. Pierpont Morgan Library, *Children's Literature; an Exhibition, November 19, 1954 through February 28, 1955* (NY: The Library, 1954).

35. Pierpont Morgan Library, *Early Children's Books and Their Illustration* (NY: The Library, 1975).

36. National Book League, London, *Children's Books of Yesterday and Today: a Catalogue of an Exhibition Held at 7 Albemarle Street, London During May 1946*, new ed., rev. and en., comp. by P.H. Muir (Detroit: Singing Tree, 1970).

37. Walter Schatzki, *Children's Books Old and Rare* (Detroit: Gale Research, 1974).

38. H.W. Wilson Company, *Children's Catalog* (NY: Wilson, 1909 to date).

39. British Museum. Department of Printed Books, *General Catalogue of Printed Books*, 263 vols. plus supplements (London: Trustees of the British Museum, 1959–).

40. Carolyn A. Allen, "Early American Children's Books at the American Antiquarian Society," *Horn Book* 52 (April 1976): 117–31.

41. S.A. Egoff, "Books of Yesterday," *Library Journal* 77 (February 15, 1952): 273–77.

42. "When Rare Books are Children's Treasures," *Grade Teacher* 87 (November 1969): 139–44.

43. *Wilson Library Bulletin* 50 (October 1975).

44. University of Florida Libraries, Gainesville, *Index to the Baldwin Library of Books in English Before 1900, Primarily for Children*, 3 vols. (Boston: G. K. Hall, 1981).

45. Andrew W. Tuer, *Pages and Pictures From Forgotten Children's Books* (London: The Leadenhall Press, Ltd., 1898; reprint ed., Detroit: Singing Tree Press, 1969).

46. Andrew W. Tuer, *Stories From Old Fashioned Children's Books* (New York: Scribner, 1899).

47. Andrew W. Tuer, *1000 Quaint Cuts* (New York: Scribner, 1886).

48. Philip James, *Children's Books of Yesterday* (London: The Studio, 1933).

49. F.J. Harvey Darton, *Children's Books in England: Five Centuries of Social Life*, 2d ed. (Cambridge: Cambridge University Press, 1960).

50. Bess Porter Adams, *About Books and Children: Historical Survey of Children's Literature* (New York: Holt, 1953).

51. Cornelia L. Meigs, et al., *A Critical History of Children's Literature* (New York: MacMillan, 1953).

52. Mary F. Thwaite, *From Primer to Pleasure: An Introduction to the History of Children's Books in England From the Invention of Printing to 1900* (London: The Library Association, 1963).

53. Barton Currie, *Fishers of Books* (Boston: Little, Brown, 1931).

54. Louise F. Field, *The Child and His Book; Some Account of the History and Progress of Children's Literature in England*, 2d ed. (London: Wells Garner, Darton, 1892; reprint ed., Detroit: Singing Tree Press, 1968).

55. Annie E. Moore, *Literature Old and New for Children: Materials for a College Course* (Boston: Houghton Mifflin, 1934).

56. Lillian Hollowell, *A Book of Children's Literature* (New York: Rinehart, 1939).

57. Montrose J. Moses, *Children's Books and Reading* (New York: Kennerley, 1923; reprint ed., Gryphon Books, 1971).

58. James D. Hart, *The Popular Book: A History of America's Literary Taste* (New York: Oxford University Press, 1950).

352   MICHELE M. REID

59. May H. Arbuthnot, "Children's Books: History and Trends," in *Children and Books*, 3d ed. (Chicago: Scott, Foresman, 1964).

60. Bertha E. Mahoney, Louise P. Latimer, and Beulah Folmsbee, comps., *Illustrators of Children's Books, 1744–1945* (Boston: Horn Book, 1947).

61. William Targ, ed., *Bibliophile in the Nursery: A Bookman's Treasury of Collector's Lore on Old and Rare Children's Books* (Cleveland: World, 1957).

62. Algernon Tassin, "Books for Children," in *Cambridge History of American Literature*, Vol. 2 (MacMillan, 1933).

63. Earl N. Saucier, "Significant Firsts in Children's Literature," *Peabody Journal of Education* 19 (November 1941): 141–47.

64. Caroline Burnite, "The Beginnings of a Literature for Children," *Library Journal* 31 (July 1906): 107–12.

65. Paul Hazard, *Books, Children & Men* (Boston: Horn Book, 1960).

66. Roger L. Green, *Tellers of Tales: Children's Books and Their Authors, 1800–1964*, 4th ed. (London: Ward, 1965).

67. Florence V. Barry, *A Century of Children's Books* (New York: Doran, 1923).

68. Smith, p. 41.

69. Rosalie V. Halsey, *Forgotten Books of the American Nursery: A History of the Development of the American Story Book* (Boston: Goodspeed, 1911; reprint ed., Detroit: Singing Tree Press, 1969).

70. Monica M. Kiefer, *American Children Through Their Books, 1700–1835* (Philadelphia: University of Pennsylvania Press, 1948).

71. Anne S. MacLeod, *A Moral Tale: Children's Fiction and American Culture, 1820–1860* (Hamden, Conn.: Shoestring, 1975).

72. James H. Fraser, ed., *Society & Children's Literature: Papers Presented on Research, Social History and Children's Literature* (Boston: Godine, 1978).

73. Siri Andrews, ed., *The Hewins Lectures, 1947–1962* (Boston: Horn Book, 1963).

74. Alice M. Jordan, *From Rollo to Tom Sawyer and Other Papers* (Boston: Horn Book, 1948).

75. Arnold E. Grade, *The Merrill Guide to Early Juvenile Literature* (Ohio: Merrill, 1970).

76. Mary Cadogan and Patricia Craig, *You're a Brick, Angela: A New Look at Girls' Fiction From 1839 to 1975* (London: Gollancz, 1976).

77. Lee Ash, comp., *Subject Collections: A Guide to Special Book Collections and Subject Emphases as Reported by University, College, Public, and Special Libraries and Museums in the United States and Canada*, 5th ed., rev. and enl. (New York: Bowker, 1978).

78. Carolyn W. Field, *Subject Collections in Children's Literature* (New York: Bowker, 1969).

79. James D. Hart, *The Oxford Companion to American Literature* (New York: Oxford University Press, 1948).

80. Samuel A. Allibone, *A Critical Dictionary of English Literature and British and American Authors*, 5 vols. (Lippincott, 1858–91; reprint ed., Detroit: Gale Research, 1965).

81. *Yesterday's Authors of Books for Children: Facts and Pictures About Authors and Illustrators of Books for Young People, From Early Times to 1960*, 2 vols. (Detroit: Gale Research, 1977–8).

82. Elva S. Smith, *History of Children's Literature: a Syllabus with Selected Bibliographies* (Chicago: ALA, 1937).

83. Virginia Haviland, *Children's Literature: a Guide to Reference Sources* (Washington, D.C.: GPO, 1966). Supplements were published in 1972 and 1977.

84. Irving P. Leif, *Children's Literature: a Historical and Contemporary Bibliography* (Troy, N.Y.: Whitston, 1977).

85. Anne Pellowski, *The World of Children's Literature* (New York: Bowker, 1968).
86. Esther Stalloman, "Books About Children's Literature: an Introductory Bibliography," *Peabody Journal of Education* 19 (November 1944): 124–30.
87. Bohdan S. Wynar, *Introduction to Cataloging and Classification*, 6th ed. (Littleton, Colo.: Libraries Unlimited, 1980), p. 640.
88. Welch, p. lviii.
89. Actually, she was Scottish, but is included here for convenience.
90. Originally from England, Mrs. Hughs emigrated to Philadelphia and is considered an American here.

APPENDIX

Biographical Sources

ALL   Allibone, S. Austin. A CRITICAL DICTIONARY OF ENGLISH LITERATURE AND BRITISH AND AMERICAN AUTHORS. 3 vols. Philadelphia: Lippincott, 1858–71; reprint ed., Detroit: Gale Research, 1965.

ALLSUP   Kirk, John F. A SUPPLEMENT TO ALLIBONE'S CRITICAL DICTIONARY OF ENGLISH LITERATURE AND BRITISH AND AMERICAN AUTHORS. 2 vols. Philadelphia: Lippincott, 1891; reprint ed., Detroit: Gale Research, 1965.

AMB   AMERICAN AUTHORS AND BOOKS, 1640 TO THE PRESENT DAY. 3rd rev. ed. NY: Crown, 1972.

AMAU   Kunitz, Stanley J., and Haycroft, Howard, eds. AMERICAN AUTHORS: 1600–1900, A BIOGRAPHICAL DICTIONARY OF AMERICAN LITERATURE. NY: Wilson, 1938.

AP   APPLETON'S CYCLOPAEDIA OF AMERICAN BIOGRAPHY. Vols. 1, 5. NY: Appleton, 1894.

BIB   BIBLIOPHILE DICTIONARY. NY: International Bibliophile Society, 1904; reprint ed., Detroit: Gale Research, 1966.

BIO   Warner, Charles D., ed. BIOGRAPHICAL DICTIONARY AND SYNOPSIS OF BOOKS ANCIENT AND MODERN. Akron, Ohio: Werner, 1902; reprint ed., Detroit: Gale Research, 1965.

BRIT   Kunitz, Stanley J. BRITISH AUTHORS OF THE
            NINETEENTH CENTURY. NY: Wilson, 1936.

CA   CASSELL'S ENCYCLOPAEDIA OF WORLD
            LITERATURE. rev. and enl. in 3 vols. NY: Morrow,
            1973.

CH   CHILDREN'S AUTHORS AND ILLUSTRATORS:
            AN INDEX TO BIOGRAPHICAL DICTIONARIES.
            2n ed. Detroit: Gale Research, 1978.

CY   Duyckinck, Evert A. and Duyckinck, George L.
            CYCLOPAEDIA OF AMERICAN LITERATURE.
            2 vols. NY: Scribner, 1856.

DIC AM   Adams, Oscar F. DICTIONARY OF AMERICAN
            AUTHORS. 5th ed., rev. and enl. Boston: Houghton
            Mifflin, 1904; reprint ed., Detroit: Gale Research, 1969.

DAB   DICTIONARY OF AMERICAN BIOGRAPHY. NY:
            Scribner, 1974.

DIC EN   Adams, W. Davenport. DICTIONARY OF ENGLISH
            LITERATURE. 2d ed. London: Cassell Petter & Galpin,
            n.d.; reprint ed., Detroit: Gale Research, 1966.

DIC LIT   DICTIONARY OF LITERATURE IN THE ENGLISH
            LANGUAGE FROM CHAUCER TO 1940. 2 vols.
            Oxford: Pergamon, 1970.

DNB   Stephen, Leslie, and Lee, Sidney, eds. DICTIONARY
            OF NATIONAL BIOGRAPHY. London: Oxford Uni-
            versity Press, 1938.

DIC NA   Wallace, W. Stewart, comp. DICTIONARY OF
            NORTH AMERICAN AUTHORS DECEASED
            BEFORE 1950. Toronto: Ryerson Press, 1951; reprint
            ed., Detroit: Gale Research, 1968.

EV   EVERYMAN'S DICTIONARY OF LITERARY
            BIOGRAPHY, ENGLISH & AMERICAN. London:
            Dent, NY: Dutton, 1962.

MEB   Boase, Frederick. MODERN ENGLISH BIOGRAPHY. London: Cass, 1965.

NC   NATIONAL CYCLOPAEDIA OF AMERICAN BIOGRAPHY. NY: White, 1892–

NEW   Barnhart, C.L., ed. NEW CENTURY HANDBOOK OF LITERATURE. rev. ed. NY: Appleton, Century, Crofts, 1967.

OX EN   Harvey, Sir Paul, comp. and ed. OXFORD COM— PANION TO ENGLISH LITERATURE. 4th ed. rev. Oxford: Oxford University Press, 1967.

PE   Daiches, D., ed. PENGUIN COMPANION TO ENGLISH LITERATURE. NY: McGraw-Hill, 1971.

RE   Hertzberg, Max J. READER'S ENCYCLOPAEDIA OF AMERICAN LITERATURE. NY: Crowell, 1962.

SV   Blant, M., and Huber, M.B. STORY AND VERSE FOR CHILDREN. 3rd ed. NY: McMillan, 1965.

TT   Green, R.L. TELLERS OF TALES: BRITISH AUTHORS OF CHILDREN'S BOOKS FROM 1800 to 1964. rev. ed. NY: Franklin Watts, 1964.

WW   Doyle, Brian, comp. and ed. WHO'S WHO OF CHILDREN'S LITERATURE. London: Evelyn, 1968.

OX AM   Hart, James D. OXFORD COMPANION TO AMERICAN LITERATURE. 4TH ED. NY: Oxford University Press, 1965.

LIST OF SOURCE ABBREVIATIONS

BALDWIN   Baldwin Collection card catalog

BLANCK   *Bibliography of American Literature*

BLANCK-P   *Peter Parley to Penrod*

BM   British Museum. Dept. of Printed Books. *General Catalog of Printed Books*

BRUNTJEN   *Checklist of American Imprints for 1831–1833.*

COOPER   *Checklist of American Imprints for 1830.*

EVANS   *American Bibliography*

FREE   Free Library of Philadelphia *Checklist*

KELLY   *American Catalogue*

LITWRITAM   *Literary Writings in America: A Bibliography.* Millwood, NY: KTO Press, 1977.

SABIN   *Bibliotheca Americana.*

SHAW   *American Bibliography*

SHOE   Shoemaker, *Checklist of American Imprints*

THOMPSON   *New Sabin*

WRIGHT   *American Fiction* (volume number depends on date of item)

BIOGRAPHICAL SKETCH
OF THE CONTRIBUTORS

Michael Binder, Director of the Library at Fairleigh Dickenson University, Rutherford, has a strong interest in technology relating to libraries. In his community he works for the advancement of libraries and was a delegate from New Jersey to the White House Conference on Libraries.

Mary M. Diebler, Service Development Specialist for the Public Service Satellite Consortium, developed on-line data based archives for the experimental NASA Communication Technology Satellite. Active in the Library Information and Technology Association, she speaks frequently to groups interested in communication technology.

Leonard Kerson, a doctoral candidate at the School of Library Science, Columbia University, has library experience gained overseas and in this country. His areas of interest are library management, planning, library education, and a special interest in the film and film archives.

Michael E. D. Koenig, of the faculty of the School of Library Service, Columbia University was formerly Vice President for Operations of Swets North America. His fields of interest include information systems, long range planning and research productivity. He has written professionally for the Special Library Association and Library Journal.

Richard G. King Jr., of Systemwide Administration University of California, does research on and writes about preservation and conservation of library materials. An avid book collector, his special interest is in the type and development of 19th Century bookbinder's cloth.

Deanna Marcum of the Council on Library Resources is both a student and interpreter of Modern Library Management Philosophy. Acting as lecturer, consultant or author, she advances the expertise of sound management for all librarians.

Murray S. Martin, University Librarian of Tufts University has long been a prolific contributor to library literature. His areas of expertise reflect the concerns of modern librarians including issues relating to the use of automation, organizing information, and library administration. His professional dedication is not so consuming that it leaves no time for attention to the contemporary literature of his native New Zealand, and he is quite comfortable discussing the poetry of that far off land.

Charles B. Osburn, Vice Provost for the University of Cincinnati Libraries, lectures frequently on the techniques of collection development. Formerly, Assistant Librarian for Collection Development at Northwestern University, he brings sound experience to his audiences both orally and in print.

Michelle M. Reid, Circulation and Interlibrary Loan Librarian of New Jersey Institute of Technology, was a student until recently at the University of South Florida. Her interest in bibliographic research led her to the somewhat neglected area of children's literature of the nineteenth century.

Tom G. Watson, Assistant to the Vice Chancellor, University of the South, was formerly University Librarian for the institution. Active in the American Library Association with most recent service as a member of the Committee on Accreditation, he has written on that subject for the ALA yearbook, 1981. He has been a frequent speaker before professional groups on management subjects.

Robert L. White, Assistant University Librarian for Planning and Budget, University of California, Santa Cruz, brings a fresh viewpoint to library management coupled with an expertise acquired in actual experience. His range of interests include health sciences with occasional service as a consultant to local hospital libraries.

John Wilkinson, Professor of Library Science at the University of Toronto, has a special interest in library administration and personnel management, and writes on these subjects. For several years, he directed the Center for Research in Librarianship at the University of Toronto.

Delmus E. Williams, Associate Director of Libraries at Western Illinois University, began his career in technical services. His reflective thinking on the principles of management is illustrated in his interest in organizational change and planning. Control of microforms, bibliographically, is an intriguing area to which he also has given attention.

AUTHOR INDEX

SUBJECT INDEX

367

Foundations in
LIBRARY AND INFORMATION SCIENCE

A Series of Monographs, Texts and Treatises

Series Editor: **Robert D. Stueart**
Dean, Graduate School of Library and Information Science
Simmons College, Boston

New!

Government Information Quarterly

An International Journal of Resources Services, Policies, and Practices

Editor: **Peter Hernon**
Graduate School of Library and Information Science, Simmons College
Associate Editor: **Charles R. McClure**
School of Library Science, University of Oklahoma

Editorial Board: Sandra K. Paull, *New Mexico State Library,* **Mary K. Fetzer,** *Alexander Library, Rutgers University,* **Peter I. Hajnal,** *Government Publications Section, University of Toronto Library,* **David C. Heisser,** *Wessell Library, Tufts University,* **Judy E. Myers,** *Central Campus Library, University of Houston,* **Harold C. Relyea,** *Congressional Research Service, Library of Congress.*

SCOPE AND PURPOSE

The journal will cover those issues, trends, developments, and information resources of interest to librarians, researchers, government administrators, record managers, students, and others interested in the role of government information (published and unpublished) in society. This interdisciplinary journal provides a forum for theoretical and philosophical analyses, the presentation of research findings and practical applications, and a discussion of current policies and practices as well as new developments for all levels of government: United States (federal, state, and local), United Nations and international organizations, and other countries.

REGULAR FEATURES

Editorial Opinion

Refereed Articles (articles in some issues will be devoted to a symposium covering different aspects of the same topic)

Refereed Articles appearing under the heading "Documents Librarianship" will focus on techniques, practices, and physical arrangement of documents collections; some of these articles may comprise pictorial essays.

Biographical Statements on Each Author.

Columns featuring Reprinted, Key Speeches and Reports, Communications (To the Editor), and Reviews of Monographs, Microforms, and Government Publications. Some reviews will, in fact, comprise review essays.

The last issue of each volume will comprise an annual review of selected topics, the literature, and research needs. In addition, this issue will carry the regular columns and an author and subject index.

DATE OF PUBLICATION

Volume 1, Number 1, will be published during the spring 1984.

FORTHCOMING ARTICLES (Selected)

Peter Hernon, **GPO Depository Library Program: Descriptive Characteristics;** *Charles R. McClure,* **Collection Development for Health Science Government Publications;** *John Phillips,* **Agriculture Department Publications;** *Susanna Schweizer,* **Computerized Management Information Systems for Government Publications, a symposium on National Security and Information Policy.**

JAi **JAI PRESS INC., 36 Sherwood Place, P.O. Box 1678**
Greenwich, Connecticut 06836
Telephone: 203-661-7602   Cable Address: JAIPUBL